T0334402

FEATURE ENGINEERING FOR MACHINE LEARNING AND DATA ANALYTICS

Chapman & Hall/CRC
Data Mining and Knowledge Series

Series Editor: Vipin Kumar

RapidMiner
Data Mining Use Cases and Business Analytics Applications
Markus Hofmann and Ralf Klinkenberg

Computational Business Analytics
Subrata Das

Data Classification
Algorithms and Applications
Charu C. Aggarwal

Healthcare Data Analytics
Chandan K. Reddy and Charu C. Aggarwal

Accelerating Discovery
Mining Unstructured Information for Hypothesis Generation
Scott Spangler

Event Mining
Algorithms and Applications
Tao Li

Text Mining and Visualization
Case Studies Using Open-Source Tools
Markus Hofmann and Andrew Chisholm

Graph-Based Social Media Analysis
Ioannis Pitas

Data Mining
A Tutorial-Based Primer, Second Edition
Richard J. Roiger

Data Mining with R
Learning with Case Studies, Second Edition
Luís Torgo

Social Networks with Rich Edge Semantics
Quan Zheng and David Skillicorn

Large-Scale Machine Learning in the Earth Sciences
Ashok N. Srivastava, Ramakrishna Nemani, and Karsten Steinhaeuser

Data Science and Analytics with Python
Jesus Rogel-Salazar

Feature Engineering for Machine Learning and Data Analytics
Guozhu Dong and Huan Liu

For more information about this series please visit:
https://www.crcpress.com/Chapman--HallCRC-Data-Mining-and-Knowledge-Discovery-Series/book-series/CHDAMINODIS

FEATURE ENGINEERING FOR MACHINE LEARNING AND DATA ANALYTICS

Edited by
Guozhu Dong and Huan Liu

CRC Press
Taylor & Francis Group
Boca Raton   London   New York

CRC Press is an imprint of the
Taylor & Francis Group, an **informa** business
A CHAPMAN & HALL BOOK

MATLAB® is a trademark of The MathWorks, Inc. and is used with permission. The MathWorks does not warrant the accuracy of the text or exercises in this book. This book's use or discussion of MATLAB® software or related products does not constitute endorsement or sponsorship by The MathWorks of a particular pedagogical approach or particular use of the MATLAB® software.

CRC Press
Taylor & Francis Group
6000 Broken Sound Parkway NW, Suite 300
Boca Raton, FL 33487-2742

First issued in paperback 2020

© 2018 by Taylor & Francis Group, LLC
CRC Press is an imprint of Taylor & Francis Group, an Informa business

No claim to original U.S. Government works

ISBN-13: 978-0-367-57185-6 (pbk)
ISBN-13: 978-1-138-74438-7 (hbk)

Version Date: 20180301

This book contains information obtained from authentic and highly regarded sources. Reasonable efforts have been made to publish reliable data and information, but the author and publisher cannot assume responsibility for the validity of all materials or the consequences of their use. The authors and publishers have attempted to trace the copyright holders of all material reproduced in this publication and apologize to copyright holders if permission to publish in this form has not been obtained. If any copyright material has not been acknowledged please write and let us know so we may rectify in any future reprint.

Except as permitted under U.S. Copyright Law, no part of this book may be reprinted, reproduced, transmitted, or utilized in any form by any electronic, mechanical, or other means, now known or hereafter invented, including photocopying, microfilming, and recording, or in any information storage or retrieval system, without written permission from the publishers.

For permission to photocopy or use material electronically from this work, please access www.copyright.com (http://www.copyright.com/) or contact the Copyright Clearance Center, Inc. (CCC), 222 Rosewood Drive, Danvers, MA 01923, 978-750-8400. CCC is a not-for-profit organization that provides licenses and registration for a variety of users. For organizations that have been granted a photocopy license by the CCC, a separate system of payment has been arranged.

Trademark Notice: Product or corporate names may be trademarks or registered trademarks, and are used only for identification and explanation without intent to infringe.

Visit the Taylor & Francis Web site at
http://www.taylorandfrancis.com

and the CRC Press Web site at
http://www.crcpress.com

To my family, especially baby Hazel [G. D.]

To my family [H. L.]

To all contributing authors [G. D. & H. L.]

Contents

3 Feature Extraction and Learning for Visual Data   55

Parag S. Chandakkar, Ragav Venkatesan, and Baoxin Li

4 Feature-Based Time-Series Analysis   87

Ben D. Fulcher

10 Pattern-Based Feature Generation   245

Yunzhe Jia, James Bailey, Ramamohanarao Kotagiri, and Christopher Leckie

11 Deep Learning for Feature Representation   279

Suhang Wang and Huan Liu

Preface

Feature engineering plays a vital role in big data analytics. Machine learning and data mining algorithms cannot work without data. Little can be achieved if there are few features to represent the underlying data objects, and the quality of results of those algorithms largely depends on the quality of the available features. Data can exist in various forms such as image, text, graph, sequence, and time series. A common way to represent data for data analytics is to use feature vectors. Feature engineering meets the needs in the generation and selection of useful features, as well as several other issues.

This book is devoted to feature engineering. It covers various aspects of feature engineering, including feature generation, feature extraction, feature transformation, feature selection, and feature analysis and evaluation. It presents concepts, methods, examples, as well as applications.

Feature engineering is often data type specific and application dependent. This calls for multiple chapters on different data types that require specialized feature engineering techniques to meet various data analytic needs. Hence, this book contains chapters on feature engineering for major data types such as texts, images, sequences, time series, graphs, streaming data, software engineering data, Twitter data, and social media data. It also contains generic feature generation approaches, as well as methods for generating tried-and-tested, hand-crafted, domain-specific features.

This book contains many useful feature engineering concepts and techniques, which are an important part of machine learning and data analytics. They can help readers to meet their needs in multiple scenarios: (a) generate features to represent the data when there are no features, (b) generate effective features when (one may be concerned that) existing features are not good/competitive enough, (c) select features when there are too many features, (d) generate and select effective features for specific types of applications, and (e) understand the challenges associated with, and the needed approaches to handle, various data types. This list is certainly not exhaustive.

The first chapter is an introduction, which defines the concepts of features and feature engineering, offers an overview of the book, and provides pointers to topics not covered in this book. The next six chapters are devoted to feature engineering, including feature generation, for specific data types, namely texts, images, sequences, time series, graphs, and streaming data. The subsequent four chapters cover generic approaches for feature engineering, namely feature selection, feature transformation-based feature engineering, deep learning–based feature engineering, and pattern-based feature generation and engineering. The last three chapters discuss feature engineering for social bot detection, software management, and Twitter-based applications respectively.

Getting familiar with the concepts and techniques covered in this book will boost one's understanding and expertise in machine learning and big data analytics. This book can be used as a reference for data analysts, big data scientists, data preprocessing workers, project managers, project developers, prediction modelers, professors, researchers, graduate students, and upper-level undergraduate students. This book can be used as the primary text for courses on feature engineering, and as supplementary materials for courses on machine learning, data mining, and big data analytics.

We wish to express our profound gratitude to the contributing authors of the chapters of the book; without their expertise and dedicated efforts, this book would not be possible. We are grateful to Randi Cohen and Veronica Rodriguez who provided guidance and assistance on the publishing side of this effort. We are indebted to Jiawei Han, Jian Pei, Nicholas Skapura, Xintao Wu, and Junjie Zhang who kindly suggested domain experts as potential authors and so on, and also to Vineeth Rakesh Mohan who provided useful feedback on parts of this book.

Guozhu Dong, Dayton, Ohio

Huan Liu, Phoenix, Arizona

Contributors

Charu Aggarwal
IBM Research
Yorktown Heights, New York, USA

Hussein S. Al-Olimat
Wright State University
Dayton, Ohio, USA

James Bailey
The University of Melbourne
Parkville, Victoria, Australia

Lakshika Balasuriya
Wright State University
Dayton, Ohio, USA

Shreyansh Bhatt
Wright State University
Dayton, Ohio, USA

Parag S. Chandakkar
Arizona State University
Phoenix, Arizona, USA

Clayton A. Davis
Indiana University
Bloomington, Indiana, USA

Guozhu Dong
Wright State University
Dayton, Ohio, USA

Lei Duan
Sichuan University
Chengdu, Sichuan, China

Alessandro Flammini
Indiana University

Bloomington, Indiana, USA

Ben D. Fulcher
Monash University
Melbourne, Victoria, Australia

Manas Gaur
Wright State University
Dayton, Ohio, USA

Chase Geigle
University of Illinois at
    Urbana-Champaign
Urbana-Champaign, Illinois, USA

Yunzhe Jia
The University of Melbourne
Parkville, Victoria, Australia

Ramamohanarao Kotagiri
The University of Melbourne
Parkville, Victoria, Australia

Christopher Leckie
The University of Melbourne
Parkville, Victoria, Australia

Baoxin Li
Arizona State University
Phoenix, Arizona, USA

Tao Li
Nanjing University of Posts and
    Telecommunications
Nanjing, Jiangsu, China

Yun Li
Nanjing University of Posts and
    Telecommunications
Nanjing, Jiangsu, China

Huan Liu
Arizona State University
Phoenix, Arizona, USA

David Lo
Singapore Management University
Singapore

Jian Lu
Nanjing University
Nanjing, Jiansu, China

Yao Ma
Michigan State University
East Lansing, Michigan, USA

Qiaozhu Mei
University of Illinois at
    Urbana-Champaign
Urbana-Champaign, Illinois, USA

Filippo Menczer
Indiana University
Bloomington, Indiana, USA

Jyrki Nummenmaa
University of Tampere
Tampere, Finland

Amit Sheth
Wright State University
Dayton, Ohio, USA

Jiliang Tang
Michigan State University
East Lansing, Michigan, USA

Krishnaprasad Thirunarayan
Wright State University
Dayton, Ohio, USA

Hanghang Tong
Arizona State University
Phoenix, Arizona, USA

Onur Varol
Indiana University
Bloomington, Indiana, USA

Ragav Venkatesan
Arizona State University
Phoenix, Arizona, USA

Suhang Wang
Arizona State University
Phoenix, Arizona, USA

Sanjaya Wijeratne
Wright State University
Dayton, Ohio, USA

Xin Xia
Monash University
Melbourne, Victoria, Australia

Feng Xu
Nanjing University
Nanjing, Jiansu, China

Yuan Yao
Nanjing University
Nanjing, Jiansu, China

Amir Hossein Yazdavar
Wright State University
Dayton, Ohio, USA

ChengXiang Zhai
University of Illinois at
    Urbana-Champaign
Urbana-Champaign, Illinois, USA

Peng Zhang
Sichuan University
Chengdu, Sichuan, China

Chapter 1

Preliminaries and Overview

Guozhu Dong

Wright State University, Dayton, Ohio, USA

Huan Liu

Arizona State University, Phoenix, Arizona, USA

> At the end of the day, some machine learning projects succeed
> and some fail. What makes the difference? Easily the most
> important factor is the features used.
> Feature engineering is the key.
>
> Pedro Domingos, 2012 [2].

This chapter first provides preliminaries on the basic concepts related to features, feature engineering, and data analytic tasks. It then gives an overview of this book. Finally, it offers pointers to other feature engineering topics not covered in other chapters of this book.

1.1 Preliminaries

1.1.1 Features

In machine learning, data mining, and data analytics, a *feature* is an attribute or variable used to describe some aspect of individual data objects.

1

Example features include age and eye color for persons, and major and grade point average for students.

Informative features are the basis for data analytics. They are useful for describing the underlying objects, and for distinguishing and characterizing different (explicit or latent) groups of objects. They are also vital for producing accurate and easy-to-explain predictive models, and yielding good results in various data analytic tasks. "Feature," "variable," and "attribute" are often used as synonyms.

For a given application and a fixed point in time, often a fixed set of features is implicitly chosen to describe all underlying data objects; each object takes a particular value for each of those features. This results in a feature-vector-based representation of the data objects.

Features are divided into several *feature types*, including categorical, ordinal, and numerical. Different feature types require different kinds of analysis, due to structural differences in their domains.

- The domain of a categorical feature is a set of discrete values. For example, *color* is a categorical feature whose domain is $\{black, blue, brown, green, red, white, yellow\}$.

- A special type of categorical feature is binary, whose domain has exactly two values.

- The domain of an ordinal feature is a set of ordered values. The *degree* feature is an ordinal feature whose domain is $\{Bachelor, Master, PhD\}$ and the three values are ordered as follows: $Bachelor < Master < PhD$.

- The domain of a numerical feature is a set of numerical values. A numerical feature is also called quantitative or continuous. For example, the *age* feature is a numerical one whose domain is the set of integers between 0 and 150.

  There is a less-than (denoted by $<$) relationship between each pair of numerical values, e.g., $3 < 4$. This relationship and the implied nearbyness among numerical values are often exploited in machine learning and data analytics.

- A numerical feature is a ratio-scaled feature if the following is true: a value u is twice as much as a value v with respect to some meaning (e.g., warmness or length) associated with the feature, whenever it is the case that $u = 2 * v$.

In many applications categorical features are represented as numerical values. Care is needed in such cases as the order implied by the numerical values is typically meaningless. In R packages categorical variables are treated as factors. A so-called "one-hot encoding" is often used to transform such features.

The usefulness of a feature is measured ultimately in terms of the improvement the feature adds to the data analytic task at hand. For example, in classification this is mostly in terms of the improvement in classification accuracy. The understandability and interpretability of the feature are also of significant interest.

1.1.2 Feature Engineering

This book uses a very general definition for *feature engineering*. It includes the topics of feature transformation, feature generation, feature extraction, feature selection, feature analysis and evaluation, general automatic feature engineering methodology, and feature engineering applications. We briefly explain these concepts below.

(1) Feature transformation is about constructing new features from existing features; this is often achieved using mathematical mappings.

(2) Feature generation is about generating new features that are often not the result of feature transformations. For example, assuming that one does not view a pixel in an image as a feature, one generates new features for images. Moreover, it makes sense to say that features defined from patterns are generated features. Many domain-specific ways for defining features also belong in the feature generation category. Sometimes the term feature extraction is used for feature generation.

(3) Feature selection is about selecting a small set of features from a very large pool of features. The reduced feature set size makes it computationally feasible to use certain algorithms. Feature selection may also lead to improved quality on the result of those algorithms.

(4) Feature analysis and evaluation is about concepts, methods, and measures for evaluating the usefulness of features and feature sets. This is often included as part of feature selection.

(5) General automatic feature engineering methodology is about generic approaches for automatically generating a large number of features and selecting an effective subset of the generated features.

(6) Feature engineering applications involve feature engineering but the focus is to solve some other data analytic tasks in specific contexts. Examples include analyzing Twitter data to improve the quality of disaster response and relief efforts.

1.1.3 Machine Learning and Data Analytic Tasks

Generally speaking, all machine learning, data mining, and data analytic tasks rely on and can benefit from effective feature engineering. Specific tasks include classification, regression, clustering, outlier detection, pattern/rule mining, predictive modeling, contrasting and characterizing data classes, concept discovery, distance learning, probability estimation, ontology/taxonomy construction, information retrieval, business intelligence, and so on. Below we provide basic concepts for some of these tasks. More information can be found in textbooks on machine learning and data mining such as [6, 7, 26, 30].

Classification is the task of learning a function f that maps each data object x to one member of some given set of predefined class labels y. The resulting function f is often referred to as a classification model. For a given application, the learning of a classification model is achieved by applying some method to a training dataset, namely a set of (x, y) pairs where x is a data object and y is a class label.

Regression is similar to classification except that y is a numerical attribute instead of a class label.

Clustering is the task of partitioning a given dataset D into a number of subsets (the clusters) so that the objects within a cluster are highly similar to each other and objects in different clusters are highly different from each other. Similarity is often measured using a distance function, but other approaches also exist. Clustering is also referred to as segmentation and as concept discovery.

Outlier detection (also called anomaly detection) is the task of identifying objects that do not conform to an expected pattern exhibited by the majority of objects in a given dataset.

Pattern mining is the task of identifying patterns that are interesting in some sense. A pattern can be viewed as a condition of individual objects that can be evaluated as true or false. The pattern mining process can be applied to one dataset, in which case one wants to mine interesting frequent patterns; it can also be applied to multiple datasets (e.g., classes), in which case one wants to mine interesting patterns that distinguish one of the datasets from the other datasets.

1.2   Overview of the Chapters

This book has three parts, together with this introductory chapter. Part 1 consists of six chapters (2 to 7) on feature engineering for various data types. Part 2 contains four chapters (8 to 11) on general feature engineering techniques which are not specific to data types. Part 3 includes three chapters (12 to 14) on feature engineering in special applications.

Chapter 2 provides a systematic review of the main techniques for feature representations for text data. Text data can be regarded as data reported by human sensors, which are supplementary to data collected by physical sensors. Text data are useful in many applications especially for supporting decision making and analyzing people's opinions and preferences. This chapter discusses (a) the dominant *bag of words*–based text representation, (b) approaches that use multiple words as features, and (c) structural features that require natural language processing techniques or statistical pattern analysis methods. It further describes how to learn latent semantic representations using methods such as probabilistic topic models and neural networks, and how text data can be analyzed together with non-textual context data to extract contextualized text representations.

A majority of visual computing tasks involve prediction, regression or decision making using features extracted from the original, raw visual data (images or videos). **Chapter 3** presents a hierarchy of feature representations for image data, starting with classic, hand-crafted features. The classic features are designed by human experts and they are based on task-specific prior knowledge. They are easily interpretable and characterize fundamental aspects of images such as color, texture and shape. The features at the next level are latent feature representations. Such features represent task-specific structures in the feature space such as sparsity, decorrelation of reduced dimension, low rank, etc.

Time series is an important type of data that are frequently encountered in data analytics. **Chapter 4** provides an overview of a vast literature of representations and analysis methods for time series. It first presents discussion on global distances between time-series values including Euclidean and elastic distance measures like DTW. It then discusses three kinds of features, namely subsequences that provide more localized shape-based information, global features that capture higher order structure, and interval features that capture discriminative properties in time-series subsequences. It also discusses factors that influence the selection of the most useful method for a given task.

Chapter 5 provides an overview of feature engineering for streaming data, with a focus on streaming feature construction and selection. It first summarizes the typical streaming settings and their corresponding formal definitions. Then it reviews automated feature construction algorithms including linear and non-linear methods. Next it gives an overview of feature selection algorithms with different streaming settings. Finally it discusses some open questions and possible research directions about feature engineering for data streams.

Sequence data occur in many applications including bioinformatics, music, literature, health care, and security. **Chapter 6** first discusses the basic concepts for sequence data. It then discusses three major classes of sequence features, namely traditional pattern-based sequence features, general pattern-based features, and sequence features that do not involve the use of patterns. It presents several approaches for using sequence patterns as sequence features, and it provides an overview of sequence pattern types as well as methods to mine such patterns. It also considers factors that are important for selecting patterns as features.

Graph and network data are essential for various graph analysis tasks such as social network analysis, protein–protein interaction analysis, and chemical molecule toxicity analysis. **Chapter 7** focuses on feature generation for graphs and networks. It first discusses the feature types for graphs, including neighborhood-level features and global-level features. Next, it describes existing feature generation methods, divided into feature extraction approaches and feature learning approaches. Finally, it presents several applications to illustrate graph feature usages, including the applications of multi-label classification on nodes, link prediction, anomaly detection, and visualization.

Feature selection is one of the key problems for machine learning and data mining. **Chapter 8** reviews recent developments on this topic. A brief historical background of the field is given, followed by a selection of topics which are of particular current interests, such as stable feature selection, multi-view feature selection, distributed feature selection, multi-label feature selection, online feature selection and adversarial feature selection. The chapter then reviews recent research advances of these topics.

The process of predictive modeling requires extensive feature engineering. It often involves the transformation of a given feature space, typically using mathematical functions, with the objective of reducing the modeling error for a given target. However, there is no well-defined basis for performing effective feature engineering. It involves domain knowledge, intuition, and most of all, a lengthy process of trial and error. The human attention involved in overseeing this process significantly influences the cost of model generation. Moreover, when the data presented is not well described and labeled, effective manual feature engineering becomes an even more prohibitive task. **Chapter 9** discusses ways to algorithmically tackle the problem of feature engineering using transformation functions in the context of supervised learning.

Frequent patterns are combinations of conditions on features that have a high frequency of co-occurrence, which can represent interesting interaction relationships among features in a given dataset. Features generated using patterns can be more discriminative than individual features. **Chapter 10** provides a systematic overview on pattern-based feature generation. Specifically, it presents approaches for generating patterns, techniques for pruning large pattern sets, strategies for constructing new features using patterns, and applications of pattern-based feature generation for classification and clustering.

Deep learning methods have become increasingly popular in recent years because of their tremendous success in image classification, speech recognition and natural language processing tasks. The great success of deep learning mainly comes from specially designed structures of deep nets, which are able to learn discriminative non-linear features that can facilitate the task at hand. In essence, the majority of existing deep learning algorithms can be used as powerful feature learning/extraction tools, i.e., the latent features extracted by deep learning algorithms are the learned new representations. **Chapter 11** reviews various classical and popular deep learning algorithms and explains how they can be used for feature representation learning. It also discusses how they are used for hierarchical and disentangle representation learning, and how they can be applied for various domains.

Increasing evidence suggests that social platforms like Twitter accommodate an increasing number of autonomous entities known as social bots, which are controlled by software that generates content and establishes interactions with other accounts. **Chapter 12** considers feature engineering for social bot detection in the context of social media. It describes the setting of such detection, and it presents various kinds of features, some of which are unique for social media, including their definition, selection, and usefulness for social bot detection. It also describes a system called Botometer that analyzes public information about a Twitter account, extracting over a thousand features describing the account and its neighbors, and discusses experiments where the extracted features were used to build classifiers for bot detection.

Chapter 13 considers feature generation and engineering for software analytics. It shows how domain-specific features can be designed and used to automate three software engineering tasks: (1) detecting defective software modules, (2) identifying a crashing mobile app release, and (3) predicting who will leave a software team. For each task, different sets of features are extracted from a diverse set of software artifacts, and used to build predictive models. The chapter also discusses recent advances as well as their potential.

Chapter 14 presents studies concerning feature engineering for Twitter-based applications. It first discusses how Twitter data can be downloaded from the Twitter Application Programming Interface (API) and the kinds of data available in the downloaded tweets. Then, it discusses various textual features, image and video features, Twitter metadata-related features, and network features that can be extracted. Next, it discusses the uses of different feature types along with an analysis of why certain features perform well in the context of informal short text messages typically found in tweets. It then presents five real-world Twitter applications that utilize different feature types. For each application, it also highlights the features that perform well in the corresponding application setting. Finally, it concludes the chapter by discussing Twitris, a real-time semantic social web analytics platform that has already been commercialized, and its use of Twitter features.

1.3 Beyond this Book

No single book can give due attention to the rich variety of topics of feature engineering. This section provides some pointers to topics not covered in other parts of the book. It includes topics on speech features, music features, malware detection data features, log data features, transfer learning–based feature engineering, numerical feature discretization, feature engineering inside machine learning and data analytic algorithms, and early papers and books on feature engineering. Due to the broadness of the feature engineering field, this chapter is certainly not complete.

1.3.1 Feature Engineering for Specific Data Types

There have been numerous studies on speech feature generation (e.g., [11,22]), often conducted as part of speech recognition (see [20]). Reference [28] gives an account of acoustic features used for emotional speech recognition; these features include the pitch, the formants, the vocal-tract cross-section areas, the mel-frequency cepstral coefficients, the Teager energy operator-based features, the intensity of the speech signal, and the speech rate.

Music data mining and analysis have attracted a lot of attention [13, 29], whose tasks include genre classification, emotion and mood detection [25], instrument detection, and music characteristic identification. Within a piece of music one may be interested in analyzing emotion or mood differences between different parts [12], and finding repeating patterns [8]. Music data is quite complex, as it includes an acoustic part (pitch, intensity, etc.), a music score part, and a text part (the lyrics). Music data can be treated as large sequences, although the alphabet of the sequences is quite large and different elements are related to each other in significant ways, and one needs to consider issues such as the handling of several concurrent sequences for each of the acoustic, music score and lyrics parts. Music data and speech data are also related. Chapter 4 on time series analysis and Chapter 6 on sequence feature engineering are related to music data analysis.

Analyzing executable codes to detect malware is an important problem. Several types of static features were used in [23], namely DLL-related features, system call features, and string/sequence features. The DLL-related features include the DLLs contained in the binary code, the DLL function calls, and the number of different system calls used within each DLL. Function length features were used for malware classification in [27], and network behavior features were used in [18]. Reference [5] gives a survey of malware classification.

Another kind of data with distinct characteristics is the execution and network navigation log data. An example is network intrusion data such as the 1999 KDD Cup dataset [10]. This KDD Cup dataset contains logs (raw TCP dump data) collected from a typical LAN. Reference [9] discusses generating and selecting features for this dataset; it considered four types of features, namely basic features (e.g., those derived from packet headers without inspecting the payload), content features, time-based traffic features, and host-based traffic features.

Analyzing game-related data can be useful in several ways, including understanding human behavior, designing winning game playing strategies, and improving game designs. However, game-play data lack structure and has big volumes. Reference [1] discusses issues related to feature generation and selection for game-play data.

1.3.2 Feature Engineering on Non-Data-Specific Topics

Transfer learning can be used to find effective features for a new dataset from another dataset, although algorithms in this field are often originally designed for other data analytic tasks such as classification and clustering. Transfer learning can also help avoid much expensive data labeling efforts. Transfer learning can also mine similar structures such as shared decision trees [3]. For a survey, see [19].

Feature discretization (also called binning) of numerical data is useful for feature transformation and feature generation, and sometimes feature selection. Feature discretization is about constructing informative categorical representations of numerical features so that the categorical values retain as much information in the original numerical values as possible. Representative research includes [4, 15]. Reference [21] is a recent a survey on feature discretization. This is still an active field of research [17, 24].

Implicit feature generation/transformation is often a part of machine learning and data mining algorithms aimed at solving specific problems. Often new features are automatically constructed and selected for use in machine learning systems such as deep learning (see Chapter 11). Also, meta classification uses predicted values of other classifiers as features [14].

Reference [16] is an early book that was devoted to several aspects of feature engineering. It contains chapters on feature selection, feature extraction, and feature construction. For example, it includes chapters on feature extraction using adaptive wavelets and using neural networks, feature transformation by function decomposition, and automatic fractal feature extraction for image recognition. This current book is more complete and more up to date; it covers a wider range of topics and techniques for feature engineering, and it includes many hand-crafted domain-specific feature generation techniques.

Bibliography

[1] Alessandro Canossa. Meaning in gameplay: Filtering variables, defining metrics, extracting features and creating models for gameplay analysis. In *Game Analytics*, pages 255–283. Springer, 2013.

[2] Pedro Domingos. A few useful things to know about machine learning. *Communications of the ACM*, 55(10):78–87, 2012.

[3] Guozhu Dong and Qian Han. Mining accurate shared decision trees from microarray gene expression data for different cancers. In *Proceedings of the International Conference on Bioinformatics & Computational Biology (BIOCOMP)*, 2013.

[4] Usama Fayyad and Keki Irani. Multi-interval discretization of continuous-valued attributes for classification learning. In *Proceedings of the 13th International Joint Conference on Artificial Intelligence (IJ-CAI)*, pages 1022–1029, 1993.

[5] Ekta Gandotra, Divya Bansal, and Sanjeev Sofat. Malware analysis and classification: A survey. *Journal of Information Security*, 5(02):56, 2014.

[6] Jiawei Han, Jian Pei, and Micheline Kamber. *Data Mining: Concepts and Techniques*. Elsevier, 2011.

[7] David J Hand, Heikki Mannila, and Padhraic Smyth. *Principles of Data Mining*. MIT Press, 2001.

[8] Jia-Lien Hsu, Arbee LP Chen, and C-C Liu. Efficient repeating pattern finding in music databases. In *Proceedings of the Seventh International Conference on Information and Knowledge Management*, pages 281–288. ACM, 1998.

[9] H Günes Kayacik, A Nur Zincir-Heywood, and Malcolm I Heywood. Selecting features for intrusion detection: A feature relevance analysis on KDD 99 intrusion detection datasets. In *Proceedings of the Third Annual Conference on Privacy, Security and Trust*, 2005.

[10] KDD Cup. 1999. http://kdd.ics.uci.edu/databases/kddcup99

[11] Yelin Kim, Honglak Lee, and Emily Mower Provost. Deep learning for robust feature generation in audiovisual emotion recognition. In *IEEE International Conference on Acoustics, Speech and Signal Processing (ICASSP)*, pages 3687–3691. IEEE, 2013.

[12] Hua-Fu Li. Memsa: Mining emerging melody structures from music query data. *Multimedia Systems*, 17(3):237–245, 2011.

[13] Tao Li, Mitsunori Ogihara, and George Tzanetakis. *Music Data Mining*. CRC Press, 2011.

[14] Wei-Hao Lin and Alexander Hauptmann. News video classification using SVM-based multimodal classifiers and combination strategies. In *Proceedings of the Tenth ACM International Conference on Multimedia*, pages 323–326. ACM, 2002.

[15] Huan Liu, Farhad Hussain, Chew Lim Tan, and Manoranjan Dash. Discretization: An enabling technique. *Data Mining and Knowledge Discovery*, 6(4):393–423, 2002.

[16] Huan Liu and Hiroshi Motoda. *Feature Extraction, Construction and Selection: A Data Mining Perspective*, volume 453. Springer Science & Business Media, 1998.

[17] Robert Moskovitch and Yuval Shahar. Classification-driven temporal discretization of multivariate time series. *Data Mining and Knowledge Discovery*, 29(4):871–913, 2015.

[18] Saeed Nari and Ali A Ghorbani. Automated malware classification based on network behavior. In *International Conference on Computing, Networking and Communications (ICNC)*, pages 642–647. IEEE, 2013.

[19] Sinno Jialin Pan and Qiang Yang. A survey on transfer learning. *IEEE Transactions on Knowledge and Data Engineering*, 22(10):1345–1359, 2010.

[20] Lawrence R Rabiner and Biing-Hwang Juang. *Fundamentals of Speech Recognition*. Prentice Hall, 1993.

[21] Sergio Ramírez-Gallego, Salvador García, Héctor Mouriño-Talín, David Martínez-Rego, Verónica Bolón-Canedo, Amparo Alonso-Betanzos, José Manuel Benítez, and Francisco Herrera. Data discretization: Taxonomy and big data challenge. *Wiley Interdisciplinary Reviews: Data Mining and Knowledge Discovery*, 6(1):5–21, 2016.

[22] Bjorn Schuller, Stephan Reiter, and Gerhard Rigoll. Evolutionary feature generation in speech emotion recognition. In *IEEE International Conference on Multimedia and Expo*, pages 5–8. IEEE, 2006.

[23] Matthew G Schultz, Eleazar Eskin, F Zadok, and Salvatore J Stolfo. Data mining methods for detection of new malicious executables. In *Proceedings of IEEE Symposium on Security and Privacy*, pages 38–49. IEEE, 2001.

[24] Nicholas Skapura and Guozhu Dong. Distribution skew-based binning: Towards mining highly discriminative patterns from EEG/EMG time series. In *IEEE 15th International Conference on Bioinformatics and Bioengineering (BIBE)*, pages 1–6. IEEE, 2015.

[25] Yading Song, Simon Dixon, and Marcus Pearce. Evaluation of musical features for emotion classification. In *Proceedings of International Society for Music Information Retrieval Conference*, pages 523–528, 2012.

[26] Pang-Ning Tan, Michael Steinbach, and Vipin Kumar. Data mining cluster analysis: Basic concepts and algorithms. *Introduction to Data Mining*, Pearson, 2013.

[27] Ronghua Tian, Lynn Margaret Batten, and SC Versteeg. Function length as a tool for malware classification. In *3rd International Conference on Malicious and Unwanted Software (MALWARE 2008)*, pages 69–76. IEEE, 2008.

[28] Dimitrios Ververidis and Constantine Kotropoulos. Emotional speech recognition: Resources, features, and methods. *Speech Communication*, 48(9):1162–1181, 2006.

[29] Claus Weihs, Dietmar Jannach, Igor Vatolkin, and Guenter Rudolph. *Music Data Analysis: Foundations and Applications*. CRC Press, 2016.

[30] Ian H Witten, Eibe Frank, Mark A Hall, and Christopher J Pal. *Data Mining: Practical Machine Learning Tools and Techniques*. Morgan Kaufmann, 2016.

Part I

Feature Engineering for Various Data Types

Chapter 2

Feature Engineering for Text Data

Chase Geigle

Department of Computer Science, University of Illinois at Urbana-Champaign

Qiaozhu Mei

School of Information, University of Michigan

ChengXiang Zhai

Department of Computer Science, University of Illinois at Urbana-Champaign

2.1 Introduction

Text data broadly refers to all kinds of natural language data, including both written text and spoken language. Recent years have seen a dramatic growth of online text data with many examples such as web pages, news articles, scientific literature, emails, enterprise documents, and social media such as blog articles, forum posts, product reviews, and tweets. Text data contain rich knowledge about the world, including human opinions and preferences. Because of this, mining and analyzing vast amounts of text data ("big text data") can enable us to support user tasks and optimize decision making in all application domains.

Nearly all text data is generated by humans and for human consumption. It is useful to imagine that text data is generated by humans operating as intelligent subjective sensors: we humans observe the world from a particular perspective (and thus are subjective) and we express our observations in the form of text data. When we take this view, we can see that as a special kind of big data, text data has unique values. First, since all domains involve humans, text data are useful in all applications of big data. Second, because text data are subjective, they offer opportunities for mining knowledge about people's behaviors, attitudes, and opinions. Finally, text data directly express knowledge about our world, so small text data are also useful (provided computers can understand it).

As data generated by human sensors, text data should in general be combined with all the related data generated by other non-human sensors in all big data applications. As such, it is desirable to convert raw text data into some form of representation that can be easily integrated with other non-text data. One way to achieve this goal is to extract features that are relevant to a problem from the text data so as to transform the unstructured raw text data into a more structured form of representation that can be directly combined with features extracted from other non-text data in a machine learning framework. As is the case for all supervised machine learning and predictive modeling applications, identification and extraction of effective features from text data (i.e., feature engineering for text data) is a very important initial step in all applications using text data. Without an effective feature representation that provides the needed discrimination for an application task, no matter how advanced a machine learning model may be, it is impossible to obtain satisfactory application performance. The techniques for computing features from text data have been developed by researchers in multiple communities, especially information retrieval, natural language processing, and data mining. This chapter provides a systematic review of all the major techniques developed in these communities over the years for computing a wide range of features from text data. We emphasize techniques that are relatively general and robust since such techniques can be potentially applied to text data on any topic and in any natural language.

2.2 Overview of Text Representation

The problem of feature engineering for text data is very closely related to the problem of text representation as the set of features extracted from the data essentially serves as a representation of the original data from a particular perspective. Text representation is at the foundation of virtually all text data applications, including search, recommendation, text categorization, text clustering, and text-based prediction [81]. Text representation has been studied in the information retrieval (IR) community ever since the birth of the field. In IR, a central issue is to determine what information we should retain from a text document in the indexing phase in order to effectively support matching any user query with the document to assess how likely a document is relevant to the query. More specifically, the decision is to choose appropriate terms from a document for indexing, and the idea of using statistical approaches to select appropriate terms was initially proposed by Luhn [39], where he proposed the idea of using the term frequencies in a document to choose good indexing terms (the specific idea is to choose terms that are neither too frequent nor too rare). This idea laid the foundation for automatic indexing, which enabled a computer to automatically match a user's query with the automatically selected indexing terms from a document and return to the user those documents that match the query well (i.e., the search engine application). The IR community has studied text representation extensively since Luhn's pioneering work and has proposed many ideas for text representation based on various features, notably the bag of words representation, statistical phrase indexing [14], syntactic phrase indexing [13,14,69], and latent semantic indexing [11], as well as some important heuristics for assigning feature values, notably the TF-IDF weighting and document length heuristics [15]. Because of the emphasis on robustness and generality in search engine applications, the techniques developed in the IR community tend to be shallow, but often very robust with the bag of words remaining the dominant text representation approach in modern search engines as well as many other text applications such as categorization and clustering.

While the bag of words representation tends to be very effective and is often sufficient for topic-based tasks such as topic categorization or information retrieval (especially with appropriate term weighting), such a shallow representation is generally insufficient for more sophisticated tasks. For example, stylistic analysis [16] and author attribution [28, 29, 68] require text representations that consider syntactic structure. For many such tasks, it is necessary to obtain features that reflect more understanding of text content by using natural language processing (NLP) techniques; for example, we may obtain syntactic structures or even semantic representations from text data. Due to the potential errors made by an NLP algorithm, features computed based on results generated by an NLP tool may be noisy, but they can potentially provide the much more powerful discrimination needed for some application tasks. The techniques for feature engineering in this line include features such as various syntactic phrase-based features [13], parse-tree-based features [1, 4, 16, 28, 29, 46], and entity-relation features [24]. Pure statistical approaches [79] can also be applied to extract patterns composed of multiple words from text data, which can be used as features; such features are generally more discriminative than single words, thus enabling finer granularity of discrimination. Examples of such patterns include statistical phrases (i.e., frequent n-grams), frequent word sets, and frequent sequential word patterns.

A third line of techniques of feature representation for text data stemmed from the seminal work of latent semantic indexing using SVD [11], where features and feature representations are learned using optimization or unsupervised machine learning. This work can be regarded as a pioneering work in the now very active direction of representation learning. It also inspired the line of work on probabilistic topic modeling, initially with probabilistic latent semantic indexing [23], and later latent Dirichlet allocation [2]. This further opened up a new direction in development of various topic models for obtaining sophisticated semantic representations of text data. Most recently, representation learning has been extensively studied in the context of both unsupervised learning (notably word embeddings [53], which enable convenient computation of a text representation in a low-dimensional vector space), and supervised learning (notably via neural networks such as convolutional and recurrent neural networks [20]), which enables optimization of the learned features for a particular application task.

These three lines of techniques can be combined with each other to form a rich feature representation of text data. Below we will systematically discuss all these techniques with increasing complexity in feature representation.

2.3 Text as Strings

The most basic and general representation of text data is the representation of text as a sequence of bytes. Such a representation is how a computer storage system "sees" text data—fundamentally, a document on disk is an ordered sequence of bytes. The generality of such a representation enables computers to store and process all kinds of text data in any natural language. Such generality is, however, at the cost of lack of meaning.

If the text is written in English, these individual bytes might be sufficient to represent the individual characters that occur in the text—this is commonly referred to as ASCII-encoded text. This particular byte-encoding for the characters of predominately English text is compatible with the UTF-8 encoding standard: any ASCII-encoded text document is a valid UTF-8 encoded text document (but this relationship is only one way). UTF-8 encoded text supports a much broader range of characters[1] than ASCII, and it has been continuously updated to be able to be utilized to represent text in nearly every written language on the planet. It does this by representing individual characters with a variable-length *sequence* of bytes. UTF-8 encoding is arguably the most commonly encountered encoding of text today (as it is the most common encoding for HTML content), but there are other variants of UTF encodings such as UTF-16 (commonly used in Windows) and UTF-32. The basic idea remains the same across all encodings, however: the document is a sequence of bytes that can be interpreted according to some encoding standard to eventually correspond to the written characters or glyphs that we eventually see displayed on a screen or physical printout.

Representing text as a sequence of characters is often called a "string" representation. Given a sufficient text encoding scheme like UTF-8, a sequence of bytes can be interpreted into a sequence of the individual characters of any written language (the string). Thus, this particular form of text representation is general in the sense that any text document in any language can be represented as a string.

Despite clearly not capturing much information about meaning, this kind of shallow representation actually has a number of different applications. For example, this representation can be used to answer questions about how similar two pieces of text are in terms of their Levenshtein edit distance [34], which computes the minimum number of operations from a certain set (typically insertion, deletion, and substitution of individual characters) required to transform one string into another. Levenshtein edit distance can be used as a component in systems for spelling correction, where the edit distance from a misspelled word to other words in a dictionary is used to rank suitable replacement words. It can also be used for approximate string matching with applications like spam detection (how close is this message to a known spam message?) and plagiarism detection (how difficult is it to "align" subsequences of two texts via edit distance?).

2.4 Sequence of Words Representation

While the string representation of text is sufficiently general to represent all possible text documents, it is not a particularly useful representation when we are concerned with applications that seek to understand the meaning of

---

[1]It is perhaps more appropriate to call them "glyphs" than characters.

the text. A sequence of characters is not how we typically think about natural language. We know, intuitively, that there is a hierarchical structure to any natural language text. Words, the base unit, are combined into phrases, which are further combined into sentences, which further combine into paragraphs, which eventually comprise documents. Humans derive meaning from written language by consuming this hierarchical structure. Individual characters are indeed important in written language in order to distinguish individual words from one another, but simply reading an individual character does not itself convey much meaning unless it is further interpreted (most of the time with other characters) as a word.

The most basic representation of text that can start to provide notions of meaning would then have to at least consider the document as consisting of individual words. A natural generalization of the string representation of documents might be to change the granularity of the sequence from the character/glyph level to the level of individual words. Each document, then, would be an ordered sequence of the words that comprise it.

To extract this representation, we need an algorithm that can ingest strings (character sequences) in some particular natural language and produce a list of boundaries into that sequence that can be used to segment the text into individual words. In English, this algorithm is fairly trivial as words are already segmented in text by whitespace and punctuation marks, but this task is not always trivial. For example, it is not immediately obvious how to divide a string of Chinese characters into individual words due to the lack of whitespace or punctuation between all words, requiring the use of more sophisticated modeling techniques to perform the segmentation [56, 67, 77, 83].

This process of ingesting a document and converting it into a sequence of individual word tokens is often referred to as "lexical analysis" or "tokenization." How one chooses to define a word changes the eventual representation you have for a document, and there are many things to consider when making this decision that, while on the surface may seem trivial, can have significant impact on the performance of downstream tasks. For example, should the word "Cubs" be treated as a separate word from "cubs," or are they the same word? Keeping them separate might aid you in tasks where you try to detect proper nouns like "Chicago Cubs," but treating differently capitalized words as entirely separate vocabulary items can also inflate the size of the vocabulary and thus your resulting feature set size. A similar question might be whether or not "running" should be treated as a separate word than "runs," or whether they should both be collapsed to some base form such as "run." This collapsing is referred to as stemming or lemmatization, and many techniques exist for this in a variety of different languages. A very popular stemmer in English is the Porter/Porter2 stemmer written by Martin Porter [58], who also spearheaded a project called Snowball that provides stemmers for a variety of different languages.[2] In some cases, it may also make sense to discard

---

[2] http://snowballstem.org

some common but uninformative words, like articles, determiners, and other such commonly used "function words" that contribute to the grammaticality of sentences but not substantially to their underlying meaning. Removing such words, often called "stop-word removal," can reduce the size of the vocabulary under consideration and thus the eventual feature set size.

Word sequences are the most fundamental building blocks of natural language processing (NLP) techniques that seek to infer the hidden hierarchical structure of the underlying text. We will revisit word sequences in Section 2.6 where they will be used in combination with NLP techniques to extract structural representations of text.

2.5   Bag of Words Representation

By far the most dominant approach for text representation is the "bag of words" representation. This approach summarizes the word sequence representations for documents by computing a histogram over words for a document's word sequence. Suppose we have a natural language with a vocabulary set $V = \{v_1, v_2, \ldots\}$ consisting of all of the possible words in that language. A document d would be represented as a $|V|$ dimensional vector

$$\vec{d} = \begin{pmatrix} c(v_1, d) & c(v_2, d) & \ldots & c(v_{|V|-1}, d) & c(v_{|V|}, d) \end{pmatrix}^T$$

where $c(v, d)$ is the number of times word type v appears in the word sequence for document d (the count of the word in the document). Note that this very high-dimensional vector will nearly always be sparse in practice for natural language documents; both taking advantage of and counteracting this sparsity will become a theme in this chapter. For example, a document's vector representation will almost always be stored in a way that takes advantage of the sparsity of the vector by storing only the non-zero count information, as storing the full vector for each document is almost certainly out of the question due to the memory consumption that would be required.

Most text data applications require discrimination of text data (e.g., distinguishing positive reviews from negative reviews or news articles covering different events). While the criteria for distinguishing different classes of text objects may be different from application to application, an ideal text representation for any such application should always map text objects that should be in the same class to the same or a very similar representation and those that should be in different classes to very different representations. Thus one way to assess whether a particular text representation is good is to examine its impact on computing similarity of text objects. We thus will discuss the effectiveness of the bag of words representation by examining the question of how to define an optimal similarity function.

The bag of words representation naturally supports discrimination of text objects based on content. Specifically, if we have two documents d_1 and d_2 that have similar content in terms of their word usage, but use the words in a different order than the other, the bag of words representation would produce vector representations $\vec{d_1}$ and $\vec{d_2}$ that are close to each other in the $|V|$-dimensional vector space induced by such a representation. This is advantageous from a machine learning perspective—anything we might learn about document d_1 by leveraging its representation $\vec{d_1}$ will transfer over when we use the similar document d_2's representation $\vec{d_2}$. At the same time, this representation is clearly naïve: it ignores all word order and structure. However, the ease with which it is induced and its ability to help machine learning methods generalize to new documents that use similar words to those already seen make it a powerful tool that is surprisingly sufficient for many different tasks.

2.5.1   Term Weighting

As discussed earlier, obtaining an optimal text representation is closely related the question of defining an optimal similarity function in most applications. For example, a similarity function is a critical sub-component of machine learning algorithms such as clustering (in the case of unsupervised learning) and k-nearest neighbor classification (in the case of supervised learning); performance of such algorithms is primarily determined by the effectiveness of the similarity function used. Designing an optimal similarity function for text objects was first studied in the information retrieval community via the vector space retrieval model [62], wherein the problem of generating a ranked list of documents in response to a query (the fundamental problem of information retrieval) can be solved by computing the similarity of each document's vector representation with a vector representation of a user's query.

The most natural approach to computation of similarity of two text objects would be to use some vector-space similarity measure on their corresponding vector representations, such as the dot product similarity. Many of the techniques for optimizing the similarity function in information retrieval can be regarded as techniques for optimizing the vector-space representation of the documents when dot product similarity is used. Because of the emphasis on generality in a retrieval application, these techniques developed in the IR community tend to be applicable to many other text data applications, especially those involving topic-based representation of text data. Below we will discuss some of the most important techniques developed; a more thorough discussion of such techniques can be found in Spärck Jones and Willett [66] as well as Zhai and Massung [81].

If we start with the basic vector-space representation we introduced earlier, the dot product similarity of d_1 and d_2 can be computed as

$$sim(\vec{d_1}, \vec{d_2}) = \vec{d_1} \cdot \vec{d_2} = \sum_{v \in V} c(v, d_1) \times c(v, d_2).$$

Under this measure, we would intuitively say that two documents are now considered as being similar if they share similar terms, and dissimilar if their term usage is disjoint from one another. One reason we might prefer to use the dot-product similarity over other kinds of similarity measures in this vector space is that it can efficiently take advantage of the sparsity present in the vectors $\vec{d_1}$ and $\vec{d_2}$. If either $c(v, d_1)$ or $c(v, d_2)$ is 0, we know that their contribution to the dot product will be 0, so they can be safely ignored. By using this idea, we can safely transform our similarity to be

$$sim(\vec{d_1}, \vec{d_2}) = \sum_{v \in d_1 \cap d_2} c(v, d_1) \times c(v, d_2)$$

where $d_1 \cap d_2$ indicates the intersection of the vocabulary sets constructed from words $v \in V$ such that $c(v, d_i) > 0$. In other words, we can now take our summation only over terms that occur in both documents, safely ignoring any term that does not occur in either document, or does not occur in one of the two documents. This can be a substantial speed increase over other similarity measures that may need to do work for unmatched terms across the two documents.

This may sound great, but there are a number of issues with this similarity function. Consider for a moment what would happen if we had two documents d_1 and d_2 that shared only one common word. Furthermore, let's assume that document d_1 uses the shared word only one time, but document d_2 uses it thousands of times. Should d_1 be considered similar to d_2? Should it be considered more similar to d_2 than a third document d_3 that shares five different unique terms with d_1? The problem with the current formulation is that the contribution from the term frequency within a document to the similarity is unbounded: one can artificially increase the similarity of a document with d_1 by blindly repeating one single matched term. This motivates our first transformation of the weights in our bag of words representation, called "term frequency (TF) transformation." The main idea here is to limit the contribution of repeated occurrences of a single matched term to the similarity. The first time we observe a matched term, it should contribute quite a bit to our belief that it is similar to the query document. As we see more and more occurrences of this matched term, however, each successive occurrence should contribute less and less to our overall belief of similarity. Thus, we would like to use a sub-linear function to transform our term frequency weights. There have been many TF transformation functions considered in the literature, but some of the most common [60, 63, 64] are illustrated in Figure 2.1.

The last function in Figure 2.1 is of some interest. It comes from the Okapi BM25 scoring function [60] and has the important property that it has a strict upper bound that is controlled by the parameter k. Most other TF transformations do not have this unique property, and BM25's TF function remains one of the best performing to date.

One remaining issue with the similarity function, even when we apply a sub-linear (or strictly upper-bounded) TF transformation, is that it treats

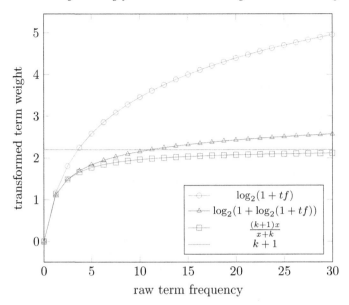

Figure 2.1: Examples of TF transformations. Note how the last function approaches an asymptote of $k+1$, while the others remain unbounded. $k = 1.2$ in this example.

matching *any* word from the vocabulary as equally important. This violates our intuition slightly—we should expect that matching a query word that occurs only in a few documents in our entire collection should be more important than matching a word that occurs in nearly every document in our collection. For example, if our query was "Ron Santo biography," matching "Santo" should be more important than matching the more generic word "biography." The basic idea here is called "term specificity," and a specific statistical interpretation with application to information retrieval was first presented by Karen Spärck Jones [25]. A term that is highly specific occurs in only a few documents, whereas a term that has low specificity occurs in many documents. Thus, we can re-weight our terms by leveraging the "document frequency" (DF) for each term, which is simply the number of documents in the collection that contain said term. We want to use the inverse document frequency (IDF) to re-weight our terms so as to allow more specific terms (higher IDF) to have higher scores overall. A commonly used IDF factor is

$$IDF(v) = \log \frac{|D|}{df(v)} = \log \frac{|D|}{|\{d \mid c(v, d) > 0\}|}.$$

There are a number of interpretations for this function, but one theoretical justification is the following. Notice that if we let X_v be a binary random variable that is equal to 1 if a document d sampled uniformly at random from

D contains v, we have

$$IDF(v) = \log \frac{|D|}{df(v)} = \log \frac{1}{p(X_v = 1 \mid D)} = -\log P(X_v = 1 \mid D)$$

which can be seen as a measure of the amount of information gained by observing an event where $X_v = 1$. Terms v with low $p(X_v = 1 \mid D)$ are more "surprising" to see than others, and will have a higher IDF weighting. One potential problem with this exact formulation is that the IDF of a term that appears in every document would be zero (because we gain no information if we observe $X_v = 1$ for that term). If we use this as a term weighting function, we would eliminate that term entirely from our computation. Should this not be desirable, an easy fix is to instead use

$$IDF(v) = \log \frac{|D| + 1}{df(v)}.$$

Most bag of words representations will combine a TF and an IDF factor by multiplying the two weights for a term, resulting in a weighting canonically referred to as a TF-IDF weighting.[3]

A final issue with this formulation, even if we use a TF-IDF transformation of the term weights, is that long documents will have a higher probability of scoring highly relative to shorter documents, even if the shorter document is more clearly similar to the query. For example, let's suppose we have a query "presidential campaign." A document that uses that phrase four times and has a length of only 1,000 words seems like it should be more relevant than a document that uses the phrase four times, but has 1,000,000 words. In this case, the second document just so happened to include the phrase "presidential campaign" a few times due to its massive length, but it does not really accurately define that document's content. This issue arises because the similarity function only considers the matched terms and their corresponding weights. A longer document has a higher chance of mentioning the query terms, even though the document is not truly about that query's content. We require some way of penalizing long documents, to normalize this effect. The most popular and effective normalization to account for the document length effect is known as "pivoted" document length normalization [63]. The main idea here is to reward short documents and penalize long documents by defining a "pivot" around which the reward/penalty changes. Typically, we define the pivot to be the average document length in the collection ($avgdl$), meaning we want to reward documents shorter than average and penalize

---

[3]TF-IDF weighting is ubiquitous. As we have discussed, however, there are many different formulations for both the TF and IDF factors. Literature often does not make clear which TF-IDF formulation was used; in this case one is forced to guess what the author's weighting scheme was. In many cases, the formulation is likely raw TF multiplied by the IDF formulation we discussed in this section but, frustratingly, one has no way of truly knowing.

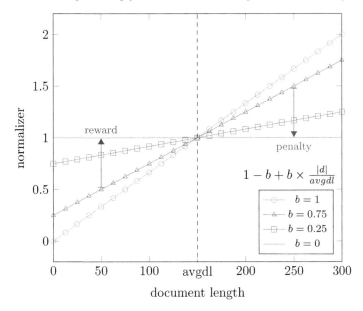

Figure 2.2: Pivoted document length normalization with varying parameter b. Note how documents below *avgdl* will be rewarded and documents above *avgdl* are penalized; *avgdl* is the pivot in this case.

documents longer than average. We'll do this by dividing the TF factor by our normalization

$$1 - b + b \times \frac{|d|}{avgdl},$$

where $b \in [0, 1]$ is a parameter controlling the slope around the pivot. This is illustrated in Figure 2.2.

If we combine all of these factors together, we can arrive at some of the best performing TF-IDF similarity functions. The traditional pivoted length normalization scoring function [63, 64] would be

$$pln(q, d) = \sum_{w \in q \cap d} c(w, q) \times \frac{\log_2(1 + \log_2(1 + c(w, d)))}{1 - b + b \times \frac{|d|}{avgdl}} \times \log_2 \frac{|D| + 1}{df(w)},$$

and the Okapi BM25 similarity function [15, 60] would be

$$bm25(q, d) = \sum_{w \in q \cap d} c(w, q) \times \frac{(k + 1) \times c(w, d)}{c(w, d) + k \times (1 - b + b \times \frac{|d|}{avgdl})} \times \log_2 \frac{|D| + 1}{df(w)}.$$

The TF-IDF transform for these two similarity functions is just the second two multiplicative terms. The second is a pivoted document length normalized TF factor (computed slightly differently between *pln* and *bm25*), and the third is a standard logarithmic IDF factor. We can use this re-weighting for all of the terms in our bag of words representation to great effect.

2.5.2 Beyond Single Words

While the bag of words representation is generally quite effective for tasks involving topic discrimination (notably information retrieval, text categorization and text clustering), there are several obvious limitations. First, word order is completely ignored, and thus it would be impossible to distinguish "education data mining" and "data mining education," which have very different meanings. Second, a single word is sometimes not specific enough to ensure accuracy of matching text; for example, "computer virus" may be matched with "computer" and "virus" separately in a document with a sentence such as "according to computer records in major hospitals, there are more cases infected by the virus this year than last year."

To address these limitations, it makes sense to go beyond single words and use phrases as units for text representation. Phrases can be identified using either natural language processing techniques or pure statistical analysis. For example, in Evans and Zhai [13], a parser is first used to identify all the noun phrases including those with prepositional phrases, which are then used to derive potentially many "smaller" phrases, e.g., two-word phrases where one word is a modifier of the other (called "head-modifier" pairs [69]). All such phrases can be used together with single words to achieve multi-resolution representation of text data. Parsing noun phrases to further obtain head-modifiers (e.g., we want "fast text processing" to generate "text processing" and "fast processing," but not "fast text") can also be done using a pure statistical approach [79]. The idea of using phrases as indexing terms has been studied extensively in information retrieval [13, 14, 36, 69]. An early study [14] compared syntactic phrases and statistical phrases and concluded that there was no significant difference between the two and the benefit of phrase indexing seems marginal, but more positive results from phrase indexing were reported in later studies [13, 69, 79].

Frequent pattern mining algorithms can be used to discover frequent patterns of word combinations (e.g., frequent word sets or frequent sequential word patterns), which can also be more informative/discriminative units for text representation than using single words as units. For example, a word set {*"learning," "algorithm," "classification"*} would be a more discriminative unit than the three words used individually as separate units. An advantage of a frequent pattern-based representation is that the word combination can be more flexible than in phrases that generally require words to be adjacent. For example, matching a pair of words like (*"water," "fish"*) by only requiring the two words to occur in a small window of text in any order (often called collocations [41]) can indicate the mention of a topic defined by the two words. While an exact phrase like "fish in water" might also capture that topic, it only applies when those three words are used in that exact order and thus will fail to match another topical segment such as "water with fish." Frequent pattern representations have been shown to be effective for text categorization [5].

In general, phrases and frequent word patterns can be expected to be beneficial when used together with single-word representations in various studies due to the additional discrimination achieved by such larger units. This specificity achieved by larger units is both a benefit and a detriment: these larger units are inevitably less frequently observed in text data as a direct consequence of their higher specificity. Using such larger units alone would therefore suffer from poor coverage of all text data and cause overfitting in supervised learning. The simultaneous inclusion of single-word-based features is generally essential to alleviate the problem of overfitting and insufficient coverage of text data. In other words, such larger units may be regarded as supplementary with the bag of words representation. A special case where phrases should be used to replace single words is lexical atoms or non-compositional compounds such as "hot dog" or "blue chip," where the meaning of a whole phrase is very different from the meaning of each individual word. Such lexical atoms can be automatically discovered using statistical approaches based on word associations [37, 78]. Some experiments [82], however, did not show a significant impact of such units on information retrieval, perhaps due to the low coverage of these larger units in typical user queries.

2.6   Structural Representation of Text

A major limitation of the bag of words representation (and many of its extensions mentioned above) is that it discards much of the hierarchical structure of natural language. It does not consider word order at all, and it does not consider how phrases combine together into sentences. In many cases this information is not needed in order to achieve good performance on downstream tasks, but there are many tasks that do require knowledge about the structure of the language itself. For example, in the domain of non-native text analysis [45] it is quite important to understand how non-native speakers of a language construct their sentences in order to provide suggestions for automated grammatical error correction, or to detect what the native background of a speaker might be. In the domain of authorship attribution [68] the need is similar—in order to understand who likely wrote a piece of text of unidentified authorship, it is often important to understand the text at the level of syntactic constructions as different authors will tend to have different sentence construction styles. Thus, it is important to be able to extract features from text documents that can capture something about their structural representation.

In order to construct this representation, we will start with the sequence of words representation from Section 2.4. From this representation, we will employ several different natural language processing (NLP) techniques to further refine our understanding of the word sequence. We should note that each of

$$\text{I}_{PRP} \quad \text{eat}_{VBP} \quad \text{pizza}_{NNS} \quad \text{with}_{IN} \quad \text{pepperoni}_{NNS} \quad \text{.}$$

Figure 2.3: A POS-tagged sentence. The tags for each word are indicated in the subscript and are example tags from the Penn Treebank corpus [43].

these steps is likely not completely accurate, as NLP is not an entirely solved subfield. Nevertheless, NLP techniques today are quite powerful, and in many cases they are still useful for describing a document, even if one particular technique makes some mistakes in its analysis.

The first thing we must do is identify sentence boundaries. This can be done for most languages with very high accuracy [59] by looking for punctuation marks and employing a set of rules or simple regular expressions. Most natural language processing toolkits [42, 44] provide this functionality as a preprocessing step. Once we have individual sentences, we then need to start building up a hierarchical representation of the individual sentences. As a first step, we will need to identify the parts of speech for each word in the sentence, known as POS tagging the sentence. While accuracies for this step vary across different languages, for English this step has around 97% accuracy[4] (approaching that of the annotator agreement between linguists [40]). There are a number of different models that have achieved this level of accuracy [6, 8, 40], and the functionality is provided in most NLP toolkits. We can extract some meaningful features about the structure of the language from a POS-tagged sequence-of-words representation. For example, we can consider adjacent n-grams of POS tags as giving us a shallow representation of the "style" of the sentence constructions the author tends to use [16, 29].

However, to go further and understand the hierarchical structure of the text, it is necessary to parse the sentence to produce a syntactic parse tree. A simple syntactic parse tree is given in Figure 2.4. This tells us exactly how the sentence is decomposed into phrases hierarchically, which is incredibly useful for extracting features that describe an author's choices in sentence construction. One simple feature set would simply be to count the number of occurrences of each non-terminal node in the tree to construct a bag of non-terminals [4].

A slightly more sophisticated feature would be to consider the "rewrite rules" of the tree [1]. A rewrite rule is simply one step in the production of the tree, so it considers a single expansion of a non-terminal node (e.g., NP → NP PP). Each rewrite rule occurrence would then be counted up and a document could be represented as a bag of rewrite rules. Extracting rewrite rule features from a parse tree is straightforward and can be done via a simple tree traversal.

Another possibility is to use a feature set consisting of all possible *subtrees* encountered in some training data set of parsed sentences. This can be seen as generalizing the rewrite rule to a depth greater than one. Unfortunately, this

---

[4]See: `https://aclweb.org/aclwiki/POS_Tagging_(State_of_the_art)`

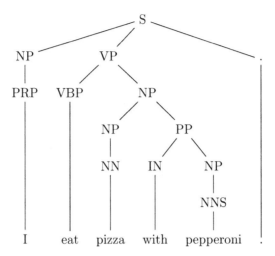

Figure 2.4: An example syntactic parse tree.

will produce an exponential number of features, so clever techniques for computing the dot product of the feature vectors that would be induced for two parse trees (also called a tree kernel) have been designed [9, 55]. Considering only the structure of the subtrees is a way of reducing the feature space [46]. Essentially, the idea is to consider subtree features where the syntactic category and surface words are deleted. Thus, two trees that are structurally the same but have different internal nodes would be collapsed down into the same feature. One can also consider keeping only certain syntactic categories; a semi-skeleton feature keeps only the root syntactic category and eliminates all of the others.

As another generalization of a rewrite rule, one can consider k-embedded edge (k-*ee*) subtree patterns [28, 29]. These are defined as a set of subtrees that are connected via at most k embedded edges. An embedded edge is a pair of nodes $e = (a, d)$ where a and d share an ancestor-descendant relationship. Unfortunately, there are again an exponential number of these features that could be extracted, so careful pattern growth and pruning algorithms must be applied in order to efficiently extract useful features of this kind.

2.6.1   Semantic Structure Features

Analogously to syntactic structure features, we may also obtain semantic structure features by performing entity-relation extraction and semantic role labeling. Structure-based features, including both syntactic and semantic structure features, can all be combined with word sequence-based features in a unified graph representation framework [24] to facilitate definition of potentially many interesting "hybrid" features that may consist of words combined with related substructures. For example, a hybrid feature may be defined as a co-occurrence of a PERSON entity and a LOCATION entity in a substructure that contains the preposition "in," which may be useful for relation extraction from text data. Features representing a sentence from multiple perspectives, including surface words and parse trees, have been systematically studied for the task of relation extraction [24], and the conclusion was that a combination of features of different levels of complexity and from different sentence representations, coupled with task-oriented feature pruning, tends to give the best performance.

2.7 Latent Semantic Representation

When we consider using individual words as features in documents, we can encounter trouble due to polysemy—the same symbol (word) can mean different things depending on its context. One way of distinguishing the meaning of a polysemous word may be to use grammatical structure or the part of speech, but this may fail to tease apart the differences between the "bank" that you deposit your paycheck at and the "bank" of the river where you go fishing as both are nouns. Sophisticated NLP techniques may be able to determine that the first "bank" is a location, but this is also true for the second! In practice, many of these polysemous words are conflated and treated as a single feature even when they mean dramatically different things.

Further complicating things is the "vocabulary mismatch" problem: because language is so free, there are often many different ways to refer to the same thing. In many cases, this freedom of expression allows for completely disjoint word usage to refer to the same object, which presents a huge challenge for word-based feature representations to overcome. For example, if a query obtained by a search engine uses one set of words to refer to the concept desired, and the documents use another, we are unlikely to obtain meaningful results because the relevant documents won't have any term overlap with the query, despite being *semantically* similar. These issues prompted a number of document representation methods that seek to bridge this vocabulary gap and mismatch problem.

2.7.1 Latent Semantic Analysis

The first major method is called Latent Semantic Analysis (LSA) [11]. The central idea in LSA is to try to perform dimensionality reduction on the term-document matrix (often with weights transformed using TF-IDF weighting) to obtain a representation of documents in a lower-dimensional *semantic* vector space, rather than staying in the original *word-based* vector space. This is achieved via the application of truncated singular value decomposition on

$$\underbrace{\begin{pmatrix} w_{1,1} & \cdots & w_{1,|D|} \\ w_{2,1} & \cdots & w_{2,|D|} \\ \vdots & \cdots & \vdots \\ w_{|V|,1} & \cdots & w_{|V|,|D|} \end{pmatrix}}_{\mathbf{W} \in \mathbb{R}^{|V| \times |D|}} \approx$$

$$\underbrace{\begin{pmatrix} t_{1,1} & \cdots & t_{1,k} \\ t_{2,1} & \cdots & t_{2,k} \\ \vdots & \cdots & \vdots \\ t_{|V|,1} & \cdots & t_{|V|,k} \end{pmatrix}}_{\mathbf{T} \in \mathbb{R}^{|V| \times k}} \times \underbrace{\begin{pmatrix} s_{1,1} & & & \\ & s_{2,2} & & \\ & & \ddots & \\ & & & s_{k,k} \end{pmatrix}}_{\mathbf{S} \in \mathbb{R}^{k \times k}} \times \underbrace{\begin{pmatrix} d_{1,1} & \cdots & d_{1,|D|} \\ d_{2,1} & \cdots & d_{2,|D|} \\ \vdots & \cdots & \vdots \\ d_{k,1} & \cdots & d_{k,|D|} \end{pmatrix}}_{\mathbf{D} \in \mathbb{R}^{k \times |D|}}$$

Figure 2.5: A visual depiction of the matrices involved in the truncated SVD for performing LSA on a corpus. $\mathbf{W}$ is the term-document matrix where each column vector represents a document, $\mathbf{T}$ is the term-factor matrix, $\mathbf{S}$ is the diagonal matrix of the top k singular values, and $\mathbf{D}$ is the factor-document matrix.

the term-document matrix (for which there exist efficient randomized algorithms [22]). The goal of SVD is to find a decomposition of the input matrix $\mathbf{M}$ into a multiplication of three matrices $\mathbf{U\Sigma V}$, where $\mathbf{U}$ is the matrix of *left singular vectors*, $\mathbf{\Sigma}$ is a diagonal matrix of *singular values*, and $\mathbf{V}$ is the matrix of *right singular vectors*. If we stop the computation after finding only the first k singular values, we have the truncated SVD. The example input and output of the truncated SVD for LSA is given in Figure 2.5. Geometrically, we can think of the left singular vectors (multiplied with the singular values matrix) as mapping each *term* into a reduced k-dimensional space. Similarly, we can think of the right singular vectors (multiplied by the singular values matrix) as mapping each *document* into a reduced k-dimensional space. Each dimension in this reduced space can be thought of as representing a latent concept.

We can now compute document-document similarity using the right singular vectors as follows. Assuming we are using dot-product similarity, we can compute the similarity between all pairs of documents from the original matrix $\mathbf{W}$ as $\mathbf{W}^T\mathbf{W}$, as each element of this matrix would now represent the similarity between the i-th and the j-th document. Using our approximation, we would have

$$\mathbf{W}^T\mathbf{W} \approx (\mathbf{TSD})^T\mathbf{TSD}$$
$$\approx \mathbf{D}^T\mathbf{S}^T\mathbf{T}^T\mathbf{TSD}$$
$$\approx \mathbf{D}^T\mathbf{S}^2\mathbf{D}$$

due to the fact that $\mathbf{T}$ is orthonormal and $\mathbf{S}$ is diagonal. Thus, we can treat $\mathbf{D}^T\mathbf{S}$ as a k-dimensional representation of our documents and compute dot products in this space to compute similarities.

How do we compute similarity to an unseen document (queries)? We can leverage the matrix $\mathbf{T}$ to create a mapping from the term vector for the unseen document to the k-dimensional document space. Let q be the $|V|$ vector representation for the unseen document. Then, we can compute

$$\hat{q} = q^T\mathbf{T}$$

and compute dot products against the elements of $\mathbf{D}^T\mathbf{S}$. This effectively amounts to placing q at the centroid of the factor vectors for its terms extracted from $\mathbf{T}$.

There are several advantages to this representation. Because it is abstracting at a higher level than that of individual words, issues arising from the vocabulary gap are mitigated, as words that are synonymous will have similar vector representations in $\mathbf{T}$, resulting in queries about a particular topic sharing a similar vector representation despite potentially using disjoint words. It is also computationally useful to instead use the reduced size document representations obtained from $\mathbf{D}^T\mathbf{S}$ to compute similarity scores between documents for clustering and other unsupervised learning techniques.

However, it does a poor job at resolving the problem of polysemy. Because each term is represented with exactly one vector, a word like "bank" will end up represented as a weighted average of two different meanings. Queries using "bank" will still have trouble with fetching documents that are about the wrong meaning because of this. It is also hard to interpret the meaning of the document and term vectors in the reduced space, as the vector entries are unconstrained real numbers.

2.7.2 Probabilistic Latent Semantic Analysis

To address these issues, a generative model called Probabilistic Latent Semantic Analysis (PLSA) was introduced [23]. PLSA seeks to uncover a latent semantic representation of documents just like LSA, but it does so by constructing a probability model for the corpus and representing documents under that probability model. Thus, document representations obtained by PLSA can be interpreted by inspection because the parameters of a PLSA model are parameters of well-formed probability distributions.

PLSA assumes that there exist K latent concepts in a corpus (alternatively called topics) of M documents. Each of these concepts is represented as a categorical distribution over words ϕ_k. Simply inspecting the distribution ϕ_k can be informative for interpreting the meaning of the k-th latent concept. Each document d is modeled as a mixture over these K components and associated with a categorical distribution θ_d over each of the K topics. Inspecting the vector θ_d thus provides insight into the mixing proportions over the K topics for this document. The generative process for the content of a document is to,

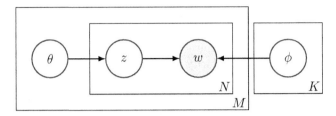

Figure 2.6: Plate notation for the PLSA graphical model. $M = |D|$ is the number of documents in the corpus, N is the number of words in a document, and K is the number of concepts/topics.

for each word, draw a concept $z \sim Categorical(\theta_d)$, and then draw the word $w \sim Categorical(\phi_z)$. This process is shown using plate notation in Figure 2.6.

The goal is then to infer the parameters $\phi_{1:K}$ and $\theta_{1:M}$ from a corpus of documents. Unfortunately, there is no closed-form solution for doing so, but one can appeal to the expectation maximization algorithm (EM algorithm) to obtain a maximum likelihood estimate of the parameters [12]. The essential idea is this: start with random guesses for $\phi_{1:K}$ and $\theta_{1:M}$ and then infer the expectation of the latent variables z for each document (E-step). Then, given this expectation, re-compute the most appropriate guess for $\phi_{1:K}$ and $\theta_{1:M}$ in a hill-climbing approach (M-step). This is guaranteed to converge to a local maximum. In practice, one can re-start the algorithm from multiple starting points and take the result that achieved highest data likelihood as a reasonable work-around for finding an inappropriate local maximum.

How does PLSA address polysemy? If we consider the "bank" example again, this word may occur in several of the different ϕ_k, each of which would correspond to some semantically coherent collection of words. In this case, we can distinguish the river bank from the financial institution by considering the other words in the topic: if it occurs with things like "river," "water," and "fishing" we can safely assume that "bank" in that context is referring to the edge of a river. If instead it appears alongside the words "interest," "rate," and "mortgage" in the same topic, we can safely assume that "bank" in that context is referring to the financial institution.

In a similar way to LSA, similarities between documents can be computed by computing the similarity of their concept vectors θ_d, which in the case of PLSA represent distributions over the K topics. This representation abstracts a bit beyond the surface-level words and in much the same way as LSA allows for us to bridge the vocabulary gap somewhat by comparing topical similarity instead of comparing individual word occurrences directly.

To compute similarities against a new document q, we can "fold in" the document into the model and perform iterations of the EM algorithm where we only update the parameters for θ_q, leaving all others fixed in the M-step of the algorithm. However, this can be somewhat unsatisfying from a theoretical point of view as this is not a "fully generative" process. We have to pretend

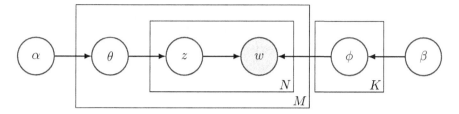

Figure 2.7: Plate notation for the LDA graphical model. $M = |D|$ is the number of documents in the corpus, N is the number of words in a document, and K is the number of concepts/topics. Notice that θ and ϕ now have Dirichlet prior distributions.

as though the model has an additional $K - 1$ parameters and re-fit that part of the model for each new document we see.

2.7.3 Latent Dirichlet Allocation

A complete generative process for topic modeling to fix this potential deficiency was proposed as Latent Dirichlet Allocation [2], where the PLSA model is modified to incorporate a Dirichlet prior over the topic proportions $\theta_{1:M}$ and the topics $\phi_{1:K}$ themselves. LDA is depicted using plate notation in Figure 2.7, and the generative process of LDA can be described as follows:

1. Sample a document topic proportion $\theta \sim \text{Dirichlet}(\alpha)$.

2. For each word w_n in the document,

    (a) sample a topic assignment $z_n \sim \text{Multinomial}(\theta)$, and
    (b) sample a word $w_n \sim \text{Multinomial}(\phi_{z_n})$.

Under this model, $\theta_{1:M}$ and $\phi_{1:K}$ are now *latent variables* rather than parameters, so they must be inferred rather than optimized. Because of this, however, we can easily adapt to new documents by applying the same inference process we applied to the training documents—from the perspective of the model, there is no difference between an "observed" training document and a "held out" testing document. Both require an inference method to be run to infer their θ_d distributions.

Unfortunately, however, performing exact inference in the LDA model (and many models like it) is intractable, so in order to estimate the parameters one must appeal to approximate inference methods. Two approaches dominate: (mean field) variational inference [2] and Markov chain Monte Carlo (MCMC) methods [21]. In the variational inference methods, one approximates the posterior distribution of interest by creating a simpler distribution that drops many of the problematic conditional dependencies between variables[5] and

---

[5]In many cases, this distribution is chosen to be fully factorized.

framing inference as an optimization problem: find the set of parameters for the surrogate distribution that most closely approximates the distribution of interest by minimizing the KL-divergence [30] between the two. This creates a deterministic hill-climbing algorithm for inference under the LDA model whose approximation will depend on the type of surrogate distribution chosen. If one marginalizes out θ and ϕ to create a "collapsed" distribution, one can perform variational inference in that setting and obtain a better approximation guarantee [73].

The other most common approach also leverages this "collapsed" distribution obtained after integrating out θ and ϕ and is called collapsed Gibbs sampling [21]. Here, the inference problem is posed as a sampling procedure over the latent variables z. Starting from some arbitrary initialization, each of the individual z variables is re-sampled from the full conditional distribution which depends on all of the *other* latent variable assignments. An iteration of the procedure finishes when each of the latent variables for the whole corpus has been sampled in turn. After a sufficient number of iterations, samples of θ and ϕ can be obtained from the current state of the z assignments. If enough iterations are performed, these samples are guaranteed to be accurate samples from the true posterior.

In the end, this produces a similar representation to that obtained from PLSA, but the incorporation of the priors can make LDA slightly more flexible. In PLSA one obtains a maximum likelihood estimate, but in LDA one can compute expectations with respect to the full underlying distribution, naturally supporting computation of representation of unseen new text data, which can only be achieved via heuristic approaches with PLSA. Furthermore, the priors can be used to encode additional information in order to guide the model in the right direction. Proper setting of these parameters is quite important in practice [38, 75].

A related technique for solving the vocabulary gap problem is document expansion [65, 72], where the idea is to expand the vector representation of a text object with additional words that occur in other related text objects. This can be generally done by computing the similarity between the current text object and other text objects in a large collection and interpolating the feature vector of the current object with the vectors of other similar text objects to obtain an "expanded" vector representation for the current object that can be expected to have more terms with non-zero weight. This achieves an effect where it is as if many more (related) words occurred in the current text object. In the special case of a query as the current text object, such a method would achieve query expansion based on the top-ranked retrieved documents, an important technique for improving retrieval results called pseudo-relevance feedback [32, 76, 80].

2.8   Explicit Semantic Representation

The major shortcoming of the latent semantic representations discussed earlier is that interpreting the latent space into which the documents were mapped can be challenging. While this is less of a problem with the PLSA and LDA models, there is still some amount of interpretation work that must be done to understand the meaning of each topic.

An alternative would be to assume that there exists some *explicit* semantic space which we can map documents into. This space would have the benefit of being inherently interpretable because its dimensions correspond directly to known concepts. This approach is called explicit semantic analysis (ESA) [18,19]. Typically, the dimensions chosen for the explicit semantic space correspond to concepts from some knowledge base. Wikipedia is a common choice for the semantic space, where each individual article is assumed to represent a distinct concept.

How do we map new documents into this semantic space? We can do so by leveraging an inverted index (like one that may be constructed to create a search engine over the underlying knowledge base). For each term w in the document, we can obtain a list of Wikipedia articles that contain that term along with a TF-IDF weight associated with that (d, w) pair from the inverted index. We can then represent the word w as a $|D|$-dimensional vector whose values are the TF-IDF scores for each document $d \in D$ from Wikipedia. To compute the representation for an entire document, we can take the (weighted) average of all of these vectors for all of the words in a document.

One interesting side-effect of this method is that we are actually obtaining a vector-space representation for individual *words* rather than for individual documents. This gives us the ability to encode potentially transferable knowledge about individual words in a way that is not tied directly to the surface form. If we learn something about a word that occurs in three Wikipedia articles d_1, d_2 and d_3, we can transfer that knowledge to other words that occur in any of $d_{1:3}$.

2.9   Embeddings for Text Representation

One persistent problem in most text representations is how to generalize knowledge obtained about one particular word to other words that are somehow similar. In the previous two sections we discussed ways of attempting to address this by mapping documents into a semantic space which is either treated as latent (LSA, PLSA) or explicit (ESA). The last method, ESA, provided us with an interesting property that each individual *word* was mapped to a point in a high-dimensional vector space, allowing us to potentially transfer knowledge between words that occur in similar knowledge base documents. The size of this vector space depends on the number of documents that occur in your knowledge base, and in many cases is a very high dimensional space. The quality of the vector space also depends on the quality of the knowledge base. This hurts our ability to generalize across semantically similar words.

What if we again treat the semantic space as being latent and attempt to map *individual words* into this latent semantic space, rather than documents? Our goal is to obtain a vector representation for each word, and we desire a latent space that has a small number of dimensions relative to the total number of words in our vocabulary. We want this space to be such that words that are similar semantically are close together in this low-dimensional vector space. Approaches taking this view are called word embedding methods, as the goal is to "embed" the words into some vector space.

You might be thinking that we have already solved this problem in Section 2.7 when we discussed Latent Semantic Analysis. One side effect of the SVD that was performed as part of LSA was indeed the creation of a low-dimensional vector space that each word was implicitly mapped into, but it makes a particular assumption about the definition of what it means for two words to be semantically related. In particular, LSA says two words are semantically similar if they occur in similar documents. ESA also exhibits this property, where instead two words are similar if they occur in similar knowledge base articles.

But is this the right choice? An alternative definition would be one proposed by John Rupert Firth [17] which states:

> You shall know a word by the company it keeps.

In essence, this codifies the intuition we teach our children: using "context clues," we can infer the meaning of an unknown word by the words that surround it in some context. That context may be a window surrounding the word, the sentence it occurs in, or the paragraph that contains it. In LSA and ESA, we take perhaps the broadest possible definition of "context" as that of the entire document, but it arguably makes more sense to limit our definition of context somewhat to match how we ourselves actually learn the meaning of unknown words as we encounter them in written text. We typically do not rely on the entire document to understand a word's meaning, instead choosing a much more restrictive context window to help our understanding.

2.9.1   Matrix Factorization for Word Embeddings

Perhaps the first meaningful attempt we can make at solving this problem, then, is to re-frame the technique of LSA to instead occur on a term-term co-occurrence matrix rather than a term-document co-occurrence matrix. The meaning of the semantic representation obtained for our words will depend on how we define term-term co-occurrence. The most common approach is to simply consider a window of a fixed size around each word of a document and say that all other words that appear within the window co-occurred. These co-occurrence counts can then be aggregated across all words in all documents in some training set to construct the large co-occurrence matrix.

Much like it was useful to apply TF-IDF weighting to our term-document co-occurrence matrix before running SVD in LSA, it is also important in the word embedding case. A common weighting is called pointwise mutual information (PMI) [7] which is computed as

$$PMI(w, c) = \log \frac{P(w, c)}{P(w)P(c)},$$

the log-ratio of the joint probability of seeing word w in the context of word c to the probability of seeing w and c individually assuming they were independent. This value will be large when the two words are highly correlated. One issue with this weighting is that there will be many entries where $PMI(w, c) = \log 0 = -\infty$. Two common workarounds exist: either set $PMI(w, c) = 0$ for all unobserved (w, c) pairs, or instead drop all entries in the matrix where $PMI(w, c) < 0$, keeping only the positive pointwise mutual information (PPMI) values [3]. The result is a large sparse matrix where each word is a vector whose entries correspond to the PPMI measure between that word in the context of each of the other words. This can be useful directly, but just as in LSA it is common to perform SVD on this matrix to instead produce a much lower-dimensional, dense representation for each word. Under this decomposition, one can obtain two different vectors for each word: one that describes the word directly when it is the "target" word in a window (obtained from the left singular vectors), and another that describes the word when it is observed as a "context" word in a window (obtained from the right singular vectors).

While this representation performs well in practice [35], one could question whether a more direct method of representation learning might be more effective. If we want to capture relationships between words in a meaningful way in the underlying vector space, it would make sense to directly construct an objective that optimizes towards this goal. GloVe [57] is an approach in this direction. It begins by considering how one can understand the relationship between the two words "ice" and "steam" by considering their co-occurrence probabilities with various other probe words k. Let $P(k \mid i)$ be the probability of observing a word k in the context of another word i. GloVe observes that the co-occurrence probability *ratios* are very meaningful. In particular, we can discover that the word "solid" is more related to "ice" as compared to "steam" by observing that the ratio $P(\text{solid} \mid \text{ice})/P(\text{solid} \mid \text{steam})$ is large. Similarly, the word "gas" is more related to "steam" than "ice" because the ratio $P(\text{gas} \mid \text{ice})/P(\text{gas} \mid \text{steam})$ is very small. The goal in GloVe is to ensure that vector-space operations on the learned word representations can capture the meaning encoded in these co-occurrence probability ratios. Much like SVD, GloVe will learn two different sets of vectors, $\mathbf{w}_i$ for the "target" word representation for word i and $\tilde{\mathbf{w}}_i$ for the "context" word representation for word i. Both sets of vectors will belong to some low-dimensional real-valued vector space whose dimensions are chosen in advance as a hyper-parameter for the model. Conceptually, GloVe seeks to learn a function

$$F((\mathbf{w_i} - \mathbf{w_j}) \cdot \tilde{\mathbf{w}}_{\mathbf{k}}) \approx \frac{P(k \mid i)}{P(k \mid j)}$$

where the *vector difference* between the "target" word vector representations for i and j is used to represent their relationship to the context word representation for k via dot-product similarity. After some algebraic manipulations to ensure exchangability of word representations and the addition of bias terms, they arrive at the objective

$$\mathbf{w_i} \cdot \tilde{\mathbf{w}}_{\mathbf{k}} + b_i + \tilde{b}_k \approx \log \mathbf{X_{i,k}}$$

where b_i and $\tilde{b}_k$ are the bias terms and $\mathbf{X_{i,k}}$ is the co-occurrence count for term k appearing in the context of word i. To ensure that both rare and very frequent co-occurrences are not over-weighted in the objective, a weighting function G is introduced of the form

$$G(x) = \begin{cases} \left(\frac{x}{x_{max}}\right)^{\alpha} & x < x_{max} \\ 1 & \text{otherwise,} \end{cases}$$

where x_{max} and α are hyper-parameters with suggested defaults of 100 and 0.75 respectively. This results in the overall loss

$$J = \sum_{i,j} G(\mathbf{X_{i,j}})(\mathbf{w_i} \cdot \tilde{\mathbf{w}}_j + b_i + \tilde{b}_j - \log \mathbf{X_{i,j}})^2$$

which is minimized by using stochastic gradient descent.

2.9.2   Neural Networks for Word Embeddings

A different approach to word embeddings called `word2vec` [53, 54] discovers vector representations for words by constructing a neural network for a prediction task. They propose two different models: "continuous bag of words" (CBOW) and "skip-gram." In CBOW, the input to the neural network is the set of "context" words within a certain window surrounding a "target" word. The goal of the network is to predict what word should belong in the "target" position. In the skip-gram model, this prediction task is flipped: the goal is to predict each "context" based on the "target" word that appears at the center of the window. In both cases, we again learn real-valued, low-dimensional target vectors $\mathbf{w_i}$ and context vectors $\tilde{\mathbf{w}}_{\mathbf{i}}$ for each word i in the vocabulary. The dimensionality of the vector space is again a hyper-parameter.

In practice, however, training a neural network for either the CBOW or the skip-gram models can be prohibitively expensive due to the need to compute the normalizing constant for the softmax output layer, which involves a sum over the entire vocabulary. Mikolov et al. [54] provide some tricks to improve the computational efficiency of this step via the use of a "hierarchical softmax" approach which reduces the complexity of computing the softmax output layer from $O(|V|)$ to $O(\log |V|)$.

However, the dominant approach for computing word vectors today is actually via the use of another trick Mikolov et al. proposed called "negative sampling." This is actually a model that is related to, but not the same as, the original skip-gram model. Here, the objective is changed to instead produce a network that can determine whether a (word, context) pair came from the training data or was generated randomly (a "negative sample"). This is done by producing a number of these random examples for each true training pair obtained from the data, and training the neural network to distinguish the "true" sample from the randomly generated ones. More formally, given a sequence of training words $v_1, v_2, \ldots v_T$, they optimize the following objective:

$$\frac{1}{T} \sum_{t=1}^{T} \sum_{-c \leq j \leq c, j \neq 0} \left(\log \sigma(\tilde{\mathbf{w}}_{\mathbf{v_{t+j}}} \cdot \mathbf{w_{v_t}}) - \sum_{i=1}^{K} E_{k \sim P_n(w)} \left[\log \sigma(-\tilde{\mathbf{w}}_{\mathbf{k}} \cdot \mathbf{w_{v_t}}) \right] \right)$$

where the expectation is computed with respect to a noise distribution $P_n(w)$ over the words in the vocabulary. This is typically chosen such that

$$P_n(w) \propto \left(\frac{\#(w)}{T} \right)^{3/4}$$

where $\#(w)$ denotes the frequency of word type w in the training data. In practice, this objective is fast to train and results in high-quality word vectors [35].

2.9.3 Document Representations from Word Embeddings

In the above two sections we detailed several ways for deriving vector space representations for *words* rather than for *documents*. How can we go from these word embeddings to a full-fledged document representation? One straightforward approach is to simply embed a document at the centroid of all of its word vectors by taking the average. Another approach would be to take the minimum value in each vector dimension across all words in the document, and yet another would be to take the maximum. In practice, approaches like these can work well for short documents [10] such as tweets, but leave something to be desired for longer texts.

One could in principle represent a document as a bag of word vectors. Kusner et al. [31] used this representation and defined a function to measure the distance between two documents by computing the minimum amount of distance required in order to "move" the embedded words from one document to the embedded words of another. They called this distance the Word Mover's Distance and showed that it can be reduced to the well-studied Earth Mover's Distance.

What that approach does not give us, however, is a directly useful document representation for other purposes: it only allows us to define a distance function $dist(d_1, d_2)$ between two documents. However, one can directly construct representations for sentences and documents via slight modifications of the CBOW and Skip-Gram models. Le and Mikolov [33] proposed two "paragraph vector" models for document representation. The first, "paragraph vectors with distributed memory" (PV-DM), modifies the CBOW model by adding an additional paragraph "word" to the context. More concretely, each paragraph in the text is associated with a paragraph context vector $\tilde{\mathbf{p}}$. This vector is added in as an additional context vector in the standard CBOW model, and a representation is learned for the paragraph itself that helps it predict the individual target words for each target word in the entire paragraph. Intuitively, this is like adding a unique "pseudo-word" to the context window for every word within a paragraph, and then representing the paragraph with the context vector learned for the "pseudo-word."

The other model proposed, "paragraph vectors with distributed bag of words" (PV-DBOW), modifies the Skip-Gram model. Here, the prediction task for the network is to output the words obtained from a randomly sampled small window of words within the paragraph by using the paragraph's vector $\mathbf{p}$. This is similar to the Skip-Gram model where we have replaced the "target" word with the paragraph vector, and the goal is to predict the "context" words that occur in our randomly sampled window. A robust representation for the paragraph can be obtained by concatenating the PV-DM vector $\tilde{\mathbf{p}}$ with the PV-DBOW vector $\mathbf{p}$. A document representation can then be obtained by averaging (or taking the minimum, or the maximum) of the dimensions of paragraph vectors that comprise it. Alternatively, one could set the "paragraph" to be the entire document and directly learn an embedding for the document itself. Document representations obtained via paragraph vectors have been shown to outperform bag of words representations for certain tasks [33].

2.10   Context-Sensitive Text Representation

Text data are always associated with rich context information. For a piece of text, its context can be loosely defined as the situations in which it was originally produced. Some types of situations are explicit and can be observed from the metadata, such as the time, the source, the author, and the audience of the text. Some of the situations are implicit and need to be inferred from the text itself, such as the sentiment the author wanted to express and the topics they wanted to discuss. Some contexts are global and the entire document belongs to the same context; some contexts are fine-grained and apply to a local region of text, such as a phrase, a sentence, or an arbitrary window of adjacent words.

Different contexts can be correlated to or dependent on each other. For example, time points and geographic locations have natural orders and structures. Various contexts can even form a complex system, such as a social network of authors. It is worth mentioning that in computational linguistics, the word *context* usually refers to the linguistic context, or the text surrounding a linguistic unit, which is useful for inferring the meaning of that unit. A linguistic context also defines a "situation" in which the language unit was produced. We refer the reader to Mei [47] for a more detailed discussion of text and context.

There can be many such situations in a text data set, such as a time stamp, a location, an author, a topic, and the presence of a word, a phrase, an entity, or a sentiment. Without loss of generality, every situation defines a subset of the text data: that is, the portion of data produced under that situation. The union or intersection of multiple such unit contexts is also a (more complex) context, which defines a new subset (e.g., a time stamp and a location, a large range of time, or a community of scientists).

The approach of modeling context alongside text, or the practice of *contextual text mining*, is powerful and can be used to solve many important text mining problems, such as evolutionary analysis, temporal and spatiotemporal analysis, personalized analysis, topic analysis, sentiment analysis, and network analysis of text data. These have lots of applications for real-world text such as news, social media, scientific literature, customer reviews, electronic health records, etc. In particular, learning context-sensitive representations of text allows us to select the most relevant signal for downstream tasks, identify the differences or changes of content across contexts, and better infer the internal structures of language from the unstructured text data.

Formally, let us denote c as a context corresponding to one of such simple or complex situations, and C as the set of all possible contexts. Let D be the entire set of text data and D_c be the subset of data that falls into the context c. If we define a textual feature as w (e.g., a word, a phrase, or a distribution) and the set of all textual features as W, then the contextual features are some sort of interaction between W and C.

When text is represented as a certain structure of discrete features (e.g., bags or sequences of words, phrases, or parts of speech), a context-sensitive representation can be easily obtained as the same structure of contextual features, where a contextual feature can be defined as the interaction of the discrete text feature w and the context c, $\langle w, c \rangle$. For a given piece of text data d, the features have a nonzero weight if both $w \in d$ and $d \in D_c$ and a zero weight otherwise.

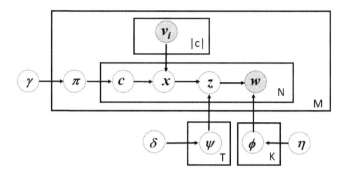

Figure 2.8: The multi-contextual LDA (mLDA) model [71], an example of a contextualized topic model for text. In the graphical structure, variables c and x denote a context type and a particular context of that type, which define a partition of the text data and a subset of the text data, respectively.

When a distributional representation is used (e.g., a document represented as a unigram language model), a context-sensitive counterpart can be obtained by a distribution of the same type, but *conditioned* on the context. That says, if we represent a piece of text as a word distribution $\{p(w)\}$, then a contextual word distribution $\{p(w \mid c)\}$ can be used to represent the piece of text that falls into a context c. These contextual distributions can be learned either from the contextualized subset of data D_c (e.g., documents of a certain year) [51], or through specialized graphical models that consider context variables in the generative process of text [50, 52, 61, 71], such as the example in Figure 2.8.

When a distributed representation is used (e.g., a document represented as a vector in a latent semantic space or by a higher layer of a neural network), a context-sensitive representation can be obtained either from the contextualized subset of text D_c or through machine learning methods that directly consider the context dimensions of data, such as tensor factorization [26] or contextualized neural networks [57, 70]. An example of such a contextualized deep neural network can be found in Figure 2.9.

While drilling down the data into contexts provides great flexibility to capture the differences among the situations, these contextualized representations inevitably suffer from the problem of data sparseness. Indeed, the interaction between text and context significantly increases the degree of freedom of the feature representations, and the contexualized subsets further reduce the information available to learn these representations. Overfitting appears to be a major concern for learning the context-sensitive representations. In literature, smoothing and regularization are common approaches to alleviating the data sparseness issue of contextual text mining [47]. In particular, network regularizations have been used to achieve the smoothness of text models over social network structures [48]; backoff techniques are used to smooth the personal-

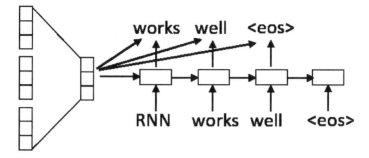

Figure 2.9: The gated context to sequence model (gC2S) [70], an example of a contextualized neural network for text. A multi-layer neural network is used as the encoder of the context and an RNN is used as the decoder, with skip-connections from contexts to words that are controlled by a gating function.

ized language models with models learned from larger crowds [49]. It is also common to model text representations of lower-level contexts as variations of those with higher-level contexts, and eventually variations of the global text representation [74]. These smoothed context-sensitive representations appear to be very effective in downstream contextual text mining tasks.

Since in many "big data" applications, it is desirable to exploit all kinds of data, including both text and non-text data, joint analysis of text and related non-text data (instead of analyzing text data without consideration of non-text data) is also generally desirable since it can facilitate construction of more effective features for such applications. For example, text data can be analyzed with a time series as "context" to discover topics that are correlated with the changes of the time series (called "causal topics" even though they are really correlated topics) [27]. This was done by iteratively constructing and refining topics that can both maximize the likelihood of the text data and have high correlations with the time-series variable. Experiment results show that the method can be used to discover topics from news articles that are "adaptive" to the context of a stock time series; such contextualized topics can be more effective features for prediction of stock trends than the features extracted from solely the text data.

2.11   Summary

Text data has rich semantics, making it necessary to go beyond the surface string representation to "deeper" representations reflecting meaning. In this chapter, we systematically reviewed the main techniques for computing text representation with a large portion of the content devoted to the bag of words representation, which by far remains the dominant text representation approach and appears to be effective and robust for a wide range of tasks. The effectiveness of such a seemingly simple approach is due to the fact that words are the "natural units" in human communications that are both sufficiently "small" to ensure coverage of all kinds of content in text data and semantically well defined to ensure meaningful matching of text data. However, additional features based on multiple words that can be obtained using either natural language processing techniques or statistical pattern analysis methods may be beneficial for some tasks especially when combined with single word representation. In some applications, text should be represented more from the perspective of syntactic structures or styles than the perspective of content, for which syntactic structure-based features would be useful. Statistical learning methods can be used to map text data into a latent vector space corresponding to latent variables in a generative model or hidden layers of neural networks which tends to have excellent generalization capacity, thus facilitating machine learning. Text data may also be mapped to an "external" explicit concept space to achieve interpretable representations. Finally, text data can be analyzed together with any non-textual context data to extract contextualized text representations; such joint analysis of text and non-text data is important in many "big data" applications where we generally have access to both kinds of data and it is desirable to use all the data for analysis and decision support. All these different methods for computing features for text data can be combined flexibly to obtain a very rich universe of features with variable granularities and perspectives for representing text data. While theoretically speaking, we can potentially feed all the features in such a large universe to a machine learning algorithm and let the algorithm take care of feature selection based on the training data, in reality, due to the inevitable data sparsity, we should only feed the subset of those features that can be expected to be most effective for a particular application. However, how to identify such an optimal subset remains a significant open challenge in feature engineering for text data that requires a combination of feature selection techniques and human supervision at the feature level.

Acknowledgments

The authors would like to thank Jian Tang and editors of the book for their useful feedback on early drafts of this manuscript. This material is based upon work supported by the National Science Foundation Graduate Research Fellowship Program under Grant Number DGE-1144245 and by the National Science Foundation research program under grant numbers IIS-1054199, IIS-1629161, CNS-1513939, and CNS-1408944.

Bibliography

[1] Harald Baayen, Hans van Halteren, and Fiona Tweedie. Outside the cave of shadows: using syntactic annotation to enhance authorship attribution. *Literary and Linguistic Computing*, 11(3):121–132, 1996.

[2] David M. Blei, Andrew Y. Ng, and Michael I. Jordan. Latent dirichlet allocation. *Journal of Machine Learning Research*, 3:993–1022, March 2003.

[3] John A. Bullinaria and Joseph P. Levy. Extracting semantic representations from word co-occurrence statistics: A computational study. *Behavior Research Methods*, 39(3):510–526, Aug 2007.

[4] Miao Chen and Klaus Zechner. Computing and evaluating syntactic complexity features for automated scoring of spontaneous non-native speech. In *Proceedings of the 49th Annual Meeting of the Association for Computational Linguistics: Human Language Technologies*, pages 722–731, Portland, Oregon, USA, June 2011.

[5] Hong Cheng, Xifeng Yan, Jiawei Han, and Chih-Wei Hsu. Discriminative frequent pattern analysis for effective classification. In *Proceedings of IEEE ICDE 2007*, pages 716–725, 2007.

[6] Jinho D. Choi. Dynamic feature induction: The last gist to the state-of-the-art. In *Proceedings of the 2016 Conference of the North American Chapter of the Association for Computational Linguistics: Human Language Technologies*, pages 271–281, San Diego, California, June 2016.

[7] Kenneth Ward Church and Patrick Hanks. Word association norms, mutual information, and lexicography. *Computational Linguistics*, 16(1):22–29, March 1990.

[8] Michael Collins. Discriminative training methods for hidden markov models: Theory and experiments with perceptron algorithms. In *Proceedings of the ACL Conference on Empirical Methods in Natural Language Processing*, EMNLP '02, pages 1–8, 2002.

[9] Michael Collins and Nigel Duffy. New ranking algorithms for parsing and tagging: Kernels over discrete structures, and the voted perceptron. In *Proceedings of 40th Annual Meeting of the Association for Computational Linguistics*, pages 263–270. Association for Computational Linguistics, July 2002.

[10] Cedric De Boom, Steven Van Canneyt, Thomas Demeester, and Bart Dhoedt. Representation learning for very short texts using weighted

word embedding aggregation. *Pattern Recognition Letters*, 80(C):150–156, September 2016.

[11] Scott Deerwester, Susan T. Dumais, George W. Furnas, Thomas K. Landauer, and Richard Harshman. Indexing by latent semantic analysis. *Journal of the American Society for Information Science*, 41(6):391–407, 9 1990.

[12] A. P. Dempster, N. M. Laird, and D. B. Rubin. Maximum likelihood from incomplete data via the em algorithm. *Journal of the Royal Statistical Society. Series B (Methodological)*, 39(1):1–38, 1977.

[13] David A. Evans and ChengXiang Zhai. Noun-phrase analysis in unrestricted text for information retrieval. In *Proceedings of the 34th annual meeting on Association for Computational Linguistics*, 1996.

[14] Joel L Fagan. *Experiments in automatic phrase indexing for document retrieval: a comparison of syntactic and non-syntactic methods.* 1987. Cornell University.

[15] Hui Fang, Tao Tao, and ChengXiang Zhai. A formal study of information retrieval heuristics. In *Proceedings of the 27th Annual International ACM SIGIR Conference on Research and Development in Information Retrieval*, SIGIR '04, pages 49–56, 2004.

[16] Song Feng, Ritwik Banerjee, and Yejin Choi. Syntactic stylometry for deception detection. In *Proceedings of the 50th Annual Meeting of the Association for Computational Linguistics (Volume 2: Short Papers)*, pages 171–175, Jeju Island, Korea, July 2012.

[17] J. R. Firth. *A Synopsis of linguistic Theory, 1930-1955.* 1957.

[18] Evgeniy Gabrilovich and Shaul Markovitch. Overcoming the brittleness bottleneck using wikipedia: Enhancing text categorization with encyclopedic knowledge. In *Proceedings of the 21st National Conference on Artificial Intelligence - Volume 2*, AAAI'06, pages 1301–1306, 2006.

[19] Evgeniy Gabrilovich and Shaul Markovitch. Computing semantic relatedness using wikipedia-based explicit semantic analysis. In *Proceedings of the 20th International Joint Conference on Artifical Intelligence*, IJCAI'07, pages 1606–1611, 2007.

[20] Yoav Goldberg. *Neural Network Methods for Natural Language Processing.* Synthesis Lectures on Human Language Technologies. Morgan & Claypool Publishers, 2017.

[21] Thomas L. Griffiths and Mark Steyvers. Finding scientific topics. *Proceedings of the National Academy of Sciences*, 101:5228–5235, 2004.

[22] Nathan P. Halko, Per-Gunnar Martinsson, and J. A. Tropp. Finding structure with randomness: Probabilistic algorithms for constructing approximate matrix decompositions. *Society for Industrial and Applied Mathematics Review*, 53(2):217–288, May 2011.

[23] Thomas Hofmann. Probabilistic latent semantic indexing. In *Proceedings of the 22Nd Annual International ACM SIGIR Conference on Research and Development in Information Retrieval*, SIGIR '99, pages 50–57, 1999.

[24] Jing Jiang and ChengXiang Zhai. A systematic exploration of the feature space for relation extraction. In *Human Language Technology Conference of the North American Chapter of the Association of Computational Linguistics, Proceedings, April 22-27, 2007, Rochester, New York, USA*, pages 113–120, 2007.

[25] Karen Spärck Jones. A statistical interpretation of term specificity and its application in retrieval. *Journal of Documentation*, 28(1):11–21, 1972.

[26] Alexandros Karatzoglou, Xavier Amatriain, Linas Baltrunas, and Nuria Oliver. Multiverse recommendation: n-dimensional tensor factorization for context-aware collaborative filtering. In *Proceedings of the fourth ACM conference on Recommender systems*, pages 79–86. ACM, 2010.

[27] Hyun Duk Kim, Malu Castellanos, Meichun Hsu, ChengXiang Zhai, Thomas A. Rietz, and Daniel Diermeier. Mining causal topics in text data: iterative topic modeling with time series feedback. In *Proceedings of the 22nd ACM international conference on Information and knowledge management*, pages 885–890, 2013.

[28] Sangkyum Kim, Hyungsul Kim, Tim Weninger, and Jiawei Han. Authorship classification: A syntactic tree mining approach. In *Proceedings of the ACM SIGKDD Workshop on Useful Patterns*, UP '10, pages 65–73, 2010.

[29] Sangkyum Kim, Hyungsul Kim, Tim Weninger, Jiawei Han, and Hyun Duk Kim. Authorship classification: A discriminative syntactic tree mining approach. In *Proceedings of the 34th International ACM SIGIR Conference on Research and Development in Information Retrieval*, SIGIR '11, pages 455–464, 2011.

[30] S. Kullback and R. A. Leibler. On information and sufficiency. *The Annals of Mathematical Statistics*, 22(1):79–86, 03 1951.

[31] Matt J. Kusner, Yu Sun, Nicholas I. Kolkin, and Kilian Q. Weinberger. From word embeddings to document distances. In *Proceedings of the 32nd International Conference on International Conference on Machine Learning - Volume 37*, ICML'15, pages 957–966, 2015.

[32] Victor Lavrenko and W. Bruce Croft. Relevance based language models. In *Proceedings of the 24th Annual International ACM SIGIR Conference on Research and Development in Information Retrieval*, SIGIR '01, pages 120–127, New York, NY, USA, 2001. ACM.

[33] Quoc Le and Tomas Mikolov. Distributed representations of sentences and documents. In *Proceedings of the 31st International Conference on Machine Learning (ICML-14)*, pages 1188–1196, 2014.

[34] Vladimir I. Levenshtein. Binary codes capable of correcting deletions, insertions, and reversals. *Soviet Physics Doklady*, 10(8):707–710, 1966. (English translation).

[35] Omer Levy, Yoav Goldberg, and Ido Dagan. Improving distributional similarity with lessons learned from word embeddings. *Transactions of the Association for Computational Linguistics*, 3:211–225, 2015.

[36] David D. Lewis. *Representation and learning in information retrieval.* 1992. Diss. University of Massachusetts at Amherst.

[37] Dekang Lin. Automatic identification of non-compositional phrases. In *Proceedings of the 37th Annual Meeting of the Association for Computational Linguistics on Computational Linguistics*, ACL '99, pages 317–324, Stroudsburg, PA, USA, 1999. Association for Computational Linguistics.

[38] Yue Lu, Qiaozhu Mei, and ChengXiang Zhai. Investigating task performance of probabilistic topic models: an empirical study of plsa and lda. *Information Retrieval*, 14(2):178–203, Apr 2011.

[39] H. P. Luhn. The automatic creation of literature abstracts. *IBM J. Res. Dev.*, 2(2):159–165, April 1958.

[40] Christopher D. Manning. Part-of-speech tagging from 97% to 100%: Is it time for some linguistics? In *Computational Linguistics and Intelligent Text Processing: 12th International Conference, CICLing 2011, Proceedings, Part I*, pages 171–189, February 2011.

[41] Christopher D. Manning and Hinrich Schütze. *Foundations of Statistical Natural Language Processing.* MIT Press, Cambridge, MA, USA, 1999.

[42] Christopher D. Manning, Mihai Surdeanu, John Bauer, Jenny Finkel, Steven J. Bethard, and David McClosky. The Stanford CoreNLP natural language processing toolkit. In *Association for Computational Linguistics (ACL) System Demonstrations*, pages 55–60, 2014.

[43] Mitchell Marcus, Grace Kim, Mary Ann Marcinkiewicz, Robert MacIntyre, Ann Bies, Mark Ferguson, Karen Katz, and Britta Schasberger. The penn treebank: Annotating predicate argument structure. In *Proceedings of the Workshop on Human Language Technology*, HLT '94, pages 114–119, 1994.

[44] Sean Massung, Chase Geigle, and ChengXiang Zhai. MeTA: A unified toolkit for text retrieval and analysis. In *Proceedings of ACL-2016 System Demonstrations*, pages 91–96, Berlin, Germany, August 2016. Association for Computational Linguistics.

[45] Sean Massung and ChengXiang Zhai. Non-native text analysis: A survey. *Natural Language Engineering*, 22(2):163–186, 2016.

[46] Sean Massung, ChengXiang Zhai, and Julia Hockenmaier. Structural parse tree features for text representation. In *2013 IEEE Seventh International Conference on Semantic Computing*, pages 9–16, Sept 2013.

[47] Qiaozhu Mei. *Contextual text mining*. PhD thesis, University of Illinois at Urbana-Champaign, 2009.

[48] Qiaozhu Mei, Deng Cai, Duo Zhang, and ChengXiang Zhai. Topic modeling with network regularization. In *Proceedings of the 17th international conference on World Wide Web*, pages 101–110. ACM, 2008.

[49] Qiaozhu Mei and Kenneth Church. Entropy of search logs: how hard is search? with personalization? with backoff? In *Proceedings of the 2008 International Conference on Web Search and Data Mining*, pages 45–54. ACM, 2008.

[50] Qiaozhu Mei, Xu Ling, Matthew Wondra, Hang Su, and ChengXiang Zhai. Topic sentiment mixture: modeling facets and opinions in weblogs. In *Proceedings of the 16th international conference on World Wide Web*, pages 171–180. ACM, 2007.

[51] Qiaozhu Mei and ChengXiang Zhai. Discovering evolutionary theme patterns from text: an exploration of temporal text mining. In *Proceedings of the eleventh ACM SIGKDD international conference on Knowledge discovery in data mining*, pages 198–207. ACM, 2005.

[52] Qiaozhu Mei and ChengXiang Zhai. A mixture model for contextual text mining. In *Proceedings of the 12th ACM SIGKDD international conference on Knowledge discovery and data mining*, pages 649–655. ACM, 2006.

[53] Tomas Mikolov, Kai Chen, Greg Corrado, and Jeffrey Dean. Efficient estimation of word representations in vector space. *CoRR*, abs/1301.3781, 2013.

[54] Tomas Mikolov, Ilya Sutskever, Kai Chen, Greg S Corrado, and Jeff Dean. Distributed representations of words and phrases and their compositionality. In *Advances in Neural Information Processing Systems 26*, pages 3111–3119. 2013.

[55] Alessandro Moschitti. Making tree kernels practical for natural language learning. In *Proceedings of the 11th Conference of the European Chapter of the Association for Computational Lingusitics*, pages 113–120, April 2006.

[56] Fuchun Peng, Fangfang Feng, and Andrew McCallum. Chinese segmentation and new word detection using conditional random fields. In *Proceedings of the 20th International Conference on Computational Linguistics*, COLING '04, 2004.

[57] Jeffrey Pennington, Richard Socher, and Christopher D. Manning. GloVe: Global vectors for word representation. In *Proceedings of the 2014 Conference on Empirical Methods in Natural Language Processing (EMNLP)*, pages 1532–1543, 2014.

[58] Martin F. Porter. An algorithm for suffix stripping. *Program*, 14(3):130–137, 1980.

[59] Jonathon Read, Rebecca Dridan, Stephan Oepen, and Lars Jørgen Solberg. Sentence boundary detection: A long solved problem? In *Proceedings of COLING 2012: Posters*, pages 985–994, Mumbai, India, December 2012.

[60] Stephen Robertson and Hugo Zaragoza. The probabilistic relevance framework: Bm25 and beyond. *Foundations and Trends in Information Retrieval*, 3(4):333–389, April 2009.

[61] Michal Rosen-Zvi, Thomas Griffiths, Mark Steyvers, and Padhraic Smyth. The author-topic model for authors and documents. In *Proceedings of the 20th conference on Uncertainty in artificial intelligence*, pages 487–494. AUAI Press, 2004.

[62] G. Salton, A. Wong, and C. S. Yang. A vector space model for automatic indexing. *Commun. ACM*, 18(11):613–620, November 1975.

[63] Amit Singhal, Chris Buckley, and Mandar Mitra. Pivoted document length normalization. In *Proceedings of the 19th Annual International ACM SIGIR Conference on Research and Development in Information Retrieval*, SIGIR '96, pages 21–29, 1996.

[64] Amit Singhal, John Choi, Donald Hindle, David D. Lewis, and Fernando Pereira. At&t at trec-7. In *TREC*, 1999.

[65] Amit Singhal and Fernando Pereira. Document expansion for speech retrieval. In *Proceedings of the 22Nd Annual International ACM SIGIR Conference on Research and Development in Information Retrieval*, SIGIR '99, pages 34–41, New York, NY, USA, 1999. ACM.

[66] Karen Spärck Jones and Peter Willett, editors. *Readings in Information Retrieval*. Morgan Kaufmann Publishers Inc., San Francisco, CA, USA, 1997.

[67] Richard Sproat and Thomas Emerson. The first international chinese word segmentation bakeoff. In *Proceedings of the Second SIGHAN Workshop on Chinese Language Processing - Volume 17*, SIGHAN '03, pages 133–143, 2003.

[68] Efstathios Stamatatos. A survey of modern authorship attribution methods. *Journal of the American Society for Information Science and Technology*, 60(3):538–556, March 2009.

[69] Tomek Strzalkowski. Natural language information retrieval. *Information Processing and Management*, 31(3):397–417, 1995.

[70] Jian Tang, Yifan Yang, Sam Carton, Ming Zhang, and Qiaozhu Mei. Context-aware natural language generation with recurrent neural networks. *arXiv preprint arXiv:1611.09900*, 2016.

[71] Jian Tang, Ming Zhang, and Qiaozhu Mei. One theme in all views: modeling consensus topics in multiple contexts. In *Proceedings of the 19th ACM SIGKDD international conference on Knowledge discovery and data mining*, pages 5–13. ACM, 2013.

[72] Tao Tao, Xuanhui Wang, Qiaozhu Mei, and ChengXiang Zhai. Accurate language model estimation with document expansion. In *Proceedings of the 14th ACM International Conference on Information and Knowledge Management*, CIKM '05, pages 273–274, New York, NY, USA, 2005. ACM.

[73] Yee W. Teh, David Newman, and Max Welling. A collapsed variational bayesian inference algorithm for latent dirichlet allocation. In *Advances in Neural Information Processing Systems 19*, pages 1353–1360. 2006.

[74] Ivan Titov and Ryan McDonald. Modeling online reviews with multigrain topic models. In *Proceedings of the 17th international conference on World Wide Web*, pages 111–120. ACM, 2008.

[75] Hanna M. Wallach, David M. Mimno, and Andrew McCallum. Rethinking lda: Why priors matter. In *Advances in Neural Information Processing Systems 22*, pages 1973–1981. 2009.

[76] Jinxi Xu and W. Bruce Croft. Query expansion using local and global document analysis. In *Proceedings of the 19th Annual International ACM SIGIR Conference on Research and Development in Information Retrieval*, SIGIR '96, pages 4–11, New York, NY, USA, 1996. ACM.

[77] Nianwen Xue et al. Chinese word segmentation as character tagging. *Computational Linguistics and Chinese Language Processing*, 8(1):29–48, 2003.

[78] ChengXiang Zhai. Exploiting context to identify lexical atoms – a statistical view of linguistic context. In *Proceedings of 1997 International and Interdisciplinary Conference on Modelling and Using Context*, pages 119–129, 1997.

[79] ChengXiang Zhai. Fast statistical parsing of noun phrases for document indexing. In *Proceedings of the 5th Conference on Applied Natural Language Processing*, pages 312–319, 1997.

[80] Chengxiang Zhai and John Lafferty. Model-based feedback in the language modeling approach to information retrieval. In *Proceedings of the Tenth International Conference on Information and Knowledge Management*, CIKM '01, pages 403–410, New York, NY, USA, 2001. ACM.

[81] ChengXiang Zhai and Sean Massung. *Text Data Management and Analysis: A Practical Introduction to Information Retrieval and Text Mining*. Association for Computing Machinery and Morgan & Claypool, New York, NY, USA, 2016.

[82] Chengxiang Zhai, Xiang Tong, Natasa Milic-Frayling, and David A. Evans. Evaluation of phrase-based index – CLARIT TREC-5 NLP track report. In *Proceedings of the Fifth Text REtrieval Conference (TREC-5)*, pages 347–357, 1997.

[83] Xiaoqing Zheng, Hanyang Chen, and Tianyu Xu. Deep learning for Chinese word segmentation and POS tagging. In *Proceedings of the 2013 Conference on Empirical Methods in Natural Language Processing*, pages 647–657, Seattle, Washington, USA, October 2013.

Chapter 3

Feature Extraction and Learning for Visual Data

Parag S. Chandakkar

Arizona State University

Ragav Venkatesan

Arizona State University

Baoxin Li

Arizona State University

Most visual computing tasks involve prediction, regression or decision making using *features* extracted from the original, raw visual data (images or videos). Feature engineering typically refers to this (often creative) process of extracting new representations from the raw data that are more conducive to a computing task. Indeed, the performance of many machine learning algorithms heavily depends on having insightful input representations that expose the underlying explanatory factors of the output for the observed input [6]. An effective data representation would also reduce data redundancy and adapt to undesired, external factors of variation introduced by sensor noise, labeling errors, missing samples, etc. In the case of images or videos, dimensionality reduction is often an integral part of feature engineering, since the raw data are typically high dimensional. Over the years, many feature engineering schemes have been proposed and researched for producing good representations of raw images and videos. Many existing feature engineering approaches may be categorized into one of three broad groups:

1. **Classical, sometimes hand-crafted, feature representations:** In general, these may refer to rudimentary features such as image gradients as well as fairly sophisticated features from elaborate algorithms such as the histogram of oriented gradients feature [13]. More often than not, such features are designed by domain experts who have good knowledge about the data properties and the demands of the task. Hence sometimes such features are called hand-crafted features. Hand-engineering features for each task requires a lot of manual labor and domain knowledge, and optimality is hardly guaranteed. However, it allows integration of human knowledge of the real world and of that specific task into the feature design process, hence making it possible to obtain good results for the said task. These types of features are easy to interpret. Note that it is not completely correct to call all classical features as being hand-crafted, since some of them are general-purpose features with little task-specific tuning (such as outputs of simple gradient filters).

2. **Advanced, latent-feature representations.** While the raw data may be of high dimensions, the factors relevant to a computing task may lie on a lower dimensional space. Latent representations may expose the underlying properties of data that exist but cannot be readily measured from the original data. These features usually seek a specific structure such as sparsity, decorrelation of reduced dimension, low rank, etc. The structure being enforced depends on the task. The sparsity and low dimensionality of these representations is often encouraged as real-world visual data have naturally sparse representations with respect to some basis (e.g., Fourier basis) and may also be embedded in a lower-dimensional manifold [66]. However, obtaining latent representations is often a difficult optimization process that may require extensive reformulation and/or clever optimization techniques such as alternating minimization.

3. **Deep representations through end-to-end learning.** Deep representations are obtained by passing raw input data with minimal preprocessing through a *learned* neural network, often consisting of a stack of convolutional and/or fully connected layers. As the input is propagated through each network layer, different data representations are obtained that abstract higher-level concepts. These networks are being

trained iteratively by minimizing a task-specific loss that alters the parameters/weights in all layers. Recently, deep features have been found extremely effective in many visual computing tasks, leading to tremendous gain in performance. Their most attractive property is their ability to learn from raw input with minimal pre-processing. Moreover, it appears that such learned representations can provide a reasonable performance on many tasks, alleviating the need for domain experts for each task. However, learning deep representations needs not only huge computational resources but also large data collections, making them suitable primarily only for computing clusters or servers with powerful GPUs, and for applications where abundant labeled data are readily available.

Exemplar feature representations from all these three broad categories will be elaborated in the remainder of this chapter.

3.1 Classical Visual Feature Representations

Images are the most common form of visual data in many visual computing applications. An image is a collection of pixels where each pixel is represented as a multidimensional array. Depending on the dimensionality of the pixels, images can be gray-scale, color or in other higher-dimensional forms such as RGBD (with RGB for color and D for depth). Raw pixel intensities can be viewed as the simplest form of feature representation. However, this is sensitive to many factors such as viewpoint change, lighting change, image interpolation, etc. Moreover, if each pixel value is treated as a separate feature, then that would result in a high-dimensional feature space. In turn, increased processing time and large amounts of training data are needed to make an inference from such high-dimensional features. Hence traditionally, most visual computing tasks do not directly operate on this simple form of representation of pixels, but on features extracted from them. Depending on how features are extracted, there are many feature extractors. Some categories include spatial versus frequency domain approaches, global versus local, appearance versus geometry, point versus area, etc. In the following section, we present a few classic feature representations that illustrate a wide variety of hand-crafted feature extractors. These processes produce representations that are better tuned to particular visual computing tasks.

3.1.1 Color Features

Color is one of the most fundamental yet discriminative attributes. Color is essential to our perception of everyday objects. In this subsection, we describe

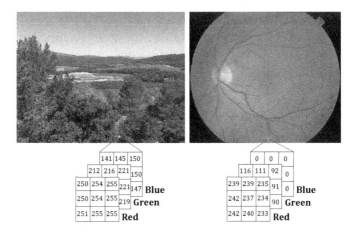

Figure 3.1: Left image shows a natural image and the right image is an example of a fundus image. Below each image, representation of a 3×3 block of pixel values is shown in a three-dimensional matrix form.

important features that characterize the color distribution in an image in a compact and efficient manner.

Color Histogram: A histogram provides a rough estimate of the underlying distribution of the data. To construct a histogram, the range of the input data is split into a number of bins. Then the number of data points falling in each bin are counted. This is followed by normalization. A histogram provides us with center, spread, skewness and number of modes present in the data. Let us consider the computation of a color histogram of an RGB image. The first step is to convert the RGB image into a single-channel image. To this end, the image is quantized such that each triplet (R,G,B) falls into a bin, converting the RGB image into a single channel image. The resulting image has as many distinct values as there were quantization bins. The quantized image is then vectorized and the histogram is computed by simply counting the occurrences of each bin. While this is the most common strategy, other alternatives also exist. For example, the histogram of each color channel can be computed separately and concatenated.

A color histogram is largely invariant to smaller changes in lighting and viewpoint. It can be computed in linear time, making it an effective feature for applications such as image retrieval [3, 4, 63]. On the other hand, its effectiveness depends on the binning strategy. For example, bins derived from a large collection of natural images are unlikely to work well for a fundus image shown in Figure 3.1 that has a predominantly red spectrum. A certain amount of *hand-crafting* is required to adapt the histogram to fundus images. To automatically derive the quantization bins for any dataset (assuming that it has sufficient number of samples), one can extract all the unique shades (i.e., RGB triplets) from the dataset and perform k-means clustering on them. The

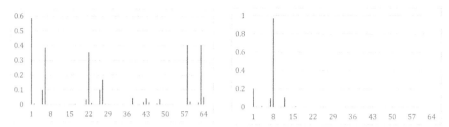

Figure 3.2: On the left: color histogram of the natural image; right: color histogram of the fundus image. Both images are obtained using a binning strategy based on the color distribution found in natural images.

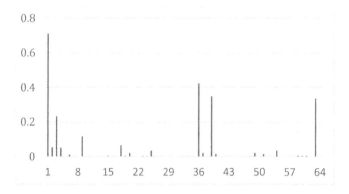

Figure 3.3: A color histogram of the fundus image using the adaptive binning strategy mentioned in [11, 59].

centroids can then be viewed as histogram bins. This approach was proposed in [59]. It produces a histogram that has more entropy than the one derived using bins based on natural images. Figure 3.2 shows a color histogram of the landscape image that uses pre-defined bins suitable for natural images. It also shows a color histogram of the fundus image using the same binning strategy. This binning strategy does not capture the color distribution in the fundus image well. By using this adaptive binning strategy, one may obtain a better histogram as shown in Figure 3.3 [10, 11, 59]. The obtained histogram has a higher entropy as it makes better utilization of the available number of bins. In practice, it has been observed that the adaptive binning strategy allows us to use fewer bins (e.g., 16 instead of 64) with almost no loss of performance [10, 11, 59].

Another drawback is that the color histogram does not model the relationship of adjacent pixels, thus failing to account for spatial distribution of different colors. As a remedy, a local color histogram (LCH) for image retrieval has been proposed [62]. To compute LCH, an image is divided into blocks and

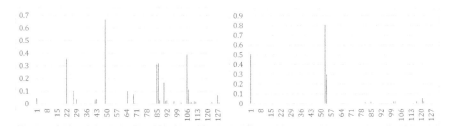

Figure 3.4: On the left: CCV of the landscape image; right: CCV of the fundus image. Both images are obtained using a binning strategy based on the color distribution of natural images.

for each, a color histogram is computed. All color histograms can then be averaged or concatenated to create the LCH. Though LCH is better at modeling regional similarities, it is sensitive to transformations such as rotation.

Color Coherence Vector: This is another feature that considers color spatial distribution. Color Coherence Vector (CCV) computation involves blurring the image with either a mean or a Gaussian filter. The image is then quantized using binning strategies similar to those mentioned above. Each pixel is classified as coherent or incoherent, where a pixel is considered coherent if it has a higher connected component count than a user-specified threshold. Repeating this for each bin produces CCVs. Alhough CCV models spatial distribution of different colors, it is possible that two different connected component patterns produce the same CCV. To overcome this, the relative position of the components is usually added as another feature dimension. Figure 3.4 shows CCVs for the landscape image and the fundus image. The same pattern can be observed here that the same binning strategy fails

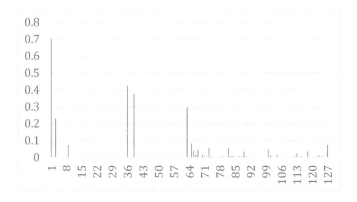

Figure 3.5: CCV of the fundus image using the adaptive binning strategy mentioned in [11, 59]

to work well for both the images. Figure 3.5 shows CCVs of the fundus image obtained with the adaptive binning strategy, which has a higher entropy.

Histogram of Color Moments: This feature is invariant to scaling and rotation. Color moments uniquely characterize the color distribution in an image. Color moments are computed on a per-channel basis. The first moment is just the average color of an image, whereas the next two moments describe the variance and the shape of the color distribution. These three moments provide sufficient information to carry out effective image retrieval [68]. Color moments work well under dynamic lighting conditions but fail under occlusion.

Color Correlogram: The above features do not lead to a compact representation that models both local as well as global distribution of colors in an image. Color histograms and CCVs fail when there is a large lighting change [30]. To overcome these drawbacks, color correlograms (CC) were proposed in [30]. The CC measures the global distribution of local correlation of colors. The rough procedure to compute the color correlogram is as follows:

1. Quantize the image into n colors (using the adaptive binning strategy, if applicable).

2. Pick a set of distance values denoted by $d \in \mathbb{N}$.

3. For each bin b_i, compute the probability that a bin b_j lies at a distance of d_k.

If only those pairs where $i = j$ are considered, then the feature is called an auto color correlogram, which has proven to be effective for image retrieval [30]. Repeating this for every distance value d_k and for all pairs of bins gives us a CC feature of size $m^2|d|$, where m is the number of bins and $|d|$ is the cardinality of the distance set. Efficient algorithms exist to compute CC in $O(n^2|d|)$ time. Extensive image retrieval experiments performed in [30] show that the CC is superior to the CCV and color histogram. The advantages of adaptive binning also carry over to the CC feature, providing a similar increase in performance [11, 59].

3.1.2 Texture Features

Another important descriptor of visual data is their textural properties. Some of the texture analysis approaches use spatial frequency to characterize textures since coarse textures constitute low spatial frequencies and vice versa. Another option is to quantify texture as the number of edges per unit area [24]. A review of the early approaches is given in [26]. We will now review some of the popular features for texture modeling.

Gray-level Co-occurrence Matrix (GCM): The GCM [25] can be computed for any image I. Denote the GCM by M, where,

$$M_{ij} = \{\#[I_{ij}] | I_{ij} = I_{i+1,j+1}\}. \tag{3.1}$$

Here, $\#[I_{ij}]$ is the cardinality of the set of pixels (denoted by $[I_{ij}]$) that satisfy the adjacency condition $I_{ij} = I_{i+1,j+1}$.

To model textures with reasonable confidence, we need multiple observations to fill each entry in M. There are two ways to achieve this. One option is to use a small number of quantization levels so that multiple pixels could satisfy the aforementioned condition. Higher quantization will lead to greater loss of accuracy. Another option is to evaluate the above condition over a larger window. This will cause errors if the texture changes significantly inside the window. The adjacency condition mentioned above models pixels that are below and to the right of the pixels under consideration. Three more types of adjacency conditions can be defined: below and to the left, below, and to the right. Haralick proposed fourteen types of statistics to be computed from the GCM to distinguish between different textures [25].

Laws' Texture Masks: Laws developed a texture-energy based approach in which a set of local masks is convolved with the image [36]. Initially, the image is pre-processed so that the average intensity in every small window is close to zero. Then, a set of vectors is defined to detect a level, a spot, an edge and a ripple as follows:

$$
\begin{aligned}
L &= [1, 4, 6, 4, 1] \\
E &= [-1, -2, 0, 2, 1] \\
S &= [-1, 0, 2, 0, -1] \\
R &= [1, -4, 6, -4, 1]
\end{aligned}
\tag{3.2}
$$

A set of 16 masks is then created by computing an outer product between every pair of masks. Note that some of the pairs created in this manner will be symmetric. Each mask is convolved with the image to generate a response. Responses arising from symmetric pairs of masks are averaged. Finally, we obtain nine matrices of convolution responses. Thus we obtain a single feature map where each point is a 9-D vector. The resultant feature map can be viewed as a texture map that can be used to cluster an image into regions of uniform texture.

Gabor Filter: The Gabor filter was invented in 1946 by Dennis Gabor [19]. Gabor filters serve as excellent features for texture analysis. They are efficient and at the same time, they outperform pyramid-structured/tree-structured wavelet transform features [12] as well as multi-resolution simultaneous autoregressive model (MR-SAR) [40] features.

A given image is convolved with Gabor filters at different scales and with different orientations to get several magnitude arrays that represent energies at different image scales and orientations. The first two moments of these energy arrays can be used to distinguish between different textures in an image. The first two moments of all magnitude arrays can be concatenated to form a feature vector, which can then be classified into one of the texture classes using a standard classifier, such as a support vector machine (SVM).

Steerable Gaussian Filter (SGF): Oriented filters are useful in many image processing tasks such as edge/contour detection, texture modeling, etc. One can apply the same filter rotated to different angles to get the various filter responses. Given this, it is often desirable to steer a filter and examine its changing response. SGF has a set of basis filters that can be used to derive a filter of arbitrary orientation [18].

Consider a simple symmetric Gaussian function G as follows:

$$G(x, y) = \exp\left(-(x^2 + y^2)\right). \tag{3.3}$$

Let us denote the nth derivative of a Gaussian as G_n. Let f^θ denote the rotation operator such that the function f is rotated by θ around the origin. The first derivative in the x-direction of the Gaussian is given by

$$G_1^{0°} = \frac{\partial}{\partial x} \exp\left(-(x^2 + y^2)\right) = -2x \cdot \exp\left(-(x^2 + y^2)\right) \tag{3.4}$$

and, rotating the function by 90° gives us

$$G_1^{90°} = \frac{\partial}{\partial y} \exp\left(-(x^2 + y^2)\right) = -2y \cdot \exp\left(-(x^2 + y^2)\right). \tag{3.5}$$

A filter at an arbitrary orientation can now be synthesized as

$$G_1^{\theta°} = \cos(\theta)G_1^{0°} + \sin(\theta)G_1^{90°}. \tag{3.6}$$

It is clear that $G_1^{0°}$ and $G_1^{90°}$ span the set of $G_1^{\theta°}$ filters and hence are basis filters. Since convolution is a linear operation, we can also synthesize the response at an arbitrary orientation as follows.

$$
\begin{aligned}
R_1^{0°} &= G_1^{0°} * I \\
R_1^{90°} &= G_1^{90°} * I \\
R_1^{\theta°} &= \cos(\theta)R_1^{0°} + \sin(\theta)R_1^{90°}
\end{aligned}
\tag{3.7}
$$

The statistics of the responses at different orientations can reveal key structures in an image. Let us take an example of a fundus image as shown in Figure 3.1.2. We convolve the image with an SGF oriented at 225°. The response is shown in Figure 3.1.2. The anomalies in the original image (such as yellow and red spots) are captured by the SGF response. Specifically, the anomalies are represented by the peaks and valleys in the response. Analogous to Gabor filters, we can extract low-order moments of the response that will help us to quantify textures.

3.1.3 Shape Features

An image contains many well-defined objects that we encounter daily. Shape is an important attribute of these objects. In some tasks such as object

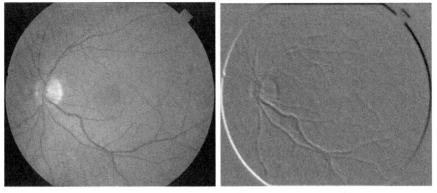

(a) A fundus image　　　　　(b) Response of an SGF oriented at 225°

Figure 3.6: A fundus image and the response of an SGF.

detection, shape is an indispensable attribute. Moreover, most of the objects come in different colors and textures, making both weak attributes for discriminating objects. On the other hand, objects can be both rigid and non-rigid. Modeling the shape of rigid objects is relatively easier, but non-rigid ones can conform to many shapes. Capturing and modeling all the shape forms is difficult. Capturing discriminative characteristics of an object using color or texture requires suitable pre-processing or large training data [38].

Shape Context: A feature that is invariant to rotation, translation and scaling is highly desirable. Shape context tries to achieve this by capturing relative positioning of all the other points with respect to a reference point [5].

Given a shape, its edge elements are first converted into a set of feature points. These feature points may not always correspond to inflection points or curvature extrema. For a point p on the contour, vectors connecting p to all the other points are computed. A histogram from the coordinates of these vectors in the polar space is computed as

$$h_i(k) = |\{p \neq q_i | (p - q_i) \in bin(k)\}|, \qquad (3.8)$$

where $|\cdot|$ denotes cardinality of a set.

Shape context features are ready to translate as everything is measured with respect to a reference point. Scale invariance can be achieved by normalizing all radial distances by the median distance between all pairs in the shape.

Shape context can be used to match two shapes because corresponding points on two shapes should have similar features. The similarity is measured by the χ^2 statistic. Suppose that p_1 and p_2 are two corresponding points on two shapes. Let the normalized shape context histograms of these two points be denoted by h_1 and h_2. The χ^2 statistic is given by

$$C = \frac{1}{2} \sum_{k=1}^{K} \frac{(h_1 - h_2)^2}{h_1 + h_2}. \tag{3.9}$$

Given a set of costs for all pairs of points, we minimize the total cost under the constraint that the matching must be one-to-one. To minimize the total cost, we permute the set of points belonging to the second shape. This is known as the square-assignment problem that can be solved in $O(N^3)$ time using the Hungarian method [35], or another efficient algorithm mentioned in [31].

Geometric Moments: The use of geometric moment invariants for two-dimensional images was first presented in [29]. Raw image moments are a projection of image $I(x,y)$ onto the basis $x^p y^q$ as follows.

$$m_{pq} = \sum_x \sum_y x^p y^q I(x,y). \tag{3.10}$$

It is clear from Equation 3.1.3 that m_{00} sums all the pixel values in the image, whereas m_{10} and m_{01} sum over x and y respectively. The centroid coordinates can then be derived as

$$\begin{aligned} \bar{x} &= \frac{m_{10}}{m_{00}}, \\ \bar{y} &= \frac{m_{01}}{m_{00}}. \end{aligned} \tag{3.11}$$

Having defined the centroid coordinates, we can now derive the central moments as

$$\mu_{pq} = \sum_{x=0}^{M-1} \sum_{y=0}^{N-1} (x - \bar{x})^p (y - \bar{y})^q I(x,y). \tag{3.12}$$

These central moments are translation and scale invariant. Although rotation invariance is difficult to achieve, complex moments defined in [1] are translation, scale and rotation invariant. It is also possible to start with complex moments and do an inverse generation of the representative shape.

Histogram of Oriented Gradients (HOG): HOG is a global feature descriptor that is obtained by concatenating features from small, local regions [13]. To obtain the HOG descriptor of an image patch, we compute the gradient vector at each pixel in an 8×8 cell. The resulting 64 gradient vectors are then binned into a 9-bin histogram. The bins range from 0 to 180 degrees with a 20-degree interval. A soft binning strategy is adopted in [13] which implies that if a gradient vector has an angle of 85 degrees, then a quarter of its magnitude is added to the bin centered at 70 degrees while the rest is added to the bin centered at 90 degrees. Soft binning prevents significant changes in the histogram given minor changes in the gradient angles that are sitting between two bins.

To make the histogram invariant to certain types of illumination changes, it is necessary that we normalize the histogram. Instead of normalizing each histogram individually, 2×2 cells are first grouped into blocks. These four histograms are concatenated to form a 36-dimensional vector, which is normalized to unit magnitude. The blocks are 50% overlapping. Since high-contrast regions tend to be localized, normalizing over smaller blocks tends to be a more effective strategy than a global one. The final HOG descriptor for the entire image can be obtained by concatenating descriptors of all the blocks. A 3,780 dimensional feature descriptor was used for person detection from a 64×128 image in [13]. HOG has since been used for many tasks, most widely in object detection [17,65] and was state-of-art [65] until deep features [20,21,44,45] surpassed its performance. HOG has also been coupled with other features such as Local Binary Pattern (LBP) to detect pedestrians in partially occluded scenarios [64].

There are many such features that have not been covered here, e.g., SIFT [42], Centrist [67], etc. However, the underlying theme remains that these features have been developed keeping a specific property in mind. Occasionally, further hand-engineering is required for tasks that have some unique characteristics. We gave an example of a fundus image where the color spectrum is predominantly red and thus conventional binning strategies that work well in a natural setting fail there. A specially designed, adaptive binning strategy worked well to capture the color distribution across a wide range of fundus image types.

3.2   Latent Feature Extraction

Direct feature extraction has its own advantages. It is (usually) computationally efficient, easy to implement and interpret, allows inclusion of prior knowledge, etc. However, hand-crafting features specific to a task demands a lot of expert labor, which can be expensive and difficult to obtain. It is desirable to obtain features (through some automated process) that satisfy certain characteristics. The automated process of discovering latent structures in the feature space should be given some target properties to achieve, often in the form of an objective function to be optimized. Some characteristics are proven to be effective across a wide range of tasks, for example, sparsity and low dimensionality. Since these structures exist but are hidden in a new (sub)-space, they are called latent features (from a Latin word "latere"). We will review some of the important latent feature types and the underlying extraction processes.

3.2.1 Principal Component Analysis

In Section 3.1 we saw that one of the simplest image features that one can conceive of is a vector of (pre-processed) pixel values. One of the major problems with that was its huge dimensionality and redundancy. Principal component analysis (PCA) employs orthogonal transformations to convert a set of correlated variables (e.g., pixel values) into a set of linearly uncorrelated variables [43]. These uncorrelated variables are called principal components. The number of principal components is equal to or (usually) less than the dimensionality of the original feature space (assuming that the number of observations are greater than the dimensionality of feature space).

Mathematically, PCA is an orthogonal linear transformation that transforms the data to a new coordinate system. The first coordinate in this new system (also called a principal component) will align with the direction that accounts for the largest variation in the data. The second principal component should be uncorrelated to the first one (and hence orthogonal) and should account for the second-largest variation in the data. In general, the nth component will be orthogonal to the first $n - 1$ components while accounting for the nth-largest variation in the data.

A simple approach to compute the principal components over the entire dataset, $X \in \mathbb{R}^{n \times d}$, containing n samples and d feature dimensions is as follows:

1. Form a mean-centered dataset by making the mean over each dimension of X to zero. The mean-centered dataset $\hat{X}$ is obtained as follows:

$$\hat{X}_i = X_i - \frac{1}{n} \sum_j X_j, \tag{3.13}$$

where X_i denotes the ith row of X.

2. Compute the covariance matrix between all dimensions as follows:

$$C = \frac{1}{n - 1} \hat{X}^T \hat{X}. \tag{3.14}$$

3. Calculate the eigenvectors and eigenvalues of the covariance matrix. The eigenvector associated with the largest eigenvalue is the first principal component. Thus the eigenvectors are ordered by their eigenvalues, highest to lowest. Eigenvectors with very small eigenvalues can be ignored, causing some loss of information but on the other hand, results in reduced dimensionality in the data.

4. The dataset in the transformed space can be obtained by multiplying the (transposed) eigenvector matrix with the data matrix. This gives us the final data matrix with dimensions along the rows and samples along the columns.

PCA has been successfully used in near real-time face recognition in an approach popularly known as Eigenfaces [56]. The main idea behind Eigenfaces is to consider face recognition as a template-matching problem. A mean-subtracted face image is represented in the form of a column vector. Then each such face image can be represented as a linear combination of the top-K eigenvectors, which the authors of [56] call eigenfaces.

This approach can be used to classify a face image. It is briefly described as follows:

1. A new mean-subtracted face image is transformed into the new coordinate system using PCA.

2. The average Eigenface representation of a class is obtained by averaging all the training images (as few as one) of that class.

3. The Euclidean distance between the transformed feature and the average Eigenface representation of each class is computed.

4. The test image is categorized into class k that minimizes the Euclidean distance.

3.2.2   Kernel Principal Component Analysis

PCA attempts to find a low-dimensional linear subspace that accounts for most of the variation in the data. However, PCA would fail to find a low-dimensional non-linear subspace if it existed. Kernel PCA tries to find this non-linear subspace [48].

While it may not be possible to linearly separate N points in $d \leq N$ dimensions, they may be linearly separated in $d \geq N$ dimensions. Thus, a mapping that maps N d-dimensional points into a higher dimension, makes it to easy to derive a separating hyperplane. The mapping can be written as,

$$\Phi(\boldsymbol{x}_i) \text{ s.t. } \Phi : \mathbb{R}^d \to \mathbb{R}^N. \tag{3.15}$$

Designing a mapping function Φ is non-trivial. In kernel PCA, we only calculate the similarity between two input points that are mapped to a higher dimensional space. Projection to a higher dimension is a pre-requisite if we are to compute similarity between those points. However, the kernel trick allows us to calculate similarity without explicitly deriving the mapping of each point as long as the similarity between two points can be expressed as a proper inner product. That is, if our kernel computing similarity between $\boldsymbol{x}$ and $\boldsymbol{x}'$ is denoted by k, and the mapping function between two spaces $\mathcal{X}$ and $\mathcal{V}$ is $\Phi : \mathcal{X} \to \mathcal{V}$ then,

$$k(\boldsymbol{x}, \boldsymbol{x}') = \langle \Phi(\boldsymbol{x}), \Phi(\boldsymbol{x}') \rangle_{\mathcal{V}}. \tag{3.16}$$

We do not need to explicitly compute the mapping $\Phi(\cdot)$, but $\mathcal{V}$ needs to be an inner product space. Since we do not ever compute the mapping, we can only obtain the projected data and not the principal components.

Experiments on object and character recognition were performed in [48] using a polynomial PCA followed by *linear* SVM. Results showed that kernel PCA consistently outperformed standard PCA and in some cases, it even outperformed non-linear SVMs.

3.2.3 Multidimensional Scaling

Multidimensional scaling (MDS) allows us to visualize similarities between samples in a dataset. The feature representation of samples may be embedded in a much higher dimensional space. Thus MDS is a type of non-linear dimensionality reduction. MDS tries to preserve distances in a reduced dimension space. There are four types of MDS algorithms: classical, metric, non-metric, and generalized [8, 33, 34].

Metric MDS takes an input matrix of known distances between input samples and corresponding weights. It minimizes a loss function called *stress* by a process called stress majorization. The stress is defined as follows:

$$stress_D(\boldsymbol{x}_1, \cdots, \boldsymbol{x}_n) = \left(\sum_{i \neq j = 1, \cdots, N} (d_{ij} - ||\boldsymbol{x}_i - \boldsymbol{x}_j||)^2 \right)^{\frac{1}{2}}. \qquad (3.17)$$

Non-metric MDS assumes that only the ranks of the distances between samples are known instead of their actual values. Generalized MDS is an extension of the metric MDS. It can handle cases where the space of dissimilarities and the target space are two different surfaces. In such cases, GMDS finds minimum-distortion embedding of one surface into another [8].

3.2.4 Isomap

This is one of the most widely used nonlinear dimensionality reduction methods. Isomap extends MDS in the sense that it uses geodesic distances in place of straight-line Euclidean distances between samples. The inclusion of geodesic distance correctly accounts for the underlying low-dimensional structure of the manifold. For example, in the famous *Swiss roll* example, two points may be nearest neighbors in the Euclidean sense but may be far away when the actual structure of a Swiss roll is considered. The geodesic distance between two points is defined as the sum of the edge weights along the shortest path that connects two nodes. The shortest path can be computed using Dijkstra's algorithm. The isomap algorithm can be briefly described as follows:

1. Get neighbors of each point either by using a fixed radius or using the *k*NN rule.

2. Construct a neighborhood graph. Two nodes are connected if one node is a k-nearest-neighbor of another. Euclidean distance can be assigned as the edge weight.

3. Use Dijkstra's algorithm to compute the shortest path between two nodes.

4. Compute lower-dimensional embedding using metric MDS.

3.2.5 Laplacian Eigenmaps

This is a computationally efficient approach to non-linear dimensionality reduction that uses information from the neighboring data points. These points are part of a weighted graph with a set of edges connecting the neighboring data points. This approach can be outlined as follows.

1. **Graph construction:** Node i and j are connected if either (1) $||\boldsymbol{x}_i - \boldsymbol{x}_j||^2 < \epsilon$ or (2) if node j is among the k-nearest neighbors of node i. Here, $x_i \in \mathbb{R}^n$ is a representation of the ith data point in the feature space.

   The first option is geometrically intuitive, however, having to choose the parameter ϵ is a disadvantage. The second option provides us with an easier choice but is difficult to visualize.

2. **Edge Weighting:** A simple strategy is to assign a weight of 1 if an edge connects two nodes, otherwise assign 0. A soft weighting strategy is to use a kernel that assigns some weight that is proportional to the similarity between the data points i and j. A popular kernel is the heat kernel defined as

$$w_{ij} = \exp{-\frac{||\boldsymbol{x}_i - \boldsymbol{x}_j||^2}{t}}, \tag{3.18}$$

   where, w_{ij} is the weight of the edge connecting node i and j. If they are not connected, then $w_{ij} = 0$. The parameter t can be viewed as a sensitivity factor. When $t = \infty$, the heat kernel reduces to the weighting strategy mentioned earlier.

3. **Computing the optimal embedding:** Let us assume that the graph is fully connected. Compute the diagonal weight matrix D by summing the columns (or rows) of the symmetric edge weight matrix W. Compute the Laplacian matrix $L = D - W$, which is a symmetric and positive semidefinite matrix. Next, solve the generalized eigenvector problem:

$$L\boldsymbol{f} = \lambda D\boldsymbol{f}. \tag{3.19}$$

After leaving out the eigenvector $\boldsymbol{f}_0$ corresponding to the eigenvalue 0, the rest of the eigenvectors are used for an m-dimensional embedding as follows (where $m \ll n$):

$$\boldsymbol{x}_i \rightarrow (\boldsymbol{f}_1(i), \cdots, \boldsymbol{f}_m(i)). \tag{3.20}$$

In this way we can obtain an m-dimensional embedding of the original high-dimensional data while maintaining local neighborhood information.

These latent feature extraction processes often require sophisticated optimization techniques that are computationally expensive and mostly require extensive reformulation of the cost function (which is problem dependent). The hand-crafted features are, for the most part, effective enough that they are used for a variety of tasks. While this school of thought continues to be quite popular and some of these features have standardized implementations that are available for most researchers to plug and play for their tasks, they were not task-specific. Hand-crafted features were designed to be useful feature representations of images that are capable of providing cues about certain aspects of images, which are deemed to be important based on our prior knowledge. HOG and Shape Context for instance, provided shape-related information and were therefore used in tasks involving shape and structure. Features like color correlogram [10, 11, 59] provided cues on color transitions and were therefore, used in medical images and other problems where shape was not necessarily an informative feature. In the next section we will study methods for *learning* task-specific features. These feature extractors are learned directly from raw images with minimal pre-processing.

3.3 Deep Image Features

Multi-layer neural networks have long been viewed as a means of extracting hierarchical task-specific features. Ever since the early works of Rumelhart et al., it was recognized that representations learned using back-propagation had the potential to learn fine-tuned features that were task-specific [47]. Until the onset of this decade, these methods were severely handicapped by a dearth of large-scale data and large-scale parallel computing hardware to be leveraged sufficiently. This, in part, directed the creativity of computer vision scientists to develop the aforementioned general-purpose feature representations. We now have access to datasets that are large enough and graphics processing units (GPUs) that are capable of large-scale parallel computations. This has allowed an explosion of neural image features and their usage [58]. In this section we will study some of these techniques.

3.3.1   Convolutional Neural Networks

There are several types of neural networks. A neural network is a network of computational neurons and is represented as a composition of multiple functions [22]. While dealing with images, we are often concerned with the use of a convolutional neural network (CNN).

Each neuron accepts a number of inputs and produces one output, which can further be supplied to many other neurons. A typical function of a computational neuron is to weight all the inputs, sum all the weighted inputs and generate an output depending on the strength of the summed weighted inputs. Neurons are organized in groups, where each group typically receives input from the same sources. These groups are called as layers. Layers come in three varieties, each characterized by its own type of neuron. They are the dot-product or the fully connected layer, the convolutional layer and the pooling layer.

3.3.1.1   The Dot-Product Layer

Consider a $1D$ vector of inputs $\mathbf{x} \in [x_0, x_1, \ldots x_d]$ of d dimensions. This may be a vectorized version of the image or may be the output of a preceding layer. Consider a dot-product layer containing n neurons. The jth neuron in this layer will simply perform the following operation,

$$z_j = \alpha \left(\sum_{i=0}^{d-1} x_i \times w_i^j \right), \tag{3.21}$$

where α is typically an element-wise monotonically increasing function that scales the output of the dot-product. α is commonly referred to as the activation function. The neuron output that has been processed by an activation layer is also referred to as an *activity*. Inputs can be processed in batches or mini-batches through the layer. In these cases $\mathbf{x}$ is a matrix in $\mathbb{R}^{b \times d}$, where b is the batch size. Together, the vectorized output of the layer is the dot-product

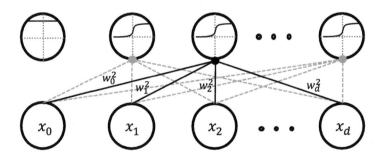

Figure 3.7: A typical dot-product layer.

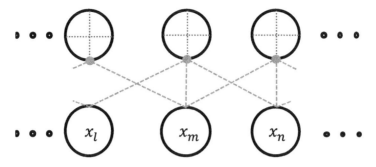

Figure 3.8: Locally connected neurons with a receptive field of $r = 3$.

operation between the weight matrix of the layer and the input signal batch,

$$\mathbf{z} = \alpha(\mathbf{x} \cdot \mathbf{w}), \tag{3.22}$$

where $\mathbf{z} \in \mathbb{R}^{b \times n}$, $\mathbf{w} \in \mathbb{R}^{d \times n}$ and the $(i, j)^{\text{th}}$ element of $\mathbf{z}$ represents the output of the jth neuron for the ith sample of input. Figure 3.7 shows such a connectivity of a typical dot-product layer. This layer takes an input of d dimensions and produces an output of n dimensions. From the figure, it should be clear as to why dot-product layers are also referred to as fully connected layers. These weights are typically *learned* using back-propagation and gradient descent [47].

3.3.1.2 The Convolution Layer

Fully connected layers require a huge amount of memory to store all their weights. They involve a lot of computation as well. Vitally, they are not ideal for use as feature extractors for images. This is because a dot-product layer has an extreme receptive field. A receptive field of a neuron is the range of input flowing into the neuron. It is the view of the input that the neuron has access to. In our definition of the dot-product layer, the receptive field of a neuron is the length of the signal d. Most image features such as SIFT or HOG have small receptive fields that are typically a few tens of pixels such as 16×16. A convolution layer also has a small receptive field. This idea of having a small receptive field is often referred to as *local connectivity*.

Locality arises in this connection because the input dimensions are organized in some order of spatial significance of the input itself. This implies that adjacent dimensions of inputs are locally related. Consider a neuron that has a local receptive field of $r = 3$. Figure 3.8 illustrates this connectivity. Each neuron in this arrangement is only capable of detecting a pattern in an image that is local and small. While each location in an image might have spatially independent features, most often in images, we find that spatial independence doesn't hold. This implies that one feature learned from one location of the image can be reasonably assumed to be useful at all locations.

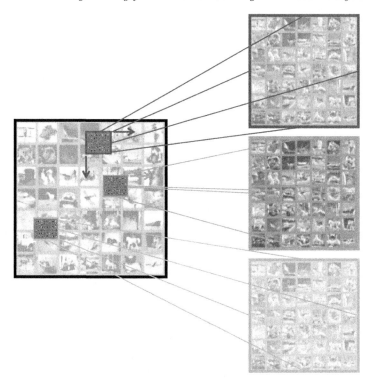

Figure 3.9: A typical convolution layer.

Although Figure 3.8 shows the neurons being independent, typically several neurons share weights. In the representation shown in Figure 3.8, all the neurons share the same weights. Even though we produce $n - r + 1$ outputs, we only use r unique weights. The convolutional layer shown here takes a $1 - D$ input and is therefore a $1 - D$ convolutional layer. Figure 3.9 illustrates a $2 - D$ convolutional layer. This figure does not show independent neurons and their connectivities but instead illustrates a convolutional filter that slides over the entire image. In other words, its weight is shared across all locations in the image. In cases where the input has more than one channel, convolution happens along all channels independently and the outputs are summed location-wise.

The $2D$ convolution layer typically performs the following operation:

$$z(j, d_1, d_2) = \alpha \left[\sum_{c=0}^{C-1} \sum_{u=0}^{r-1} \sum_{v=0}^{r-1} x_{c,d_1+u,d_2+u} \times w_{u,v}^j \right],$$

$$\forall j \in [0, 1, \dots n] \text{ and } \forall d_1, d_2 \in [0, 1, \dots d], \quad (3.23)$$

where the weights $\mathbf{w} \in \mathbb{R}^{j,r,r}$ are j sets of weights, each set being shared by several neurons, each with a receptive field of r working on an input $x \in \mathbb{R}^{d_1 \times d_2}$.

Since we have j sets of weights shared by several neurons, we will produce j activation *images* each (due to boundary conditions) of size $\mathbb{R}^{d-r+1 \times d-r+1}$.

In the context of convolution layers, the activations are also referred to as feature maps. Figure 3.9 shows three feature maps being generated at the end of the layer. The convolutional layer's filters are also *learned* by back-propagation and gradient descent. Once learned, these filters typically work as pattern detectors. Each filter produces one feature map. The feature map is a spatial map of confidence values for the existence of the pattern that the filter has adapted to detect.

The Pooling Layer The convolution layer creates activations that are $d-r+1$ long on each axis. Adjacent activities in each of these feature maps are often related to each other. This is because, in imaging contexts, most patterns spread across a few pixels. We want to avoid storing (and processing) these redundancies and preferably only use the most prominent of these features.

This is typically accomplished by using a pooling or a sub-sampling operation. Pooling is done typically using non-overlapping sliding windows, where each window will sample one activation. In the context of images, pooling by maximum (max-pooling) is typically preferred. Pooling by p (widow size of p) reduces the sizes of activations by p-fold. A pooling layer has no learnable components.

3.3.2 CNN Architecture Design

Analogous to model design in most of machine learning and to the practice of hand-crafting features, CNNs also involve some degree of skilled hand-crafting. Most hand-crafting involves the design of the architecture of the network. This involves choosing the types and number of layers and types of activations and number of neurons in each layer. One important design choice that arises particularly in image data and CNNs, is the design of the receptive fields.

The receptive field is typically guided by the size of filters (weights) in each layer and by the use of pooling layers. The effective receptive field (in relation to the input image) grows after each layer as the range of the signal received from the input layer grows progressively. There are typically two philosophies relating to the choice of filter sizes and therefore to the receptive fields. The first was designed by Yann LeCun et al. [37,38] and was later re-introduced and widely preferred in modern-day object categorization by Alex Krizhevsky et al. [32]. They employ a *relatively* large receptive field at the earlier layers and continue growing with the rate of growth reducing by a magnitude. Consider AlexNet [32]. This network won the ImageNet (ILSVRC) challenge in 2012 which involves recognizing objects belonging to 1000 categories with each image being 224×224 in size [14]. This network has a first layer with 11×11 convolutional filters (applied with a stride of 4 pixels), followed by a 3×3 pooling (applied with a stride of 2 pixels). The next layer is 5×5, followed by 3×3, each with their own respective pooling layers.

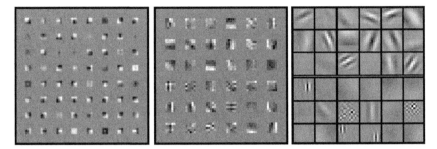

Figure 3.10: Some filters learned by various CNNs at the first layer that is closest to the image. From left to right are filters learned by VGG (3×3), a typical Yann LeCun style LeNet (5×5) and a AlexNet (11×11).

The second of these philosophies is increasing the receptive field as minimally as possible. These were pioneered by the VGG group [50] and one particular implementation won the 2014 ImageNet competition [14]. These networks have a fixed filter size, typically of 3×3, and have a fixed pooling size of 2×2 at some checkpoint layers. These philosophies aim to hierarchically learn better filters over various growth of small receptive fields. The classic LeNet from Yann LeCun is a trade-off between these two case studies [38]. Figure 3.10 shows various filters that were learned by each of these philosophies. It can be noticed that although most first-layer filters adapt themselves to simple edge filters and Gabor filters, the 3×3 filters are simpler lower-dimensional corner detectors while the larger receptive field filters are complex high-dimensional pattern detectors.

Although we studied some popular network architecture design and philosophies, several other styles of networks also exist. In this section we have only studied those that feed-forward from the input layer to the task layer (whatever that task might be) and there is only one path for gradients to flow during back-propagation. Recently, several networks such as GoogleNet [54] and the newer implementations of the inception layer [53,55], Residual Net [27] and Highway Nets [51], have been proposed that involve creating DAG-style networks that allow for more than one path to the target. One of these paths typically involves directly feeding forward the input signal. This allows for the gradient to not attenuate and help in solving the vanishing gradient problems [7].

3.3.3 Fine-Tuning Off-the-Shelf Neural Networks

While we studied the components of a typical CNN and some of their idiosyncrasies, we didn't detail the task-specific nature of the back-propagation learning strategy. At the top end of all these neural networks is a logistic regressor that feeds off of the last layer of activations, be it from a fully connected layer as is conventional or a convolutional layer such as in some recent network implementations used in image segmentation [41]. Often, this regressor is also referred to as a dot-product layer, for logistic regression is simply a dot-product layer using a softmax activation. A typical softmax layer is capable of producing the probability distribution over the labels $y \in [0, 1, \ldots c]$ that we want to predict. Given an input image $\mathbf{x}$, $P(y|\mathbf{x})$ is as follows,

$$
\begin{bmatrix} P(y = 1|\mathbf{x}) \\ \vdots \\ P(y = c|\mathbf{x}) \end{bmatrix} = \frac{1}{\sum\limits_{p=1}^{c} e^{w^p N'(\mathbf{x})}} \begin{bmatrix} e^{w^1 N'(\mathbf{x})} \\ \vdots \\ e^{w^c N'(\mathbf{x})} \end{bmatrix}, \tag{3.24}
$$

where $\mathbf{w}$ is the weight matrix of the last softmax layer with w^p representing the weight vector that produces the output of the class p and $N'(\mathbf{x})$ is the output of the layer in the network N, immediately preceding the softmax layer. The label that the network predicts, $\hat{y}$, is the maximum of these probabilities,

$$
\hat{y} = \arg\max_{y} P(y|\mathbf{x}). \tag{3.25}
$$

If e were a measure of error in this prediction, in order to learn any weight w, we can acquire its gradient $\frac{\partial e}{\partial w}$, for every weight w in the network using the chain rule of differentiation. Once we have this error gradient, we can iteratively learn the weights using the following gradient descent update rule:

$$
w^{\tau+1} = w^{\tau} - \eta \frac{\partial e}{\partial w}, \tag{3.26}
$$

where η is some predefined rate of learning and τ is the iteration number.

It can be clearly noticed in the back-propagation strategy outlined above that the features of a CNN are learned with only one objective—to minimize the prediction error. It is therefore to be expected that the features learned thusly, are specific only to those particular tasks. Paradoxically, in deep CNNs trained using large datasets, this is often not the typical observation. In most CNNs, we observe as illustrated in Figure 3.11 that the anatomy of the CNN and the ambition of each layer is contrived meticulously. The features that are close to the image layer are more general (such as edge detectors or Gabor filters) and those that are closer to the task layer are more task specific.

Given this observation among most popular CNNs, modern-day computer vision engineers prefer to simply *download* off-the-shelf neural networks and fine-tune them for their task. This process involves the following steps. Consider that a stable network N is well trained on some task T using ample amounts of data. Consider that the target for an engineer is to build a network n that can make inferences on task t. Also assume that these two tasks are somehow related; perhaps T was visual object categorization on ImageNet and t on the COCO dataset [39] or the Caltech-101/256 Datasets [16,23]. To learn the task on t, one could simply *download* N, randomly reinitialize the last few layers (at the extreme case reinitialize only the softmax layer) and

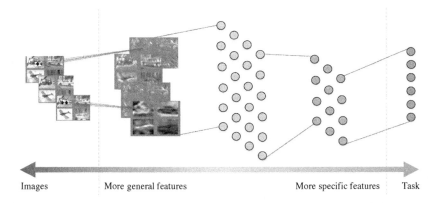

Images   More general features   More specific features   Task

Figure 3.11: The anatomy of a typical CNN.

continue back-propagation of the network to learn the task t with a smaller η. It is expected that N is very well trained already and that they could serve as good initializations to begin *fine-tuning* the network for this new task. In some cases where enough computation is not available to update all the weights, we may simply choose to update only a few of the layers close to the task and leave the others as is. The first few layers that are not updated are now treated as feature extractors much the same way as HOG or SIFT.

Some networks capitalized on this idea and created off-the-shelf download-able networks that are designed specifically to work as feed-forward determin-istic feature extractors. Popular off-the-shelf networks were the DECAF [15] and the Over Feat [49]. Over Feat in particular was used for a wide-variety of tasks from pulmonary nodule detection in CT scans [57] to detecting people in crowded scenes [52]. While this has been shown to work to some degree and has been used in practice constantly, it is not a perfect solution and some problems are known to exist. One problem in particular is that of dataset generality [60]. In this article, the authors show that a network learned on T, might not necessarily be a good initializer for t. This was particularly striking when using a network trained on visual object categorization and fine-tuned for tasks in medical imaging.

Another concern with this philosophy of using off-the-shelf network as feature extractors is that the network n is also expected to be of the same size as N. In some cases, we might desire a network of a different architecture. One strategy to learn a different network using a pre-trained network is by using the idea of distillation [2, 28]. The idea of distillation works around the use of a temperature-raised softmax, defined as follows:

$$\begin{bmatrix} P(y=1|\mathbf{x},\Gamma) \\ \vdots \\ P(y=c|\mathbf{x},\Gamma) \end{bmatrix} = \frac{1}{\sum\limits_{p=1}^{c} e^{\frac{w^P N'(\mathbf{x})}{\Gamma}}} \begin{bmatrix} e^{\frac{w^1 N'(\mathbf{x})}{\Gamma}} \\ \vdots \\ e^{\frac{w^c N'(\mathbf{x})}{\Gamma}} \end{bmatrix}. \tag{3.27}$$

This temperature-raised softmax for $\Gamma > 1$ ($\Gamma = 1$ is simply the softmax described in equation 3.24) provides a softer target which is smoother across the labels. It reduces the probability of the most probable label and provides rewards for the second and third most probable labels also, by equalizing the distribution. Using this *dark knowledge* to create the errors e (in addition to the error over predictions as discussed above), knowledge can be transferred from N, during the training of n. This idea can be used to learn different types of networks. One can learn shallower [61] or deeper [46] networks through this kind of mentoring. Learning a neural network with small datasets is extremely unstable. This kind of distillation-based learning acts as a strong regularizer. This can also be extended to simply learn many layers of n to match some activations of particular layers in N. Suppose we have a pre-determined set of probes B, which is a set of tuples of layers from (N, n). The overall network cost is

$$e = \alpha_\tau e + \beta_\tau \sum_{\forall(l,j)\in B} \Psi(l, j) + \gamma_\tau \Psi(n, m), \qquad (3.28)$$

where α_τ and β_τ weigh the two losses together to enable balanced training and γ_τ is the weight of the probe between the two (temperature) softmax layers. $\alpha_\tau = g_\alpha(\tau)$, $\beta_\tau = g_\beta(\tau)$ and $\gamma_\tau = g_\gamma(\tau)$ are annealing functions parametrized by the iteration τ under progress, where

$$\Psi(l, j) = \sqrt{\frac{1}{a} \sum_{i=0}^{a} (N(l, i) - n(j, i))^2} \qquad (3.29)$$

is the probing error function. This idea can also be used to learn new types of networks, for instance, unrolling a recurrent neural network into a feed-forward deep network [9].

3.3.4 Summary and Conclusions

In this chapter, we explored a hierarchy of feature representations starting with classic, hand-crafted features. These features are designed by human experts and have task-specific prior knowledge. These features are easily interpretable and characterize fundamental aspects of images such as color, texture and shape. The next-level in this hierarchy is latent feature representations. Latent features discover task-specific structures in the feature space such as sparsity, decorrelation of reduced dimension, low rank, etc. However, to discover these structures, complex optimization procedures are required that are computationally expensive.

While these features have been in prominence and have shown tremendous success recently, computer vision has now pivoted toward learning features from data, where new feature representations are typically learned using CNNs. The learned features in layers closer to the input layer can function as general feature extractors and be task specific at layers closer to the task layer.

Leveraging this observation, several off-the-shelf networks have been created that have been used widely as a replacement for HOG-style deterministic feature extractors, as have been discussed in this chapter. These network learning strategies culminate in learning neural networks that provide task-specific image features that require minimal hand-crafting and domain knowledge.

Bibliography

[1] Yaser S Abu-Mostafa and Demetri Psaltis. Image normalization by complex moments. *IEEE Trans. on Pattern Analysis and Machine Intelligence*, (1):46–55, 1985.

[2] Anoop Korattikara Balan, Vivek Rathod, Kevin P Murphy, and Max Welling. Bayesian dark knowledge. In *Advances in Neural Information Processing Systems (NIPS)*, pages 3438–3446, 2015.

[3] EA Bashkov and NS Kostyukova. Effectiveness estimation of image retrieval by 2d color histogram. *Journal of Automation and Information Sciences*, 8(11):74–80, 2006.

[4] Evgenity A Bashkov and Natalya S Shozda. Content-based image retrieval using color histogram correlation. *Graphicon Proceedings*, pages 458–461, 2002.

[5] Serge Belongie, Jitendra Malik, and Jan Puzicha. Shape context: A new descriptor for shape matching and object recognition. In *Advances in Neural Information Processing Systems (NIPS)*, pages 831–837, 2001.

[6] Yoshua Bengio, Aaron Courville, and Pascal Vincent. Representation learning: A review and new perspectives. *IEEE Trans. on Pattern Analysis and Machine Intelligence*, 35(8):1798–1828, 2013.

[7] Yoshua Bengio, Patrice Simard, and Paolo Frasconi. Learning long-term dependencies with gradient descent is difficult. *IEEE Transactions on Neural Networks*, 5(2):157–166, 1994.

[8] Alexander M Bronstein, Michael M Bronstein, and Ron Kimmel. Generalized multidimensional scaling: A framework for isometry-invariant partial surface matching. *Proceedings of the National Academy of Sciences*, 103(5):1168–1172, 2006.

[9] William Chan, Nan Rosemary Ke, and Ian Lane. Transferring knowledge from a RNN to a DNN. *arXiv preprint arXiv:1504.01483*, 2015.

[10] Parag S Chandakkar, Ragav Venkatesan, and Baoxin Li. MIrank-KNN: Multiple-instance retrieval of clinically relevant diabetic retinopathy images. *Journal of Medical Imaging*, 4(3):034003, 2017.

[11] Parag S Chandakkar, Ragav Venkatesan, Baoxin Li, and HK Li. Retrieving clinically relevant diabetic retinopathy images using a multi-class multiple-instance framework. In *SPIE Medical Imaging*, pages 86700Q–86700Q. International Society for Optics and Photonics, 2013.

[12] Tianhorng Chang and C-CJ Kuo. Texture analysis and classification with tree-structured wavelet transform. *IEEE Transactions on Image Processing*, 2(4):429–441, 1993.

[13] Navneet Dalal and Bill Triggs. Histograms of oriented gradients for human detection. In *Proceedings of the IEEE Conf. on Computer Vision and Pattern Recognition (CVPR)*, volume 1, pages 886–893. IEEE, 2005.

[14] Jia Deng, Wei Dong, Richard Socher, Li-Jia Li, Kai Li, and Li Fei-Fei. Imagenet: A large-scale hierarchical image database. In *Proceedings of the IEEE Conf. on Computer Vision and Pattern Recognition (CVPR)*, pages 248–255. IEEE, 2009.

[15] Jeff Donahue, Yangqing Jia, Oriol Vinyals, Judy Hoffman, Ning Zhang, Eric Tzeng, and Trevor Darrell. DECAF: A deep convolutional activation feature for generic visual recognition. In *Proceedings of the ACM Intl. Conf. on Machine Learning (ICML)*, pages 647–655, 2014.

[16] Li Fei-Fei, Rob Fergus, and Pietro Perona. One-shot learning of object categories. *IEEE Trans. on Pattern Analysis and Machine Intelligence*, 28(4):594–611, 2006.

[17] Pedro F Felzenszwalb, Ross B Girshick, David McAllester, and Deva Ramanan. Object detection with discriminatively trained part-based models. *IEEE Trans. on Pattern Analysis and Machine Intelligence*, 32(9):1627–1645, 2010.

[18] William T Freeman, Edward H Adelson, et al. The design and use of steerable filters. *IEEE Trans. on Pattern Analysis and Machine Intelligence*, 13(9):891–906, 1991.

[19] Dennis Gabor. Theory of communication. part 1: The analysis of information. *Journal of the Institution of Electrical Engineers-Part III: Radio and Communication Engineering*, 93(26):429–441, 1946.

[20] Ross Girshick. Fast r-cnn. In *Proceedings of the IEEE Intl. Conf. on Computer Vision (ICCV)*, pages 1440–1448, 2015.

[21] Ross Girshick, Jeff Donahue, Trevor Darrell, and Jitendra Malik. Rich feature hierarchies for accurate object detection and semantic segmentation. In *Proceedings of the IEEE Conf. on Computer Vision and Pattern Recognition (CVPR)*, pages 580–587, 2014.

[22] Ian Goodfellow, Yoshua Bengio, and Aaron Courville. *Deep Learning*. MIT Press, 2016. http://www.deeplearningbook.org.

[23] Gregory Griffin, Alex Holub, and Pietro Perona. Caltech-256 object category dataset. 2007.

[24] Robert M Haralick. Statistical and structural approaches to texture. *Proceedings of the IEEE*, 67(5):786–804, 1979.

[25] Robert M Haralick, Karthikeyan Shanmugam, et al. Textural features for image classification. *IEEE Transactions on Systems, Man, and Cybernetics*, (6):610–621, 1973.

[26] Joseph K Hawkins. Textural properties for pattern recognition. *Picture Processing and Psychopictorics*, pages 347–370, 1970.

[27] Kaiming He, Xiangyu Zhang, Shaoqing Ren, and Jian Sun. Deep residual learning for image recognition. In *Proceedings of the IEEE Conf. on Computer Vision and Pattern Recognition (CVPR)*, pages 770–778, 2016.

[28] Geoffrey Hinton, Oriol Vinyals, and Jeff Dean. Distilling the knowledge in a neural network. *arXiv preprint arXiv:1503.02531*, 2015.

[29] Ming-Kuei Hu. Visual pattern recognition by moment invariants. *IRE Transactions on Information Theory*, 8(2):179–187, 1962.

[30] Jing Huang, S Ravi Kumar, Mandar Mitra, Wei-Jing Zhu, and Ramin Zabih. Image indexing using color correlograms. In *Proceedings of the IEEE Conf. on Computer Vision and Pattern Recognition (CVPR)*, pages 762–768. IEEE, 1997.

[31] Roy Jonker and Anton Volgenant. A shortest augmenting path algorithm for dense and sparse linear assignment problems. *Computing*, 38(4):325–340, 1987.

[32] Alex Krizhevsky, Ilya Sutskever, and Geoffrey E Hinton. Imagenet classification with deep convolutional neural networks. In *Advances in Neural Information Processing Systems (NIPS)*, pages 1097–1105, 2012.

[33] Joseph B Kruskal. Multidimensional scaling by optimizing goodness of fit to a nonmetric hypothesis. *Psychometrika*, 29(1):1–27, 1964.

[34] Joseph B Kruskal. Nonmetric multidimensional scaling: A numerical method. *Psychometrika*, 29(2):115–129, 1964.

[35] Harold W Kuhn. The Hungarian method for the assignment problem. *Naval Research Logistics (NRL)*, 2(1-2):83–97, 1955.

[36] Kenneth I Laws. Textured image segmentation. Technical report, University of Southern California, Los Angeles, Image Processing Institute, 1980.

[37] Yann LeCun, Bernhard E Boser, John S Denker, Donnie Henderson, Richard E Howard, Wayne E Hubbard, and Lawrence D Jackel. Handwritten digit recognition with a back-propagation network. In *Advances in Neural Information Processing Systems (NIPS)*, pages 396–404, 1990.

[38] Yann LeCun, Léon Bottou, Yoshua Bengio, and Patrick Haffner. Gradient-based learning applied to document recognition. *Proceedings of the IEEE*, 86(11):2278–2324, 1998.

[39] Tsung-Yi Lin, Michael Maire, Serge Belongie, James Hays, Pietro Perona, Deva Ramanan, Piotr Dollár, and C Lawrence Zitnick. Microsoft Coco: Common objects in context. In *Proceedings of the European Conf. on Computer Vision (ECCV)*, pages 740–755. Springer, 2014.

[40] Fang Liu and Rosalind W Picard. Periodicity, directionality, and randomness: Wold features for image modeling and retrieval. *IEEE Trans. on Pattern Analysis and Machine Intelligence*, 18(7):722–733, 1996.

[41] Jonathan Long, Evan Shelhamer, and Trevor Darrell. Fully convolutional networks for semantic segmentation. In *Proceedings of the IEEE Conf. on Computer Vision and Pattern Recognition (CVPR)*, pages 3431–3440, 2015.

[42] David G Lowe. Object recognition from local scale-invariant features. In *Proceedings of the IEEE Intl. Conf. on Computer Vision (ICCV)*, volume 2, pages 1150–1157. IEEE, 1999.

[43] Karl Pearson. Liii. on lines and planes of closest fit to systems of points in space. *The London, Edinburgh, and Dublin Philosophical Magazine and Journal of Science*, 2(11):559–572, 1901.

[44] Joseph Redmon, Santosh Divvala, Ross Girshick, and Ali Farhadi. You only look once: Unified, real-time object detection. In *Proceedings of the IEEE Conf. on Computer Vision and Pattern Recognition (CVPR)*, pages 779–788, 2016.

[45] Shaoqing Ren, Kaiming He, Ross Girshick, and Jian Sun. Faster R-CNN: Towards real-time object detection with region proposal networks. In *Advances in Neural Information Processing Systems (NIPS)*, pages 91–99, 2015.

[46] Adriana Romero, Nicolas Ballas, Samira Ebrahimi Kahou, Antoine Chassang, Carlo Gatta, and Yoshua Bengio. Fitnets: Hints for thin deep nets. *arXiv preprint arXiv:1412.6550*, 2014.

[47] David E Rumelhart, Geoffrey E Hinton, and Ronald J Williams. Learning internal representations by error propagation. Technical report, California Univ San Diego La Jolla Inst for Cognitive Science, 1985.

[48] Bernhard Schölkopf, Alexander Smola, and Klaus-Robert Müller. Nonlinear component analysis as a kernel eigenvalue problem. *Neural Computation*, 10(5):1299–1319, 1998.

[49] Pierre Sermanet, David Eigen, Xiang Zhang, Michaël Mathieu, Rob Fergus, and Yann LeCun. Over Feat: Integrated recognition, localization and detection using convolutional networks. *arXiv preprint arXiv:1312.6229*, 2013.

[50] Karen Simonyan and Andrew Zisserman. Very deep convolutional networks for large-scale image recognition. *arXiv preprint arXiv:1409.1556*, 2014.

[51] Rupesh Kumar Srivastava, Klaus Greff, and Jürgen Schmidhuber. Highway networks. *arXiv preprint arXiv:1505.00387*, 2015.

[52] Russell Stewart, Mykhaylo Andriluka, and Andrew Y. Ng. End-to-end people detection in crowded scenes. In *Proceedings of the IEEE Conf. on Computer Vision and Pattern Recognition (CVPR)*, June 2016.

[53] Christian Szegedy, Sergey Ioffe, Vincent Vanhoucke, and Alexander A Alemi. Inception-v4, inception-resnet and the impact of residual connections on learning. In *Proceedings of the AAAI Conf. on Artificial Intelligence*, pages 4278–4284, 2017.

[54] Christian Szegedy, Wei Liu, Yangqing Jia, Pierre Sermanet, Scott Reed, Dragomir Anguelov, Dumitru Erhan, Vincent Vanhoucke, and Andrew Rabinovich. Going deeper with convolutions. In *Proceedings of the IEEE Conf. on Computer Vision and Pattern Recognition (CVPR)*, pages 1–9, 2015.

[55] Christian Szegedy, Vincent Vanhoucke, Sergey Ioffe, Jon Shlens, and Zbigniew Wojna. Rethinking the inception architecture for computer vision. In *Proceedings of the IEEE Conf. on Computer Vision and Pattern Recognition (CVPR)*, pages 2818–2826, 2016.

[56] Matthew Turk and Alex Pentland. Eigenfaces for recognition. *Journal of Cognitive Neuroscience*, 3(1):71–86, 1991.

[57] Bram van Ginneken, Arnaud AA Setio, Colin Jacobs, and Francesco Ciompi. Off-the-shelf convolutional neural network features for pulmonary nodule detection in computed tomography scans. In *IEEE 12th International Symposium on Biomedical Imaging (ISBI)*, pages 286–289. IEEE, 2015.

[58] R. Venkatesan and B. Li. *Convolutional Neural Networks in Visual Computing: A Concise Guide*. Data-Enabled Engineering. Taylor & Francis Group, 2017.

[59] Ragav Venkatesan, Parag Chandakkar, Baoxin Li, and Helen K Li. Classification of diabetic retinopathy images using multi-class multiple-instance learning based on color correlogram features. In *Engineering in Medicine and Biology Society (EMBC), 2012 Annual International Conference of the IEEE*, pages 1462–1465. IEEE, 2012.

[60] Ragav Venkatesan, Vijetha Gatupalli, and Baoxin Li. On the generality of neural image features. In *IEEE International Conference on Image Processing*. IEEE, 2016.

[61] Ragav Venkatesan and Baoxin Li. Diving deeper into mentee networks, 2016, arXiv:1604.08220[cs.LG].

[62] Shengjiu Wang. A robust CBIR approach using local color histograms, Department of Computer Science Technical Report TR01-13, University of Alberta.

[63] Xiang-Yang Wang, Jun-Feng Wu, and Hong-Ying Yang. Robust image retrieval based on color histogram of local feature regions. *Multimedia Tools and Applications*, 49(2):323–345, 2010.

[64] Xiaoyu Wang, Tony X Han, and Shuicheng Yan. An HOG-LBP human detector with partial occlusion handling. In *Proceedings of the IEEE Intl. Conf. on Computer Vision (ICCV)*, pages 32–39. IEEE, 2009.

[65] Xiaoyu Wang, Ming Yang, Shenghuo Zhu, and Yuanqing Lin. Regionlets for generic object detection. In *Proceedings of the IEEE Intl. Conf. on Computer Vision (ICCV)*, pages 17–24, 2013.

[66] John Wright, Yi Ma, Julien Mairal, Guillermo Sapiro, Thomas S Huang, and Shuicheng Yan. Sparse representation for computer vision and pattern recognition. *Proceedings of the IEEE*, 98(6):1031–1044, 2010.

[67] Jianxin Wu and Jim M Rehg. Centrist: A visual descriptor for scene categorization. *IEEE Trans. on Pattern Analysis and Machine Intelligence*, 33(8):1489–1501, 2011.

[68] Hui Yu, Mingjing Li, Hong-Jiang Zhang, and Jufu Feng. Color texture moments for content-based image retrieval. In *IEEE International Conference on Image Processing*, volume 3, pages 929–932. IEEE, 2002.

Chapter 4

Feature-Based Time-Series Analysis

Ben D. Fulcher

Monash Institute for Cognitive and Clinical Neurosciences, Monash University, Melbourne, Victoria, Australia.
School of Physics, Sydney University, NSW, Australia.

4.1 Introduction

4.1.1 The Time Series Data Type

The passing of time is a fundamental component of the human experience and the dynamics of real-world processes is a key driver of human curiosity. On observing a leaf in the wind, we might contemplate the burstiness of the wind speed, whether the wind direction now is related to what it was a few seconds ago, or whether the dynamics might be similar if observed tomorrow. This line of questioning about dynamics has been followed to understand a wide range of real-world processes, including in seismology (e.g.,

recordings of earthquake tremors), biochemistry (e.g., cell potential fluctuations), biomedicine (e.g., recordings of heart rate dynamics), ecology (e.g.,
animal population levels over time), astrophysics (e.g., radiation dynamics),
meteorology (e.g., air pressure recordings), economics (e.g., inflation rates variations), human machine interfaces (e.g., gesture recognition from accelerom-
eter data), and industry (e.g., quality control sensor measurements on a production line). In each case, the dynamics can be captured as a set of repeated
measurements of the system over time, or a *time series*. Time series are a fundamental data type for understanding dynamics in real-world systems. Note
that throughout this work we use the convention of hyphenating "time-series"
when used as an adjective, but not when used as a noun (as "time series").

In general, time series can be sampled non-uniformly through time, and
can therefore be represented as a vector of time stamps, t_i, and associated measurements, x_i. However, time series are frequently sampled uniformly through
time (i.e., at a constant sampling period, Δt), facilitating a more compact
representation as an ordered vector $x = (x_1, x_2, ..., x_N)$, where N measurements have been taken at times $t = (0, \Delta t, 2\Delta t, ..., (N-1)\Delta t)$. Representing
a uniformly sampled time series as an ordered vector allows other types of
real-valued sequential data to be represented in the same way, such as spec-
tra (where measurements are ordered by frequency), word length sequences
of sentences in books (where measurements are ordered through the text),
widths of rings in tree trunks (ordered across the radius of the trunk cross
section), and even the shape of objects (where the distance from a central
point in a shape can be measured and ordered by the angle of rotation of
the shape) [46]. Some examples are shown in Fig. 4.1. Given this common
representation for sequential data, methods developed for analyzing time series (which order measurements by time), can also be applied to understand
patterns in any sequential data.

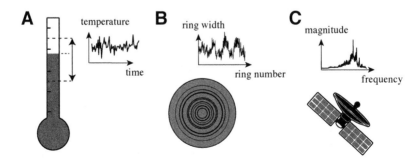

Figure 4.1: Sequential data can be ordered in many ways, including **A** temperature measured over time (a *time series*), **B** a sequence of ring widths,
ordered across the cross section of a tree trunk, and **C** a frequency spectrum
of astrophysical data (ordered by frequency). All of these sequential measurements can be analyzed by methods that take their sequential ordering into
account, including time-series analysis methods.

While the time series described above are the result of a single measurement taken repeatedly through time, or *univariate* time series, measurements are frequently made from multiple parts of a system simultaneously, yielding *multivariate* time series. Examples of multivariate time series include measurements of the activity dynamics of multiple brain regions through time, or measuring the air temperature, air pressure, and humidity levels together through time. Techniques have been developed to model and understand multivariate time series, and infer models of statistical associations between different parts of a system that may explain its multivariate dynamics. Methods for characterizing inter-relationships between time series are vast, including the simple measures of statistical dependencies, like linear cross correlation, mutual information, and to infer causal (directed) relationships using methods like transfer entropy and Granger causality [82]. A range of information-theoretic methods for characterizing time series, particularly the dynamics of information transfer between time series, are described and implemented in the excellent Java Information Dynamics Toolkit (JIDT) [53]. Feature-based representations of multivariate systems can include both features of individual time series, and features of inter-relationships between (e.g., pairs of) time series. However, in this chapter we focus on individual univariate time series sampled uniformly through time (that can be represented as ordered vectors, x_i).

4.1.2 Time-Series Characterization

As depicted in the left box of Fig. 4.2, real-world and model-generated time series are highly diverse, ranging from the dynamics of sets of ordinary differential equations simulated numerically, to fast (nanosecond timescale) dynamics of plasmas, the bursty patterns of daily rainfall, or the complex fluctuations of global financial markets. How can we capture the different types of patterns in these data to understand the dynamical processes underlying them? Being such a ubiquitous data type, part of the excitement of time-series analysis is the large interdisciplinary toolkit of analysis methods and quantitative models that have been developed to quantify interesting structures in time series, or *time-series characterization.*

We distinguish the characterization of *unordered* sets of data, which is restricted to the distribution of values, and allows questions to be asked like the following: Does the sample have a high mean or spread of values? Does the sample contain outliers? Are the data approximately Gaussian distributed? While these types of questions can also be asked of time series, the most interesting types of questions probe the temporal dependencies and hence the dynamic processes that might underlie the data, e.g., How bursty is the time series? How correlated is the value of the time series to its value one second in the future? Does the time series contain strong periodicities? Interpreting the answers to these questions in their domain context provides understanding of the process being measured.

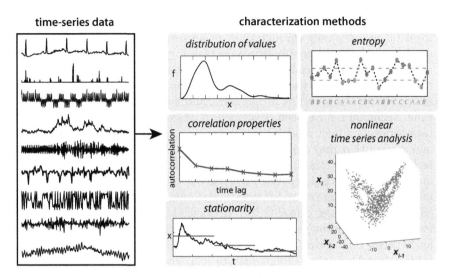

Figure 4.2: **Time-series characterization.** *Left*: A sample of nine real-world time series reveals a diverse range of temporal patterns [25, 29]. *Right*: Examples of different classes of methods for quantifying different types of structure, such as those seen in time series on the left: (i) *distribution* (the distribution of values in the time series, regardless of their sequential ordering); (ii) *autocorrelation properties* (how values of a time series are correlated to themselves through time); (iii) *stationarity* (how statistical properties change across a recording); (iv) *entropy* (measures of complexity or predictability of the time series quantified using information theory); and (v) *nonlinear time-series analysis* (methods that quantify nonlinear properties of the dynamics).

Some key classes of methods developed for characterizing time series are depicted in the right panel of Fig. 4.2, and include autocorrelation, stationarity, entropy, and methods from the physics-based nonlinear time-series analysis literature. Within each broad methodological class, hundreds of time-series analysis methods have been developed across decades of diverse research [29]. In their simplest form, these methods can be represented as algorithms that capture time-series properties as real numbers, or *features*. Many different feature-based representations for time series have been developed and been used in applications ranging from time-series modeling, forecasting, and classification.

4.1.3   Applications of Time-Series Analysis

The interdisciplinary reach of the time-series analysis literature reflects the diverse range of problem classes that involve time series. *Time-series modeling* is perhaps the most iconic problem class. Statistical models can provide

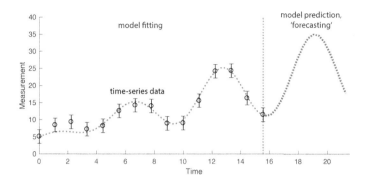

Figure 4.3: **Time-series modeling and forecasting.** The figure shows a uniformly sampled time series, a model fit, and predictions of the fitted model.

understanding of statistical relationships in the data (e.g., autocorrelation structure, seasonality, trends, nonlinearity, etc.), whereas mechanistic models use domain knowledge to capture underlying processes and interactions as equations that can be simulated in an attempt to reproduce properties of the observed dynamics. Comparing the quality of fit between different models allows inference of different types of processes that may underlie the data. Models that fit the observed data well can be simulated forward in time to make predictions about the future state of the system, a task known as *forecasting* [35], depicted in Fig. 4.3. For example, forecasting could be used to predict the value of a stock in an hour's time, the air temperature at noon tomorrow, or an individual's depression severity in a week. The range of statistical modeling approaches is vast [14,16,35], with different applications and data types favoring different approaches, including simple exponential smoothing [37], autoregressive integrated moving average (ARIMA) models, generalized autoregressive conditional heteroscedastic (GARCH) models, Gaussian Process models [4], and neural networks [83].

Problems in time-series data mining have received much research attention [23], and typically center around quantifying the similarity between pairs of time series using an appropriate *representation* and *similarity metric* [75]. This allows one to tackle problems including: *query by content*, in which known patterns of interest are located in a time-series database [24]; *anomaly detection*, in which unusual patterns in a time-series database are detected, such as unusual (possibly fraudulent) patterns of credit card transactions [77]; *motif discovery*, in which commonly recurring subsequences in a time series are identified [17,60]; *clustering*, in which time series are organized into groups of similar time series [44,47]; and *classification*, in which different labeled classes of time series are distinguished from each other [9].

Time-series classification, depicted in Fig. 4.4, is a much-studied problem that we revisit throughout this chapter. The figure depicts the goal of classi-

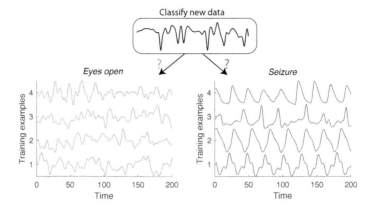

Figure 4.4: **In time-series classification, time series are assigned to categories.** In this example, involving EEG signals of two types, the aim is to distinguish data corresponding to "eyes open" from "seizure" [2]. Time-series classification algorithms quantify discriminative patterns in training examples (which the reader may be able to see), and use them to classify new data into one of the predefined groups.

fying a new time series as being measured from a subject in one of two states: (1) at rest with "eyes open" or (2) during a "seizure" [2]. The aim is to learn the most discriminative differences between the classes from labeled training examples, and use this information to accurately classify new data. The same framework can be used to detect faults on a production line using time-series sensor recordings ("safe" versus "fault"), or diagnose heart rate dynamics of a patient with congestive heart failure from a healthy control ("healthy" versus "heart failure"). Note that while most applications have considered a categorical target variable, this problem can also be placed in a *regression* framework when the target variable is continuous [29,54] (see Sec. 4 of the supplementary text of [29]). For example, rather than predicting whether a patient has "high" or "low" blood pressure (as in a classification framework), this can allow the direct prediction of blood pressure from a physiological time series.

4.2 Feature-Based Representations of Time Series

In this section, we motivate feature-based representations of time series using the problem of defining a measure of similarity between pairs of time series, which is required for many applications of time-series analysis, including many problems in time-series data mining [43, 47, 75]. As we saw above in time-series classification, new time series are classified by matching them to the most similar training time series and then inferring their class label (cf. Fig. 4.4). What is meant by "similar" in the context of this problem—and hence the motivation for defining a similarity metric—determines the classification results. Despite the pursuit of algorithms that perform "best" (on general datasets), the No-Free-Lunch theorem identifies that good performance of an algorithm on any class of problems is offset by poorer performance on another class [78, 79]. In the context of time-series representations, this implies that there is no "best" representation or similarity metric in general; the most useful measure depends on the data and the questions being asked of it [5]. For example, it may sometimes be useful to define similar time series as those with similar frequency content, while for other applications it may be more useful to define and quantify a burst rate, and define similar time series as those with similar burst rates.

For time series of equal length, perhaps the simplest measure of time-series similarity captures how similar time-series values are across the time period, depicted in Fig. 4.5A. This approach judges two time series as similar that have similar values at similar times, and can be quantified using simple metrics like the Euclidean distance between the two time-series vectors. Many more sophisticated similarity measures that capture the similarity of time-series values through time have been developed, including "elastic" distance measures like dynamic time warping (DTW) that do not require time series to be aligned precisely in time [11, 13, 51, 64, 75]. Across typically studied time-series classification problems, DTW combined with one-nearest-neighbor classification (i.e., classifying new time series by the time series in the training set with the smallest DTW distance) can yield high classification performance [7].

While optimizing performance (e.g., classification accuracy) is the main objective in many real-world applications of machine learning, providing understanding of why performance is good is often preferable, especially for applications in scientific research. Although comparing sequential values through time can yield high classification accuracy for some applications, nearest neighbor classifiers involve computing distances from a new time series to many training time series (which can be computationally expensive) and, most importantly, does not provide deeper understanding of the characteristics of time series in different classes that drive successful classification. An alternative is to use a *feature-based representation*, which reframes the problem in terms of interpretable features. Timmer et al. wrote: *"The crucial problem is not the classification function (linear or nonlinear), but the selection of well-discriminating features. In addition, the features should contribute to an understanding ..."* [72]. Similar sentiments have been mirrored by others, who have argued that research aiming to improve classification performance should focus on transformations of time series into useful (e.g., feature-based) spaces, rather than trying to develop and apply new and complex classifiers in spaces that may not best represent the data for the desired application [6,8,27,34]. A

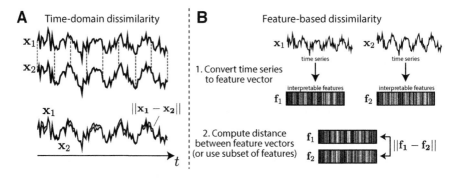

Figure 4.5: **Time-domain and feature-based dissimilarity measures for pairs of time series.** **A** Dissimilarity between two time series, x_1 and x_2, can be computed in the time domain as a simple Euclidean distance, e.g., $||x_1 - x_2||_2$. This judges two time series as similar that have similar values at similar times. **B** An alternative similarity metric involves computing a set of interpretable features from each time series (such as properties of their distribution, correlation properties, etc.), and then computing the dissimilarity between their features, as $||f_1 - f_2||_2$. This judges two time series as similar that have similar sets of global properties.

feature-based approach to time-series classification is illustrated in Fig. 4.5B, in which each time series is converted to a set of global features (such as measures of its trend, entropy, distribution), which are used to define the similarity between pairs of time series [27]. Understanding which feature-based representations provide good performance for a given task can provide conceptual understanding of the properties of the data that drive accurate decision making, information that can in turn be used to inform domain understanding and motivate future experiments.

Feature-based representations of time series can be used to tackle a wide range of time-series analysis problems in a way that provides interpretability, with the choice of feature-based representation determining the types of insights that can be gained about the problem at hand. For example, in the case of global features derived from time-series analysis algorithms, understanding comes from the features which encode deeper theoretical concepts (like entropy, stationarity, or Fourier components, described in Sec. 4.3.1 below), e.g., the researcher may learn that patients with congestive heart failure have heart rate intervals with lower entropy. If features are instead derived from the shapes of time-series subsequences, understanding comes from the time-series patterns in discriminatory time intervals, e.g., the researcher may learn that patients with congestive heart failure have characteristic shapes of ECG fluctuations following the onset of atrial depolarization. As different time-series similarity metrics are introduced through the following sections, the reader should keep in mind the benefits of each representation in terms of the understanding it can provide to a given problem.

4.3 Global Features

Global features refer to algorithms that quantify patterns in time series across the full time interval of measurement (e.g., rather than capturing shorter subsequences). Global features can thus distill complicated temporal patterns that play out on different timescales and can be produced by a variety of complex underlying mechanisms, into interpretable low-dimensional summaries that can provide insights into the generative processes underlying the time series. Representing a time series in terms of its properties judges two time series to be similar that have similar global properties, and can thereby connect dynamics in time series to deeper theoretical ideas. Global features can be applied to time series of variable lengths straightforwardly, and allows a time-series dataset to be represented as a time series (rows) × features (columns) data matrix, which can form the basis of traditional statistical learning (e.g., machine learning) methods. An example is shown in Fig. 4.6.

4.3.1 Examples of Global Features

There is a vast literature of time-series analysis methods for characterizing time-series properties [29] that can be leveraged to extract interpretable features from a time series. In this section we list some examples of specific global time-series features from some of the major methodological classes to give a flavor for the wide, interdisciplinary literature of time-series analysis [29] (cf. Fig. 4.2).

Simple measures of the *distribution* of time-series values (which ignore their time ordering) can often be informative. Examples include the mean, variance, fits to distribution types (e.g., Gaussian), distribution entropy, and measures of outliers. A simple example is the (unbiased) sample variance:

$$s_x^2 = \frac{1}{N-1} \sum_{i=1}^{N} (x_i - \bar{x})^2, \tag{4.1}$$

for a time series, x, of length N with mean $\bar{x}$. Note how the variance is independent of the ordering of values in x.

A *stationary* time series is produced from a system with fixed and constant parameters throughout the recording (or probability distributions over parameters that do not vary across the recording). Measures of stationarity capture how temporal dependences vary over time. For example, the simple

StatAv metric provides a measure of mean stationarity [63]:

$$\text{StatAv}(\tau) = \frac{\text{std}(\{\overline{x_{1:w}}, \overline{x_{w+1:2w}}, ..., \overline{x_{(m-1)w+1:mw}}\})}{\text{std}(x)}, \tag{4.2}$$

where the standard deviation is taken across the set of means computed in m non-overlapping windows of the time series, each of length w. Time series in which the mean in windows of length w vary more than the full time series as a whole have higher values of StatAv at this timescale relative to time series in which the windowed means are less variable.

Autocorrelation measures the correlation between time-series values separated by a given time lag. The following provides an estimate:

$$C(\tau) = \langle x_t x_{t+\tau} \rangle = \frac{1}{s_x^2(N-\tau)} \sum_{t=1}^{N-\tau} (x_t - \bar{x})(x_{t+\tau} - \bar{x}), \tag{4.3}$$

at a time lag τ, for a time series, x, with variance s_x^2 and mean $\bar{x}$. Nonlinear generalizations can also be computed, for example, as the automutual information [36,40]. Apart from autocorrelation values at specific time lags, other features aim to quantify the structure of the autocorrelation function, such as the earliest time lag at which it crosses zero.

The (discrete-time) *Fourier transform* allows a time series to be represented as a linear combination of frequency components, with each component given by

$$\tilde{x}_k = \frac{1}{\sqrt{N}} \sum_{n=1}^{N} x_n e^{2\pi i k n / N}, \tag{4.4}$$

where the real and complex parts of $\tilde{x}_k$ encode the amplitude and phase of that component, $e^{2\pi i k n / N}$, for frequencies $f_k = k/N\Delta t$, where Δt is the sampling interval. Other basis function decompositions, such as *wavelet decompositions*, use a wavelet basis set under variations in temporal scaling and translation, to capture changes in, e.g., frequency content through time (using a Morlet wavelet) [32].

Given that linear systems of equations can only produce exponentially growing (or decaying) or (damped) oscillatory solutions, irregular behavior in a linear time series must be attributed to a stochastic external drive to the system. An alternative explanation is that the system displays nonlinearity; deterministic nonlinear equations can produce irregular (chaotic) dynamics which can be quantified using methods from the physics-based *nonlinear time-series analysis* literature [40]. These algorithms are typically based on a phase space reconstruction of the time series, e.g., using the method of delays [71], and include measures of the Lyapunov exponent, correlation dimension, correlation entropy, and others.

Entropy measures are derived from information theory and have been used to quantify predictability in a time series, with specific examples including

Approximate Entropy (ApEn) [62], Sample Entropy (SampEn) [65], and Permutation Entropy (PermEn) [10]. For example, ApEn(m, r) is defined as the logarithmic likelihood that the sequential patterns of the data (of length m) that are close to each other (within a threshold, r), will remain close for the next sample, $m + 1$. An unstructured time series has high ApEn, and can be distinguished from a regular deterministic signal, which has a higher probability of similar sequences remaining similar (and thus low ApEn). Representing time series as a time-delay embedding in terms of a set of vectors u_m, which each contain m consecutive values of the time series [40], ApEn(m, r) is defined as

$$\text{ApEn}(m, r) = \Phi^m(r) - \Phi^{m+1}(r), \tag{4.5}$$

where

$$\Phi^m(r) = \frac{1}{N - m + 1} \sum_{i=1}^{N-m+1} \ln C_r^m(i), \tag{4.6}$$

and

$$C_i^m(r) = \frac{A_i}{N - m + 1}. \tag{4.7}$$

A_i is the number of vectors, u_m, within a distance r of u_m (for a given distance function) [62].

Scaling algorithms capture the power-law scaling of time-series fluctuations over different timescales, as would be produced by a self-affine or fractal process [40]. A stationary time series with long-range correlations can be interpreted as increments of a diffusion-like process and integrated (as a cumulative sum through time) to form a self-similar time series, i.e., a time series that statistically resembles itself through rescaling in time. So-called "short-range correlations," Eq. (4.3), decay exponentially as $C(\tau) \sim e^{-\lambda\tau}$; whereas "long-range correlations" decay as a power law, $C(\tau) \sim \tau^{-\gamma}$. Detrended fluctuation analysis [39, 61] is one method that allows estimation of the correlation exponent, γ, via the fluctuation function:

$$F(s) = \left[\frac{1}{N} \sum_{j=1}^{N} z_i(s)^2 \right]^{1/2}, \tag{4.8}$$

which is computed over a range of scales, s, for a fluctuation function $z_i(s) = y_i - y_{\text{fit},i}$, for the integrated time series, y, non-overlapping subsequences labeled with the index i, and (e.g., linear or quadratic) trends, $y_{\text{fit},i}$, subtracted from each subsequence. Scaling as $F(s) \sim s^\alpha$ quantifies long-range power law scaling of time-series fluctuations, with α related to the correlation exponent, γ, as $\alpha = 1 - \gamma/2$ [39].

Statistical *time-series models* can be fit to data to better understand complex dynamical patterns. The range of models is extensive, and includes exponential smoothing models, autoregressive models, moving average models, and Gaussian process models [14, 16, 35]. For example, an exponential smoothing model makes predictions about future values of a time series using a weighted sum of its past values, using a smoothing parameter, α:

$$\hat{x}_{t+1} = \alpha x_t + \alpha(1 - \alpha)x_{t-1} + \alpha(1 - \alpha)^2 x_{t-2} + ..., \qquad (4.9)$$

for a prediction of the value at the next time step, $\hat{x}_{t+1}$, with $0 < \alpha \leq 1$ such that values further into the past are weighted (exponentially) less in the prediction [35]. Many different types of features can be extracted from time-series models, including the model parameters (e.g., the optimal α of an exponential smoothing model), and goodness-of-fit measures (e.g., as the autocorrelation of residuals).

4.3.2 Massive Feature Vectors and Highly Comparative Time-Series Analysis

Given the large number of global features that can be used to characterize different properties of a time series, the selection of which features best capture the relevant dynamics of a given dataset typically follows the expertise of a data analyst. Examples of using manually curated feature sets are numerous, and include:

- Timmer et al. [72] characterized hand tremor time series using a variety of time- and frequency-domain features;

- Nanopoulos et al. [58] used the mean, standard deviation, skewness, and kurtosis of the time series and its successive increments as features to classify synthetic control chart patterns used in statistical process control;

- Mörchen [56] used features derived from wavelet and Fourier transforms to classify classes within each of 17 time-series datasets, including buoy sensor data, ECGs, currency spot prices, and gene expression;

- Wang et al. [73] used thirteen features containing measures of trend, seasonality, periodicity, serial correlation, skewness, kurtosis, chaos, nonlinearity, and self-similarity to represent time series, an approach that has since been extended to multivariate time series [74];

- Bagnall et al. [6] represented time series as a power spectrum, autocorrelation function, and in a principal components space, demonstrating the potential for a large increase in classification accuracy for feature-based representations (and leveraging different representations together in an ensemble).

In each application listed above—as is typical of data analysis in general—the choice of which features to use to characterize a time series is subjective and non-systematic. Thus, it is difficult to determine whether the features selected by one researcher might differ had they been selected by a different researcher, and therefore whether the feature set presented for a given task is better than existing alternatives [27–29]. The problem is well illustrated by the problem of distinguishing EEG time series during a seizure, for which existing studies had used features derived from a discrete wavelet transform [69] or a neural network classifier using a multistage nonlinear pre-processing filter with Lyapunov exponents, relative spike amplitude and spike occurrence frequency features [33]; although implicit, it is difficult to establish whether these complicated methodological approaches outperform simpler alternatives. Indeed, it has been shown that a threshold on the simple standard deviation computed for each time series provides comparable classification performance on this problem, undermining the need for computing nonlinear features or using complex classification algorithms [29].

Comprehensive methodological comparison—which is rarely done, even on a small scale [43]—is required to determine whether alternative feature-based representation of time series could be simpler and/or outperform a manually selected representation. A difficulty in performing such a comparison is the vast, interdisciplinary nature of the time-series analysis literature, that has been developed over many decades and spanning methods and models used to inform policy decisions from economic time series and those developed to diagnose disease from biomedical time series. Could it be possible to distill decades of time-series analysis research spanning thousands of studies, datasets, and applications into a unified feature set that would allow us to judge progress through comprehensive methodological comparison? Such a resource would not only allow us to partially automate the comparison of features, but would also allow us to understand previously uncharacterized methodological connections between an interdisciplinary literature and to judge whether newly developed methods for time-series analysis outperform existing alternatives (and understand what types of time-series analysis problems they perform well on).

The problem of unifying and structuring the interdisciplinary literature on global time-series features was addressed in 2013 by Fulcher, Little, and Jones [29], who collected and implemented hundreds of methods for characterizing time series from across science into a consolidated framework, operationalizing each method as a feature (or set of features), and comparing the behavior of over more than 9 000 such features using their behavior on a large dataset of more than 30 000 empirical time series collected from across science. As the approach involves comprehensive comparison across the time-series analysis literature, it was termed *highly comparative time-series analysis*. In this framework, time series (rows of the matrix in Fig. 4.6) are represented as diverse feature vectors of their properties measured using thousands of time-series analysis methods, while time-series analysis methods (columns of the matrix in Fig. 4.6) are represented in terms of their behavior across a wide range of empirical time series. This representation of time-series data in terms of their properties, and time-series analysis methods in terms of their

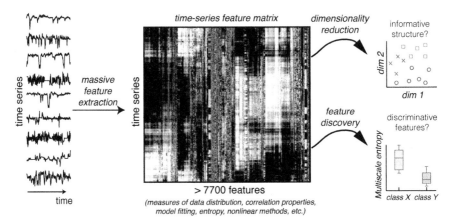

Figure 4.6: **Massive feature extraction for time-series datasets.** In this example, we show how a time-series dataset (left) can be converted to a time series × feature matrix. Each feature captures a different interpretable property of each time series, and the resulting feature matrix can be used to enable a range of analysis tasks, including visualizing low-dimensional structure in the dataset [29] or learning discriminative features for time-series classification [27]. Code for computing features and performing a range of analyses and visualizations is in the *hctsa* software package [28].

empirical behavior, facilitates a range of new approaches to time-series analysis, including the following:

- *Contextualize empirical time-series data*: using a feature-based representation of time series to find clusters of similar time series (e.g., to automatically visualize structure a time-series dataset), or search for types of time-series data similar to a given target (e.g., to find model-generated time series with properties similar to real data).

- *Contextualize algorithms for time-series analysis* in terms of their cross-disciplinary interrelationships: using the behavior of time-series analysis methods across a large number of time series to find clusters of similar analysis methods (e.g., to organize an interdisciplinary literature), or search for types of methods similar to a given target method (e.g., to automatically connect features developed in different disciplines).

- *Automate the selection of useful feature-based representations of time series*: searching across a comprehensive feature set for supervised learning tasks such as classification or regression.

When analyzing a specific dataset, the highly comparative approach allows a feature-based representation for time series to be learned systematically, tailoring it to the problem at hand using the empirical behavior of a large number of analysis methods (shown schematically in Fig. 4.6). This process can be used to guide the data analyst in their task of selecting and interpreting relevant analysis methods. Applications of the highly comparative approach to supervised and unsupervised time-series analysis problems include: classifying time series using a large range of time-series data mining datasets [27]; diagnosing phoneme audio recordings from individuals with Parkinson's disease [29]; automatically retrieving and organizing a relevant literature of features for distinguishing heart rate interval sequences of patients with congestive heart failure [29]; labeling the emotional content of speech [29]; distinguishing earthquakes from explosions [29]; projecting a database of EEG recordings into a low-dimensional feature space that revealed differences in seizure-related states [29]; estimating the scaling exponent of self-affine time series, the Lyapunov exponent of Logistic Map time series, and the noise variance added to periodic time series [29]; deciding whether to intervene during labor on the basis of cardiotocography data [26]; distinguishing *C. elegans* genotypes from movement speed dynamics [15,28]; learning differences between male and female flies during day or night from tracking their movement [28,30]; and determining the dynamical correlates of brain connectivity from fMRI data in anesthetized mice [68]. In these diverse disciplinary applications, the highly comparative approach has there characteristics (i) it selects features based on their performance on a time-series dataset in a systematic and unbiased way, (ii) the selected features facilitate interpretable insights into each time-series dataset, (iii) features are often selected from unexpected literatures (drawing attention to novel features), (iv) classifiers are often constructed using a novel combination of interdisciplinary features (e.g., combining features developed in economics with others developed in biomedical signal processing), (v) classifiers have high accuracy, comparable to state-of-the-art approaches, (vi) the concise, low-dimensional feature-based representations of time series aid data mining applications.

A MATLAB®-based computational framework for evaluating a refined set of more than 7700 interpretable global time-series features, as well as a suite of computational and analysis functions for applying the results to time-series classification tasks, for example, is available as the software implementation, *hctsa* [28] at github.com/benfulcher/hctsa. The work is accompanied by an interactive website for comparing data and methods for time-series analysis [25]. On a smaller scale than *hctsa*, the related python-based package, *tsfresh*, includes implementations of hundreds of features and includes univariate relevance scoring feature selection methods designed around applications in data mining [18].

Comparative approaches to selecting global features for time series, described above, are limited to features that have already been developed and devised, i.e., there is no scope to devise completely new types of features for a given dataset. Automated feature construction for time series, such as the genetic programming (GP)-based approach *Autofead* (using combinations of interpretable transformations, like Fourier transforms, filtering, nonlinear transformations, and windowing) are powerful in their ability to adapt to particular data contexts to generate informative features [34]. However, features generated automatically in this way can be much more difficult to interpret, as they do not connect the data to interpretable areas of the time-series analysis literature.

4.4   Subsequence Features

The previous section outlined how time series can be converted from a sequential set of measurements to a feature vector that captures interpretable global dynamical properties of a time series. However, for some classification problems, time-series properties may differ only within a specific time interval such that a most efficient representation captures these more temporally specific patterns. We refer to a subsequence, s, of length l, taken from a time series, x, of length N, as $s = (x_k, x_{k+1}, ..., x_{k+l-1})$, for $1 \leq k \leq m - l + 1$, where $l \leq N$. Different approaches to quantifying subsequences and extracting meaningful and interpretable features from them depend on the application and are summarized through this section.

4.4.1   Interval Features

As depicted in Fig. 4.7, some time-series classification problems may involve class differences in time-series properties that are restricted to specific discriminative time intervals. Interval classifiers seek to learn the location of discriminative subsequences and the features that separate different classes, which can be learned by computing simple features across many subsequences, and then building classifiers by searching over both features and time intervals [21, 66].

Deng et al. [21] used three simple features to capture the properties of time-series subsequences (for an interval $t_1 \leq x \leq t_2$) to aid interpretability and computational efficiency: the mean, $\frac{1}{t_2-t_1+1} \sum_{i=t_1}^{t_2} x_i$, standard deviation, cf. Eq. (4.3), and the slope (computed from a least squares regression line through the interval). Differences in these properties are shown visually in Fig. 4.7. In this way, each time-series subsequence is represented by the values of these three features, after which thresholds are learned on interval feature values using an entropy gain-splitting criterion (and breaking ties by taking the split that maximizes the margin between classes). After random sampling of time intervals and accumulating many decision trees, a resulting time-series forest classifier was used to classify new time series (as the majority vote from all individual decision trees). To gain interpretable understanding, the contribution of each feature to the performance of the classifier at each time point was calculated (in terms of the entropy gain of that feature at a given time point),

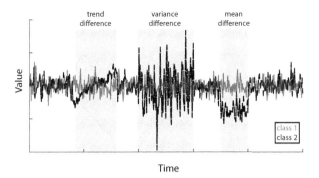

Figure 4.7: **Discriminating interval features**. Computing simple features in subsequences of a time series allows interpretable differences to be identified and used to distinguish labeled classes of time series. In this example, representative samples from two classes are shown, and periods of time in which they differ in their linear trend, variance, and mean, are highlighted. Quantifying these features and the specific time intervals at which they are most discriminative provides interpretable understanding of how, and when, the two data classes differ.

yielding an importance curve that indicates which of the three simple features contribute most to classification at each time point. For example, for times at which spread differs between the classes, the standard deviation feature will have high temporal importance, but where there are differences in location between the two series, the mean will have high importance. This information can be used to understand which time-series properties drive successful classification at each time point. Recent work has used feature-feature covariance matrices to capture subsequence properties for classification [22].

4.4.2 Shapelets

Another representation for time series is in terms of the individual subsequences themselves. In the context of time-series classification, subsequences that are highly predictive of class differences are known as *shapelets* [57, 81], and provide interpretable information about the types of sequential patterns (or shapes) that are important to measure for a given problem. The problem of shapelet discovery can be framed around determining subsequences, s, that best distinguish different classes of time series by their distance to the shapelet, $d(s, x)$. The distance between a time series, x, and a subsequence, s, of length l, can be defined as the minimum Euclidean distance across translation of the subsequence across the time series:

$$d(s, x) = \min_k d(s, x_{k,...,k+l}), \tag{4.10}$$

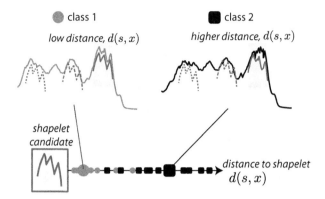

Figure 4.8: **The distance between a time series, x, and a subsequence pattern, or *shapelet*, s, or $d(s,x)$, can be used as the basis of classifying time series.** The distance, $d(s,x)$, is defined as the minimum Euclidean distance across translation of the subsequence across the time series. In this example, the candidate shapelet is closer to the time series of class 1 (picking up the shape of the peaks toward the end of the time series), but further from class 2, which has a different peak shape. An example time series from class 1 (circles) and class 2 (squares) is plotted to illustrate [$d(s,x)$ for the two plotted examples are shown as a larger circle/square]. The shapelet is an interpretable subsequence that can be used to quantify and understand subsequence patterns that differ between classes of time series.

for a Euclidean distance function, d. This distance, $d(s,x)$, can be thought of as the "feature" extracted from the time series. The problem is illustrated in Fig. 4.8, where the depicted shapelet candidate captures the class difference in the shape of the peaks toward the end of the time series, which better matches the time series of class 1, yielding a lower $d(s,x)$ for class 1. In this way, shapelet-based classifiers can learn interpretable discriminative subsequences for time-series classification problems. Shapelets: (i) provide directly interpretable subsequence patterns that are discriminative of time-series classes, (ii) allow efficient classification of new data using simple rules based on a small set of learned shapelets (avoiding the need to compare to a large training set of time series), and (iii) ignore shapes in the time series that are not informative of class differences, thereby helping to improve generalization and robustness to noise.

In early work by Geurts [31], interpretable classification rules were learned based on patterns in subsequences after transforming time series piecewise constant representations. Taking subsequences from time series in the dataset, Geurts noted the difficulty of determining the best subsequences from the vast space of all possible subsequences (across all possible subsequence lengths); instead taking subsequences from a single, randomly chosen instance from each class and used a piecewise constant representation to reduce the search space. The problem was revisited by Ye and Keogh [81], who introduced an algorithmic framework for feasibly searching across the massive space of all possible candidate time-series subsequences represented in a dataset. They framed the classification problem in terms of the discovery of subsequences whose distance to a time series is informative of its class label, defining a *shapelet* as the most informative such subsequence [81]. Discriminability was quantified using information theory in one dimension, with a single threshold used to compute the *optimal split point* as the split that maximizes the *information gain* between classes, or using multiple splits in a decision tree framework for multiclass problems. The framework has been applied widely and extended, for example, to incorporate multiple shapelets (as logical combinations of individual shapelets, as *and* and *or* [57]), using genetic algorithms to improve subsequences [70], and defining representative patterns as subsequences that appear frequently in a given class of time series and are discriminative between classes [76]. Lines et al. [50] implemented a shapelet transform that extracts a set of optimal shapelets, independent of any decision-tree-based classification system, which could then be used to transform a given time series into a feature-based representation, where k features are the set of distances to k shapelets extracted from the dataset. This shapelet distance feature-based representation of the dataset was then fed into a standard classification algorithm (like a random forest or support vector machine) [50].

4.4.3 Pattern Dictionaries

While shapelets can capture how well a subsequence matches to a time series (and are well-suited to short, pattern-based time series), they cannot capture how many times a given subsequence is represented across an extended time-series recording. For example, consider two types of time series that differ in their frequency of short, characteristic subsequence patterns across the recording, depicted in Fig. 4.9. In this case, class 1 has many occurrences of an increasing and then decreasing pattern (highlighted using circles), whereas class 2 features a characteristic oscillatory pattern. Learning these discriminative patterns, and then characterizing each time series by the frequency of each pattern across the recording, provides useful information about the frequency of discriminative subsequences between classes of time series. This representation is likely to be important in capturing stereotypical dynamic motifs, such as characteristic movement patterns in different strains of the nematode *C. elegans* [8]. In analogy to the bag-of-words representation of texts that judges two documents as similar that have similar relative frequencies of specific words, the time-series pattern dictionary approach judges pairs of time series as similar that contain similar frequencies of subsequence patterns. It thus represents time series as a histogram that counts the number of matches to a given set of subsequence patterns across the full recording (ignoring their relative timing).

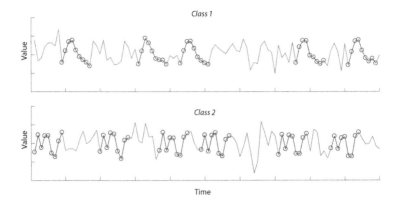

Figure 4.9: Capturing differences between two classes of time series by the frequency of shorter motifs. Characteristic motifs of each class are highlighted using circles in this idealized example; representing each class by the frequency of these motifs can be used as the basis for classification.

Variations on this basic approach have been used to tackle a range of problems. The histogram-based bag of patterns approach of Lin et al. [49] represents time series using the frequency of shorter patterns, summed across a discretized SAX transformation of the time series [48]. Schäfter [67] analyzed a symbolic representation of the time series in each window (based on a Symbolic Fourier Approximation), with an overall histogram across all sliding windows used to represent the time series as a whole. Baydogan et al. [12] computed mean, slope, and variance features in time-series subsequences (as Deng et al. [21]), as well as start and end points for the subsequence, after which all classified subsequences were combined as histograms to form a codebook to represent and assign each time series.

4.5   Combining Time-Series Representations

Thus far we have seen how the similarity of pairs of time series can be defined in terms of interpretable, extracted features that can provide different types of interpretable understanding of class differences (beyond simply computing differences in the time-series values across the full recording). As well as global feature-based representations, we have also seen how meaningful differences can be quantified in terms of characteristic time-series subsequences. Some time-series similarity measures do not fit into these two types of representations, such as the compression-based dissimilarity measure [45], which uses algorithms to compress each time series and defines time-series similarity based on the Kolmogorov complexity. Other, hybrid approaches combine feature-based representations with conventional time-domain similarity measures. For example, Batista et al. [11] used a global feature of "complexity," CE, measured simply as the length of outstretched lines connecting successive points in a time series:

$$CE = \sqrt{\sum_{i=1}^{N-1} (x_{i+1} - x_i)^2}, \tag{4.11}$$

for time series, x, of length N, to re-weight Euclidean distances between pairs of time series. In this way, pairs of time series are similar when they both: (i) have similar values through time, and (ii) have similar global "complexity." Kate [41] used time-domain distances to form a feature-based representation of time series, as the set of (e.g., dynamic time warping, DTW) distances to a set of training time series.

Comparing the large number of representations for time series, researchers have started to more comprehensively characterize which representations are better suited to which types of problems. While it is conventionally the role of the researcher to select and interpret the data representation that provides the most interesting insights into the scientific question being asked of the data, promising recent research has combined multiple time-series representations into an ensemble, partially automating this subjective procedure. For example, Bagnall et al. [8] combined 34 classifiers based on four representations of time series: (i) eleven time-domain representations (based on different elastic distance measures), (ii) eight power spectrum classifiers, (iii) eight autocorrelation-based classifiers, and (iv) eight shapelet classifiers, in a simple ensemble named a Flat Collective of Transformation-based Ensembles, or *Flat-COTE*. This was later extended as a Hierarchical Vote Collective of Transformation-based Ensembles, or *HIVE-COTE* [52], which yields a single probabilistic prediction from five domains: (i) time domain, (ii) time-series forest based on simple interval features, (iii) shapelets, (iv) dictionary-based bag-of-SFA-symbols [67], and (v) random interval spectral features. As we have seen, large collections of global time-series features can automate the selection of informative features for specific time-series problems [18, 27–29]. Continuing in this direction, we may eventually be able to compare a large number of time-series representations automatically in order to understand which representations best suit a given problem. The results of such a comparison would yield multiple interpretable perspectives on the dataset, rather than those obtained from a small number of manually selected methods.

4.6   Feature-Based Forecasting

In the final section of this chapter, we describe the use of time-series features for tackling time-series forecasting, as depicted in Fig. 4.3. Forecasting is typically tackled by fitting a statistical model to the data and then simulating it forward in time to make predictions. A feature-based approach avoids training a model directly on sequences of time-series values, but instead uses features computed in reduced time intervals to make the prediction. Many of the time-series features characterized above (in the context of time-series similarity measures for classification) could also be applied to forecasting problems. For example, a feature-based approach to weather prediction by Paras et al. [59] involved training neural networks on weighted averages, trend, and moments of the distribution in windows of time-series data. Similarly, other work has used shapelets for forecasting [55, 80].

Just as recent advances in time-series similarity metrics described above (e.g., for classification) have recognized that no single time-series representation can perform best on all problems [7, 78, 79], in the context of forecasting, no single time-series representation or forecasting method can perform best on all types of time series. Recognizing this, hybrid approaches, such as *rule-based forecasting*, first measure time-series features to characterize the data and then weight predictions of different time-series forecasting models accordingly [1, 3, 19]. This approach has been extended to learn relevant features from data using grammars, and then using feature selection and machine learning methods to generate predictions [20]. Following this idea further, a detailed investigation was performed recently by Kang et al. [38], who questioned whether the types of time series studied in classic forecasting datasets represent the diversity (and therefore the true challenge) of forecasting new types of real-world data. In this work, each time series is represented as a vector containing six features (spectral entropy, trend, seasonality, seasonal period, lag-1 autocorrelation, and the optimal Box-Cox transformation parameter), after which the full time-series dataset was projected to a two-dimensional principal components feature space in which time series with different properties occupy different parts of the space. For example, some parts of the space contain time series with decreasing trend, where other parts contain time series with strong seasonality. After embedding time-series data in a meaningful feature space, the performance of different forecasting algorithms was visualized in the space, providing an understanding of (i) which algorithms are best suited to which types of time series, (ii) how the results may generalize to new datasets (in which time series may occupy different parts of the space), and (iii) which types of time series are the most challenging to forecast, and therefore where future development of forecasting algorithms should be focused. Perhaps most interestingly, Kang et al. [38] also introduce a method for correcting for potential bias in datasets of time series that may be overrepresented by time series of a certain type, i.e., by generating new time-series instances in sparse parts of the instance space. The problem of visualizing and generating new time series with a given set of feature-based characteristics is ongoing [42].

4.7 Summary and Outlook

In this chapter, we have provided an overview of a vast literature of representations and analysis methods for time series. We have encountered global distances between time-series values (including Euclidean and elastic distance measures like DTW), subsequences that provide more localized shape-based information, global features that capture higher-order structure, and interval features that capture discriminative properties in time-series subsequences. The most useful method for a given task is determined by the structure of the data (e.g., whether time series are of the same length, are phase-aligned, or whether class differences are global or restricted to specific intervals), and the context of the problem (e.g., whether accuracy or interpretability is more important, and what type of understanding would best address the domain question of interest).

We have seen how the large and interdisciplinary toolset for characterizing time-series properties has been adapted for problems ranging from classification, regression, clustering, forecasting, and time-series generation, as well as how more tailored approaches based on time-series subsequences have been developed. A growing literature acknowledges that modern machine learning approaches can overcome some of the limitations of traditional data analysis, which is often plagued by subjective choices and small-scale comparison. This includes the use of large, interdisciplinary databases of features that can be compared systematically based on their empirical performance to automate feature selection, for example [18, 27–29], and the use of ensemble methods that try to understand the properties of a time series or time-series dataset that make it suitable for a particular representation or algorithm [6,8,34,38]. These approaches acknowledge that no algorithm can perform well on all datasets [78,79], and use modern statistical approaches to tailor our methods to our data. While complex machine learning methods are sometimes criticized for being difficult to interpret, these examples show how feature-based statistical learning approaches can allow analysts to leverage the power and sophistication of diverse interdisciplinary methods to automatically glean interpretable understanding of their data. The future of modern data analysis, including for problems involving time series, is likely to embrace such approaches that partially automate human learning and understanding of the complex dynamical patterns in the time series we measure from the world around us.

Bibliography

[1] M. Adya, F. Collopy, J.S. Armstrong, and M. Kennedy. Automatic identification of time series features for rule-based forecasting. *Int. J. Forecasting*, 17(2):143–157, 2001.

[2] Ralph G. Andrzejak, Klaus Lehnertz, Florian Mormann, Christoph Rieke, Peter David, and Christian E. Elger. Indications of nonlinear deterministic and finite-dimensional structures in time series of brain electrical activity: Dependence on recording region and brain state. *Phys. Rev. E*, 64(6):061907, 2001.

[3] J. Scott Armstrong, Monica Adya, and Fred Collopy. *Rule-Based Forecasting: Using Judgment in Time-Series Extrapolation*, pages 259–282. Springer US, Boston, MA, 2001.

[4] Sofiane B.-B. and Amine B. Gaussian process for nonstationary time series prediction. *Comput. Stat. Data Anal.*, 47(4):705–712, 2004.

[5] Anthony Bagnall, Aaron Bostrom, James Large, and Jason Lines. Simulated data experiments for time series classification part 1: Accuracy comparison with default settings. *arXiv*, page 1703.09480, 2017.

[6] Anthony Bagnall, Luke Davis, Jon Hills, and Jason Lines. Transformation based ensembles for time series classification. In *Proceedings of the 2012 SIAM International Conference on Data Mining*, pages 307–318. SIAM, 2012.

[7] Anthony Bagnall, Jason Lines, Aaron Bostrom, James Large, and Eamonn Keogh. The great time series classification bake off: a review and experimental evaluation of recent algorithmic advances. *Data Min. Knowl. Disc.*, 31(3):606–660, 2017.

[8] Anthony Bagnall, Jason Lines, Jon Hills, and Aaron Bostrom. Time-series classification with cote: the collective of transformation-based ensembles. *IEEE Trans. Knowl. Data Eng.*, 27(9):2522–2535, 2015.

[9] B.R. Bakshi and G. Stephanopoulos. Representation of process trends—IV. Induction of real-time patterns from operating data for diagnosis and supervisory control. *Comput. & Chem. Eng.*, 18(4):303–332, 1994.

[10] Christoph Bandt and Bernd Pompe. Permutation entropy: A natural complexity measure for time series. *Phys. Rev. Lett.*, 88(17):174102, 2002.

[11] G.E.A.P.A. Batista, E.J. Keogh, O.M. Tataw, and V.M.A. De Souza. Cid: An efficient complexity-invariant distance for time series. *Data Min. Knowl. Discov.*, 28(3):634–669, 2014.

[12] M.G. Baydogan, G. Runger, and E. Tuv. A bag-of-features framework to classify time series. *IEEE Trans. Pattern Anal. Machine Intell.*, 35(11):2796–2802, 2013.

[13] D. Berndt and James Clifford. Using dynamic time warping to find patterns in time series. In *KDD Workshop*, volume 10, pages 359–370, Seattle, WA, USA, 1994.

[14] G.E.P. Box, G.M. Jenkins, G.C. Reinsel, and G.M. Ljung. *Time Series Analysis: Forecasting and Control.* John Wiley & Sons, 2015.

[15] André E. X. Brown, Eviatar I. Yemini, Laura J. Grundy, Tadas Jucikas, and William R. Schafer. A dictionary of behavioral motifs reveals clusters of genes affecting *Caenorhabditis elegans* locomotion. *Proc. Natl. Acad. Sci. USA*, 110(2):791–796, 2013.

[16] C. Chatfield. *Time-Series Forecasting.* CRC Press, 2000.

[17] Bill Chiu, Eamonn Keogh, and Stefano Lonardi. Probabilistic discovery of time series motifs. In *Proceedings of the Ninth ACM SIGKDD International Conference on Knowledge Discovery and Data Mining*, pages 493–498. ACM, 2003.

[18] Maximilian Christ, Andreas W. Kempa-Liehr, and Michael Feindt. Distributed and parallel time series feature extraction for industrial big data applications. *arXiv*, page 1610.07717, 2016.

[19] Fred Collopy and J. Scott Armstrong. Rule-based forecasting: Development and validation of an expert systems approach to combining time series extrapolations. *Manag. Sci.*, 38(10):1394–1414, 1992.

[20] A.M. De Silva and P.H.W. Leong. *Grammar-Based Feature Generation for Time-Series Prediction.* Springer, 2015.

[21] H. Deng, G. Runger, E. Tuv, and M. Vladimir. A time series forest for classification and feature extraction. *Informat. Sci.*, 239:142–153, 2013.

[22] Hamza Ergezer and Kemal Leblebicioğlu. Time series classification with feature covariance matrices. *Knowl. Inf. Sys.*, pages 1–24, 2017.

[23] Philippe Esling and Carlos Agon. Time-series data mining. *ACM Computing Surveys (CSUR)*, 45(1):12, 2012.

[24] Christos Faloutsos, Mudumbai Ranganathan, and Yannis Manolopoulos. Fast subsequence matching in time-series databases. In *SIGMOD '94 Proceedings of the 1994 ACM SIGMOD International Conference on Management of Data*, volume 23, pages 419–429. ACM, 1994.

[25] B. D. Fulcher and N. S. Jones. Comp-engine time series (http://www.comp-engine.org/timeseries/), 2017.

[26] B.D. Fulcher, A.E. Georgieva, C.W.G. Redman, and N.S. Jones. Highly comparative fetal heart rate analysis. *34th Ann. Int. Conf. IEEE EMBC*, pages 3135–3138, 2012.

[27] B.D. Fulcher and N.S. Jones. Highly comparative feature-based time-series classification. *IEEE Trans. Knowl. Data Eng.*, 26(12):3026–3037, 2014.

[28] B.D. Fulcher and N.S. Jones. *hctsa*: A computational framework for automated time-series phenotyping using massive feature extraction. *Cell Systems (accepted)*, 2017.

[29] B.D. Fulcher, M.A. Little, and N.S. Jones. Highly comparative time-series analysis: The empirical structure of time series and their methods. *J. Roy. Soc. Interface*, 10(83):20130048, 2013.

[30] Quentin Geissmann, Luis Garcia Rodriguez, Esteban J. Beckwith, Alice S. French, Arian R. Jamasb, and Giorgio F. Gilestro. Ethoscopes: An Open Platform for High-Throughput Ethomics. *bioRxiv*, page 113647, 2017.

[31] Pierre Geurts. Pattern extraction for time series classification. In Luc De Raedt and Arno Siebes, editors, *Principles of Data Mining and Knowledge Discovery*, volume 2168 of *Lecture Notes in Computer Science*, pages 115–127. Springer Berlin / Heidelberg, 2001.

[32] A. Graps. An introduction to wavelets. *IEEE Comput. Sci. Eng.*, 2(2):50–61, 1995.

[33] Nihal Fatma Güler, Elif Derya Übeyli, and Inan Güler. Recurrent neural networks employing Lyapunov exponents for EEG signals classification. *Expert Syst. Appl.*, 29(3):506–514, 2005.

[34] D.Y. Harvey and M.D. Todd. Automated feature design for numeric sequence classification by genetic programming. *IEEE Trans. Evolut. Comput.*, 19(4):474–489, 2015.

[35] R.J. Hyndman and G. Athanasopoulos. *Forecasting: Principles and Practice*. OTexts, 2014.

[36] Jaeseung Jeong, John C. Gore, and Bradley S. Peterson. Mutual information analysis of the EEG in patients with Alzheimer's disease. *Clin. Neurophysiol.*, 112(5):827–835, 2001.

[37] Everette S.G. Jr. Exponential smoothing: The state of the art—Part II. *Int. J. Forecasting*, 22(4):637 – 666, 2006.

[38] Y. Kang, R.J. Hyndman, and K. Smith-Miles. Visualising forecasting algorithm performance using time series instance spaces. *Int. J. Forecasting*, 33(2):345–358, 2017.

[39] Jan W. Kantelhardt, Eva Koscielny-Bunde, Henio H. A. Rego, Shlomo Havlin, and Armin Bunde. Detecting long-range correlations with detrended fluctuation analysis. *Physica A*, 295(3-4):441–454, 2001.

[40] Holger Kantz and Thomas Schreiber. *Nonlinear Time Series Analysis*, volume 7. Cambridge university press, 2004.

[41] R.J. Kate. Using dynamic time warping distances as features for improved time series classification. *Data Min. Knowl. Discov.*, 30(2):283–312, 2016.

[42] Lars Kegel, Martin Hahmann, and Wolfgang Lehner. Feature-driven time series generation. In *29th GI-Workshop on Foundations of Databases*, 2017.

[43] E. Keogh and S. Kasetty. On the need for time series data mining benchmarks: A survey and empirical demonstration. *Data Min. Knowl. Disc.*, 7:349–371, 2003.

[44] E. Keogh, J. Lin, and W. Truppel. Clustering of time series subsequences is meaningless: Implications for previous and future research. In *Third IEEE International Conference on Data Mining (ICDM)*, pages 115–122. IEEE, 2003.

[45] E. Keogh, S. Lonardi, and C.A. Ratanamahatana. Towards parameter-free data mining. In *Proceedings of the 10th ACM SIGKDD International Conference on Knowledge Discovery and Data Mining*, pages 206–215, New York, NY, USA, 2004. ACM.

[46] Eamonn Keogh, Li Wei, Xiaopeng Xi, Sang-Hee Lee, and Michail Vlachos. Lb_keogh supports exact indexing of shapes under rotation invariance with arbitrary representations and distance measures. In *Proceedings of the 32nd International Conference on Very Large Data Bases*, pages 882–893. VLDB Endowment, 2006.

[47] T. W. Liao. Clustering of time series data: A survey. *Pattern Recogn.*, 38(11):1857–1874, 2005.

[48] J. Lin, E. Keogh, L. Wei, and S. Lonardi. Experiencing SAX: A novel symbolic representation of time series. *Data Min. Knowl. Disc.*, 15(2):107–144, 2007.

[49] J. Lin, R. Khade, and Y. Li. Rotation-invariant similarity in time series using bag-of-patterns representation. *J. Intel. Informat. Sys.*, 39(2):287–315, 2012.

[50] J. Lines, L. Davis, J. Hills, and A. Bagnall. A shapelet transform for time series classification. In *Proceedings of the 18th International Conference on Knowledge Discovery in Data and Data Mining (ACM SIGKDD 2012)*, 2012.

[51] Jason Lines and Anthony Bagnall. Time series classification with ensembles of elastic distance measures. *Data Min. Knowl. Disc.*, 29(3):565–592, 2015.

[52] Jason Lines, Sarah Taylor, and Anthony Bagnall. HIVE-COTE: The hierarchical vote collective of transformation-based ensembles for time series classification. In *Data Mining (ICDM), 2016 IEEE 16th International Conference on*, pages 1041–1046. IEEE, 2016.

[53] J.T. Lizier. JIDT: An information-theoretic toolkit for studying the dynamics of complex systems. *Front. Robot. AI*, 1:1085, 2014.

[54] A.W. Kempa-Liehr M. Christ, B.D. Fulcher. What lies beyond time series classification? Regression of exogenous variables from time series and other signals. (in preparation), 2017.

[55] A. McGovern, D.H. Rosendahl, R.A. Brown, and K.K. Droegemeier. Identifying predictive multi-dimensional time series motifs: An application to severe weather prediction. *Data Min. Knowl. Discov.*, 22(1):232–258, 2011.

[56] F. Mörchen. Time series feature extraction for data mining using DWT and DFT. Technical report, Philipps-University Marburg, 2003.

[57] Abdullah Mueen, Eamonn bi, and Neal Young. Logical-shapelets: An expressive primitive for time series classification. In *Proceedings of the 17th ACM SIGKDD International Conference on Knowledge Discovery and Data Mining*, pages 1154–1162. ACM, 2011.

[58] Alex Nanopoulos, Rob Alcock, and Yannis Manolopoulos. *Information Processing and Technology*, Feature-based classification of time-series data, pages 49–61. Nova Science Publishers, Inc., Commack, NY, USA, 2001.

[59] S. M. Paras, A. Kumar, and M. Chandra. A feature based neural network model for weather forecasting. *Int. J. Comput. Intelligence*, 4(3), 2009.

[60] Pranav Patel, Eamonn Keogh, Jessica Lin, and Stefano Lonardi. Mining motifs in massive time series databases. In *Data Mining, 2002. ICDM 2003. Proceedings. 2002 IEEE International Conference on*, pages 370–377. IEEE, 2002.

[61] C. K. Peng, S. V. Buldyrev, A. L. Goldberger, S. Havlin, R. N. Mantegna, M. Simons, and H. E. Stanley. Statistical properties of DNA sequences. *Physica A*, 221(1-3):180–192, 1995.

[62] S. M. Pincus. Approximate entropy as a measure of system complexity. *Proc. Natl. Acad. Sci. USA*, 88(6):2297–2301, 1991.

[63] S.M. Pincus, T.R. Cummins, and G.G. Haddad. Heart rate control in normal and aborted-SIDS infants. *Am. J. Physiology—Regul., Int., Comp. Physiol.*, 264(3):R638–R646, 1993.

[64] C. A. Ratanamahatana and E. Keogh. Making time-series classification more accurate using learned constraints. In *SIAM Int'l Conf. Data Mining*, pages 11–22, 2004.

[65] J. S. Richman and J. R. Moorman. Physiological time-series analysis using approximate entropy and sample entropy. *Am. J. Physiol. Heart Circ. Physiol.*, 278(6):H2039–2049, 2000.

[66] J.J. Rodríguez, C.J. Alonso, and H. Boström. Boosting interval based literals. *Intell. Data Anal.*, 5(3):245–262, 2001.

[67] P. Schäfer. The BOSS is concerned with time series classification in the presence of noise. *Data Min. Knowl. Discov.*, 29(6):1505–1530, 2015.

[68] S.S. Sethi, B. Zerbi, N. Wenderoth, A. Fornito, and B.D. Fulcher. Structural connectome topology relates to regional BOLD signal dynamics in the mouse brain. *Chaos*, 27(4):047405, 2017.

[69] Abdulhamit Subasi and M. Ismail Gursoy. EEG signal classification using PCA, ICA, LDA and support vector machines. *Expert Syst. Appl.*, 37(12):8659–8666, 2010.

[70] H. Sugimura and K. Matsumoto. Classification system for time series data based on feature pattern extraction. In *IEEE International Conference on Systems, Man, and Cybernetics (SMC)*, pages 1340–1345. IEEE, 2011.

[71] Floris Takens. Detecting strange attractors in turbulence. *Lect. Notes Math.*, 898:366–381, 1981.

[72] J. Timmer, C. Gantert, G. Deuschl, and J. Honerkamp. Characteristics of hand tremor time series. *Biol. Cybern.*, 70(1):75–80, 1993.

[73] X. Wang, K. Smith, and R. Hyndman. Characteristic-based clustering for time series data. *Data Min. Knowl. Disc.*, 13:335–364, 2006.

[74] X. Wang, A. Wirth, and L. Wang. Structure-based statistical features and multivariate time series clustering. In *IEEE Int'l Conf. Data Mining*, pages 351–360. IEEE Computer Society, 2007.

[75] Xiaoyue Wang, Abdullah Mueen, Hui Ding, Goce Trajcevski, Peter Scheuermann, and Eamonn Keogh. Experimental comparison of representation methods and distance measures for time series data. *Data Min. Knowl. Disc.*, 2012.

[76] Xing Wang, Jessica Lin, Pavel Senin, Tim Oates, Sunil Gandhi, Arnold P Boedihardjo, Crystal Chen, and Susan Frankenstein. RPM: Representative pattern mining for efficient time series classification. In *Proceedings of International Conference on Extending Database Technology (EDBT)*, pages 185–196, 2016.

[77] Gary M Weiss. Mining with rarity: a unifying framework. *ACM SIGKDD Explorations Newsletter, Special Issue on Learning from Imbalanced Datasets*, 6(1):7–19, 2004.

[78] David H Wolpert. The lack of a priori distinctions between learning algorithms. *Neural Comput.*, 8(7):1341–1390, 1996.

[79] D.H. Wolpert and W.G. Macready. No free lunch theorems for optimization. *IEEE T. Evolut. Comput.*, 1(1):67–82, 1997.

[80] Zhengzheng Xing, Jian Pei, Philip S Yu, and Ke Wang. Extracting interpretable features for early classification on time series. In *Proceedings of the 2011 SIAM International Conference on Data Mining*, pages 247–258. SIAM, 2011.

[81] Lexiang Ye and Eamonn Keogh. Time series shapelets: A new primitive for data mining. In *Proc. 15th ACM SIGKDD Int'l Conf. Knowledge Discovery and Data Mining*, pages 947–956, New York, NY, USA, 2009. ACM.

[82] A. Zaremba and T. Aste. Measures of causality in complex datasets with application to financial data. *Entropy*, 16(4):2309–2349, 2014.

[83] Guoqiang Zhang, B. Eddy Patuwo, and Michael Y. Hu. Forecasting with artificial neural networks: The state of the art. *Int. J. Forecasting*, 14(1):35–62, 1998.

Chapter 5

Feature Engineering for Data Streams

Yao Ma

Michigan State University

Jiliang Tang

Michigan State University

Charu Aggarwal

IBM Research

5.1   Introduction

It is well known that the performance of machine learning algorithms strongly depends on the feature representation of the input data [4]. A good set of features provides tremendous flexibilies that allow us to choose fast and simple models. However, the raw representation of data is not usually amenable to learning [13]. Feature engineering is the process to generate new features from the existing raw features by discovering hidden patterns in the data [65]. It aims to enrich the current feature set and increase the predictive power of the learning algorithms consequently. Therefore, feature engineering plays an important role in the success of machine learning in practice: "At the end of the day, some machine learning projects succeed and some fail. What makes the difference? Easily the most important factor is the features used [13]."

A typical process of feature engineering is suggested as follows [65]:

- Feature construction: this targets to extract extra features from the raw features in the data. It can be manual—extracting features via data analysis or by taking domain knowledge into account. It also can be automated—extracting features by aggregating, combining or transforming raw features. This step can result in a rapid growth in the total number of features.

- Feature selection: With a large number of features, learning algorithms are likely to overfit because of the curse of dimensionality, leading to performance degradation. Feature selection aims to select a small subset of the most relevant features based on some relevance evaluation criterion. It has been proven that feature selection can help improve learning performance, lower computational cost, and improve model interpretability [32].

- Model evaluation: this estimates model performance on unseen data using the chosen features.

The feature construction step will generate a set of features, the feature selection step will select the most relevant feature subset, and the model evaluation phase estimates the model performance with the selected features, which could be returned to the feature construction step for the next iteration of feature engineering [65].

We have witnessed a rapid growth in our ability to gather data from various sensors and devices, in different formats, from independent or connected applications in recent years [15]. We have entered into the era of big data where new data is generated continuously and rapidly. For example, 6,000 tweets are tweeted on Twitter per second and 293,000 statuses are updated per minute on Facebook. Data arriving as streams pose tremendous challenges to feature engineering [1, 8, 64]. With new data coming, new insights and patterns are emerging. It is not practical and realistic to rerun the feature engineering algorithms when new instances or features are added or to wait until all data instances or features are available to perform the algorithms. Therefore, feature engineering algorithms should be able to capture them in real time. Meanwhile, new instances or features are consistently presented and the size of data instances or features is unknown. Thus, feature engineering algorithms should not assume the size of the data in advance. In addition, we need to maintain a huge memory to store the data either learned previously or newly introduced. Hence, algorithms requiring several passes over the data become infeasible and algorithms only needing one pass are desired.

These immense challenges have encouraged a large body of efforts dedicated to feature engineering for data streams. Therefore, in this chapter, we provide an overview of streaming feature engineering. Among the typical steps of feature engineering, there are good surveys and books about modeling streaming data [1, 18, 41, 52, 64]. However, overviews of streaming feature construction and selection are rather limited. Hence, in this book chapter, we focus on the steps of feature construction and selection of feature engineering. Feature construction can be manual or automated. Manual feature construction strongly relies on data analysis or domain knowledge. It is usually data, problem or domain specific. On the other hand, automated feature construction, especially feature transforming, is general and can be applied to multiple domains and applications. Therefore, for feature construction, we are dedicated to automated feature construction, especially feature transformation. The remaining sections of this book chapter are organized as follows:

- In Section 2, we summarize the typical streaming settings and their corresponding formal definitions.

- We review automated feature construction algorithms including linear and non-linear methods in Section 3.

- In Section 4, we give an overview of feature selection algorithms with different streaming settings.

- We discuss some open questions and possible research directions of feature engineering for data streams in Section 5.

5.2 Streaming Settings

We summarize the three scenarios of feature engineering with data streams in Figure 5.1 [16, 22, 44, 49, 60]. In some applications, the features are relatively stable and instances are continuously added. For example, in email

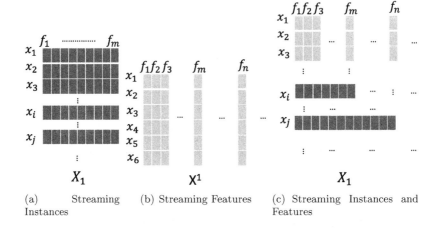

(a)   Streaming Instances   (b) Streaming Features   (c) Streaming Instances and Features

Figure 5.1: Settings for streaming feature engineering.

spam detection, the terms (or features) in the dictionary are stable but emails are rapidly generated. For these applications, we assume that the set of features is fixed while the instances are streaming as shown in Figure 5.1(a). Let $\mathcal{F} = \{f_1, \ldots, f_m\}$ be the set of m features. We use $\mathcal{X}_t = \{x_1, x_2, \ldots, x_T\}$ as the set of T instances at time t and we use a matrix $\mathbf{X}_t \in \mathbb{R}^{T \times m}$ to represent $\mathcal{X}_t$. Feature engineering in this setting aims to construct features $\mathcal{F}_t$ from $\mathcal{F}$ at t and (2) reconstruct $\mathcal{F}_t$ with a new instance x_{T+1}.

In some applications, the instances are relatively stable but new features are created. For example, in bioinformatics, the set of genes is fixed but new gene expressions are continuously observed. Thus it is reasonable to study the setting that the set of instances is fixed while the features are streaming as shown in Figure 5.1(a). Let $\mathcal{F}^t = \{f_1, \ldots, f_T\}$ be the set of features at time t. We use $\mathcal{X} = \{x_1, x_2, \ldots, x_n\}$ to denote the set of n instances and matrices $\mathbf{X}^t \in \mathbb{R}^{n \times T}$ to represent $\mathcal{X}$ at time t with $\mathcal{F}^t$. We study feature engineering with streaming features that construct $\mathcal{S}^t$ from $\mathcal{F}^t$ at t; and (2) reconstruct $\mathcal{S}^t$ with a new feature f_{T+1} .

In other applications, both instances and features are continuously introduced. For example, millions of images are uploaded to Flickr per day and new tags (or features) are generated to associate with images; and Twitter produces hundreds of millions of tweets every day and a large amount of slang words (or features) are consistently being generated. Let $\mathcal{F}^t = \{f_1, \ldots, f_T\}$ be the sets of T features at time t. We use $\mathcal{X}_t = \{x_1, x_2, \ldots, x_{n_t}\}$ as the set of n_t instances at t and we use a matrix $\mathbf{X}_t \in \mathbb{R}^{n_t \times T}$ to represent $\mathcal{X}_t$. Feature engineering with streaming features and instances aims to construct features from $\mathcal{F}^t$ at t and update selected features with new instances and features.

Data with streaming instances and features can be naturally treated as two parts—one with streaming instances and the other with streaming features. Feature engineering for data with streaming instances and features can be achieved by (1) performing feature engineering with streaming instances; and (2) performing feature engineering with streaming features. Therefore, in this book chapter, we only consider the setting of streaming instances with fixed features and the setting of streaming features with fixed instances. Without specific statements, we use the setting of streaming instances with fixed features by default.

Feature extraction is the most popular technique for automated feature construction [35]. It aims to extract a set of new features from the original features via some mapping or projections [20]. According to the chosen mapping or projection functions, feature extraction algorithms can be generally divided into linear and non-linear methods. Linear methods, such as Linear Discriminant Analysis (LDA) [38] and Principal Component Analysis (PCA) [59], map the original feature space to a new space by linear transformations (or functions), while non-linear methods, such as Locally Linear Embedding (LLE) [46], kernel learning [53], and neural networks [19], project the original features via non-linear functions. Following a similar way, we will review linear and non-linear streaming feature extraction algorithms in the following section.

5.3 Linear Methods for Streaming Feature Construction

Linear methods utilize linear projections or functions to transform original features into new features. Given their efficiency, there is a large body of literature about linear feature extraction methods such as Principal Component Analysis (PCA), Linear Discriminant Analysis (LDA), Maximum Margin Criterion (MMC) [31], and Orthogonal centroid algorithm [24]. There are many efforts to extend these traditional linear methods for data streams. In the following subsections, we will use PCA and LDA as examples to give an overview of linear feature extraction methods for data streams.

5.3.1 Principal Component Analysis for Data Streams

Principal Component Analysis (PCA), aiming to maximally preserve the data variance, has been widely used in many real-world applications such as dimension reduction, signal denoising, and correlation analysis [14,59]. Various ways can be used to describe PCA and the following one is particularly preferred under the streaming setting [6]. For $\mathbf{X} = \{\mathbf{x}_1, \mathbf{x}_2, \ldots, \mathbf{x}_n\}$ with $\mathbf{x}_i \in \mathbb{R}^T$, it targets to find $\mathbf{Y} = \{\mathbf{y}_1, \mathbf{y}_2, \ldots, \mathbf{y}_n\}$ with $\mathbf{y}_i \in \mathbb{R}^K$, which can minimize the reconstruction error as

$$\min_{\mathbf{y}_i} \min_{\mathbf{W} \in \mathcal{O}_{T,K}} \sum_{i=1}^{n} \|\mathbf{x}_i - \mathbf{W}\mathbf{y}_i\|_2^2 \tag{5.1}$$

where $\mathcal{O}_{T,K}$ denotes the set of $T \times K$ isometric embedding matrices:

$$\mathcal{O}_{T,K} = \mathbf{W} \in \mathbb{R}^{T \times K} | \forall \mathbf{y} \in \mathbb{R}^K, \|\mathbf{W}\mathbf{y}\|_2 = \|\mathbf{y}\|_2. \tag{5.2}$$

It is easy to prove that the optimal solution of $\mathbf{W}$ spans the top K left singular vectors of $\mathbf{X}$ and $\mathbf{Y} = \mathbf{W}^\top \mathbf{X}$. We use OPT_K to denote the objective function value with the optimal solution. The optimal $\mathbf{W}$ can be computed from $\mathbf{X}\mathbf{X}^\top$, which typically requires $O(nT^2)$ time and $O(T^2)$ space [27]. Moreover, to obtain $\mathbf{Y} = \mathbf{W}^\top \mathbf{X}$, several passes over the matrix $\mathbf{X}$ are demanded, which is prohibitive under the streaming setting. With a newly introduced data instance, re-running the algorithm is also not desired. Therefore, dedicated efforts have been made to adapt PCA in the streaming setting. According to the chosen techniques, we divide existing algorithms into the following major groups such as random projection, regret minimization, stochastic optimization, and matrix sketching-based methods.

Random Projection: These methods generate a matrix $\mathbf{S} \in \mathbb{R}^{T \times \ell}$ randomly and independently [11] from the data [49] and set $\mathbf{y}_i = \mathbf{S}^\top \mathbf{x}_i$. As shown in [25], $\mathbf{S}$ can exhibit the Johnson Lindenstrauss property—$\mathbf{y}_i$ approximately maintains the lengths and distances between all the vectors $\mathbf{x}_i$. Then, with constant probability for $\ell = \Theta(K/\epsilon)$:

$$\min \sum_{i=1}^{n} \|\mathbf{x}_i - \mathbf{W}\mathbf{y}_i\|_2^2 \leq (1 + \epsilon)OPT_K. \tag{5.3}$$

Hence, the solution leading to the minimal reconstruction error is $\mathbf{W} = \mathbf{X}\mathbf{Y}^+$ where $\mathbf{Y}^+$ is the Moore Penrose inverse or pseudo-inverse of $\mathbf{Y}$. For a new data instance, since we only need to update one column of $\mathbf{S}$ [11], it is efficient for the streaming setting. However, as noticed in [6], $\mathbf{W}$ obtained from random projection is typically not an isometry and due to the Johnson Lindenstrauss property, noise could also exist after data transformation.

Regret Minimization: In [43, 58], regret minimization, approaches are investigated to help PCA under the streaming setting. At time t, before receiving the data instance $\mathbf{x}_t$, the algorithms generate a projection matrix $\mathbf{P}_t \in \mathbb{R}^{T \times T}$ with rank K where $\mathbf{P}_t$ is a square projection matrix having $\mathbf{P}_t^2 = \mathbf{P}_t$. Then these algorithms ensure that $\sum_t \|\mathbf{x}_t - \mathbf{P}_t^\top \mathbf{x}_t\|_2^2$ converges to OPT_k in the usual no-regret sense. The term $\sum_t \|\mathbf{x}_t - \mathbf{P}_t^\top \mathbf{x}_t\|_2^2$ can be rewritten as

$$\sum_t \|\mathbf{x}_t - \mathbf{P}_t^\top \mathbf{x}_t\|_2^2 = \sum_t \|(\mathbf{P} - \mathbf{I})\mathbf{x}_t\|_2^2 = Tr((\mathbf{I} - \mathbf{P}) \sum_t \mathbf{x}_t \mathbf{x}_t^\top) \tag{5.4}$$

where $(\mathbf{I} - \mathbf{P})^2 = \mathbf{I} - \mathbf{P}$ is a projection matrix. Therefore, we can interpret the loss as linear in the projection matrix $\mathbf{I} - \mathbf{P}$ and the covariance matrix

$\mathbf{C} = \sum_t \mathbf{x}_t \mathbf{x}_t^\top$. Regret minimization is to obtain an algorithm whose cumulative loss over trials $t = 1, \ldots, T$ is close to the cumulative loss of the best rank K projection matrix chosen in hindsight after seeing all T instances. The maximum difference between the cumulative loss of the algorithm and the best off-line comparator is called the (worst-case) regret. In [58], a matrix version of the multiplicative update was applied to PCA, whose regret bound is logarithmic in dimension T. This algorithm uses the quantum relative entropy in its motivation and is called the Matrix Exponentiated Gradient (MEG) algorithm [55]. It does a matrix version of a multiplicative update and then projects onto constraints where the projections are with respect to the quantum relative entropy. In [43], the authors discussed algorithms based on both the Gradient Descent (GD) and Matrix Exponentiated Gradient (MEG) and provided tight upper bounds on the regret of these two algorithms.

Stochastic Optimization: Algorithms based on stochastic optimization [2, 3, 16, 40] assume the instances $\mathbf{x}_t$ are drawn i.i.d. from a fixed (and unknown) distribution. Hence, after obtaining n_0 columns of $\mathbf{x}_t$, we can efficiently calculate $U_{n_0} \in \mathcal{O}_{T,K}$ such that it approximately spans the top K singular vectors of $\mathbf{X}$. Then we set $\mathbf{y}_t = 0^k$ for $t < n_0$ and $y_t = U_{n_0} \mathbf{x}_t$ for $t \le n_0$. These algorithms are provably correct for some n_0, which is independent on n. The stochastic setting is very popular in applications where the data distribution is expected to change or at least drift over time.

Matrix Sketching: Recently there are algorithms proposed based on matrix sketching [6,27]. For $\mathbf{X}_t$, matrix sketching aims to learn $\mathbf{B}_t \in \mathbb{R}^{K \times n}$, $K \ll T$ by minimizing $\|\mathbf{X}_t^\top \mathbf{X}_t - \mathbf{B}_t^\top \mathbf{B}_t\|_F^2$ [34]. When a new instance $\mathbf{x}_{t+1} \in \mathbb{R}^T$ is added at $t + 1$, the algorithm to obtain $\mathbf{B}_{t+1}$ is presented in Algorithm 1; it performs the K truncated SVD on the concatenation of $\mathbf{B}_t$ and $\mathbf{x}_{T+1}$, and then constructs $\mathbf{B}_{t+1}$. Algorithms based on matrix sketching are designed to work with the sketching matrix $\mathbf{B}_t$ rather than the original matrix $\mathbf{X}_t$, which requires only one pass over the data.

Algorithm 1 The algorithm of matrix sketching with a new instance $\mathbf{x}_{t+1}$.

Input: $\mathbf{B}_t, \mathbf{x}_{t+1}$
Output: $\mathbf{B}_{t+1}$ $\mathbf{A}_{t+1} = [\mathbf{B}_t, \mathbf{x}_{t+1}]$
$\mathbf{U}_{t+1}, \Sigma_{t+1}, \mathbf{V}_{t+1} = SVD_K(\mathbf{A}_{t+1})$ where $\Sigma_{t+1} = diag(\sigma_1, \ldots, \sigma_K)$
$\bar{\Sigma}_{t+1} = diag(\sqrt{(\sigma_1^2 - \sigma_K^2)}, \ldots, 0)$
$\mathbf{B}_{t+1} = \bar{\Sigma}_{t+1}(\mathbf{V}_{t+1})^\top$

5.3.2 Linear Discriminant Analysis for Data Streams

Linear discriminant analysis (LDA) is powerful for supervised dimensionality reduction and has been applied successfully to many applications, including machine learning, data mining, and bioinformatics [38]. It is used to find a new feature space that best discriminates the samples from different classes. It can be achieved by addressing the following generalized eigenvalue decomposition problem: $\mathbf{S}_b \mathbf{w} = \lambda \mathbf{S}_w \mathbf{w}$ where $\mathbf{S}_b$ and $\mathbf{S}_w$ are inter-class and intra-class matrices, respectively, which are formally defined as

$$\mathbf{S}_b = \sum_{i=1}^{C} \frac{n_i}{n} (\mathbf{c}_i - \mathbf{c})(\mathbf{c}_i - \mathbf{c})^\top$$

$$\mathbf{S}_w = \sum_{i=1}^{C} \frac{n_i}{n} \sum_{x_j \in c_i} (\mathbf{x}_j - \mathbf{c}_j)(\mathbf{x}_j - \mathbf{c}_j)^\top \tag{5.5}$$

where C is the number of classes, c_i is the i-th class with the center vector $\mathbf{c}_i$ and n_i data instances, and $\mathbf{c}$ is the mean vector of all data instances.

Some efforts have been made to adapt LDA with the streaming setting via QR decomposition. In [63], the proposed IDR/QR algorithm applies regularized LDA in a projected subspace, which is spanned by the class means. In LDA, the dimension of the new subspace is equal to the number of classes, which is typical low. Hence, the IDR/QR algorithm is very efficient. However, in the first projection of IDR/QR, much information is lost. Moreover, some useful components are discarded in the updating process. In addition, it needs to pre-define an appropriate regularization parameter. In [10], a new algorithm LDA/QR for traditional linear discriminant analysis (LDA) was built. It calculates the economic QR factorization of the data matrix and then solves a lower triangular linear system. Based on LDA/QR, a new algorithm ILDA/QR was introduced for data streams. The main advantages of ILDA/QR are threefold. First, it can easily deal with the update from one new sample or a chunk of new samples. Second, it has efficient computational and space complexities. Finally, it often achieves similar performance as existing ILDA algorithms.

In [28], a different LDA algorithm, ILDA/SSS, is introduced. It utilizes sufficient spanning set approximation to update the between-class scatter matrix and the total scatter matrix. With the approximation, the principal eigenvectors and eigenvalues of these two matrices are maintained and updated, and the minor components are removed in each update. However, in ILDA/SSS, three eigenvalue thresholds are required to determine the principal components of the between-class scatter matrix, the total scatter matrix, and the optimal transformation matrix, respectively. As demonstrated in [36], it is challenging for ILDA/SSS to determine a balance between the classification performance and the computational efficiency. For example, when it discards many small components, the performance will reduce although the efficiency will increase. In addition, its performance is extremely sensitive to the setting of the approximation parameter.

QR-based methods and ILDA/SSS are approximation methods. There are methods performing exact updating whenever a new data sample is added, such as LS-ILDA [36] and ICLDA [37]. ICLDA is an approach by incrementally implementing CLDA [61] exactly. Its dimension of the reduced space of

ICLDA is equal to the rank of the total scatter matrix. As a consequence, its dimension is usually high, which leads to large computational complexity and memory requirements. Meanwhile, many items need to be updated when a new instance is added. Therefore, the space complexity is increased. In LS-LDA [62], LDA is proven to be a framework of multivariate regression and is given the least-square solution. LS-ILDA [36] is the streaming implementation of LS-LDA.

5.4 Non-Linear Methods for Streaming Feature Construction

Non-linear methods extract new features by applying non-linear transforming on the original features. Non-linear methods are able to capture complicated patterns among data and have been attracting more and more attention with the increase of data complexity in the era of big data. In the following subsections, we will review representative non-linear methods including locally linear embedding, kernel learning and deep neural networks.

5.4.1 Locally Linear Embedding for Data Streams

The LLE algorithm [46] consists of three major steps:

- For each data instance x_i, it defines its neighbor set N_i, which contains the N_i nearest neighbors of x_i. We use $|N_i|$ to denote the number of neighbors. Properly selecting $|N_i|$ is important to LLE [9]. With a larger $|N_i|$, the algorithm will lose the local nonlinear features on the manifold; while with a smaller $|N_i|$, LLE will split the continuous manifold into detached locality pieces, because the global characteristics are lost.

- The optimal weights $\{\mathbf{W}_{ij}, j \in N_i, i = 1, 2, \ldots, n\}$ are obtained by solving the following optimization problem:

$$\min \sum_{i=1}^{n} \|\mathbf{x}_i - \sum_{j \in N_i} \mathbf{W}_{ij}\mathbf{x}_j\|_2^2, \quad s.t., \quad \sum_{j \in N_i} \mathbf{W}_{ij} = 1. \quad (5.6)$$

- Let $\mathbf{y}_i \in \mathbb{R}^K$ be the new feature representation of $\mathbf{x}_i$. The new representations aim to best preserve the geometric properties of the original space. To minimize

$$\min \sum_{i=1}^{n} \|\mathbf{y}_i - \sum_{j \in N_i} \mathbf{W}_{ij}\mathbf{y}_i\|_2^2, \quad s.t., \quad \sum_{i=1}^{n} \mathbf{y}_i = 0, \quad \sum_{i=1}^{n} \mathbf{y}_i\mathbf{y}_i^\top = \mathbf{I} \quad (5.7)$$

we add constraint $\sum_{i=1}^{n} \mathbf{y}_i = 0$ to ensure that the new representations are centered and $\sum_{i=1}^{n} \mathbf{y}_i \mathbf{y}_i^\top = \mathbf{I}$ to make sure that the new representation vectors have unit covariance.

To find the matrix $\mathbf{Y} = [\mathbf{y}_1, \ldots, \mathbf{y}_n]$ under these constraints, a new sparse symmetric and positive semi-definite matrix $\mathbf{M}$ is constructed based on the matrix $\mathbf{W} : \mathbf{M} = (\mathbf{I} - \mathbf{W})^\top (\mathbf{I} - \mathbf{W})$. LLE then computes the smallest $K + 1$ eigenvectors of $\mathbf{M}$, associated with the $K + 1$ smallest eigenvalues. The vector whose eigenvalue is equal to zero is excluded. The remaining K eigenvectors yield the final embedding $\mathbf{Y}$. A comprehensive survey of LLE can be found in [9].

However, LLE cannot handle new data, which makes LLE less attractive in streaming settings, where a complete rerun of the algorithm becomes prohibitively expensive. There are attempts to extend LLE for data streams. In [50], the nearest neighbors N_{n+1} of x_{n+1} are first computed. Then the linear weights, $\mathbf{W}_{n+1}$, that best reconstruct x_{n+1} from its neighbors, are calculated. Finally, the new output $\mathbf{y}_{n+1}$ is defined as

$$\mathbf{y}_{n+1} = \sum_{i \in N_{n+1}} \mathbf{W}_{(n+1)j} \mathbf{y}_j. \tag{5.8}$$

In [5], the theoretical analysis is conducted for the algorithm.

Let $\mathbf{Y}_{n+1}$ and $\mathbf{X}_{n+1}$ be new and old representations of neighbors of x_{n+1}, respectively. Intuitively, the manifold is locally linear, therefore, it is reasonable to assume a linear relation between them as $\mathbf{Y}_{n+1} = \mathbf{Z}\mathbf{X}_{n+1}$, where $\mathbf{Z}$ is an unknown linear transformation matrix, which can be determined as $\mathbf{Z} = \mathbf{Y}_{n+1}\mathbf{X}_{n+1}^{-1}$. Because $\mathbf{X}_{n+1}$ is the neighborhood of x_{n+1} and LLE preserves local structures, the new projection can be computed as $y_{n+1} = \mathbf{Z}\mathbf{x}_{n+1}$. Many other approaches have also been introduced to learn the transformation matrix $\mathbf{Z}$ such as multivariate linear regression [26].

In [29], the authors proposed an incremental version of LLE (ILLE). First, distances between instances, which either belong to the nearest neighbors of the new instance or contain the new instance as one of their nearest neighbors, are recalculated. Then the weights for the instances whose distances have been changed are updated and the new matrix $\mathbf{M}_{new}$ is calculated by using these weights. To avoid the ill-conditioned eigen-problem, they assume that the eigenvalues of the new cost matrix $\mathbf{M}_{new}$ are the same as those of the cost matrix computed for N instances. The new coordinates are obtained by solving a $K \times K$ minimization problem

$$\min_{\mathbf{Y}_{new}} (\mathbf{Y}_{new} \mathbf{M}_{new} \mathbf{Y}_{new}^T - diag\{\lambda_1, \ldots, \lambda_K\}) \tag{5.9}$$

where λ_i are the i-th smallest eigenvalues of the cost matrix $\mathbf{M}$.

5.4.2   Kernel Learning for Data Streams

Kernel methods are one of the most popular feature transformation methods. They are typically incorporated into different algorithms for better performance such as kernel SVMs for classification [51], kernel PCA [39] and kernel K-means [12]. The basic idea of kernel methods is to transform non-linearly separable data to a discriminative and linearly separable feature space, in which the discriminative nature of the feature space is primarily ensured by tuning the parameters of the kernel. Next we will review SVM with kernel learning under the streaming setting.

The formulation of soft-margin SVM is as follows:

$$\min \frac{1}{2}\mathbf{w}^\top \mathbf{w} + C \sum_{i=1}^{n} \epsilon_i$$
$$s.t. \quad y_i(\mathbf{w}^\top \mathbf{x}_i + b) \leq 1 - \epsilon_i, i = 1, \dots, n$$
$$\epsilon_i \geq 0, i = 1, \dots, n \tag{5.10}$$

where $\mathbf{x}_i$ is the i-th training instance and its corresponding label is $y_i \in \{1, -1\}$. C is the parameter to control the allowed errors. The optimal separating function reduces to a linear combination of kernels on the training data: $f(\mathbf{x}) = \sum_i \alpha_i K(\mathbf{x}_i, \mathbf{x}) + b$. The coefficients α_i are obtained by minimizing the following objective function under constraints [56]:

$$\min_{0 \leq \alpha_i \leq C}, F = \frac{1}{2} \sum_{i,j} \alpha_i Q_{ij} \alpha_j - \sum_i \alpha_i + b \sum_i y_i \alpha_i \tag{5.11}$$

where $\mathbf{Q}_{ij} = y_i y_j K(\mathbf{x}_i \mathbf{x}_j)$. Let $g_i = \frac{\partial F}{\partial \alpha_i} = y_i f(x_i) - 1$, which partitions the training data and corresponding coefficients into three categories—the set S of margin support vectors strictly on the margin ($y_i f(\mathbf{x}_i) = 1$), the set E of error support vectors exceeding the margin (not necessarily misclassified), and the remaining set R of (ignored) vectors within the margin.

One of the earliest attempts to adapt SVM for data streams is proposed in [54]. It re-trains a new SVM by using new data instances N combined with previous support vectors S. However, the support vectors cannot describe the whole data but only the decision function. To mitigate this problem, the author in [47] proposed to make an error on the old support vectors more costly than that on new examples by adding a constant L as

$$\min \frac{1}{2}\mathbf{w}^\top \mathbf{w} + C\left(\sum_{x_i \in N} \epsilon_i + L \sum_{i \in S} \epsilon_i\right) \tag{5.12}$$

where $L = \frac{\# \text{ instances}}{\# \text{ support vectors}}$ to denote that every support vector stands for a constant fraction of all examples. The algorithm proposed in [7] is one of the earliest algorithms, which can provide the exact solution. It updates an optimal solution of an SVM training problem after one training example (x_c, y_c) is added. More details about the methods can be found in [7]. In [30], a better scheme for organization of memory and arithmetic operations in exact incremental SVM is proposed based on the gaxpy-type updates of the sensitivity vector. The algorithm proposed in [66] consists of two components: Learning

Prototypes (LPs) and Learning SVs (LSVs). LPs are to represent the original data and adapt prototypes to the concept of data continuously, and the obtained prototypes (representatives) up to now denote local neighbors of the training samples. LSVs learn the SVs with the help of LPs. The bridge between LPs and LSVs is to make the learned data more "costly."

5.4.3   Neural Networks for Data Streams

Deep neural networks have been proven to be powerful in learning representations in many domains such as speech recognition, image processing, natural language processing and social network analysis. They were not originally designed for data streams. However, most of these networks adopt Stochastic Gradient Decent (SGD) to train their models. Thus, they are naturally applicable to streaming data. In the following, we briefly review two representative deep neural networks, i.e., Autoencoder [21] and Restricted Boltzmann Machines [42, 48].

Autoencoder: An autoencoder is a feed-forward neural network. It takes the input $\mathbf{x}$ and tries to encode it to some representations $h(\mathbf{x})$ so that the input $\mathbf{x}$ can be reconstructed from the representations $h(\mathbf{x})$. The output of an autoencoder is the input itself. When the dimension of $h(\mathbf{x})$ is less than the input dimension, the autoencoder is called undercomplete. This is the case we will introduce in this chapter. An undercomplete autoencoder tries to push the input through a "bottleneck" and compresses it to a low-dimensional representation which can still reconstruct the input well.

Figure 5.2 shows an autoencoder with one hidden layer. It consists of two components : 1) the encoder that encodes the input $\mathbf{x}$ to latent representations $h(\mathbf{x})$; and 2) the decoder that decodes the latent representation $h(\mathbf{x})$ to $\hat{\mathbf{x}}$, which is supposed to be close to the input $\mathbf{x}$. The autoencoder is fully connected; $\mathbf{W}$ is the connection matrix between the input layer and the hidden layer while $\hat{\mathbf{W}}$ is the connection matrix between the hidden layer and output layer. More clearly, the relations between the layers are

$$h(\mathbf{x}) = f(\mathbf{W}\mathbf{x} + \mathbf{b}); \tag{5.13}$$

$$\hat{\mathbf{x}} = f(\hat{\mathbf{W}}^T h(\mathbf{x}) + \hat{\mathbf{b}}); \tag{5.14}$$

where $\mathbf{b}$ and $\hat{\mathbf{b}}$ are the terms of biases, and the function f is the non-linear activation function such as sigmoid.

To train the autoencoder, different loss functions could be used. For example, for real-value inputs, the squared error can be used:

$$L(\mathbf{x}, \hat{\mathbf{x}}) = \frac{1}{2}||\mathbf{x} - \hat{\mathbf{x}}||_2^2. \tag{5.15}$$

For binary inputs, the cross-entropy error can be used:

$$L(\mathbf{x}, \hat{\mathbf{x}}) = -\sum_k (x_k \log(\hat{x}_k) + (1 - x_k)\log(1 - \hat{x}_k)). \tag{5.16}$$

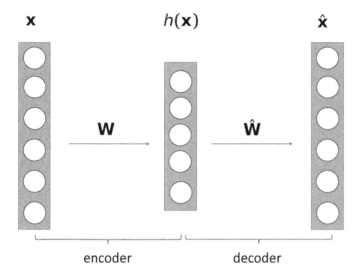

Figure 5.2: An autoencoder with one hidden layer.

Stochastic Gradient Decent (SGD) and back propagation (BP) are usually adopted to update the parameters. Let θ denote all the parameters in the model which include the connection matrices $\mathbf{W}, \hat{\mathbf{W}}$ and the bias terms $\mathbf{b}$, and $\hat{\mathbf{b}}$. For each step, the update rule can be represented as

$$\theta \leftarrow \theta - \eta \cdot \frac{\partial L(\mathbf{x}, \hat{\mathbf{x}})}{\partial \theta}, \tag{5.17}$$

where η is the learning rate.

Restricted Boltzmann Machine: The Restricted Boltzmann Machine (RBM) is a neural network with one input layer (visible layer) and one hidden layer. After training, the RBM can map the input $\mathbf{x}$ to the learned features $\mathbf{h}$. Figure 5.3 shows a Restricted Boltzmann Machine with one visible layer and one hidden layer where both layers consist of binary units. The Restricted Boltzmann Machine is fully connected between layers, while there are no connections within any given layer. The two layers are connected via the connection matrix $\mathbf{W}$.

The joint distribution of $\mathbf{x}$ and $\mathbf{h}$ can be modeled as

$$p(\mathbf{x}, \mathbf{h}) = \frac{\exp(-E(\mathbf{x}, \mathbf{h}))}{Z}, \tag{5.18}$$

where $E(\mathbf{x}, \mathbf{h})$ is the energy function

$$E(\mathbf{x}, \mathbf{h}) = -\mathbf{h}^T \mathbf{W} \mathbf{x} - \mathbf{c}^T \mathbf{x} - \mathbf{b}^T \mathbf{h}, \tag{5.19}$$

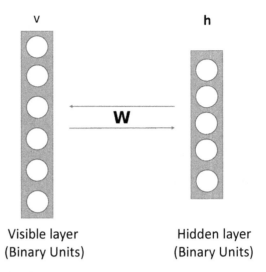

Figure 5.3: Restricted Boltzmann Machine.

and Z is the normalizing factor called the *partition function* by analogy with physical systems.

$$Z = \sum_{\mathbf{x},\mathbf{h}} \exp(-E(\mathbf{x},\mathbf{h})). \tag{5.20}$$

Then, the probability of observing $\mathbf{x}^{(i)}$ in the training set is

$$p(\mathbf{x}^{(i)}) = \sum_{\mathbf{h}} p(\mathbf{x}^{(i)}, \mathbf{h})$$

$$= \sum_{\mathbf{h}} \frac{\exp(-E(\mathbf{x}^{(i)}, \mathbf{h}))}{Z}. \tag{5.21}$$

We model the problem as a maximum likelihood problem. We need to maximize the probability of observing the training set $\prod_i p(\mathbf{v}^{(i)})$. Instead of directly maximizing it, we equivalently minimize the negative log-likelihood $-\sum_i \log p(\mathbf{v}^{(i)})$.

Stochastic Gradient Decent (SGD) is adopted to update the parameters. Let θ denote the parameters which include the connection matrix $\mathbf{W}$ and the bias terms $\mathbf{b}$ and $\mathbf{c}$. The update rule for each step is

$$\theta \leftarrow \theta - \eta \cdot \frac{\partial - \log p(\mathbf{v}^{(i)})}{\partial \theta}. \tag{5.22}$$

So, if we can calculate the derivative in (5.22), the learning procedure can be smoothly performed.

Starting from (5.21) and (5.20), we can write the derivative as follows:

$$
\frac{\partial - \log p(\mathbf{x}^{(t)})}{\partial \theta} = - \frac{\partial \log \sum_{\mathbf{h}} \exp(-E(\mathbf{x}^{(t)}, \mathbf{h}))}{\theta} + \frac{\partial \log \sum_{\mathbf{x}, \mathbf{h}} \exp(-E(\mathbf{x}, \mathbf{h}))}{\theta}
$$

$$
= + \frac{1}{\sum_{\mathbf{h}} \exp(-E(\mathbf{x}^{(t)}, \mathbf{h}))} \sum_{\mathbf{h}} \exp(-E(\mathbf{x}^{(t)}, \mathbf{h})) \frac{\partial E(\mathbf{x}^{(t)}, \mathbf{h})}{\partial \theta}
$$

$$
- \frac{1}{\sum_{\mathbf{x}, \mathbf{h}} \exp(-E(\mathbf{x}, \mathbf{h}))} \sum_{\mathbf{x}, \mathbf{h}} \exp(-E(\mathbf{x}, \mathbf{h})) \frac{\partial E(\mathbf{x}, \mathbf{h})}{\partial \theta}
$$

$$
= \sum_{\mathbf{h}} p(\mathbf{h}|\mathbf{x}^{(t)}) \frac{\partial E(\mathbf{x}^{(t)}, \mathbf{h})}{\partial \theta} - \sum_{\mathbf{h}} p(\mathbf{x}, \mathbf{h}) \frac{\partial E(\mathbf{x}, \mathbf{h})}{\partial \theta}
$$

$$
= \mathbb{E}_{\mathbf{h}} \left[\frac{\partial E(\mathbf{x}^{(t)}, \mathbf{h})}{\partial \theta} | \mathbf{x}^{(t)} \right] - \mathbb{E}_{\mathbf{x}, \mathbf{h}} \left[\frac{\partial E(\mathbf{x}, \mathbf{h})}{\partial \theta} \right]. \tag{5.23}
$$

In (5.23), the first expectation is over $\mathbf{h}$ and the second expectation is over both $\mathbf{x}$ and $\mathbf{h}$. Note that calculating $\frac{\partial E(\mathbf{x}, \mathbf{h})}{\partial \theta}$ given $\mathbf{x}$ and $\mathbf{h}$ is tractable, however, calculating the second expectation is intractable as we have to make an exponential summation over both $\mathbf{x}$ and $\mathbf{h}$. Thus, we have to approximate this term to perform the SGD efficiently.

The Gibbs Sampling is adopted to estimate the expectations. For k Gibbs steps, starting from a training example $\mathbf{v}^{(t)}$:

$$
\mathbf{x}^{(i)} \sim \hat{p}(\mathbf{x});
$$
$$
\mathbf{h}^{(i)} \sim p(\mathbf{h}|\mathbf{x}^{(i)});
$$
$$
\mathbf{x}_1 \sim p(\mathbf{x}|\mathbf{h}^{(i)});
$$
$$
\mathbf{h}_1 \sim p(\mathbf{h}|\mathbf{x}_1);
$$
$$
\mathbf{x}_2 \sim p(\mathbf{x}|\mathbf{h}_1);
$$
$$
\cdots \tag{5.24}
$$
$$
\mathbf{h}_k \sim p(\mathbf{h}|\mathbf{x}_k);
$$

where $\hat{p}(\mathbf{x})$ is the empirical distribution of the training set. The Gibbs sampling can be efficiently performed since both $p(\mathbf{x}|\mathbf{h})$ and $p(\mathbf{h}|\mathbf{x})$ can be factorized:

$$
p(\mathbf{x}|\mathbf{h}) = \prod_i p(x_i|\mathbf{h}); \tag{5.25}
$$

$$
p(\mathbf{h}|\mathbf{x}) = \prod_j p(h_j|\mathbf{x}); \tag{5.26}
$$

where x_i and h_j are the ith and jth components of $\mathbf{x}$ and $\mathbf{h}$, respectively.

Since (5.25) and (5.26) are similar, we only show that (5.26) holds.

$$
\begin{aligned}
p(\mathbf{h}|\mathbf{x}) &= \frac{p(\mathbf{x},\mathbf{h})}{\sum_{\tilde{\mathbf{h}}} p(\mathbf{x},\tilde{\mathbf{h}})} \\
&= \frac{\exp(\mathbf{h}^T\mathbf{W}\mathbf{x} + \mathbf{c}^T\mathbf{x} + \mathbf{b}^T\mathbf{h})}{\sum_{\tilde{\mathbf{h}}} \exp(\tilde{\mathbf{h}}^T\mathbf{W}\mathbf{x} + \mathbf{c}^T\mathbf{x} + \mathbf{b}^T\tilde{\mathbf{h}})} \\
&= \frac{\prod_j \exp(h_j\mathbf{W}_j.\mathbf{x} + b_j h_j)}{\prod_j \sum_{\tilde{h}_j \in \{0,1\}} \exp(\tilde{h}_j\mathbf{W}_j.\mathbf{x} + b_j\tilde{h}_j)} \\
&= \prod_j \frac{\exp(h_j\mathbf{W}_j.\mathbf{v} + b_j h_j)}{\sum_{\tilde{h}_j \in \{0,1\}} \exp(\tilde{h}_j\mathbf{W}_j.\mathbf{x} + b_j\tilde{h}_j)} \\
&= \prod_j p(h_j|\mathbf{x}). \quad (5.27)
\end{aligned}
$$

Then, $\frac{\partial E(\mathbf{x}^{(t)}, \mathbf{h}^{(t)})}{\partial \theta}$ is used to estimate the first term in (5.23) and $\frac{\partial E(\mathbf{x}_k, \mathbf{h}_k)}{\partial \theta}$ is used to estimate the second term in (5.23). Therefore, $\frac{\partial - \log p(\mathbf{v}^{(i)})}{\partial \theta}$ can be approximated as

$$
\frac{\partial - \log p(\mathbf{v}^{(i)})}{\partial \theta} \approx \frac{\partial E(\mathbf{v}^{(i)}, \mathbf{h}^{(t)})}{\partial \theta} - \frac{\partial E(\mathbf{x}_k, \mathbf{h}_k)}{\partial \theta}. \quad (5.28)
$$

With the approximation (5.28), the update (5.22) can be efficiently performed.

5.4.4   Discussion

In the step of feature construction, a large number of features can be generated. In other words, the dimension of data could be very high. It is well known that the majority of machine learning and data mining algorithms cannot work well with high-dimensional data due to the curse of dimensionality. Therefore, it is crucial and necessary to select the most relevant subset of features for feature engineering. There are two groups of feature selection algorithms designed corresponding to two streaming settings, i.e., streaming features and streaming instances. There were some attempts to design algorithms for these two settings. Next we will review some representative algorithms.

5.5   Feature Selection for Data Streams with Streaming Features

For the feature selection problem with streaming features, the number of instances is fixed while candidate features arrive one at a time; the task is to timely select a subset of relevant features from all features seen so far. A typical framework for streaming feature selection consists of *Step 1:* a new feature arrives; *Step 2:* decide whether to add the new feature to the selected features; *step 3:* determine whether to remove features from the selected features; and *Step 4:* repeat *Step 1* to *Step 3*. Different algorithms may have distinct implementations for *Step 2* and *Step 3*; next we will review some representative methods. Note that *Step 3* is optional and some streaming feature selection algorithms only provide *Step 2*.

5.5.1 The Grafting Algorithm

Grafting is a general technique that can be applied to a variety of models that are parameterized by a weight vector $\mathbf{w}$, subject to ℓ_1 regularization, One example is the following feature selection algorithm based on lasso:

$$\hat{\mathbf{w}} = \min_{\mathbf{w}} c(\mathbf{w}, \mathbf{X}) + \alpha \sum_{j=1}^{m} |\mathbf{w}_j|. \tag{5.29}$$

When we have all features, *penalty* $(\mathbf{w})$ penalizes all weights in $\mathbf{w}$ equally for feature selection. It is applied for streaming features by [45]. In Eq. (5.29), a non-zero weight $\mathbf{w}_j$ added to the model will lead to a penalty of $\alpha|\mathbf{w}_j|$. Hence, we add the feature to the model when the loss of $c(\cdot)$ is larger than the regularizer penalty. The grafting technique will only take $\mathbf{w}_j$ non-zero if:

$$\frac{\partial c}{\partial \mathbf{w}_j} > \alpha, \tag{5.30}$$

otherwise it will set the weight to zero (or excluding the feature).

5.5.2 The Alpha-Investing Algorithm

To control the false discovery rate, alpha-investing dynamically adjusts a threshold on the p-statistic for a new feature to enter the model [67]. It is described as follows:

- initialize w_0, $i = 0$, selected features in the model $SF = \emptyset$;

- get a new feature f_i;

- set $\alpha_i = w_i/(2i)$;

-
$$w_{i+1} = w_i - \alpha_i \qquad \text{if } pvalue(x_i, SF) \geq \alpha_i,$$
$$w_{i+1} = w_i + \alpha_\triangle - \alpha_i, \quad SF = SF \cup f_i \quad \text{otherwise,}$$

- $i = i + 1$ and repeat.

where α_i is the probability of selecting a spurious feature in the i-th step. It is adjusted by the wealth w_i, which denotes the current acceptable number of future false positives. Wealth is increased when a feature is added to the model, and it is decreased when a feature is not selected. The p-value is the probability that a feature coefficient may be judged as non-zero when it is actually zero. It is computed relying on the fact that $\triangle$-Loglikelihood is equivalent to t-statistics. Alpha-investing is to adaptively adjust the threshold to select features, for example, when new features are added, one "invests" α increasing the wealth, raising the threshold, and allowing a slightly higher future chance of incorrect inclusion of features. Each time a feature is tested and found to be insignificant, wealth is "spent," reducing the threshold to keep the guarantee of not selecting more than a target fraction of spurious features.

5.5.3   The Online Streaming Feature Selection Algorithm

For the grafting algorithm, we need to know all features in advance to determine the value of α. For the α-investing algorithm, we require some prior knowledge about the feature space structure to heuristically control the choice of candidate features; however, it is hard to obtain such information under the streaming setting. Therefore, the online streaming feature selection algorithm (OSFS) is proposed to solving these challenging issues [60].

We can divide an entire feature set into four basic disjoint subsets: (1) irrelevant features, (2) redundant features, (3) weakly relevant but non-redundant features, and (4) strongly relevant features. An optimal feature selection algorithm should select non-redundant and strongly relevant features. For streaming features, it is difficult to find all strongly relevant and non-redundant features. OSFS aims to find such an optimal subset using a two-phase scheme—online relevance analysis and redundancy analysis. A general framework of OSFS is presented as follows:

- Initialize $BCF = \emptyset$.

- Add a new feature f_i.

- Online relevance analysis:

> Disregard f_i, if f_i is irrelevant to the class labels.
> $BCF = BCF \cup f_i$ otherwise.

- Online Redundancy Analysis.

- Repeat until the stopping criteria are satisfied.

In the phase of online relevance analysis, OSFS adds strongly and weakly relevant features into best candidate features (BCFs). If a new coming feature is irrelevant, it is discarded, otherwise it is added to BCFs.

In the phase of online redundancy analysis, OSFS dynamically eliminates redundant features from the selected set. For each feature f_i in BCFs, if there is a subset within BCFs, which makes f_k and the class label conditionally independent, f_i is eliminated from BCFs. One way to improve the efficiency is to further divide this phase into two types of analysis—inner-redundancy analysis and outer-redundancy analysis. In the inner-redundancy analysis, OSFS only re-examines the feature newly added into BCFs, while the outer-redundancy analysis re-examines each feature of BCFs only when we stop the process of adding new features.

5.5.4   Unsupervised Streaming Feature Selection in Social Media

Most existing streaming feature selection algorithms utilize label information to guide the feature selection process. However, in reality, it is time and labor consuming for labeling; but, it is easy to amass vast quantities of unlabeled data. The USFS algorithm is proposed to handle large-scale unlabeled data in social media [33]. USFS takes advantage of extra sources such as link information to enable unsupervised streaming feature selection. USFS first discovers hidden factors via link information by a mixed membership stochastic blockmodel [17]. With the latent factors $\mathbf{\Pi} \in \mathbb{R}^{n \times k}$, USFS uses them as constraints for feature selection. At a given timestamp t, let $\mathbf{X}^{(t)}$ and $\mathbf{W}^{(t)}$ denote the corresponding feature matrix and feature coefficient, respectively. USFS constructs a graph $\mathcal{G}$ to represent feature similarity and $\mathbf{A}^{(t)}$ denotes its adjacency matrix; $\mathbf{L}^{(t)}$ is the corresponding Laplacian matrix from $\mathbf{X}^{(t)}$. Then we use the following formulation to achieve feature selection at the time step t:

$$\min_{\mathbf{W}^{(t)}} \frac{1}{2}||\mathbf{X}^{(t)}\mathbf{W}^{(t)} - \mathbf{\Pi}||_F^2 + \alpha \sum_{i=1}^{k} ||(\mathbf{w}^{(t)})^i||_1 + \frac{\beta}{2}||\mathbf{W}^{(t)}||_F^2 + \frac{\gamma}{2}||(\mathbf{X}^{(t)}\mathbf{W}^{(t)})'(\mathbf{L}^{(t)})^{\frac{1}{2}}||_F^2,$$

$$(5.31)$$

where α controls the sparsity and γ balances contributions from different sources. Assume at $t+1$ a new feature arrives; to test new features, USFS uses a strategy similar to grafting. Specifically, if the inclusion of the new feature will reduce the objective function value in Eq. (5.31), the feature is added; otherwise the new feature will be removed. When new features are continuously being generated, some existing features may become outdated, therefore, USFS also investigates removing selected features by re-optimizing the model via BFGS.

5.6   Feature Selection for Data Streams with Streaming Instances

In this subsection, we review feature selection with streaming instances where the set of features is fixed, while new instances are consistently and continuously arriving.

5.6.1   Online Feature Selection

An online feature selection algorithm (OFS) for binary classification is proposed in [57]. Let $\{\mathbf{x}_1, \mathbf{x}_2, ..., \mathbf{x}_t...\}$ and $\{y_1, y_2, ..., y_t...\}$ denote a sequence of data instances and their corresponding class labels where $\mathbf{x}_i \in \mathbb{R}^d$. OFS learns a linear classifier $\mathbf{w}^{(t)} \in \mathbb{R}^d$ that can classify each instance $\mathbf{x}_i$ by as $\text{sign}(\mathbf{w}^{(t)}\mathbf{x}_i)$. To achieve feature selection, the linear classifier $\mathbf{w}^{(t)}$ has at most B-nonzero elements, i.e., $\|\mathbf{w}^{(t)}\|_0 \leq B$. With a regularization parameter λ and a step size η, OFS works as follows: (1) get a new data instance $\mathbf{x}_t$ and its class label y_t; (2) predict the class label for the new instance as $\text{sign}(\mathbf{w}^{(t)}\mathbf{x}_t)$; (3) if $y_i\mathbf{w}^{(t)}\mathbf{x}_t < 0$ (or $\mathbf{x}_t$ is misclassified), $\tilde{\mathbf{w}}_{t+1} = (1-\lambda\eta)\mathbf{w}_t + \eta y_t\mathbf{x}_t$, $\hat{\mathbf{w}}_{t+1} = \min\{1, 1/\sqrt{\lambda}\|\tilde{\mathbf{w}}_{t+1}\|_2\}\tilde{\mathbf{w}}_{t+1}$, and $\mathbf{w}_{t+1} = Truncate(\hat{\mathbf{w}}_{t+1}, B)$; and (4) $\mathbf{w}_{t+1} = (1-\lambda\eta)\mathbf{w}_t$. In particular, when an instance $\mathbf{x}_t$ is misclassified, $\mathbf{w}_t$ is first updated by online gradient descent and then it is projected to a ℓ_2-norm ball to ensure that the classifier is bounded. After that, the new classifier $\hat{\mathbf{w}}_{t+1}$ is truncated by taking the most important B features. It outputs a subset of B features at each time stamp. The process repeats until no new data instances can be added.

5.6.2   Unsupervised Feature Selection on Data Streams

A novel unsupervised feature selection method (FSDS) is proposed to timely select a subset of relevant features when unlabeled data is continuously being generated [23]. It requires only one pass over the data with limited storage. FSDS uses matrix sketching to efficiently maintain a low-rank approximation of the current observed data and then apply regularized regression to achieve feature selection. In particular, when some orthogonality conditions are satisfied, the ridge regression can replace the lasso for feature selection. Assume that at a specific time step t, $\mathbf{X}^{(t)} \in \mathbb{R}^{n_t \times d}$ denotes the data matrix and the feature coefficients can be obtained as

$$\min_{\mathbf{W}^{(t)}} \|\mathbf{B}^{(t)}\mathbf{W}^{(t)} - \{\mathbf{e}_1, ..., \mathbf{e}_k\}\|_F^2 + \alpha\|\mathbf{W}^{(t)}\|_F^2, \qquad (5.32)$$

where $\mathbf{B}^{(t)} \in \mathbb{R}^{\ell \times d}$ denotes the matrix sketch of $\mathbf{X}^{(t)}$ ($\ell \ll n_t$), and $\mathbf{e}_i \in \mathbb{R}^\ell$ is a vector with its i-th location as 1 and other locations as 0.

5.7   Discussions and Challenges

In this section, we briefly discuss some challenges and open issues in feature engineering for data streams.

5.7.1 Stability

Algorithms of feature engineering are often evaluated through the impact on the accuracy performance of classification and clustering. However, the stability of algorithms is also an important consideration when developing feature engineering methods. A motivating example is from bioinformatics, where the domain experts would like to see the same or at least a similar set of genes, i.e., features to be constructed, each time they obtain new samples in the presence of a small amount of perturbation. Otherwise they will not trust the algorithm when they get different sets of features while the datasets are drawn for the same problem. Therefore, the stability of feature engineering algorithms is very important. However, efforts on this topic is rather limited.

5.7.2 Number of Features

For most feature extraction and selection algorithms, we typically need to pre-define the number of features to extract and select. However, it is often unknown what is the optimal number of features. A large number of features will increase the risk of including some noisy, redundant and irrelevant features that may jeopardize the learning performance. On the other hand, it is also not good to include too small a number of features, which may not be sufficient to capture the complexity of data. In practice, we usually adopt a heuristic way to grid search the number of features and pick the number that has the best classification or clustering performance, but the whole process is computationally expensive. It is still an open and challenging problem to determine the optimal number of features.

5.7.3 Heterogeneous Streaming Data

In addition to volume and velocity, another characteristic of big data is variety, i.e., data with diverse and heterogeneous information. For example, images in Flickr are often associated with tags and text descriptions, while recent advancements in bioinformatics reveal the existence of some non-coding RNA species in addition to RNA. Hence, in reality, data is related to multiple streams. On the one hand, heterogeneous data streams challenge the majority of traditional feature engineering algorithms that are designed for homogeneous data. On the other hand, the availability of multiple data sources makes it possible to solve some problems unsolvable with homogeneous data especially under unsupervised scenarios. Therefore, there are both challenges and opportunities from feature engineering for heterogeneous data streams.

Acknowledgments

This material is based upon work supported by, or in part by, the National Science Foundation (NSF) under grant number IIS-1714741 and IIS-1715940.

Bibliography

[1] Charu C Aggarwal. *Data Streams: Models and Algorithms*, volume 31. Springer Science & Business Media, 2007.

[2] Raman Arora, Andy Cotter, and Nati Srebro. Stochastic optimization of pca with capped msg. In *Advances in Neural Information Processing Systems*, pages 1815–1823, 2013.

[3] Akshay Balsubramani, Sanjoy Dasgupta, and Yoav Freund. The fast convergence of incremental pca. In *Advances in Neural Information Processing Systems*, pages 3174–3182, 2013.

[4] Yoshua Bengio, Aaron Courville, and Pascal Vincent. Representation learning: A review and new perspectives. *IEEE Transactions on Pattern Analysis and Machine Intelligence*, 35(8):1798–1828, 2013.

[5] Yoshua Bengio, Jean-françois Paiement, Pascal Vincent, Olivier Delalleau, Nicolas L Roux, and Marie Ouimet. Out-of-sample extensions for lle, isomap, mds, eigenmaps, and spectral clustering. In *Advances in Neural Information Processing Systems*, pages 177–184, 2004.

[6] Christos Boutsidis, Dan Garber, Zohar Karnin, and Edo Liberty. Online principal components analysis. In *Proceedings of the Twenty-Sixth Annual ACM-SIAM Symposium on Discrete Algorithms*, pages 887–901. Society for Industrial and Applied Mathematics, 2015.

[7] Gert Cauwenberghs and Tomaso Poggio. Incremental and decremental support vector machine learning. In *Advances in Neural Information Processing Systems*, pages 409–415, 2001.

[8] Shiyu Chang, Yang Zhang, Jiliang Tang, Dawei Yin, Yi Chang, Mark A Hasegawa-Johnson, and Thomas S Huang. Positive-unlabeled learning in streaming networks. In *Proceedings of the 22nd ACM SIGKDD International Conference on Knowledge Discovery and Data Mining*, pages 755–764. ACM, 2016.

[9] Jing Chen and Yang Liu. Locally linear embedding: a survey. *Artificial Intelligence Review*, 36(1):29–48, 2011.

[10] Delin Chu, Li-Zhi Liao, Michael Kwok-Po Ng, and Xiaoyan Wang. Incremental linear discriminant analysis: a fast algorithm and comparisons. *IEEE Transactions on Neural Networks and Learning Systems*, 26(11):2716–2735, 2015.

[11] Kenneth L Clarkson and David P Woodruff. Numerical linear algebra in the streaming model. In *Proceedings of the Forty-First Annual ACM Symposium on Theory of Computing*, pages 205–214. ACM, 2009.

[12] Inderjit S Dhillon, Yuqiang Guan, and Brian Kulis. Kernel k-means: spectral clustering and normalized cuts. In *Proceedings of the Tenth ACM SIGKDD International Conference on Knowledge Discovery and Data Mining*, pages 551–556. ACM, 2004.

[13] Pedro Domingos. A few useful things to know about machine learning. *Communications of the ACM*, 55(10):78–87, 2012.

[14] George H Dunteman. *Principal Components Analysis*. Number 69. Sage, 1989.

[15] Wei Fan and Albert Bifet. Mining big data: current status, and forecast to the future. *ACM sIGKDD Explorations Newsletter*, 14(2):1–5, 2013.

[16] Jiashi Feng, Huan Xu, and Shuicheng Yan. Online robust pca via stochastic optimization. In *Advances in Neural Information Processing Systems*, pages 404–412, 2013.

[17] Wenjie Fu, Le Song, and Eric P Xing. Dynamic mixed membership blockmodel for evolving networks. In *Proceedings of the 26th Annual International Conference on Machine Learning*, pages 329–336. ACM, 2009.

[18] Lukasz Golab and M Tamer Özsu. Issues in data stream management. *ACM Sigmod Record*, 32(2):5–14, 2003.

[19] Ian Goodfellow, Yoshua Bengio, and Aaron Courville. *Deep Learning*. MIT Press, 2016. http://www.deeplearningbook.org.

[20] Isabelle Guyon and André Elisseeff. An introduction to feature extraction. *Feature Extraction*, pages 1–25, 2006.

[21] Geoffrey E Hinton and Richard S Zemel. Autoencoders, minimum description length and helmholtz free energy. In *Advances in Neural Information Processing Systems*, pages 3–10, 1994.

[22] Kazuyuki Hiraoka, Ken-ichi Hidai, Masashi Hamahira, Hiroshi Mizoguchi, Tanaka Mishima, and Shuji Yoshizawa. Successive learning of

linear discriminant analysis: Sanger-type algorithm. In *Pattern Recognition, 2000. Proceedings. 15th International Conference on*, volume 2, pages 664–667. IEEE, 2000.

[23] Hao Huang, Shinjae Yoo, and Shiva Prasad Kasiviswanathan. Unsupervised feature selection on data streams. In *Proceedings of the 24th ACM International on Conference on Information and Knowledge Management*, pages 1031–1040. ACM, 2015.

[24] Moongu Jeon, Haesun Park, and J Ben Rosen. Dimension reduction based on centroids and least squares for efficient processing of text data. In *Proceedings of the 2001 SIAM International Conference on Data Mining*, pages 1–13. SIAM, 2001.

[25] William B Johnson and Joram Lindenstrauss. Extensions of lipschitz mappings into a hilbert space. *Contemporary Mathematics*, 26(189-206):1, 1984.

[26] Samuel Kadoury and Martin D Levine. Face detection in gray scale images using locally linear embeddings. *Computer Vision and Image Understanding*, 105(1):1–20, 2007.

[27] Zohar Karnin and Edo Liberty. Online pca with spectral bounds. In *Conference on Learning Theory*, pages 1129–1140, 2015.

[28] Tae-Kyun Kim, Shu-Fai Wong, Bjorn Stenger, Josef Kittler, and Roberto Cipolla. Incremental linear discriminant analysis using sufficient spanning set approximations. In *Computer Vision and Pattern Recognition, 2007. CVPR'07. IEEE Conference on*, pages 1–8. IEEE, 2007.

[29] Olga Kouropteva, Oleg Okun, and Matti Pietikäinen. Incremental locally linear embedding. *Pattern Recognition*, 38(10):1764–1767, 2005.

[30] Pavel Laskov, Christian Gehl, Stefan Krüger, and Klaus-Robert Müller. Incremental support vector learning: Analysis, implementation and applications. *Journal of Machine Learning Research*, 7(Sep):1909–1936, 2006.

[31] Haifeng Li, Tao Jiang, and Keshu Zhang. Efficient and robust feature extraction by maximum margin criterion. In *Advances in Neural Information Processing Systems*, pages 97–104, 2004.

[32] Jundong Li, Kewei Cheng, Suhang Wang, Fred Morstatter, Robert P Trevino, Jiliang Tang, and Huan Liu. Feature selection: A data perspective. *arXiv preprint arXiv:1601.07996*, 2016.

[33] Jundong Li, Xia Hu, Jiliang Tang, and Huan Liu. Unsupervised streaming feature selection in social media. In *Proceedings of the 24th ACM International on Conference on Information and Knowledge Management*, pages 1041–1050. ACM, 2015.

[34] Edo Liberty. Simple and deterministic matrix sketching. In *Proceedings of the 19th ACM SIGKDD International Conference on Knowledge Discovery and Data Mining*, pages 581–588. ACM, 2013.

[35] Huan Liu and Hiroshi Motoda. Feature transformation and subset selection. *IEEE Intell Syst Their Appl*, 13(2):26–28, 1998.

[36] Li-Ping Liu, Yuan Jiang, and Zhi-Hua Zhou. Least square incremental linear discriminant analysis. In *Data Mining, 2009. ICDM'09. Ninth IEEE International Conference on*, pages 298–306. IEEE, 2009.

[37] Gui-Fu Lu, Jian Zou, and Yong Wang. Incremental complete lda for face recognition. *Pattern Recognition*, 45(7):2510–2521, 2012.

[38] Aleix M Martínez and Avinash C Kak. Pca versus lda. *IEEE Transactions on Pattern Analysis and Machine Intelligence*, 23(2):228–233, 2001.

[39] Sebastian Mika, Bernhard Schölkopf, Alex J Smola, Klaus-Robert Müller, Matthias Scholz, and Gunnar Rätsch. Kernel pca and de-noising in feature spaces. In *Advances in Neural Information Processing Systems*, pages 536–542, 1999.

[40] Ioannis Mitliagkas, Constantine Caramanis, and Prateek Jain. Memory limited, streaming pca. In *Advances in Neural Information Processing Systems*, pages 2886–2894, 2013.

[41] Shanmugavelayutham Muthukrishnan et al. Data streams: Algorithms and applications. *Foundations and Trends® in Theoretical Computer Science*, 1(2):117–236, 2005.

[42] Vinod Nair and Geoffrey E Hinton. Rectified linear units improve restricted boltzmann machines. In *Proceedings of the 27th International Conference on Machine Learning (ICML-10)*, pages 807–814, 2010.

[43] Jiazhong Nie, Wojciech Kotlowski, and Manfred K Warmuth. Online pca with optimal regret. *Journal of Machine Learning Research*, 17(173):1–49, 2016.

[44] Simon Perkins, Kevin Lacker, and James Theiler. Grafting: Fast, incremental feature selection by gradient descent in function space. *Journal of Machine Learning Research*, 3(Mar):1333–1356, 2003.

[45] Simon Perkins and James Theiler. Online feature selection using grafting. In *Proceedings of the 20th International Conference on Machine Learning (ICML-03)*, pages 592–599, 2003.

[46] Sam T Roweis and Lawrence K Saul. Nonlinear dimensionality reduction by locally linear embedding. *Science*, 290(5500):2323–2326, 2000.

[47] Stefan Ruping. Incremental learning with support vector machines. In *Data Mining, 2001. ICDM 2001, Proceedings IEEE International Conference on*, pages 641–642. IEEE, 2001.

[48] Ruslan Salakhutdinov, Andriy Mnih, and Geoffrey Hinton. Restricted boltzmann machines for collaborative filtering. In *Proceedings of the 24th International Conference on Machine Learning*, pages 791–798. ACM, 2007.

[49] Tamas Sarlos. Improved approximation algorithms for large matrices via random projections. In *Foundations of Computer Science, 2006. FOCS'06. 47th Annual IEEE Symposium on*, pages 143–152. IEEE, 2006.

[50] Lawrence K Saul and Sam T Roweis. Think globally, fit locally: unsupervised learning of low dimensional manifolds. *Journal of Machine Learning Research*, 4(Jun):119–155, 2003.

[51] Bernhard Schölkopf and Alexander J Smola. *Learning with Kernels: Support Vector Machines, Regularization, Optimization, and Beyond*. MIT press, 2002.

[52] Jonathan A Silva, Elaine R Faria, Rodrigo C Barros, Eduardo R Hruschka, André CPLF de Carvalho, and João Gama. Data stream clustering: A survey. *ACM Computing Surveys (CSUR)*, 46(1):13, 2013.

[53] Sören Sonnenburg, Gunnar Rätsch, Christin Schäfer, and Bernhard Schölkopf. Large scale multiple kernel learning. *Journal of Machine Learning Research*, 7(Jul):1531–1565, 2006.

[54] Nadeem Ahmed Syed, Syed Huan, Liu Kah, and Kay Sung. Incremental learning with support vector machines. 1999.

[55] Koji Tsuda, Gunnar Rätsch, and Manfred K Warmuth. Matrix exponentiated gradient updates for on-line learning and bregman projection. *Journal of Machine Learning Research*, 6(Jun):995–1018, 2005.

[56] Vladimir Vapnik. *The Nature of Statistical Learning Theory*. Springer science & business media, 2013.

[57] Jialei Wang, Peilin Zhao, Steven CH Hoi, and Rong Jin. Online feature selection and its applications. *IEEE Transactions on Knowledge and Data Engineering*, 26(3):698–710, 2014.

[58] Manfred K Warmuth and Dima Kuzmin. Randomized online pca algorithms with regret bounds that are logarithmic in the dimension. *Journal of Machine Learning Research*, 9(Oct):2287–2320, 2008.

[59] Svante Wold, Kim Esbensen, and Paul Geladi. Principal component analysis. *Chemometrics and Intelligent Laboratory Systems*, 2(1-3):37–52, 1987.

[60] Xindong Wu, Kui Yu, Hao Wang, and Wei Ding. Online streaming feature selection. In *Proceedings of the 27th International Conference on Machine Learning (ICML-10)*, pages 1159–1166, 2010.

[61] Jian Yang and Jing-yu Yang. Why can lda be performed in pca transformed space? *Pattern Recognition*, 36(2):563–566, 2003.

[62] Jieping Ye. Least squares linear discriminant analysis. In *Proceedings of the 24th International Conference on Machine Learning*, pages 1087–1093. ACM, 2007.

[63] Jieping Ye, Qi Li, Hui Xiong, Haesun Park, Ravi Janardan, and Vipin Kumar. Idr/qr: An incremental dimension reduction algorithm via qr decomposition. *IEEE Transactions on Knowledge and Data Engineering*, 17(9):1208–1222, 2005.

[64] PHILIP S Yu, H Wang, and J Han. Mining data streams. *The Data Mining and Knowledge Discovery Handbook*, 2005.

[65] Zdenek Zabokrtsky. Feature engineering in machine learning. 2015.

[66] Jun Zheng, Furao Shen, Hongjun Fan, and Jinxi Zhao. An online incremental learning support vector machine for large-scale data. *Neural Computing and Applications*, 22(5):1023–1035, 2013.

[67] Jing Zhou, Dean Foster, Robert Stine, and Lyle Ungar. Streaming feature selection using alpha-investing. In *Proceedings of the eleventh ACM SIGKDD International Conference on Knowledge Discovery in Data Mining*, pages 384–393. ACM, 2005.

Chapter 6

Feature Generation and Feature Engineering for Sequences

Guozhu Dong

Department of Computer Science & Engineering, Wright State University, Dayton, USA

Lei Duan

School of Computer Science, Sichuan University, Chengdu, China

Jyrki Nummenmaa

Faculty of Natural Sciences, University of Tampere, Finland

Peng Zhang

School of Computer Science, Sichuan University, Chengdu, China

6.1   Introduction

Sequence data are ubiquitous in people's daily lives and they are often used in data analytics. Figure 6.1 gives examples of sequence data from several types of applications including biomedicine, music, literature, and health care. We now use several other examples to illustrate what kinds of sequence data analysis people may be interested in.

- Major computer companies are interested in determining what combinations of events may lead to computer crashes. This can be performed by examining computer log entries written before such crashes.

- Log data is also useful for cyber security and for optimizing internet navigation processing.

- For music data analysis, we may want to determine which kind of music pieces often cause happiness and what may cause sadness, from the symbolic representation of music pieces. One may also want to find out the unique patterns of music composed by Mozart. These typically require that we use sequence features to represent the music pieces.

- For biological sequence analysis, a typical task is to identify biologically important sites (e.g., start sites [13], cleavage sites [26], and binding sites [22]). Useful information for this task is often located in the upstream region of potential sites.

For sequence analytics, one often needs to represent sequences as feature vectors. The need for automatic sequence feature generation was recognized early in [14].

Compared with other data types, distinguishing characteristics of sequence data include:

- The number of elements comprising a sequence can range from very small to very large. In particular, there are very long sequences. For example, the length of a typical DNA/protein sequence is often in the tens of thousands.

- The order of elements in a sequence is fixed. In other words, exchanging the positions of two different elements in a sequence produces a different sequence. For example, if we exchange the positions of any two different words in a sentence, the whole sentence changes, which may also dramatically change the meaning of the sentence.

- Even the position of elements in sequences can be important. For example, the promotional region of a gene starting site in DNA needs to occur some fixed number of positions before the start site.

tgctatcctgacagttgtcacgctgattggtgtcgttacaatctaacgcatcgccaa

(a) E. coli promoter gene sequence

Data mining has attracted a great deal of attention in the information industry and in society as a whole in recent years, due to the wide availability of huge amounts of data

(b) Text

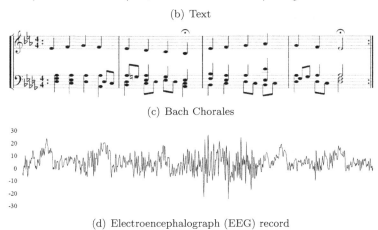

(c) Bach Chorales

(d) Electroencephalograph (EEG) record

Figure 6.1: Examples of sequence data.

Due to the unique characteristics and importance of sequence data, mining sequence data has attracted numerous researchers' attention (see e.g., [8, 32]) and has produced a set of results that is fairly different from that for other kind of data.

In this chapter, we first discuss the basics of sequence data and then present three major classes of sequence features: traditional pattern-based sequence features, general pattern-based features, and sequence features that are not defined by patterns. We also discuss several ways that sequence patterns can be used as sequence features. We present an overview of sequence pattern types and then give brief discussions on how to mine them. Finally, we consider factors that are important for selecting patterns as features.

Patterns are often referred to as "motifs" in biological data analysis (see e.g., [2]). Often, pattern matching, pattern discovery, and pattern utilization for knowledge transfer between different domains, have been performed by sequence alignment (see e.g., [9]). However, some studies do use motifs and patterns as features (e.g., [10, 18, 23]) explicitly.

6.2   Basics on Sequence Data and Sequence Patterns

Broadly speaking, a sequence is an ordered list of elements over some given alphabet. It is generally assumed that within one sequence the elements are of the same data type. There is a rich variety of data types that are used to construct sequences. The following are factors that influence the complexity of a given sequence type: the structure of the underlying alphabet (e.g., the existence of a total order on the alphabet, or whether the elements are simple or complex), the cardinality of the underlying alphabet, and the limits, if any, on the length of the sequences.

In Figure 6.1 for example, we have sequences made of DNAs (represented by characters), words, musical notation, and numerical values. In the simplest case, the sequences have only basic elements one after another. The other cases are more complex: we have a sequence (text) of sequences (words); we have a sequence of itemsets for music (sets of notes representing pitch and duration); we have a sequence where each element (a numerical value) is associated with a timestamp. Sequence elements can even be graphs (e.g., representing a snapshot of the evolution of the network of Facebook users), or relations. In some situations, each element in a sequence is associated with some attributes (e.g., a timestamp or a location). The elements in the alphabet of the sequences for a given application can be structured in some way. For example, one music sequence element can be viewed as larger than another since the former is higher in sound.

The following is a list of some typical types of sequence data.

Symbolic (plain) sequences: Each element is just an item. Examples of symbolic sequences include DNA/Protein sequences where each element represents a nucleotide or an amino acid, and text, where each element is a character string. More complex symbolic sequences also exist.

Time series: Each element is a numeric value associated with a timestamp. Examples of time series include EEG records, stock exchange index price histories, and temperature histories for given locations.

Event sequences: Each element is a symbol representing an event. However, different from symbolic sequences, each element in an event sequence is associated with a timestamp or a time interval representing the start and the end of the event. Examples include system logs, where each element represents an event happening in the system at a certain time or during a time interval, and trajectory data, where each element is a geographic location associated with a timestamp.

Among various kinds of sequence data types, the symbolic sequences are the most basic. Many other sequence types can be converted into symbolic sequences using preprocessing. For example, numeric-valued sequences can be mapped to symbolic sequences using various binning techniques. In this chapter, we focus on feature engineering for symbolic sequences.

We now turn to the preliminary concepts for sequence data. Let Σ be a finite set of distinct items representing an alphabet. The elements can be used to form sequences. A sequence S over Σ is an ordered list of items with the form $S = < e_1 e_2 \ldots e_n >$, where $e_i \in \Sigma$ for $1 \leq i \leq n$. Each integer $i \in \{1, \ldots, n\}$ is called a *position* of S. We denote by $S_{[i]}$ the element of S at position i. The number of elements in S is the *length* of S, denoted by $|S|$.

For two sequences S and S' satisfying $|S| \geq |S'|$, S' is called a *subsequence* of S (also S is a *super-sequence* of S'), denoted by $S' \sqsubseteq S$, if there exist integers $1 \leq k_1 < k_2 < \cdots < k_{|S'|} \leq |S|$, such that $S'_{[i]} = S_{[k_i]}$ for all $1 \leq i \leq |S'|$. S' is a proper *subsequence* of S (denoted by $S' \sqsubset S$), if $S' \sqsubseteq S$ and $|S'| < |S|$. S' is a *substring* of S, if $S' \sqsubseteq S$ and $k_{j+1} = k_j + 1$ for all $1 \leq j < |S'|$.

Example 1 *For DNA sequences the alphabet Σ is $\{\mathrm{a, c, g, t}\}$. For the DNA sequence S shown in Figure 6.1(a), $|S| = 57$, $S_{[1]} = \mathrm{t}$, and $S_{[2]} = \mathrm{g}$. Moreover, ttt is a subsequence, but not a substring, of S.*

Starting from the next section we will be referring to sequence patterns. So we define such patterns here.

A *sequence pattern* is just a sequence. As will be discussed later, one can use constraints (such as gap limitations) when matching sequence patterns with sequences.

6.3   Approaches to Using Patterns in Sequence Features

A pattern-defined sequence feature is the combination of a sequence pattern P and a way W of describing how to use the pattern to derive feature values for a given sequence S. The ways W include the following:

Cumulative way: Here a pattern P leads to just one feature for each S, whose value typically is the count of occurrences of P in S. A cumulative feature describes a property of the entirety of a given sequence.

Interval-specific way: Here S is divided into several (say k) intervals (following some common scheme for the sequences of the application). We have k features for P; there is one feature for each interval, whose value is typically the count of occurrences of P in that interval.

An interval-specific feature describes a property of the corresponding interval in a given sequence. Such features can help to spot differences in the density of subsequences that match given patterns in different intervals.

Position-specific way: Here there are $|S|$ features for P, one for each position in S, with the ith indicating if P occurs at position i in S. A position-specific feature describes a property of the corresponding position in a given sequence. Clearly, position-specific features can only have 0 or 1 as values.

Running cumulative way: This is a combination of "cumulative" and "position specific": For each position i in S we get a feature from P whose value represents the cumulative count of occurrences of P from position 1 to position i. (Reference [37] used such features.)

Sliding-window-based way: Some fixed window size, say w, is used. For each position i in S we get a feature from P whose value represents the count of occurrences of P in the sliding window around (sometimes the window immediately before) position i of size w.

Sliding-window-based features can be used to spot differences in the density of subsequences that match given patterns in different parts of the sequences. They can be helpful in finding unusual positions (or sites) in sequences. Sliding-window-based features are more flexible than interval-specific features.

Sliding-window-based features are related to moving averages for time series. They can also be used to define time-series-like numerical series from sequences.

We illustrate these ways in the next section.

Due to the richness of sequences, there are clearly many other ways to use sequence patterns as sequence features.

6.4   Traditional Pattern-Based Sequence Features

We now describe some frequently used traditional pattern-based sequence features, using the DNA sequence S in Figure 6.1(a) to illustrate them. We note that the patterns in this section are all simple ones defined in terms of the underlying alphabet using some fixed positional relationships; they are not the result of pattern mining.

Single-element features: These features are those defined by single sequence elements as patterns. These patterns can be combined with different ways, as discussed in Section 6.3, to form features.

For example, each element and position combination can be a position-specific feature. For DNA sequences with length 57 over $\{a, c, g, t\}$ such as the one in Figure 6.1(a), there are a total of $57 * 4$ position-specific features (e.g., $(t, 1)$). If we divide the 57 positions into the 3 intervals of $1 \ldots 19$, $20 \ldots 38$, and $39 \ldots 57$, each element and interval combination can be an interval-specific feature, and there are a total of $4 * 3$ interval-specific features. There are a total of 4 cumulative features, one for each element in the alphabet. The value for each such feature for a given sequence is typically the total number of occurrences of the element in the sequence.

k-gram features: A k-gram feature is a sequence over the alphabet of length k, where k is a positive integer. A k-gram can be used in position-specific, interval-specific, or cumulative features. For the sequence in Figure 6.1(a), the 3-gram 'atc' has a value of 3 for S (since it occurs 3 times in S) if it is used as a cumulative feature. In DNA analysis, 3-grams are frequently used due to the close relationship between 3-grams and proteins.

k-gapped-pair features: A k-gapped pair is a pair of sequence elements e and e', with a gap of length k between them when considering matching it to sequences. Again k-gapped-pair features can be position-specific, interval-specific, etc. When used as cumulative features, the value of a k-gapped pair is the k-*gapped occurrence frequency* in S, defined by

$$F(ee', k) = \frac{|\{i \mid S_{[i]} = e, S_{[i+k+1]} = e', 1 \le i \le |S| - k - 1\}|}{|S| - k - 1}.$$

For $F(ee', k)$, the numerator is the number of matches of e, e' in S as a k-gapped pattern, and the denominator is the maximal number of matches possible. Observe that, when $k = 0$, a k-gapped pair is a 2-gram. For the sequence in Figure 6.1(a), $F(\text{tc}, 0) = \frac{5}{56}$, $F(\text{tc}, 1) = \frac{3}{55}$, $F(\text{tc}, 2) = \frac{8}{54}$.

Substring features: Substring features are defined by subsequences that are viewed as substrings. Unique substring features were used in [21,35], to identify signature patterns for given sequences. Shared substrings (for a number of sequences), as well as repeating substrings, can also be used as features.

6.5   Mined Sequence Patterns for Use in Sequence Features

Mined sequence patterns can be a rich source for sequence features. They can be better than the alphabet-based features described in Section 6.4, as they can be mined from the data to be used in a given analytic task (e.g., classification) and hence they can be more relevant to the task at hand.

Numerous sequence pattern types have been studied. This section presents several major sequence pattern types for the purpose of using them as features. The presented sequence pattern types include frequent sequence patterns, closed sequential patterns, partial-order patterns, periodic sequence patterns, and distinguishing sequence patterns. This section also discusses several sequence-specific characteristics, such as gap, in connection with sequence patterns. Section 6.6 discusses several issues that should be considered when selecting patterns as features.

As mentioned earlier, a sequence pattern is just a sequence. Constraints may be used to limit the matching of sequence patterns to sequences.

6.5.1   Frequent Sequence Patterns

The supermarket customer example of people who finish by (1) paying at the checkout, then (2) taking goods they bought to their car, and then (3) returning the shopping cart to a designated place is meant to be an example of frequent sequence patterns. Informally it may be easy to accept this as a meaningful frequent pattern. However, an obvious question is how to decide if some pattern is frequent or not. For this, we need some definitions.

The *support* of a sequence S in a set of sequences D is the ratio of the number of sequences containing S to the total number of sequences in D:

$$Sup_D(S) = \frac{|\{S' \in D \mid S \sqsubseteq S'\}|}{|D|}.$$

For the sake of simplicity, we denote $Sup_D(S)$ as $Sup(S)$ when the sequence set is clear from the context.

There are two typical ways to define what kinds of sequence patterns are frequent.

- By thresholds: given a minimum support threshold α, a sequence pattern P is *frequent* if $Sup(P) \geq \alpha$.

- By top-k: given an integer k, a sequence pattern P is *frequent* if $|\{P' \mid Sup(P') > Sup(P)\}| < k$.

We will focus on the first way below.

Example 2 *Consider the sequence dataset D in Table 6.1. Using the minimum support threshold $\alpha = 0.8$, the frequent patterns appearing in D_+ and D_- are given in Tables 6.2 and 6.3, respectively. Clearly, all the patterns whose support is 1.0 are top-k for any k. Since there are 10 patterns with support of 1.0 in D_+, the rest of the patterns in Table 6.2 are top-11 (since they all have the same support of 0.8).*

Different sequence datasets often have different sets of frequent patterns. Hence, for use as features, we should mine the frequent sequence patterns from the dataset that we want to analyze.

Table 6.1: Sequence dataset D. D_+ denotes the subset of D in $+$ and D_- denotes the subset of D in $-$

ID	Sequence	Class	ID	Sequence	Class
S_1	*tatgagcata*		S_6	*tcgtggatgg*	
S_2	*ctaacagttg*		S_7	*ctgagtgctt*	
S_3	*acgctttta*	$+$	S_8	*gctttcttgt*	$-$
S_4	*tagcgggaag*		S_9	*gacagattca*	
S_5	*tgacgctgca*		S_{10}	*atccatctac*	

Table 6.2: Complete set of frequent sequence patterns in D_+

Sup_{D_+}	Frequent Sequence Pattern
0.8	$< at >, < ct >, < cg >, < tc >, < tt >, < tg >, < ga >,$ $< gc >, < gt >, < gg >, < act >, < acg >, < aga >,$ $< agc >, < agt >, < agg >, < cta >, < taa >, < tac >,$ $< tag >, < tca >, < tgg >, < gca >, < agca >, < taca >,$ $< tagg >$
1.0	$< a >, < c >, < t >, < g >, < aa >, < ac >, < ag >,$ $< ca >, < ta >, < aca >$

There exists an anti-monotone property for frequent sequence patterns. For example, $< aca >$ is a frequent sequence pattern in Table 6.2, and all subsequences of the pattern, i.e., $< a >, < c >, < ac >, < ca >$, and $< aa >$ are also frequent sequence patterns; this is because every sequence containing $< aca >$ also contains all these subsequences of $< aca >$ as well. The anti-monotone property is useful to improve the efficiency of mining frequent sequence patterns, since all super-sequences of non-frequent sequences are not frequent.

Given a sequence set D, for any sequence $S \sqsubseteq S'$, $Sup_D(S') \leq Sup_D(S)$.

Table 6.3: Complete set of frequent sequence patterns in D_-

Sup_{D_-}	Frequent Sequence Pattern
0.8	$< a >, < g >, < at >, < ca >, < cc >, < cg >, < gg >,$ $< gt >, < ta >, < cat >, < cta >, < ctc >, < cgt >,$ $< tct >, < ttc >, < ttt >, < gtt >, < ggt >, < cttc >,$ $< tctt >$
1.0	$< c >, < t >, < ct >, < tc >, < tt >, < ctt >$

Table **6.4**: Complete set of closed sequential patterns in D_+

Sup_{D_+}	Closed Sequential Pattern
0.8	$< tt >$, $< act >$, $< acg >$, $< agt >$, $< cta >$, $< agca >$, $< taca >$, $< tagg >$
1.0	$< ag >$, $< ta >$, $< aca >$

Table **6.5**: Complete set of closed sequential patterns in D_-

Sup_{D_-}	Closed Sequential Pattern
0.8	$< cat >$, $< cta >$, $< cgt >$, $< gtt >$, $< ggt >$, $< cttc >$, $< tctt >$
1.0	$< tc >$, $< ctt >$

Mining frequent sequence patterns has been investigated extensively. Several efficient algorithms for frequent sequence pattern mining were proposed, such as *GSP* [24], *PrefixSpan* [19], *SPADE* [36], *SPAM* [1], and *DISC* [4].

Reference [23] used frequent subsequences as features for the prediction of outer membrane proteins.

6.5.2 Closed Sequential Patterns

Redundant information may exist among the frequent sequence patterns. For example, in Table 6.2, the support of $< ac >$ is equal to the supports of two of its subsequences, $< a >$ and $< c >$, implying that these three patterns match the same subset of sequences.

Definition 1 (Closed sequential pattern) *A   sequential   pattern P is closed if there is no pattern P' such that $P \sqsubset P'$ and $Sup(P) = Sup(P')$.*

It is lossless to remove the non-closed sequential patterns from the set of frequent sequence patterns. Indeed, from the closed sequence patterns, we can recover the information about whether a pattern Q is frequent or not and we can also determine the support of Q. This can be done as follows:

> Let C be the complete set of closed frequent sequential patterns for some given $minSup$ threshold. Let Q be a sequential pattern not in C. Then, Q is frequent if and only if there exists some closed sequential pattern P in C satisfying $Q \sqsubset P$. Moreover, the support of Q is $max\{sup(P_i) \mid P_i$ is in C and $Q \sqsubset P_i\}$.

Example 3 *Consider, again, sequence database D listed in Table 6.1. Tables 6.4 and 6.5 show the sets of closed frequent sequence patterns computed* *from D_+ and D_-, respectively, for $minSup = 0.8$. From Table 6.4, we observe that $< ca >$ is not a closed sequential pattern in D_+.*

As $< tca >$ is a closed sequential pattern such that $< ca > \sqsubset < tca >$, we know that $< ca >$ is a frequent pattern. Moreover, among all closed patterns P such that $< ca > \sqsubset P$, $P_0 = < aca >$ has the largest support. Hence $Sup(< aa >) = Sup(< aca >) = 1$ in D_+.

Observe that this procedure also shows that $Sup(< c >) = Sup(< aca >) = 1$.

Clearly, a closed sequential pattern is a concise representation of a set of frequent sequence patterns that match the same set of sequences. As the number of all closed patterns is much less than the number of all frequent patterns, the closed patterns offer a better choice as a starting pool of patterns for use in generating features.

Several algorithms have been proposed to mine closed sequential patterns, such as *BIDE* [27], *TSP* [25], and *CloSpan* [33]. Among these methods, *BIDE* is a representative one; it is an extension of *PrefixSpan* for closed sequential pattern mining.

BIDE uses a so-called BI-directional extension closure checking scheme to improve computational efficiency. Specifically, this idea helps avoid the search over many non-closed sequential patterns. For a sequential pattern S, if there exists a sequential pattern $S' = S_{[1]} \ldots S_{[|S|]}e$ (e is a sequence element in the alphabet) such that $Sup(S) = Sup(S')$, S' is called a forward-extension sequence of S, and S is non-closed. On the other hand, if there exists a sequential pattern $S'' = eS_{[1]} \ldots S_{[|S|]}$ or $S'' = S_{[1]} \ldots S_{[i]}eS_{[i+1]} \ldots S_{[|S|]}$ such that $Sup(S) = Sup(S'')$, S'' is called a backward-extension sequence of S, and S is non-closed. The information needed for the closure checking can be obtained from the projected databases used in *PrefixSpan*. Mining closed sequential patterns, instead of frequent sequence patterns, can not only reduce the number of patterns substantially, but can also reduce the mining time [27].

6.5.3 Gap Constraints for Sequence Patterns

In many applications, such as the analysis of logs, we are interested in patterns where the elements do not necessarily appear consecutively in the sequences, but there may be some other elements that are not a part of the pattern, between the elements of the pattern. For instance, referring to the example of the supermarket customers, there might be some other recorded events between paying and going to their car, like visiting an ATM.

This means that there may be gaps in the sequences between the pattern elements. There are two reasons to limit the length of such gaps. First of all, if the gap is very long, then it begins to feel more questionable if the elements really belong together. Secondly, long gaps are computationally expensive for the mining algorithms.

Table 6.6: Sequence database D'

ID	Sequence
S_1	$acegbfd$
S_2	$aegcbfd$
S_3	$acgebdf$
S_4	$agcebdf$

A *gap constraint* γ is specified by two natural numbers M and N satisfying $M \leq N$. A pattern P is said to *match* a sequence S, if there exist integers $1 \leq k_1 < k_2 < \cdots < k_{|P|} \leq |P|$, such that $P_{[i]} = S_{[k_i]}$ for all $1 \leq i \leq |P|$, and $M \leq k_{j+1} - k_j - 1 \leq N$ for all j satisfying $1 \leq j < |P|$. $< k_1, \ldots, k_{|P|} >$ is called an *instance* of P in S with gap constraint γ. Observe that, if we set $M = 0$ and $N = |S| - 2$, then having the gap constraint is equivalent to having no gap constraint.

There are no changes to other concepts regarding patterns when gap constraints are involved.

Consider the data in Table 6.1. The support of $< ca >$ is 1.0 in the set D_+ when there is no gap constraint. If we set for instance $M = 0$ and $N = 3$, then the support of $< ca >$ is 0.8 in the set D_+.

In practical applications, the choice of the right gap constraint may be difficult. Automatic search for a suitable constraint is studied in [28].

6.5.4 Partial Order Patterns

A *partial order* describes an ordering among elements existing in a given set of sequences. For example, the partial order R illustrated in Figure 6.2 is shared by all sequences in Table 6.6. From R, we can see that after an occurrence of a, one of c, e and g occurs before b in every sequence. Moreover, for each occurrence of b in a sequence, there is a d or f following it. The use of partial order is different from the use of Gap constraint in two ways. Firstly, the gap length for partial order is unlimited, and secondly, even if some frequent pattern with a gap constraint is contained in a sequence S, it is perfectly legal that S also contains the pattern in the reversed order.

Partial orders can capture information that is not explicitly available in frequent sequential patterns. A possible example are activity logs, where a partial order may exist. For instance, when observing a patient, we may be interested in knowing if he/she takes her medicine before breakfast or after. In some cases a partial order is required by law, administration, etc. Then instead of checking against patterns it is enough to check for potential violations of the partial order.

As shown in Figure 6.2, a partial order can be expressed as a directed acyclic graph. That is, each edge along with two vertices in the graph describe the preferred order between the two elements at the vertices. Now, we denote

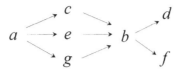

Figure 6.2: A frequent partial order R in Table 6.1.

by (x, y) the edge from x to y. Figure 6.2 represents the following partial order $R = \{(a, c), (a, e), (a, g), (a, b), (a, d), (a, f), (c, b), (c, d), (c, f), (e, b), (e, d), (e, f), (g, b), (g, d), (g, f), (b, d), (b, f)\}$.

For a sequence S, the transitive closure of S, denoted by $\mathcal{C}(S)$, is $\{(S_{[i]}, S_{[j]}) \mid 1 \leq i < j \leq |S|\}$. (The trivial pairs $(S_{[i]}, S_{[i]})$ are omitted in $\mathcal{C}(S)$.) For a given partial order R, a sequence S is said to *support* R if $R \subseteq \mathcal{C}(S)$. The *support* of R in sequence database D, denoted by $Sup(R)$, is

$$Sup(R) = \frac{|\{S \in D \mid R \subseteq \mathcal{C}(S)\}|}{|D|}.$$

Given a minimum support threshold α, R is a frequent partial order if $Sup(R) \geq \alpha$.

In practice, there are two typical scenarios of mining ordering information from given sequence data [3, 17, 20]. The first is mining frequent closed partial orders, and the second is finding one or a small number of partial orders that fit all the sequences globally.

A frequent partial order R is *closed* in a sequence database if there exists no partial order R' satisfying $R' \supset R$ and $Sup(R') = Sup(R)$. There are two strategies to discover all frequent closed partial orders in a sequence database with respect to a minimum support threshold. One strategy is transforming the sequence database into the set consisting of the transitive closures of every sequence. Then, the problem is reduced to mining frequent closed itemsets. A more efficient strategy is identifying the frequent closed partial orders in the form of transitive reductions directly from sequence data without transitive closure computing. A representative algorithm called *Frecpo* is given in [20].

There are two criteria for finding a global partial order R to fit a sequence set. On the one hand, R should be supported by as many sequences as possible. On the other hand, R should retain as much ordering information as possible. Clearly, it is not easy to satisfy these two criteria at the same time. For example, partial order (a, b) is supported by every sequence in Table 6.6. However, it contains less ordering information than the order illustrated in Figure 6.2. Take another example; the total order of S_1 fits S_1 completely, but it is not supported by other sequences. To make a tradeoff between the generality and the specificity, a greedy search method was proposed in [17]. Interested readers can refer to [17] for details.

6.5.5   Periodic Sequence Patterns

Different from frequent sequence patterns, closed sequential patterns, and partial order patterns, periodic sequence patterns are discovered from one single sequence only instead of a set of more sequences [11, 16, 38]. A periodic sequence pattern occurs in a sequence repeatedly. Finding periodic sequence patterns is useful in long activity logs.

Considering the application of a gap constraint to periodic sequence patterns, we denote by $count(S, P, \gamma)$ the count of instances of a pattern P in a sequence S with regard to a gap constraint γ, and denote by $N_{\ell,\gamma}^{S}$ the number of all possible length-ℓ instances satisfying γ in S. (A recursive way to compute $N_{\ell,\gamma}^{S}$ is given in [38].) Then, the support of P in S is defined as

$$Sup(S, P, \gamma) = \frac{count(S, P, \gamma)}{N_{|P|,\gamma}^{S}}.$$

Given a support threshold α, pattern P is a periodic sequence pattern with respect to γ if $Sup(S, P, \gamma) \geq \alpha$.

Example 4 *For the sequence $S = acdacbbc$, suppose the gap constraint is $\gamma = [2, 3]$, and the minimum support threshold is $\alpha = 0.2$. For pattern $P = <ac>$, there are two instances $<1, 5>$, $<4, 8>$ in S. For any length-2 pattern, the set of all possible instances in S with regard to γ is $\{<1, 4>, <1, 5>, <2, 5>, <2, 6>, <3, 6>, <3, 7>, <4, 7>, <4, 8>, <5, 8>\}$. That is, $N_{2,\gamma}^{S} = 9$. Then, $Sup(S, P, \gamma) = 2/9 > \alpha$. Thus, P is a periodic sequence pattern with respect to γ. The complete set of periodic sequence patterns includes: $<a>$ (2/8), $<b>$ (2/8), $<c>$ (3/8), $<ac>$ (2/9), $<cc>$ (2/9).*

6.5.6   Distinguishing Sequence Patterns

Distinguishing sequence patterns, discovered from two sets of sequences, are useful as sequence features to characterize a set of sequences and distinguish the set from other sets of sequences. (These are related to contrast patterns [6] and emerging patterns [7].) The above can also be defined in terms of one interval vs. other intervals instead of one set vs. other sets. We may, e.g., want to find distinguishing patterns in clickstream data to analyze the differences between customers who click an advertisement and customers who do not.

There are two main steps to discover distinguishing sequence patterns.

Step 1 Setting up two sets of sequences to be compared.

Step 2 Designing the contrast measure for candidate pattern evaluation.

There are many ways to set up sequences to be compared and they, naturally, depend on the domain. One is considering the class labels of sequences:

Table 6.7: Distinguishing sequence patterns discovered in D

Pattern P	$Sup_{D_+}(P)$	$Sup_{D_-}(P)$	Pattern P	$Sup_{D_+}(P)$	$Sup_{D_-}(P)$
$< aa >$	5	2	$< taca >$	4	1
$< aca >$	5	2	$< agca >$	4	1
$< acg >$	4	1	$< agc >$	4	2
$< aga >$	4	1	$< tac >$	4	2
$< gca >$	4	1	$< tgg >$	4	2
$< taa >$	4	1	$< tagg >$	4	2
$< agca >$	4	1			

a sequence database is divided into a set belonging to the target class and a set belonging to the non-target class. For example, given a collection of customers' shopping records, to analyze the special requirements of married customers, the records can be divided into the set of married ones and the set of unmarried ones. Another way to set up comparison is considering the different parts of sequences. Specifically, given a set of sequences, we compare the part at/near a given site of sequences with elsewhere in these sequences. In the case of two given sets of sequences, we can compare the part at/near a given site of sequences of the target set with the part at/near the same site of sequences of the other set. For example, the sequences around the transcription start site of one species can be compared with the sequences around the transcription start site of another species. Technically, in addition to selecting the sequences for comparison, we also select suitable subsequences.

As distinguishing sequence patterns are sequences that occur frequently in the target set but infrequently in the non-target set, the most commonly used contrast measure is the frequency (support) change in different sets. For example, given a candidate pattern P, let $Sup_{D_+}(P)$ and $Sup_{D_-}(P)$ be the supports of P in the target set and the non-target set, respectively. Then, P is a distinguishing sequence pattern if one of following conditions is satisfied: (i) $Sup_{D_+}(P) - Sup_{D_-}(P)$ is greater than the threshold; (ii) $Sup_{D_+}(P)/Sup_{D_-}(P)$ is greater than the threshold; (iii) $Sup_{D_+}(P)$ is greater than the minimum support threshold, and $Sup_{D_-}(P)$ is less than the maximum support threshold.

Example 5 *Consider the sequence dataset D listed in Table 6.1. Suppose we use the difference between $Sup_{D_+}(P)$ and $Sup_{D_-}(P)$ to measure the contrast of P. Then Table 6.7 lists all distinguishing sequence patterns such that $Sup_{D_+}(P) \geq 4$ and $Sup_{D_-}(P) \leq 2$.*

Distinguishing sequence patterns are useful for classification and mining distinguishing properties of classes. Gap constraints may also be used in distinguishing sequence pattern mining. Using closed sequences for distinguishing sequence patterns is more complicated than for frequent sequence patterns, because the Apriori property cannot be used—the distinguishing condition depends on a minimum support in the other set and the maximum set in the other.

A main approach for mining distinguishing sequence patterns is evaluating the contrast measure of each candidate pattern by traversing a lexicographic sequence tree in a depth-first or width-first manner [12, 29, 34].

6.5.7   Pattern Matching for Sequences

In the previous discussion, there was no restriction on frequent sequence pattern matching. That is, any element in the sequence can be freely used to match a pattern element. However, the occurrence of a pattern in a sequence is inherently complicated since a sequence element may match multiple pattern elements. Intuitively, different matching may result in different support values. Next, we present two types of matches.

- One-off match [15, 30]: each element in a sequence can be used only once to match an element in the pattern.

- Non-overlapping match [5, 31]: each element in a sequence can be used to match a pattern element as long as the matched pattern elements are different.

Example 6 *Given a sequence $S = abaa$, consider a pattern $P = aa$. Then, there are three occurrences of P in S when no limitations are placed for matching: $< 1, 3 >$, $< 1, 4 >$, and $< 3, 4 >$. Using the one-off match, there is only one occurrence of P in S, since no matter which of $< 1, 3 >$, $< 1, 4 >$, and $< 3, 4 >$ is selected, the other two are no longer occurrences. However, $< 1, 3 >$ and $< 3, 4 >$ are two occurrences of P in S if the non-overlapping match is used.*

When computing the support of a pattern P in a sequence database D, we can also consider the number of matches in each sequence. For example, [29] defined a support measure to consider both the number of sequences matching the pattern and the number of occurrences of the pattern in an individual sequence. This is relevant to situations where density/richness of occurrences of patterns matter; for example, in bio-sequence analysis people refer to "CpG islands" which are regions with a high frequency of CpG sites; in stock market analysis, having high frequency of large magnitude price changes in an interval of time is also of interest.

6.6   Factors for Selecting Sequence Patterns as Features

This section discusses several issues and properties associated with patterns that should be considered in evaluating/selecting patterns for use as features.

Supports: When the dataset is used for unsupervised study, the supports of the patterns should be used in pattern selection. When it is used for supervised learning, the supports of the patterns in different classes should be used; the ones with a large support difference or support ratio are discriminative against the classes.

Signal overlap: The matching datasets of patterns in a given dataset are useful in analyzing the overlap in the signals carried by patterns. Let P be a pattern and D a dataset. Then the *matching dataset* of P, denoted by $MDS(P)$, is the set of sequences in D that match P.

Two patterns having the same matching dataset can be considered as having the same signal; picking one of them is typically sufficient. It may also be necessary to pick among patterns that have very similar matching datasets.

Equivalence classes and generators: Given a pattern P, the set of all patterns Q such that $MDS(Q) = MDS(P)$ is called the *equivalence class* of P. A pattern P' is called a *minimal generator* of the equivalence class of P if there are no proper sub-patterns Q of P' such that Q is also in this equivalence class. It often suffices to pick one minimal generator from an equivalence class. This greatly reduces the number of patterns to consider for use as features, and at the same time, reduces the complexity of pattern matching and improves on pattern understandability.

The above are special factors associated with patterns that should be considered in selecting patterns for use as features. Of course one can also perform standard feature selection after computing the feature-vector representation of sequences.

6.7   Sequence Features Not Defined by Patterns

In addition to pattern-defined features, there are also features not defined by patterns. Such features can represent various properties of complete sequences, milestones at different positions, or characteristics of various intervals, of given sequences. Some of these are derived from the original sequences, and some cannot be derived in this way. We use some examples to illustrate these below.

Take national stock index histories for various countries as an example. Economic and political events can be added as features. Example events of interest to investment include economic recessions (which have start and end times), political coups, or other kinds of political turmoil. With such events as features, one can analyze their impact on stock prices.

For numerical sequences and time series, one can use regression coefficients (over the entire history or over fixed intervals) and interval averages etc. as features.

As another example, we consider long DNA sequences. Inside such a sequence there can be many positions that have significant importance, e.g., position 97 of a sequence is the start site of gene G_0 and position 905 is the start site of gene G_{25}. In the analysis of such sequences, the knowledge of those sites can help mine patterns and identify other sites.

In addition to events, tags (e.g., indicating that a given position in a particular DNA sequence is likely the start site of a medically important gene) can also be added as features for sequences. We can also include features that indicate positions where some window-based count of some pattern (e.g., GC) peaks.

A game-play sequence typically represents a sequence of moves. For instance, in the game of GO, the players take turns to make their moves. For each position in such a sequence one can consider a feature that indicates some properties, e.g., the difference between the number of white pieces and that of black pieces, or the difference between the area controlled by the white pieces and that by the black pieces.

6.8   Sequence Databases

The main sequence databases include the following three.

(a) The Entrez Global Query Cross-Database Search System[1] is a federated search engine. It provides access to many databases simultaneously with a single query string and user interface. Entrez can efficiently retrieve related sequences, structures, and references. The Entrez system can provide views of gene and protein sequences and chromosome maps. The protein database can be accessed at the link at this footnote.[2]

(b) The European Nucleotide Archive (ENA)[3] provides a comprehensive

---

[1]https://www.ncbi.nlm.nih.gov/sites/gquery
[2]https://www.ncbi.nlm.nih.gov/protein/
[3]https://www.ebi.ac.uk/ena

record of the world's nucleotide sequencing information, covering raw sequencing data, sequence assembly information and functional annotation.

(c) Genbank[4] is an annotated collection of all publicly available DNA sequences and is managed by the NIH.

6.9 Concluding Remarks

Many types of sequence features can be generated from sequences, including pattern-based ones and non-pattern-based ones. We gave examples of both of those two types. We presented several major kinds of patterns that can be used as sequence features, together with ways to mine them. We also described several approaches to using patterns as features. Finally we discussed key factors to consider when selecting sequence patterns for use as features. Chapter 4 on time series data analysis is related to this chapter, as well as Chapter 10 on pattern-based feature generation.

Bibliography

[1] Jay Ayres, Jason Flannick, Johannes Gehrke, and Tomi Yiu. Sequential pattern mining using a bitmap representation. In *Proceedings of the 8th ACM SIGKDD International Conference on Knowledge Discovery and Data Mining*, pages 429–435, 2002.

[2] Timothy L Bailey, Nadya Williams, Chris Misleh, and Wilfred W Li. Meme: discovering and analyzing DNA and protein sequence motifs. *Nucleic Acids Research*, 34(suppl_2):W369–W373, 2006.

[3] Gemma Casas-Garriga. Summarizing sequential data with closed partial orders. In *Proceedings of the SIAM International Conference on Data Mining, SDM, Newport Beach, CA, USA*, pages 380–391, 2005.

[4] Ding-Ying Chiu, Yi-Hung Wu, and Arbee L. P. Chen. An efficient algorithm for mining frequent sequences by a new strategy without support counting. In *Proceedings of the 20th International Conference on Data Engineering*, pages 375–386, 2004.

[5] Bolin Ding, David Lo, Jiawei Han, and Siau-Cheng Khoo. Efficient mining of closed repetitive gapped subsequences from a sequence database. In

---

[4]http://www.ncbi.nlm.nih.gov/Genbank/

Proceedings of the IEEE International Conference on Data Engineering, pages 1024–1035, 2009.

[6] Guozhu Dong and James Bailey. *Contrast Data Mining: Concepts, Algorithms, and Applications.* CRC Press, 2012.

[7] Guozhu Dong and Jinyan Li. Efficient mining of emerging patterns: Discovering trends and differences. In *Proceedings of the Fifth ACM SIGKDD International Conference on Knowledge Discovery and Data Mining,* pages 43–52. ACM, 1999.

[8] Guozhu Dong and Jian Pei. *Sequence Data Mining.* Springer-Verlag, Berlin, Heidelberg, 2007.

[9] Robert C Edgar. Muscle: Multiple sequence alignment with high accuracy and high throughput. *Nucleic Acids Research,* 32(5):1792–1797, 2004.

[10] Gilbert Eriani, Marc Delarue, Olivier Poch, Jean Gangloff, and Dino Moras. Partition of tnra synthetases into two classes based on mutually exclusive sets of sequence motifs. *Nature,* 347(6289):203, 1990.

[11] Jiawei Han, Guozhu Dong, and Yiwen Yin. Efficient mining of partial periodic patterns in time series database. In *Proceedings of the 15th International Conference on Data Engineering,* pages 106–115, 1999.

[12] Xiaonan Ji, James Bailey, and Guozhu Dong. Mining minimal distinguishing subsequence patterns with gap constraints. *Knowledge and Information Systems,* 11(3):259–286, 2007.

[13] Peter A Jones. Functions of DNA methylation: Islands, start sites, gene bodies and beyond. *Nature Reviews. Genetics,* 13(7):484, 2012.

[14] Daniel Kudenko and Haym Hirsh. Feature generation for sequence categorization. In *AAAI/IAAI,* pages 733–738, 1998.

[15] Hoang Thanh Lam, Fabian Moerchen, Dmitriy Fradkin, and Toon Calders. Mining compressing sequential patterns. In *Proceedings of the 12th SIAM International Conference on Data Mining,* pages 319–330, 2012.

[16] Chun Li, Qingyan Yang, Jianyong Wang, and Ming Li. Efficient mining of gap-constrained subsequences and its various applications. *ACM Transactions on Knowledge Discovery from Data,* 6(1):2, 2012.

[17] Heikki Mannila and Christopher Meek. Global partial orders from sequential data. In *Proceedings of the Sixth ACM SIGKDD International Conference on Knowledge Discovery and Data Mining, Boston, MA, USA,* pages 161–168, 2000.

[18] John C Obenauer, Lewis C Cantley, and Michael B Yaffe. Scansite 2.0: Proteome-wide prediction of cell signaling interactions using short sequence motifs. *Nucleic Acids Research*, 31(13):3635–3641, 2003.

[19] Jian Pei, Jiawei Han, Behzad Mortazavi-asl, Helen Pinto, Qiming Chen, Umeshwar Dayal, and Mei chun Hsu. PrefixSpan: Mining sequential patterns by prefix-projected growth. In *Proceedings of the 17th International Conference on Data Engineering*, pages 215–224, 2001.

[20] Jian Pei, Haixun Wang, Jian Liu, Ke Wang, Jianyong Wang, and Philip S. Yu. Discovering frequent closed partial orders from strings. *IEEE Transactions on Knowledge and Data Engineering*, 18(11):1467–1481, 2006.

[21] Jian Pei, Wush Chi-Hsuan Wu, and Mi-Yen Yeh. On shortest unique substring queries. In *Proceedings of the 29th IEEE International Conference on Data Engineering*, pages 937–948, 2013.

[22] Thomas D Schneider, Gary D Stormo, Larry Gold, and Andrzej Ehrenfeucht. Information content of binding sites on nucleotide sequences. *Journal of Molecular Biology*, 188(3):415–431, 1986.

[23] Rong She, Fei Chen, Ke Wang, Martin Ester, Jennifer L Gardy, and Fiona SL Brinkman. Frequent-subsequence-based prediction of outer membrane proteins. In *Proceedings of the Ninth ACM SIGKDD International Conference on Knowledge Discovery and Data Mining*, pages 436–445. ACM, 2003.

[24] Ramakrishnan Srikant and Rakesh Agrawal. Mining sequential patterns: Generalizations and performance improvements. In *Proceedings of the 5th International Conference on Extending Database Technology*, pages 3–17, 1996.

[25] Petre Tzvetkov, Xifeng Yan, and Jiawei Han. TSP: Mining top-k closed sequential patterns. *Knowledge and Information Systems*, 7(4):438–457, 2005.

[26] Gunnar Von Heijne. A new method for predicting signal sequence cleavage sites. *Nucleic Acids Research*, 14(11):4683–4690, 1986.

[27] Jianyong Wang and Jiawei Han. BIDE: Efficient mining of frequent closed sequences. In *Proceedings of the 20th International Conference on Data Engineering*, pages 79–90, 2004.

[28] Wentao Wang, Lei Duan, Jyrki Nummenmaa, Song Deng, Zhongqi Li, Hao Yang, and Changjie Tang. Mining frequent closed sequential patterns with non-user-defined gap constraints. In *Proceedings of the 10th International Conference on Advanced Data Mining and Applications*, pages 57–70, 2014.

[29] Xianming Wang, Lei Duan, Guozhu Dong, Zhonghua Yu, and Changjie Tang. Efficient mining of density-aware distinguishing sequential patterns with gap constraints. In *Proceedings of the 19th International Conference on Database Systems for Advanced Applications*, pages 372–387, 2014.

[30] Xindong Wu, Xingquan Zhu, Yu He, and Abdullah N. Arslan. PMBC: Pattern mining from biological sequences with wildcard constraints. *Computers in Biology and Medicine*, 43(5):481–492, 2013.

[31] Youxi Wu, Cong Shen, He Jiang, and Xindong Wu. Strict pattern matching under non-overlapping condition. *SCIENCE CHINA Information Sciences*, 60(1):12101, 2017.

[32] Zhengzheng Xing, Jian Pei, and Eamonn Keogh. A brief survey on sequence classification. *ACM Sigkdd Explorations Newsletter*, 12(1):40–48, 2010.

[33] Xifeng Yan, Jiawei Han, and Ramin Afshar. CloSpan: Mining closed sequential patterns in large datasets. In *Proceedings of the 3rd SIAM International Conference on Data Mining*, pages 166–177, 2003.

[34] Hao Yang, Lei Duan, Guozhu Dong, Jyrki Nummenmaa, Changjie Tang, and Xiaosong Li. Mining itemset-based distinguishing sequential patterns with gap constraint. In *Proceedings of the 20th International Conference on Database Systems for Advanced Applications*, pages 39–54, 2015.

[35] Kai Ye, Zhenyu Jia, Yipeng Wang, Paul Flicek, and Rolf Apweiler. Mining unique-m substrings from genomes. *Journal of Proteomics & Bioinformatics*, 3(3):99–103, 2010.

[36] Mohammed Javeed Zaki. SPADE: An efficient algorithm for mining frequent sequences. *Machine Learning*, 42(1/2):31–60, 2001.

[37] Chun Ting Zhang and Ju Wang. Recognition of protein coding genes in the yeast genome at better than 95% accuracy based on the Z curve. *Nucleic Acids Research*, 60(1):2804–2814, 2000.

[38] Minghua Zhang, Ben Kao, David W. Cheung, and Kevin Y. Yip. Mining periodic patterns with gap requirement from sequences. *ACM Transactions on Knowledge Discovery from Data*, 1(2):7, 2007.

Chapter 7

Feature Generation for Graphs and Networks

Yuan Yao

State Key Laboratory for Novel Software Technology, Nanjing University, China

Hanghang Tong

School of Computing, Informatics and Decision Systems Engineering, Arizona State University, USA

Feng Xu

State Key Laboratory for Novel Software Technology, Nanjing University, China

Jian Lu

State Key Laboratory for Novel Software Technology, Nanjing University, China

7.1   Introduction

In this chapter, we focus on the feature generation problem for graphs and networks.[1] The generated features are essential for various graph analysis tasks including node classification [5], link prediction [17], clustering [27], anomaly detection [2], etc.

We organize this chapter as follows.

- We first discuss the feature types. Based on the scope where the features are computed, existing features can be divided into neighborhood-level features (i.e., the features that can be computed from the neighborhood of a node) and global-level features (e.g., the graph diameter and density whose computations need the global knowledge of the graph).

- Next, we describe the existing feature generation methods and divide them into feature extraction approaches and feature learning approaches. For the feature extraction approach, the key is to *manually* define the functions based on which we can compute the corresponding features. In contrast, the feature learning approach[2] aims to *automatically* learn the features for graph nodes.

- Finally, we present several applications to illustrate feature usages. Specifically, we discuss the applications of multi-label classification (predicting the possible labels for a node), link prediction (predicting the missing links in a graph), anomaly detection (finding the outlier nodes), and visualization.

7.2   Feature Types

In this section, we briefly describe the feature types. As mentioned above, there has been comprehensive work studying both neighborhood-level and global-level features. Global-level features characterize the overall properties of graphs. For example, the graph diameter has been observed to be small [3] and shrink over time [15], the principal eigenvalue of the graph is shown to be informative as a vulnerability measure [32], the overall degree correlation has been shown as an indicator for graph types [40], etc.

As to neighborhood-level features, following Henderson et al. [12], we further divide them into two classes: common features, and recursive features:

---

[1] We interchangeably use graph and network in this chapter.

[2] Also widely known as graph embedding, network embedding, or network representation learning methods.

- Common features are directly computed based on each node's neighborhood (the neighborhood is also known as the egonet which includes the node, its neighbors, and any edges in the induced subgraph on these nodes). For example, common features include in-degree, out-degree, and total degree for directed graphs, as well as the number of triangles in the induced egonet, the principal eigenvalue of the induced egonet, the number of within-egonet edges, the number of edges entering and leaving the egonet, etc.

- In contrast to common features, recursive features are defined as any aggregate computed over a feature value among a node's neighbors. For example, the mean (or sum) degree value of the neighbors for a node is a typical recursive feature. It has been shown that recursive features are effective in various graph mining tasks including within- and across-network classification and identity resolution tasks [12].

In this chapter, we mainly focus on the neighborhood-level features as well as their applications in graph analysis tasks.

7.3 Feature Generation

To facilitate the analysis tasks on graphs, various types of features have been proposed. Generally, we divide existing feature generation methods for graph nodes into feature extraction approaches and feature learning approaches.

For feature extraction approaches, the key is to manually define the functions based on which we can compute the corresponding features from a node and its neighbors. For example, given a node and its neighborhood, example features include the number of neighbors, the number of triangles, the number of edges in the neighborhood, the principal eigenvalue of the adjacency matrix constructed from the neighborhood, the number of neighbors of a certain degree, etc. Therefore, we usually need to define a relatively small set of features for a specific prediction task. For example, when defining features for the anomaly detection task, features that most nodes obey while the anomaly nodes violate would be desired [2]; another example is from the link prediction problem [17], where topological features for node pairs (e.g., the number of common neighbors) are extracted and used to boost the prediction performance. When defining the features, we also need to consider the computational scalability (which matters in the extraction phase) of the features.

For feature learning approaches, the goal is to automatically learn the features for graph nodes. The basic assumption behind is that nodes in the same *context* (e.g., neighborhood) tend to be similar to each other in terms of the learned features. Therefore, the definition of context is a key problem in

Symbols	Descriptions
$G(V, E)$	graph with node set V and edge set E
$\mathbf{A}$	the adjacency matrix of graph G
$\mathbf{S}$	the similarity/proximity/weighting matrix between nodes
s_{ij}	the element of matrix $\mathbf{S}$
$\mathbf{U}$	the node embedding matrix
$\mathbf{U}^T$	the transpose of $\mathbf{U}$
$\mathbf{u}_i$	the embedding of node i
u, v, v', c, i, j	nodes u, v, v', c, i, j
$N(u)$	the neighbors of node u
f, g	functions

these methods. Typically, it is defined as the neighborhood for a given node, and other types of context such as proximity-based and similarity-based ones are also proposed. Based on the context definition, a machine learning problem can be formulated to learn the node features.

In this section, we systematically review the existing feature learning methods. We will first introduce some basic models for feature learning on graphs. These methods are *basic* in that they are designed for a simple graph. After that, we show the existing extensions on these basic models in terms of preserving the community structure, incorporating the node attributes, etc. Before describing the existing feature learning methods, we first present the symbols used in this chapter in Table 7.1. We use capital bold letters for matrices, and lower-case bold letters for vectors. For example, $\mathbf{u}_i$ stands for the $i - th$ row of $\mathbf{U}$.

7.3.1   Basic Models

Here, we roughly categorize the existing graph embedding methods for simple graphs into three classes: neural network models, factorization-based models, and regularization-based models.

(A) Neural Network Models. Recently, several researchers propose to apply the word2vec model [19, 20] to learn the node embeddings/features[3] in graphs [11, 25, 30]. The basic assumption of existing methods is from the skip-gram model in word2vec: given a node u in a graph $G(V, E)$, and its neighbors $N(u)$, the goal is to maximize

$$\sum_{u \in V} \log Pr(N(u)|f(u)) \tag{7.1}$$

where $f(u)$ is the embedding of node u. The above equation basically means that the neighborhood is determined by the central node. This idea can date back to the social theory of homophily where similar people tend to cluster together.

---

[3]We interchangeably use embedding and feature in this chapter.

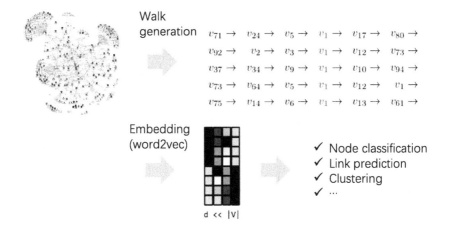

Figure 7.1: The illustration of neural network methods.

To solve the above equation, we typically assume that the nodes in $N(u)$ are conditional independent, and thus we have

$$Pr(N(u)|f(u)) = \prod_{v \in N(u)} Pr(v|f(u)) \qquad (7.2)$$

where we usually use the softmax function to estimate the conditional probability

$$Pr(v|f(u)) = \frac{exp(g(v) \cdot f(u))}{\sum_{v' \in V} exp(g(v') \cdot f(u))}. \qquad (7.3)$$

Here, $\cdot$ denotes an inner product, f is the embedding function for central nodes, and g is the embedding function for neighbor nodes. Both f and g are to be learned, which can map the node to its features. The denominator of the above equation is expensive to compute for large graphs. Therefore, negative sampling techniques are commonly used to approximate it.

Eq. (7.1) serves as the optimization framework for DeepWalk [25] and node2vec [11]. The remaining problem is how to define the context of a given node. Specifically, DeepWalk generates multiple random walks from each node; by treating a walk as a sentence, it defines the neighbors of a given node on the walk as its context. Different from DeepWalk (depth-first walking), node2vec generates the walks by combining breadth-first walking and depth-first walking. An overview of these methods is shown in Fig. 7.1. As we can see from the figure, these methods first generate walks from an input graph, define context based on the walks, and apply the word2vec (skig-gram) model to learn the embeddings for each node. Finally, these features can be used for different prediction tasks including node classification, link prediction, and clustering. Based on the figure, the key difference between DeepWalk and node2vec is in the first step, i.e., walk generation.

Next, although not explicitly stated, LINE [30] also follows the above framework in Eq. (7.1). Based on the above notations, the optimization formulation of LINE (second-order proximity) can be written as

$$\min - \sum_{(u,v)\in E} s_{ij} \cdot log \frac{exp(g(v) \cdot f(u))}{\sum_{v'\in V} exp(g(v') \cdot f(u))} \tag{7.4}$$

where s_{ij} is the edge weight. This weight also differentiates LINE from Deep-Walk and node2vec.

There also exist methods that use neural network models other than the word2vec model. For example, DNGR [7] uses a stacked autoencoder. DNGR first generates a random surfing model to capture graph structural information. Based on the results of random surfing, DNGR generates a probabilistic co-occurrence matrix, and calculates the PPMI matrix [16]. Then, a stacked denoising autoencoder is applied to learn the node embeddings. Different from DeepWalk and node2vec, DNGR uses random surfing to substitute the random walk sampling, and it uses a stacked autoencoder (on the PPMI matrix) to substitute the word2vec model.

(B) Factorization-Based Models. In addition to the neural network methods, some researchers propose to apply matrix factorization for the graph embedding task [1, 6, 33, 36, 38]. The basic idea is to first construct a node-context matrix, and then use the low-rank approximations of the matrix as the embeddings. In the early 2000s, graph embedding was related to dimensionality reduction. These methods first construct a similarity graph based on the neighborhood and then embed the nodes via dimensionality reduction. The common rationale behind this is that similar nodes are closer to each other in the embedding space. Typical examples include Laplacian Eigenmaps [4] and Locally Linear Embedding (LLE) [26].

Recently, several types of construction methods for the node-context matrix have been proposed. First, instead of the adopting the sampling procedure of DeepWalk and node2vec, some researchers propose to directly construct the node-context matrix via matrix multiplication [33, 38]. For example, Yang et al. [38] compute

$$\mathbf{S} = (\mathbf{A} + \mathbf{A}^2)/2 \tag{7.5}$$

and apply matrix factorization on the $\mathbf{S}$ matrix. Here, $\mathbf{A}$ is the normalized adjacency matrix of graph $G(V, E)$, and $\mathbf{S}$ includes all the possible 2-hop walks between two nodes. The authors mention that the matrix can be propagated through more hops, and they choose two hops due to the efficiency concern.

The second method to construct the node-context matrix is by proximity computation [24, 36]. For example, Wang et al. [36] follow the proximity definition from LINE [30] and compute the node-context matrix as follows

$$\mathbf{S} = \mathbf{S}^{(1)} + \eta \mathbf{S}^{(2)} \tag{7.6}$$

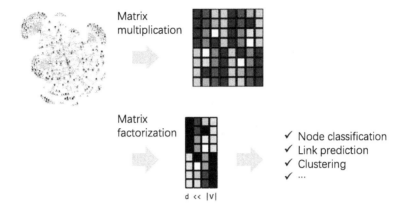

Matrix multiplication

Matrix factorization

✓ Node classification
✓ Link prediction
✓ Clustering
✓ ...

d << |V|

Figure 7.2: The illustration of factorization-based methods (GraRep [6]).

where the first-order proximity $\mathbf{S}^{(1)} = \mathbf{A}$, the second-order proximity $\mathbf{S}^{(2)}(i,j) = cos(\mathbf{A}(i,:), \mathbf{A}(j,:))$, and η is a parameter to control the relative importance. Here, $\mathbf{A}(i,:)$ denotes the $i - th$ row of $\mathbf{A}$, and cos denotes the cosine similarity. In other words, the second-order proximity assumes that nodes sharing many connections are close to each other.

The third method of node-context matrix construction is based on the PMI (pointwise mutual information) matrix [6, 16]. The PMI matrix is defined as

$$PMI(i,j) = \log(\frac{\#(i,j) \cdot |D|}{\#(i) \cdot \#(j)}) \tag{7.7}$$

where $\#(i,j)$ is the number of occurrences that node i and j are in the same context, $\#(i)$ ($\#(j)$) is the number of occurrences of node i (j), and $|D| = \sum_i \sum_j \#(i,j)$. The PMI matrix is derived from an equivalence proof between word2vec and matrix factorization [16].

Next, we describe a representative factorization-based method, and discuss its differences from the neural network methods. Afterwards, we will come back to the equivalence proof of the PMI matrix.

GraRep [6] is a typical factorization-based method for graph embedding. As shown in Fig. 7.2, it consists of three major steps. First, GraRep computes all the possible paths between nodes via k-step multiplications of the transition matrix (i.e., normalized adjacency matrix). Next, following Levy and Goldberg [16], for each k value, GraRep applies SVD on the shifted matrix derived from the optimization formulation. Finally, GraRep concatenates the resulting embeddings from all k values. We only show one specific k value in the figure.

Comparing Fig. 7.2 with Fig. 7.1, GraRep differs from the neural network methods (i.e., DeepWalk and node2vec) in the following three aspects corresponding to the three steps. First, the walks in DeepWalk and node2vec can be seen as a sampling set of all possible paths, while GraRep directly computes (the transition probabilities of) all the possible paths. Although GraRep covers more paths, it may also cause efficiency issues especially for large-scale graphs. Second, DeepWalk and node2vec directly optimize over Eq. (7.1), while GraRep chooses to adopt SVD on the derived matrix (by setting the derivative to zero) to find an approximate solution. Third, DeepWalk and node2vec compute a unique embedding for nodes, while GraRep results in several embeddings and returns the concatenation of these embeddings.

(C) Connections between Neural Network Models and Factorization-Based Models. Next, we show the equivalence proof between word2vec/DeepWalk and matrix factorization. More specifically, we are going to present the equivalence proof between the skip-gram model with negative sampling (SGNS) and matrix factorization [16, 38].

From word2vec, we have the following optimization formulation of SGNS [16, 38] to maximize

$$l = \sum_{v \in V} \sum_{c \in V_C} \#(v, c)(\log \sigma(\mathbf{v} \cdot \mathbf{c}) + k \cdot \mathbb{E}_{c_N \sim P_D}[\log \sigma(-\mathbf{v} \cdot \mathbf{c}_N)]) \quad (7.8)$$

where v is the central node, c is the context node, D contains all the node-context pairs, $\mathbf{v}$ ($\mathbf{c}$) is the embedding of v (c), $\sigma(x) = \frac{1}{1+exp(-x)}$, c_N is the negative sample, k is the number of negative samples, and P_D is the negative sampling distribution with $P_D(c_N) = \frac{\#(c_N)}{|D|}$. Note that in the above equation, each node may have two roles: the central node and the context node.

Then, taking P_D into the above equation and with $\#(v) = \sum_{c \in V_C} \#(v, c)$, we have

$$l = \sum_{v \in V} \sum_{c \in V_C} \#(v, c) \log \sigma(\mathbf{v} \cdot \mathbf{c}) + k \cdot \sum_{v \in V} \#(v) \sum_{c_N \in V_C} \frac{\#(c_N)}{|D|} \log \sigma(-\mathbf{v} \cdot \mathbf{c}_N).$$
$$(7.9)$$

Next, by substituting c_N with c in the latter term of the above equation, we have

$$l = \sum_{v \in V} \sum_{c \in V_C} \#(v, c)(\log \sigma(\mathbf{v} \cdot \mathbf{c}) + k \cdot \frac{\#(v) \cdot \#(c)}{|D|} \log \sigma(-\mathbf{v} \cdot \mathbf{c})) \quad (7.10)$$

Finally, denoting $x = \mathbf{v} \cdot \mathbf{c}$ and solving $\frac{\partial l}{\partial x} = 0$, we have

$$\mathbf{v} \cdot \mathbf{c} = x = \log \frac{\#(v, c) \cdot |D|}{\#(v) \cdot \#(c)} - \log k. \quad (7.11)$$

Here, $\log \frac{\#(v,c) \cdot |D|}{\#(v) \cdot \#(c)}$ is the well-known pointwise mutual information (PMI) for node pair (v, c). Such equivalence between word2vec and matrix factorization is widely used in existing work because matrix factorization is more flexible in terms of incorporating more information (e.g., community structure, node labels, etc.) in the graph embedding process. However, in practice, the performance of word2vec and matrix factorization may differ in specific tasks.

(D) Regularization-Based Models. In addition to the above two types of methods, regularization-based methods have also been studied [13,14]. Typically, regularization-based methods directly constrain that nodes in the same context are close to each other, e.g.,

$$\min \sum_{(i,j)\in E} s_{ij} ||\frac{\mathbf{u}_i}{\sqrt{d_i}} - \frac{\mathbf{u}_j}{\sqrt{d_j}}||_2^2 \tag{7.12}$$

where s_{ij} is the weight/similarity between two nodes, $\mathbf{u}_i$ ($\mathbf{u}_j$) is the embedding of node i (j), and d_i (d_j) is the degree of node i (j). As we can see from the above equation, if two nodes share higher similarity, the minimization problem would force the corresponding two embeddings to stay closer. Note that although we directly sum over the links in E in the above equation, we can actually construct any similarity matrix to substitute E. Further, Eq. (7.12) can be reformulated as the following maximization problem

$$\max Tr(\mathbf{U}^T \mathbf{L} \mathbf{U}) \tag{7.13}$$

where $\mathbf{L} = \mathbf{D}^{-0.5} \mathbf{S} \mathbf{D}^{0.5}$, and $\mathbf{D}$ is a diagonal matrix with sum of each row of $\mathbf{S}$ on the diagonal.

Regularization-based methods are usually combined with other types of methods in practice. For example, AANE [13] combines a regularization-based method (to capture the graph structure) with a factorization-based method (to capture the attribute similarity). SDNE [34] combines an autoencoder with regularization to learn the node embeddings. Specifically, SDNE inputs the neighbor vector of each node into the autoencoder, uses the hidden state as the embedding, and further regulates that the embeddings of connected nodes are close to each other.

7.3.2 Extensions

Next, we present and discuss the existing extensions on the basic models for graph feature learning. These extensions consider the cases including whether the community structure is preserved, whether the node attributes are incorporated, etc.

(A) Community Structure. Most of the basic models for graph embedding focus on the pairwise relationship/similarity between nodes, while the community structure is an important characteristic of graphs. Therefore, several researchers propose to incorporate the community structure when such information is available.

M-NMF [36] adopts the factorization-based method while aiming to preserve the community structure of the graph. It collectively factorizes the node similarity matrix and the community indicator matrix, and further adds an optimization term to maximize the modularity [23].

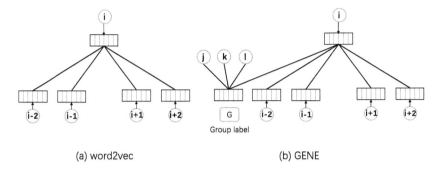

(a) word2vec   (b) GENE

Figure 7.3: The illustration of GENE [9].

Different from M-NMF, GENE [9] adopts a neural network model. GENE is built upon the word2vec/DeepWalk model. While wor2vec generates the embedding of a given node from its neighbors, GENE does so from the neighbors and the group embedding. The difference between word2vec and GENE is illustrated in Fig. 7.3. As we can see, the group embedding is incorporated when generating the embedding of the central node, and the group embedding is related to the embeddings of the nodes that belong to this group.

(B) Node Attributes. In some cases, nodes in a graph may be accompanied by some attributes (e.g., tags and descriptions). Therefore, learning the node embeddings by collectively considering the graph structure and node attributes becomes an important problem.

Yang et al. [38] propose TADW to make use of the associated textual information on nodes. By encoding the textual features in matrix $\mathbf{T}$ (where each column indicates the textual features for the corresponding node), TADW aims to optimize the following objective

$$\min_{\mathbf{U},\mathbf{V}} ||\mathbf{S} - \mathbf{U}\mathbf{V}\mathbf{T}||_F^2 \tag{7.14}$$

where $\mathbf{S}$ is defined in Eq. (7.5). A typical factorization-based method would optimize the following objective:

$$\min_{\mathbf{U},\mathbf{V}} ||\mathbf{S} - \mathbf{U}\mathbf{V}||_F^2 \tag{7.15}$$

In the above two equations, we ignore the regularization terms. As we can see, TADW follows inductive matrix completion [22] to include the node attributes. The embeddings results are contained in both $\mathbf{U}$ and $\mathbf{V}$ (or $\mathbf{V}\mathbf{T}$).

Recently, Huang et al. [13] proposed AANE to learn the node embeddings with node attributes. Based on the regularization-based method in Eq. (7.12), they further add the following constraint on the learned embeddings

$$\min_{\mathbf{U}} ||\mathbf{S} - \mathbf{U}\mathbf{U}^T||_F^2 \tag{7.16}$$

where $\mathbf{S}$ is the similarity matrix between nodes computed from the node attributes, and $\mathbf{U}$ contains the node embeddings. Later, built upon AANE, they further formulate a supervised learning problem, and use the node labels (e.g., categories) in the training data to predict the labels in the test data [14]. The basic idea is to formulate the label information as regularization terms.

(C) Directed Graphs. Some existing work pays special attention to directed graphs, as the proximity from node i to node j is different from the proximity from node j to node i in a directed graph. To this end, HOPE [24] proposes to factorize the following matrix

$$\min_{\mathbf{U}^s, \mathbf{U}^t} ||\mathbf{S} - \mathbf{U}^s\mathbf{U}^{t}||_F^2 \qquad (7.17)$$

where matrix $\mathbf{S}$ reflects the asymmetric transitivity on directed graphs, and $\mathbf{U}^s$ and $\mathbf{U}^t$ contain the embeddings as source node and target node, respectively. Here, $\mathbf{S}$ is computed by several high-order proximity measurements such as Katz Index and Adamic-Adar (please refer to [24] for more details about these measurements).

Different from HOPE, APP [42] extends the DeepWalk model by the following formulation

$$\max \sum_u \sum_v N_{uv}(\log \sigma(-\mathbf{s}_u \cdot \mathbf{t}_v)) \qquad (7.18)$$

where we ignore the negative sampling terms, and the asymmetry property is encoded in N_{uv}. Here, each node has two embeddings (i.e., $\mathbf{s}_u$ and $\mathbf{t}_u$) indicating whether it serves as the source role or the target role, and N_{uv} is the number of paths from node u to node v. In APP, N_{uv} is obtained by Monte Carlo sampling.

(D) Signed Graphs. The vast majority of existing methods are designed for unsigned graphs (with only positive links), while some graphs contain both positive links and negative links (e.g., social networks with trust and distrust). For signed graphs, a key issue is to deal with the negative links.

SNE [41] adopts the log-bilinear model to linearly combine the embeddings of the context nodes (predecessors) for a given central node. That is, the predicted embedding of node v in a path $h = [1, 2, ..., l, v]$ is defined as

$$\hat{\mathbf{u}}_v = \sum_{i=1}^{l} \mathbf{x}_i \odot \mathbf{u}_i \qquad (7.19)$$

where there are l predecessors in the path, $\odot$ denotes the element-wise multiplication, and each node i is associated with two signed-type vectors $\mathbf{x}_+$ and $\mathbf{x}_-$ depending on the sign of edge $(i, i+1)$. Then, a similar objective of Eq. (7.3) is proposed

$$\frac{exp(\hat{\mathbf{u}}_v \cdot \mathbf{u}_v + b_v)}{\sum_{v' \in V} exp(\hat{\mathbf{u}}_{v'} \cdot \mathbf{u}_{v'} + b_{v'})} \qquad (7.20)$$

where a bias term b_v is added.

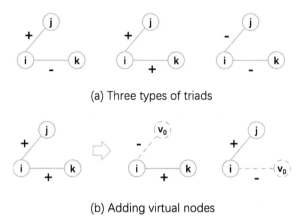

(a) Three types of triads

(b) Adding virtual nodes

Figure 7.4: The illustration of SiNE [35].

To deal with negative links, SiNE [35] concentrates on the triad structure and proposes a pairwise objective where the similarity of positively linked nodes should be higher than that of negatively linked nodes. Take Fig. 7.4 as an example. There are three types of triads as shown in the first row. For the first type, SiNE constrains that nodes with positive links are more likely to be similar:

$$f(\mathbf{u}_i, \mathbf{u}_j) \geq f(\mathbf{u}_i, \mathbf{u}_k) + \delta. \tag{7.21}$$

where δ is a threshold to regulate the difference between the two similarities. For the other two types of triads, SiNE introduces a virtual node. Take the second type as an example. As shown in the second row of Fig. 7.4, when two links in a triad are both positive, SiNE splits it into two new triads and adds a virtual node v_0 in the new triads with the following constraint

$$f(\mathbf{u}_i, \mathbf{u}_j) \geq f(\mathbf{u}_i, \mathbf{u}_0) + \delta_0 \tag{7.22}$$

Then, a minimization problem is formulated based on the above two equations. Finally, for the function f, SiNE applies neural networks with two hidden layers to compute the node similarities.

(E) Heterogeneous Graphs. Most existing graph embedding methods are proposed for homogenous graphs where the nodes/edges are of the same type. In reality, some graphs may contain nodes/edges of different types. Fig. 7.5 illustrates some examples of heterogeneous graphs. In heterogeneous graphs, there are several types of nodes (e.g., papers, venues, authors, and terms) and different types of edges exist between these nodes (e.g., paper-published-in-venue, author-writes-paper, and paper-has-terms).

PTE [29] extends the LINE model to embed heterogeneous graphs. LINE can be seen as an embedding method for homogeneous graphs that contain node-node relationships. Based on LINE, PTE further considers node-community relationships (nodes may belong to different communities) and

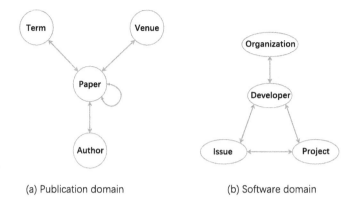

(a) Publication domain (b) Software domain

Figure 7.5: The illustration of heterogeneous networks.

node-label relationships (the labels serve as supervision information). Specially, PTE treats node (in the homogeneous graph), community, and label as three types of nodes in the generalized heterogeneous graph.

Different from PTE, Chang et al. [8] consider the heterogeneous graph where each node may have different types of attributes. The basic idea is to use neural networks to obtain the features of different attributes, and then map the features to the same space via a linear transformation. Dong et al. [10] define metapaths on the heterogeneous graph and then learn the embeddings in a way similar to DeepWalk.

(F) Supervised Methods. Finally, there are two branches of network embedding methods. The first branch aims to learn general features which can be used for different tasks. In contrast, the second branch is designed for specific tasks, and the supervision information from the tasks can be used to learn the embeddings. We call the second branch supervised methods.

In the literature, several methods can be seen as supervised methods or semi-supervised methods [29, 39]. For example, PTE [29] incorporates the known labels as input when learning the embeddings, and uses these embeddings to predict the unknown labels. MMDW [33] introduces the max-margin idea in SVM into factorization-based models. MMDW can be seen as a supervised method as it jointly optimizes the max-margin-based classifier and the network embedding formulation.

7.3.3   Summary

Overall, we summarize the existing graph embedding methods for automatic feature learning in Table 7.2. We can make several observations based on the table. First, graph embedding is a popular topic in recent years, and many methods have been proposed. Actually, graph embedding can date back to earlier years when the embedded learning was mainly related to dimen-

Methods	Year	Method Type	Extensions
DeepWalk [25]	2014	neural network method	none
GraRep [6]	2015	factorization-based method	none
LINE [30]	2015	neural network method	none
PTE [29]	2015	neural network method	heterogenous graph, supervised method
TADW [38]	2015	factorization-based method	node attributes
HNE [8]	2015	neural network method	heterogenous graph
node2vec [11]	2016	neural network method	none
DNGR [7]	2016	neural network method	none
SDNE [34]	2016	neural network + regularization-based method	community structure
HOPE [24]	2016	factorization-based method	directed graphs
GENE [9]	2016	neural network method	community structure
MMDW [33]	2016	factorization-based method	supervised method
AANE [13]	2017	regularization-based + factorization-based method	node attributes
APP [42]	2017	neural network method	directed graph
M-NMF [36]	2017	factorization-based method	community structure
LANE [14]	2017	regularization-based method	node attributes, supervised method
metapath2vec [10]	2017	neural network method	heterogenous graph
SNE [41]	2017	neural network method	signed graph
SiNE [35]	2017	neural network method	signed graph

sionality reduction [28]. In 2014, DeepWalk used the neural word2vec model for graph embedding, which has opened a new door for this area. Therefore, we focus on the work since DeepWalk in the table. Second, neural network methods are widely adopted by existing work. One possible reason is that neural network methods have been shown to have performance improvement in many tasks. Additionally, although word2vec is equivalent to matrix factorization to some extent, they still use different optimization techniques which may result in performance discrepancy. Third, recent work tends to consider various extensions (e.g., community structure, node attributes, etc.) as well as the combinations of these extensions. For example, LANE incorporates node attributes and existing labels for label prediction. From this perspective, there are several future directions including learning graph embeddings for attributed heterogeneous graphs and attributed signed graphs.

In addition to learning the embeddings for graph nodes, some researchers propose to learn the embeddings of communities/subgraphs [21, 37]. These methods first define the context among subgraphs, and then apply word2vec-like models to ensure that the embeddings of subgraphs that occur in the same context tend to be similar to each other. These methods are out of the scope of this chapter.

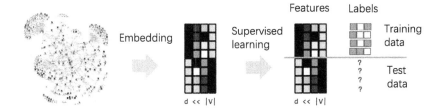

Figure 7.6: The illustration of multi-label prediction.

7.4 Feature Usages

In this section, we present some example applications to show the feature usages including multi-label classification, link prediction, anomaly detection, and visualization.

7.4.1 Multi-Label Classification

In some graphs, each node may correspond to multiple (one or more) labels from a finite set. For example, in a social network, individuals may have multiple interests or belong to multiple groups. In practice, we may want to recommend suitable news/groups for individuals based on his/her labels. However, such labels are not always available for all individuals, and it is useful to predict the labels for those individuals without labels. Compared to the cases of predicting a single label for each network node, predicting multiple labels is a more challenging task especially when the label size is large. This task is referred to as multi-label classification [31].

An illustrative example for multi-label classification is shown in Fig. 7.6. For the experimental setup, we are usually given a network of nodes, and a certain fraction of nodes with their labels in the training phase. The goal is to predict the labels for the remaining nodes. As shown in the example, we first generate the features for each network node (e.g., by network embedding) and then formulate a supervised machine learning problem (e.g., via one-vs-rest logistic regression) where the known labels are used as supervision information. Then, in the example, we can predict whether the nodes in the test set would be associated with each of the three labels.

7.4.2 Link Prediction

Link prediction is another widely studied task. In this problem, we aim to predict the potential unseen edges in a graph, and it can be used to extract missing information, identify spurious interactions, or evaluate graph evolving mechanisms. Experimentally, we can first hide a certain fraction of the edges, and the goal is to predict these missing edges.

Different from multi-label prediction, link prediction involves pairs of nodes instead of individual nodes. Typically, we need to first transfer the node features to edge features. Take node2vec [11] as an example. Given two nodes i and j, and their features $\mathbf{u}_i$ and $\mathbf{u}_j$, the node2vec method provides several binary operators over the corresponding feature vectors $\mathbf{u}_i$ and $\mathbf{u}_j$ in order to generate the features for edge (i, j). The provided operators include average, Hadamard product, etc. Next, similar to multi-label classification, a supervised machine learning problem can be formulated to learn the labels (e.g., the edge exists or not) of node pairs.

7.4.3   Anomaly Detection

In many real networks, there exist some outliers conducting anomalous behaviors. For example, outliers include spammers in a communication network, "water-army" in a social network, etc. In these networks, it is essential to identify the anomalies as their behaviors may be illegal or dangerous. Such a problem is referred to as anomaly detection.

To tackle this problem, Akoglu et al. [2] manually designed several features that can distinguish anomalous nodes from normal nodes. They define the concept of the egonet for each node: egonet includes the node, its neighbors (in k hops), and any edges in the induced subgraph on these nodes. The basic assumption is that the egonet of anomalous nodes would be different from that of normal nodes. Based on this assumption, the authors tested a dozen features and found that the number of nodes in a egonet, the number of edges in a egonet, the total weight (for weighed graphs) of a egonet, and the principal eigenvalue of the egonet's adjacency matrix are very successful in spotting anomalies.

Further, instead of directly using the features to spot anomalies (e.g., the node significantly deviates from other nodes in the feature space), the authors consider the interactions between these features. For example, they found that the number of nodes and the number of edges in a egonet follow a power law, the principal eigenvalue of the egonet's adjacency matrix and the total weight of a egonet follow a power law, etc. Based on these pairwise patterns, they flag those nodes that significantly deviate from the average patterns as anomalies. They experimentally found that such pairwise patterns are more effective for the anomaly detection problem.

7.4.4   Visualization

In addition to the prediction tasks on graphs and networks, it is meaningful to provide visualizations for a network. Based on the generated features of nodes, we can plot them in a 2D space via, for example, t-SNE [18]. Fig. 7.7 presents two examples from DeepWalk [25] and LINE [30]. The visualization

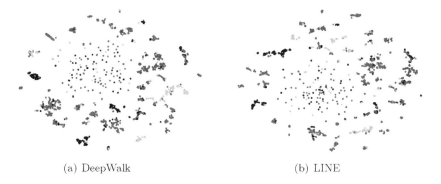

(a) DeepWalk   (b) LINE

Figure 7.7: The visualization examples.

results are from a citation network (3,312 authors and 4,732 citations) of the Citeseer data. The six colors correspond to "agents" (blue), "AI" (red), "DB" (black), "IR" (purple), "ML" (khaki), and "HCI" (green), respectively. As we can observe from the figures, the visualization results of DeepWalk and LINE are both meaningful as nodes with the same colors are distributed closer. For example, the red nodes standing for AI publications are clustered in the left part and the right part of the two figures, respectively.

7.5 Conclusions and Future Directions

In this chapter, we have discussed the existing efforts and feature generation for graphs and networks. We first discussed two types of features (neighborhood-level and global-level). Global-level features reflect the overall properties of the graphs/networks, while neighborhood-level features characterize the local neighborhood of nodes. For neighborhood-level features, we further divide them into common features which are computed based on the node's egonet, and recursive features which are computed over a feature value among the node's neighbors.

Next, we divide existing graph feature generation methods into feature extraction approaches and feature learning approaches. For the feature extraction approaches, the key is to define the feature functions. For the feature learning approaches (i.e., graph embedding), we systematically reviewed the recent progress. The basic idea of feature learning approaches is to automatically learn the features for graph nodes, based on the assumption that the nodes in the same context tend to be similar to each other. In particular, we have introduced three types of basic graph embedding models (neural network method, factorization-based method, and regularization-based method), and summarized several extensions (based on the basic models) that have been studied in the literature. The extensions include whether to preserve community structure, whether to incorporate node attributes, whether to use supervision information, as well as several special types of graphs (i.e., directed graph, signed graph, and heterogeneous graph).

Finally, we presented several applications for feature usages. We first introduce the multi-label classification task and link prediction task. The former one aims to extract node features and predict labels for each node, while the latter one needs to transfer the node features to edge features and predict the existence of edges. In these two tasks, we use the features from feature learning approaches. We then give an example application of anomaly detection which takes the feature extraction approach. Several manually designed features are explained to spot the anomalous nodes. After that, we present the visualization application of features.

For future work, there are several directions. First, we can consider fusing the feature extraction method and feature learning method. One simple way is to use both extracted features and learned features for the prediction task. Further, we may consider incorporating the manually extracted features in the learning process of feature learning. Second, while the features from feature extraction methods have clear meanings, the meanings of the features from feature learning methods are not clear. A future direction is to interpret/explain the learned features. Third, graphs and networks evolve over time; therefore, generating features in a dynamic setting is an important problem. For example, for the feature learning method, we need to incrementally update the features as new nodes and edges arrive, especially for large-scale graphs. Fourth, special treatment is needed for certain extensions. For example, when the spatial-temporal data is available, we can have some special modeling methods instead of simply treating them as node attributes.

Bibliography

[1] Amr Ahmed, Nino Shervashidze, Shravan Narayanamurthy, Vanja Josifovski, and Alexander J Smola. Distributed large-scale natural graph factorization. In *Proceedings of the 22nd International Conference on World Wide Web (WWW)*, pages 37–48. ACM, 2013.

[2] Leman Akoglu, Mary McGlohon, and Christos Faloutsos. Oddball: Spotting anomalies in weighted graphs. *Advances in Knowledge Discovery and Data Mining*, pages 410–421, 2010.

[3] Albert-László Barabási, Réka Albert, and Hawoong Jeong. Diameter of the world-wide web. *Nature*, 401(9):130–131, 1999.

[4] Mikhail Belkin and Partha Niyogi. Laplacian eigenmaps and spectral techniques for embedding and clustering. In *Advances in Neural Information Processing Systems (NIPS)*, pages 585–591, 2002.

[5] Smriti Bhagat, Graham Cormode, and S Muthukrishnan. Node classification in social networks. In *Social Network Data Analytics*, pages 115–148. Springer, 2011.

[6] Shaosheng Cao, Wei Lu, and Qiongkai Xu. Grarep: Learning graph representations with global structural information. In *Proceedings of the 24th ACM International on Conference on Information and Knowledge Management (CIKM)*, pages 891–900. ACM, 2015.

[7] Shaosheng Cao, Wei Lu, and Qiongkai Xu. Deep neural networks for learning graph representations. In *Proceedings of the Thirtieth AAAI Conference on Artificial Intelligence (AAAI)*, pages 1145–1152. AAAI Press, 2016.

[8] Shiyu Chang, Wei Han, Jiliang Tang, Guo-Jun Qi, Charu C Aggarwal, and Thomas S Huang. Heterogeneous network embedding via deep architectures. In *Proceedings of the 21th ACM SIGKDD International Conference on Knowledge Discovery and Data Mining (KDD)*, pages 119–128. ACM, 2015.

[9] Jifan Chen, Qi Zhang, and Xuanjing Huang. Incorporate group information to enhance network embedding. In *Proceedings of the 25th ACM International on Conference on Information and Knowledge Management (CIKM)*, pages 1901–1904. ACM, 2016.

[10] Yuxiao Dong, Nitesh V Chawla, and Ananthram Swami. metapath2vec: Scalable representation learning for heterogeneous networks. In *Proceedings of the 23rd ACM SIGKDD International Conference on Knowledge Discovery and Data Mining*, pages 135–144. ACM, 2017.

[11] Aditya Grover and Jure Leskovec. node2vec: Scalable feature learning for networks. In *Proceedings of the 22nd ACM SIGKDD International Conference on Knowledge Discovery and Data Mining (KDD)*, pages 855–864. ACM, 2016.

[12] Keith Henderson, Brian Gallagher, Lei Li, Leman Akoglu, Tina Eliassi-Rad, Hanghang Tong, and Christos Faloutsos. It's who you know: Graph mining using recursive structural features. In *Proceedings of the 17th ACM SIGKDD International Conference on Knowledge Discovery and Data Mining (KDD)*, pages 663–671. ACM, 2011.

[13] Xiao Huang, Jundong Li, and Xia Hu. Accelerated attributed network embedding. In *SDM*, 2017.

[14] Xiao Huang, Jundong Li, and Xia Hu. Label informed attributed network embedding. In *Proceedings of 10th ACM International Conference on Web Search and Data Mining (WSDM)*, 2017.

[15] Jure Leskovec, Jon Kleinberg, and Christos Faloutsos. Graphs over time: densification laws, shrinking diameters and possible explanations. In *Proceedings of the Eleventh ACM SIGKDD International Conference on Knowledge Discovery in Data Mining (KDD)*, pages 177–187. ACM, 2005.

[16] Omer Levy and Yoav Goldberg. Neural word embedding as implicit matrix factorization. In *Advances in Neural Information Processing Systems (NIPS)*, pages 2177–2185, 2014.

[17] David Liben-Nowell and Jon Kleinberg. The link-prediction problem for social networks. *Journal of the Association for Information Science and Technology*, 58(7):1019–1031, 2007.

[18] Laurens van der Maaten and Geoffrey Hinton. Visualizing data using t-sne. *Journal of Machine Learning Research*, 9(Nov):2579–2605, 2008.

[19] Tomas Mikolov, Kai Chen, Greg Corrado, and Jeffrey Dean. Efficient estimation of word representations in vector space. *arXiv preprint arXiv:1301.3781*, 2013.

[20] Tomas Mikolov, Ilya Sutskever, Kai Chen, Greg S Corrado, and Jeff Dean. Distributed representations of words and phrases and their compositionality. In *Advances in Neural Information Processing Systems (NIPS)*, pages 3111–3119, 2013.

[21] Annamalai Narayanan, Mahinthan Chandramohan, Lihui Chen, Yang Liu, and Santhoshkumar Saminathan. subgraph2vec: Learning distributed representations of rooted sub-graphs from large graphs. *arXiv preprint arXiv:1606.08928*, 2016.

[22] Nagarajan Natarajan and Inderjit S Dhillon. Inductive matrix completion for predicting gene–disease associations. *Bioinformatics*, 30(12):i60–i68, 2014.

[23] Mark EJ Newman. Modularity and community structure in networks. *Proceedings of the National Academy of Sciences*, 103(23):8577–8582, 2006.

[24] Mingdong Ou, Peng Cui, Jian Pei, Ziwei Zhang, and Wenwu Zhu. Asymmetric transitivity preserving graph embedding. In *Proceedings of the 22nd ACM SIGKDD International Conference on Knowledge Discovery and Data Mining (KDD)*, pages 1105–1114. ACM, 2016.

[25] Bryan Perozzi, Rami Al-Rfou, and Steven Skiena. Deepwalk: Online learning of social representations. In *Proceedings of the 20th ACM*

SIGKDD International Conference on Knowledge Discovery and Data Mining (KDD), pages 701–710. ACM, 2014.

[26] Sam T Roweis and Lawrence K Saul. Nonlinear dimensionality reduction by locally linear embedding. *Science*, 290(5500):2323–2326, 2000.

[27] Satu Elisa Schaeffer. Graph clustering. *Computer Science Review*, 1(1):27–64, 2007.

[28] Blake Shaw and Tony Jebara. Structure preserving embedding. In *Proceedings of the 26th Annual International Conference on Machine Learning (ICML)*, pages 937–944. ACM, 2009.

[29] Jian Tang, Meng Qu, and Qiaozhu Mei. PTE: Predictive text embedding through large-scale heterogeneous text networks. In *Proceedings of the 21th ACM SIGKDD International Conference on Knowledge Discovery and Data Mining (KDD)*, pages 1165–1174. ACM, 2015.

[30] Jian Tang, Meng Qu, Mingzhe Wang, Ming Zhang, Jun Yan, and Qiaozhu Mei. Line: Large-scale information network embedding. In *Proceedings of the 24th International Conference on World Wide Web (WWW)*, pages 1067–1077. ACM, 2015.

[31] Lei Tang and Huan Liu. Leveraging social media networks for classification. *Data Mining and Knowledge Discovery*, 23(3):447–478, 2011.

[32] Hanghang Tong, B Aditya Prakash, Charalampos Tsourakakis, Tina Eliassi-Rad, Christos Faloutsos, and Duen Horng Chau. On the vulnerability of large graphs. In *IEEE International Conference on Data Mining (ICDM)*, pages 1091–1096. IEEE, 2010.

[33] Cunchao Tu, Weicheng Zhang, Zhiyuan Liu, and Maosong Sun. Max-margin DeepWalk: discriminative learning of network representation. In *Proceedings of the Twenty-Fifth International Joint Conference on Artificial Intelligence (IJCAI)*, pages 3889–3895, 2016.

[34] Daixin Wang, Peng Cui, and Wenwu Zhu. Structural deep network embedding. In *Proceedings of the 22nd ACM SIGKDD International Conference on Knowledge Discovery and Data Mining (KDD)*, pages 1225–1234. ACM, 2016.

[35] Suhang Wang, Jiliang Tang, Charu Aggarwal, Yi Chang, and Huan Liu. Signed network embedding in social media. In *SDM*, 2017.

[36] Xiao Wang, Peng Cui, Jing Wang, Jian Pei, Wenwu Zhu, and Shiqiang Yang. Community preserving network embedding. In *Proceedings of the Thirtieth AAAI Conference on Artificial Intelligence (AAAI)*, pages 203–209, 2017.

[37] Pinar Yanardag and SVN Vishwanathan. Deep graph kernels. In *Proceedings of the 21th ACM SIGKDD International Conference on Knowledge Discovery and Data Mining (KDD)*, pages 1365–1374. ACM, 2015.

[38] Cheng Yang, Zhiyuan Liu, Deli Zhao, Maosong Sun, and Edward Y Chang. Network representation learning with rich text information. In *Proceedings of the 24th International Joint Conference on Artificial Intelligence (IJCAI)*, pages 2111–2117, 2015.

[39] Zhilin Yang, William Cohen, and Ruslan Salakhudinov. Revisiting semi-supervised learning with graph embeddings. In *Proceedings of The 33rd International Conference on Machine Learning*, pages 40–48, 2016.

[40] Yuan Yao, Jiufeng Zhou, Lixin Han, Feng Xu, and Jian Lü. Comparing linkage graph and activity graph of online social networks. In *SocInfo*, pages 84–97. Springer, 2011.

[41] Shuhan Yuan, Xintao Wu, and Yang Xiang. SNE: Signed network embedding. In *Pacific-Asia Conference on Knowledge Discovery and Data Mining (PAKDD)*, pages 183–195. Springer, 2017.

[42] Chang Zhou, Yuqiong Liu, Xiaofei Liu, Zhongyi Liu, and Jun Gao. Scalable graph embedding for asymmetric proximity. In *Proceedings of the Thirtieth AAAI Conference on Artificial Intelligence (AAAI)*, pages 2942–2948, 2017.

7.6   Glossary

Graph embedding: Learn the embeddings/features of graph nodes.

Part II

General Feature Engineering Techniques

Chapter 8

Feature Selection and Evaluation

Yun Li and Tao Li

School of Computer Science, Nanjing University of Posts and Telecommunications, Nanjing, China

Jiangsu Key Laboratory of Big Data Security and Intelligent Processing, Nanjing University of Posts and Telecommunications, Nanjing, China

8.1   Introduction

Feature selection is one of the important tasks in machine learning and data mining. It is an important and frequently used technique for dimension reduction by removing irrelevant and redundant information from the data set to obtain an optimal feature subset [24, 45]. It is also a knowledge discovery tool for providing insights into the problems through the interpretation of the most relevant features. Feature selection research dates back to the 1960s. Hughes used a general parametric model to study the accuracy of a Bayesian classifier as a function of the number of features [32]. Since then the research in feature selection has been a challenging field and some researchers have doubted its computational feasibility, such as in the paper [47]. Despite the computationally challenging scenario, the research in this direction continued. As of 1997, several papers on variable and feature selection were published [7, 37], however, few papers dealt with data sets with more than 40 features [24]. Nowadays, it has enjoyed increased attention due to the massive growth of data across many scientific disciplines, such as in genomic analysis [33], text mining [19], to name a few. To deal with these data, feature selection faces some new challenges. So it is timely and significant to review the relevant topics of these emerging challenges and give some suggestions to the practitioners. The discussed challenges and topics are listed in Table 1.

Feature selection brings the immediate effects of speeding up a data mining algorithm, improving learning accuracy, and enhancing model comprehensibility. However, finding an optimal feature subset is usually intractable [37] and many problems related to feature selection have been shown to be NP-hard [8]. To efficiently solve this problem, two frameworks are proposed up to now. One is the search-based framework, and the other is the correlation-based framework [45]. For the former, the search strategy and evaluation criterion are two key components. The search strategy is about how to produce a candidate feature subset, and each candidate subset is evaluated and compared with the previous best one according to a certain evaluation criterion. The process of subset generation and evaluation is repeated until a given stopping criterion is satisfied. For the latter, the redundancy and relevance of features are calculated based on some correlation measure. The entire original feature set can then be divided into four basic disjoint subsets: (1) irrelevant features, (2) redundant feature, (3) weakly relevant but non-redundant features, and (4) strongly relevant features. An optimal feature selection algorithm should select non-redundant and strongly relevant features. When the best subset is selected, generally, it will be validated by prior knowledge or different tests via synthetic and/or real-world data sets. One of the most well-known data repositories is in UCI [20], which contains many kinds of data sets with different sizes of sample and dimensionality. Feature Selection @ ASU (http://featureselection.asu.edu) also provides many benchmark data sets and source codes for different feature selection algorithms. In addition, some microarray data, such as Leukemia [22], Prostate [57], Lung [2] and Colon [3], are often used to evaluate the performance of feature selection algorithms on the high-dimensionality small sample size (HDSSS) problem.

8.2   Feature Selection Frameworks

Many feature selection algorithms have been proposed over the past decades. These algorithms are either search-based or correlation-based. We

Table 8.1: Summary of latest topics for current feature selection research

Topics
Topic 1: Stable feature selection
Topic 2: Sparsity-based feature selection
Topic 3: Multi-sources feature selection
Topic 4: Distributed feature selection
Topic 5: Multi-view feature selection
Topic 6: Multi-label feature selection
Topic 7: Online feature selection
Topic 8: Privacy preserving feature selection
Topic 9: Adversarial feature selection

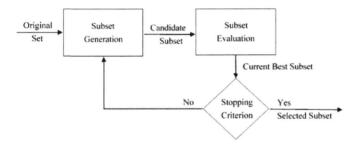

Figure 8.1: Search-based feature selection.

briefly introduce existing algorithms according to these two frameworks and show how feature selection works in each framework and what their strengths and weaknesses are.

8.2.1   Search-Based Feature Selection Framework

For the search-based framework, a typical feature selection process consists of three basic steps (shown in Fig. 1), namely, subset generation, subset evaluation, and stopping criterion. Subset generation aims to generate a candidate feature subset. Each candidate subset is evaluated and compared with the previous best one according to a certain evaluation criterion. If the newly generated subset is better than the previous one, it will be the latest best subset. The first two steps of search-based feature selection are repeated until a given stopping criterion is satisfied.

Figure 1 indicates that search-based feature selection includes two key factors: the evaluation criterion and the search strategy. According to the evaluation criterion, feature selection algorithms are categorized into filter, wrapper,

Table 8.2: Analysis of search-based feature selection algorithms

Models	Advantages	Disadvantages
Filter	Fast Scalable Independent of the classifier	Ignores interaction with the classifier
Wrapper	Simple Interacts with the classifier Models feature dependencies	Risk of overfitting Classifier dependent selection Computationally intensive
Hybrid (Embedded)	Interacts with the classifier Less complexity than Wrapper Models feature dependencies	Classifier dependent selection

and hybrid (embedded) models. Feature selection algorithms under the filter model rely on analyzing the general characteristics of data and evaluating features without involving any learning algorithms. Wrapper utilizes a predefined learning algorithm instead of an independent measure for subset evaluation. A typical hybrid algorithm makes use of both an independent measure and a learning algorithm to evaluate feature subsets. The analysis of advantages and disadvantages of filter, wrapper and hybrid models is summarized in Table 2. On the other hand, search strategies are usually categorized into complete, sequential, and random models. Complete search evaluates all feature subsets and guarantees to find the optimal result according to the evaluation criterion. Sequential search likes to add or remove features for the previous subset at a time. Random search starts with a randomly selected subset and injects randomness into the procedure of subsequent search. Some earlier studies have been categorized based on the evaluation criterion and the search strategy in [45].

Nowadays, as big data with high dimensionality are emerging, the filter model has attracted more attention than ever. Feature selection algorithms under the filter model rely on analyzing the general characteristics of data and evaluating features without involving any learning algorithms, therefore most of them do not have bias on specific learner models. Moreover, the filter model has a straightforward search strategy and feature evaluation criterion, then its structure is always simple. The advantages of the simple structure are evident: First, it is easy to design and easily understood by other researchers. Second, it is usually very fast [85], and is often appropriate for high-dimensional data.

8.2.2   Correlation-Based Feature Selection Framework

Besides search-based feature selection, another important framework for feature selection is based on the correlation analysis between features and classes. The correlation-based framework considers the feature-feature correlation and feature-class correlation. Generally, the correlation between features is known as feature redundancy, while the feature-class correlation is viewed as feature relevance. Then an entire feature set can be divided into four basic disjoint subsets: (1) irrelevant features, (2) redundant features, (3) weakly relevant but non-redundant features, and (4) strongly relevant features. An optimal feature selection algorithm should select non-redundant and strongly relevant features as shown in Fig. 2. The classical definitions for feature relevance and redundancy are introduced as follows. Let $\mathbf{F} = \{f_1, \cdots, f_d\}$ be a full set of features, C be a full set of class labels, P be the probability distribution, f_j be a feature, and $\mathbf{S}_j = \mathbf{F} - f_j$.

Definition 1 (Strong relevance) Given a class C, a feature f_j is strongly relevant iff

$$P(C|f_j, \mathbf{S}_j) \neq P(C|\mathbf{S}_j). \tag{8.1}$$

Definition 2 (Weak relevance) Given a class C, a feature f_j is weakly relevant iff

$$P(C|f_j, \mathbf{S}_j) = P(C|\mathbf{S}_j), \quad and$$

$$\exists \mathbf{S}'_j \subset \mathbf{S}_j, \quad such \quad that \quad P(C|f_j, \mathbf{S}'_j) \neq P(C|\mathbf{S}'_j). \tag{8.2}$$

Definition 3 (Irrelevance) Given a class C, a feature f_j is irrelevant iff

$$\forall \mathbf{S}'_j \subset \mathbf{S}_j, \quad P(C|f_j, \mathbf{S}'_j) = P(C|\mathbf{S}'_j). \tag{8.3}$$

Definition 4 (Redundancy) Let $\mathbf{F}$ be the current selected feature subset. A feature f_j is redundant iff it is weakly relevant and has a Markov blanket M_j within $\mathbf{F}$. M_j is said to be a Markov blanket for f_j iff

$$P(\mathbf{F} - M_j - \{f_j\}, C|f_j, M_j) = P(\mathbf{F} - M_j - \{f_j\}, C|M_j). \tag{8.4}$$

The correlation-based feature selection framework is shown in Fig. 3, which consists of two steps: relevance analysis determines the subset of relevant features, and redundancy analysis determines and eliminates the redundant features from relevant ones to produce the final subset. This framework has advantages over the search-based framework as it circumvents subset search and allows for an efficient and effective way of finding an approximate optimal subset. The most well-known feature selection algorithms under this framework are mRMR [52], Mitra's [48], CFS [27], and FCBF [79, 80].

In Section 8.2, we briefly summarized the earlier studies on feature selection. For more details about the basic knowledge of feature selection and the algorithms mentioned above, please refer to [14, 24, 25, 45, 85]. In the following section, we will focus on the recent advances in feature selection along with the newly emerged challenges in data processing.

Optimal Subset

Figure 8.2: Optimal subset for correlation-based feature selection.

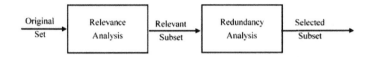

Figure 8.3: Correlation-based feature selection.

8.3 Advanced Topics for Feature Selection

Massive amounts of high-dimensional data bring about both opportunities and challenges to feature selection. Valid computational paradigms for new challenges are becoming increasingly important. Then along with the paradigms, many feature selection topics are emerging, such as feature selection for high-dimensional small sample size (HDSSS) data, feature selection for big data mining, feature selection for multi-label learning, feature selection with privacy preservation, and feature selection for streaming data mining. So we would like to survey these new ongoing topics and corresponding solutions in this section.

8.3.1 Stable Feature Selection

Problem: Various feature selection algorithms have been developed with a focus on improving classification accuracy while reducing dimensionality. Furthermore, another important issue about the stability of feature selection recently attracted much attention. *Stability* means the insensitivity of the result of a feature selection algorithm to variations of the training set [28, 46, 55]. When feature selection is adopted to identify the critical markers to explain some phenomena, the stability is very important. For instance, in microarray analysis, biologists are interested in finding a small number of features (genes or proteins) that explain the mechanisms driving different behaviors of microarray samples. A feature selection algorithm is often used to choose a subset of genes or proteins. However, the selection results will be largely different under variations in the training data, although most of results are similar to each other in terms of the classification performance [46]. Such instability dampens the confidence of domain experts in experimentally validating the selected features.

In consideration of the importance of stability in applications, several stable feature selection algorithms have been proposed, such as ensemble methods [1, 41, 55, 69], sample weighting [28, 78] and feature grouping [46, 77], to name a few. A comprehensive survey on stable feature selection can be found in [29]. We introduce these solutions in detail as follows.

Solution 1: Ensemble methods. Ensemble feature selection techniques use an idea similar to ensemble learning for classification: In the first step, a number of different feature selectors are produced, and in a final phase, the outputs of these separate selectors are aggregated and returned as the final (ensemble) result. Variation in the feature selectors can be achieved by various methods: choosing different feature selection techniques, instance-level perturbation (e.g., by removing or adding samples), feature-level perturbation (e.g., by adding noise to features), stochasticity in the feature selector, Bayesian model averaging, or combinations of these techniques. Aggregating different feature selection results can be done by weighted voting, e.g., in the case of deriving a consensus feature ranking, or by counting the most frequently selected features in the case of deriving a consensus feature subset [55].

In this paper, we present the ensemble feature weighting as an example and the framework is shown in Figure 8.4. The bootstrap-based strategy is used to train base feature selectors on m different bootstrap subsets of the original training set D. Ensemble feature weighting results are achieved by averaging the obtained outputs $\mathbf{w}_{D(\mathbf{r}_t)}$ ($t = 1, \cdots, m$) from the base feature selectors. The theoretical analysis and experimental results about the stability of ensemble feature weighting is presented in our work [42, 43].

Solution 2: Sample weighting. The main idea of this solution is to assign different weights to each sample in the training set, and the weight depends on the sample's influence on feature relevance estimation. Then it provides a weighted training set to train the feature selection method. The key point in this solution is how to determine the sample influence on feature relevance. The influence is always measured by the samples' view or local profile of feature relevance. The basic idea behind the local profile is that the central mass region containing most of the instances is clearly more important in deciding the aggregate feature weight than the outlying region with a couple of outliers. Following the ideas of importance sampling, instances with higher outlying degrees from the central mass region should be assigned lower instance weights, which leads to reducing the variance of feature weighting under training data variations. If a sample shows a noticeably distinct local profile from other samples, its absence or presence in the training data will substantially affect the feature selection result. In order to improve feature selection stability, samples

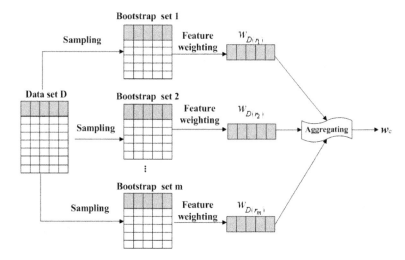

Figure 8.4: Ensemble feature weighting.

with remote local profiles need to be weighted differently from other samples. In [28, 78], the local profile of feature relevance for a given sample is measured based on the hypothesis margin; then a margin-based sample weighting algorithm is proposed to assign a weight to each sample according to the remote degree of its local profile. In [28, 78], for a sample $\mathbf{x}_i$, its hypothesis margin is always determined by the distance among $\mathbf{x}_i$, its nearest neighbor with same class label and its nearest neighbor with different class label. An intuitive interpretation of the hypothesis margin is a measure of the proportion of the features in $\mathbf{x}_i$ that can be corrupted by noise (or how much $\mathbf{x}_i$ can "move" in the feature space) before $\mathbf{x}_i$ is misclassified [12]. Of course, the local profile of a sample can be calculated using other measures, and it is an ongoing research.

Solution 3: Feature grouping. This is motivated by a key observation that intrinsic feature groups (or groups of correlated features) commonly exist in high-dimensional data, and such groups are resistant to the variations of training samples. Then, it is natural to select stable features through determining the features groups. Usually, we can approximate intrinsic feature groups by a set of consensus feature groups, and perform feature selection in the transformed feature space described by a consensus feature group. Generally, the (ensemble) clustering algorithm can be adopted to identify the consensus feature groups. For example, DRAGS is proposed in [77] to identify dense feature groups based on kernel density estimation, and treat features in each dense group as a coherent entity for feature selection. Another feature grouping method is introduced in [46] based on ensemble idea, which has two essential steps in identifying consensus feature groups:

Step 1. Create an ensemble of feature grouping results.

Step 2. Aggregate the ensemble into a single set of consensus feature groups.

In Step 1, the DGF (Dense Group Finder) in the DRAGS algorithm is considered as the base algorithm for identifying feature groups, and is applied on a number of bootstrapped training sets from a given training set. The result of this step is an ensemble of feature groupings. In Step 2, a given ensemble of feature groupings is aggregated into a final set of consensus groups. In this way, the aggregation strategy gets improved results by exploiting the strength of instance-based ensemble clustering and cluster-based ensemble clustering.

Discussion: For the solutions introduced above, Solution 1 and Solution 2 utilize the label information; then they are supervised stable feature selection solutions. Solution 3 does not rely on the label information, it belongs to unsupervised learning. One future work for stable feature selection is to combine supervised methods with unsupervised ones to obtain semi-supervised stable feature selection methods. We also observe that ensemble is a widely adopted idea to improve the stability of feature selection, such as in Solution 1 and Solution 3. However, the ensemble strategies used in Solution 1 and Solution 3 are borrowed from classification or clustering ensembles. Specific ensemble strategies for stable feature selection should be proposed in the future. Lastly, for all the aforementioned stable feature selection solutions; stability validation mainly depends on the experiment, the insight of feature selection stability is not explored completely. Although we have done some primary theoretical work on stable feature weighting in [43], the stability of feature ranking and feature subset selection is not investigated. As a result, theoretical analysis of stable feature selection still needs more attention.

8.3.2 Sparsity-Based Feature Selection

Problem: For the HDSSS data, the dimensionality is extremely high, while the sample size is very small. Sparsity-based feature selection is an efficient tool to select features from HDSSS data. The basic idea of sparsity-based feature selection is to impose a sparse penalty to select discriminative features. The L1-norm (namely Lasso, least absolution shrinkage and selection operator) [64] is effectively implemented to make the learning model both sparse and interpretable. Feature selection with L1-norm has been fully analyzed in [50]. However, Lasso tends to select only one of the pairwise correlated features and cannot induce the group effect. Then the Lasso should be largely improved.

Solution 1: In order to remedy the deficiency of Lasso and due to the importance of structural information, such as group, recently a general definition of the structured sparsity-inducing norm was proposed to incorporate the prior knowledge or structural constraints to find the suitable linear features [34]. Group Lasso [81] and elastic net [91], even the tree-guided group Lasso [36] are under the setting of structured sparsity-inducing norm. A very popular and successful approach to learn linear classifiers $\mathbf{w} = \{w_1, \cdots, w_d\}$ with structured features is to minimize a regularized empirical loss. For a given data set $D = \{\mathbf{X}, \mathbf{Y}\} = \{\mathbf{x}_i, y_i\}_{i=1}^{n}$, we choose a predictor $\mathbf{w}$ by minimizing the following empirical loss with regularized term,

$$min_{\mathbf{w}} \frac{1}{n} \sum_{i=1}^{n} L(\mathbf{w}^T \mathbf{x}_i, y_i) + \gamma \mathcal{R}(\mathbf{w}, U) \qquad (8.5)$$

where $L(.)$ is the loss function. Popular choices of $L(.)$ are least squares, hinge and logistic loss. $\mathcal{R}(.)$ is a regularization term, and γ is the regularization parameter controlling the trade-off between the $L(.)$ and the regularization. U denotes the structure of features, which includes group structure, tree structure, and graph structure. The value of elements in the learned classifier $\mathbf{w}$ can be equal to zero. Since each element in $\mathbf{w}$ corresponds to one feature, such as w_j corresponds to feature f_j, $(j = 1, \cdots, d)$, feature selection then chooses the features that correspond to elements with nonzero value in $\mathbf{w}$. The detailed summary for group structure, tree structure, and graph structure information used in the sparsity-based feature selection are presented in [62].

Solution 2: Besides the sparsity-based feature selection embedded structure information, another notable advance is the implementation of safe feature screening before sparsity-based feature selection. The safe feature screening intrinsically belongs to feature selection. For large-scale problems, solving the L1 regularized sparsity with higher accuracy remains challenging. One promising solution is first to discard ("screening") the "inactive" features. This would result in a reduced feature matrix for sparsity-based feature selection, and save the computational cost and memory size. A fast and effective sparse logistic regression screening rule (Slores) to identify the "inactive" features is proposed in [68]. The proposed screening rule detects "inactive" features by estimating an upper bound of the inner product between each feature vector and the "dual optimal solution" of the L1 regularized logistic regression. The safe screening rule has been applied to multi-task feature learning [65].

Discussion: The sparsity-based feature selection has gained much attention in machine learning and statistics. For more details about sparsity-based feature selection, please refer to the latest survey [40,62]. The sparsity strategy is also adopted in many other feature selection topics, such as online feature selection described below.

8.3.3   Multi-Source Feature Selection

Problem: The small sample size in the HDSSS problem has negative influence on the reliability of statistical analysis. An alternative way to address this issue is to utilize additional information sources to enhance our understanding of the data in hand, which leads to multi-source feature selection. How to extract and represent useful knowledge for feature selection from different sources, then obtain the uniform result, is one key problem in multi-source feature selection. As summarized in [85] and [86], the knowledge used in feature selection can usually be categorized into two kinds: the knowledge about

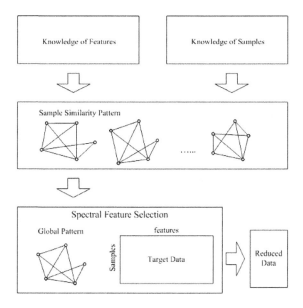

Figure 8.5: The framework for multi-source spectral feature selection.

features and the knowledge about samples. The former usually contains information about the properties of features or their relationships, and the latter usually contains sample categories or their similarity.

Solution 1: One framework for multi-source feature selection introduced in [85] is shown in Figure 8.5 where heterogeneous knowledge is commonly represented by similarity among samples via conversion operation, and the spectral feature selection algorithm is applied. The framework can be summarized as follows:

(1) Knowledge conversion. The conversion operator is adopted to extract a local specification of sample similarity matrix for each knowledge source.

(2) Knowledge integration. The multiple local sample similarity matrices are linearly combined to obtain a global similarity matrix.

(3) Feature selection. A spectral feature selection algorithm is performed on the obtained global similarity matrix.

Note that the different knowledge sources need different conversion operations. For example, if the similarity among features is given, then the feature covariance can be constructed and used in calculating the pairwise sample similarity via Mahalanobis distance [85].

Solution 2: The above framework depends on combining a local sample similarity matrix and a spectral feature selection algorithm has to be used, which is not flexible for the choice of other feature selection algorithms in handling small sample data. Another general framework, KOFS, is presented

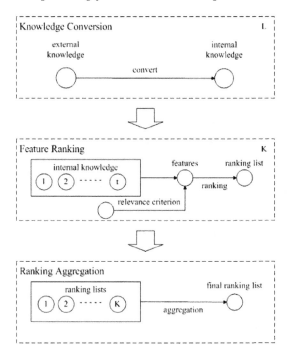

Figure 8.6: The framework of KOFS.

in [86] to address this limitation through combining the local feature selection results from different knowledge sources. KOFS consists of three components described below and is shown in Figure 6.

(1) Knowledge conversion. Transform different types of human or external knowledge into certain types of internal knowledge that can be used by feature selection algorithms.

(2) Feature ranking. Rank the features based on the internal knowledge and some given criterion. And for multiple knowledge, we can obtain several feature ranking results.

(3) Rank aggregation. Combine the multiple feature ranking results to generate the final ranking.

Discussion: Multi-source feature selection aims to utilize various knowledge sources to advance feature selection research on the HDSSS problems. The key problem for multi-source feature selection is knowledge conversion. We should convert the heterogeneous knowledge from different sources into samples or features knowledge that can be utilized by a feature selection method. Then the knowledge conversion depends on the knowledge source and the feature selection algorithm. On the other hand, the usefulness of knowledge sources for feature selection and the combination of feature selection result from different sources should be discussed.

8.3.4 Distributed Feature Selection

Given a large-scale data set containing a huge number of samples and features, the scalability of a feature selection algorithm becomes extremely important. However, most existing feature selection algorithms are proposed to deal with data sets whose sizes are under several gigabytes. In order to improve the scalability of existing feature selection methods for large-scale data sets, the feature selection is always performed in a distributed manner. It has been shown in [11] that any operation fitting the Statistical Query model can be computed in parallel based on data partitioning. Studies also showed that when the data size is large enough, parallelization based on data partitioning can result in linear speedup as computing resources increase [11].

Problem 1: When the data are located at a central database, how do we implement the distributed feature selection?

Solution: For a central data repository, efficient distributed programming models and protocols, such as MPI [59] and Google's Map-Reduce [15], are resorted. These models help implement distributed feature selection on high-performance computer grids or clusters. In general, feature selection can be parallelized in four steps as follows: (1) decompose the feature selection process into summation forms over training samples, (2) divide the data and store data partitions on nodes of the cluster, (3) compute local feature selection results in parallel on nodes of the cluster, and (4) calculate the final feature selection result by integrating the local results.

For example, spectral feature selection is parallelized on MPI as described in [88]. In addition, a novel large-scale feature selection algorithm is proposed in [87]. The algorithm chooses features by evaluating their abilities to explain data variances. The algorithm can read data in distributed form and perform parallel feature selection in both symmetric multiprocessing mode and massively parallel processing mode. The algorithm has been developed as SAS High-Performance Analytics procedure.

Problem 2: On the other hand, data are not located at a central repository, but rather distributed across a large number of nodes in a network. The next generation of Peer-to-Peer (P2P) networks provides an example. The existing feature selection algorithms cannot be directly executed under these scenarios. Therefore analysis of data in such networks will require the development of another type of distributed feature selection algorithm capable of working in such large-scale distributed environments.

Solution: In [13], a distributed feature selection algorithm on a P2P network is introduced. The proposed P2P feature selection algorithm (PAFS) incorporates three popular feature selection criteria: misclassification gain, gini index and entropy measurement. As a first step, these measurements are evaluated in a P2P network without any data centralization. Then the algorithm works based on local interactions among participating peers. The algorithm is provably correct in the sense that it converges to the correct result compared to centralization. And the proposed algorithm has low communication overhead.

Discussion: When data are distributed across a large number of nodes in a network, a distributed feature selection algorithm has to enable an information exchange and fusion mechanism to ensure that all distributed sites (or information sources) can work together to achieve a global optimization goal [71]. Local feature selection and correlations are the key steps to ensure that the results discovered from multiple information sources can be consolidated to meet the global objective. For the current distributed feature selection, the data in each node or peer have the same set of features. However, more studies are needed in distributed feature selection when the data in different nodes may have different feature representations.

8.3.5   Multi-View Feature Selection

Problem: In the era of big data, we can easily access information from different sources. For example, in a medical scenario, measurements from a series of medical examinations are documented for each subject, including clinical, imaging, immunologic, serologic, and cognitive measures. These measurements are obtained from multiple sources, and each measurement is a view of the subject. It is desirable to combine all these measurements for multi-view learning in an effective way. However, some measurements are irrelevant or noisy, even conflicting, which is unfavorable for multi-view learning. To address this issue, feature selection should be incorporated into the process of multi-view learning.

Solutions: Three strategies of multi-view feature selection are summarized in [9]: (1) concatenate features from all views in the input space, then a traditional feature selection method is adopted; (2) convert multiple views into a tensor and directly perform feature selection in the tensor product space; (3) efficiently conduct feature selection in the input space while effectively leveraging relationships between the original data and its reconstruction in the tensor product space. Methods (1) and (2) ignore the intrinsic properties of raw multi-view features and hidden relationships between the original data and its reconstruction. The problem of feature selection in the tensor product space is formulated as an integer quadratic programming problem in [58]. However, this method is limited to the interaction between two views and is hard to extend to many views, since it directly selects features in the tensor product space resulting in the curse of dimensionality. Reference [63] studies multi-view feature selection in the unsupervised setting. Taking into account the latent interactions among views in [9], the tensor product is used to organize multi-view features, and [9] studies the problem of multi-view feature selection based on SVM-RFE [26] and tensor techniques.

Discussion: In the era of big data, multi-view learning is a useful paradigm to deal with heterogeneous data. This multi-view feature selection is different from the multi-source feature selection above. If multi-source feature selection is adopted, feature selection is always conducted independently for each resource and the results from multi-source are combined to obtain the final result. This feature selection paradigm always assumes each source is sufficient to learn the target concept and ignore the relationship between sources. However, in multi-view learning, individual views can often provide complementary information to each other, and does not assume each view is sufficient to learn the target concept, which leads to improved performance in real-world applications. Moreover, the relationship between views is considered in multi-view learning, and tensor product space is always used to represent this relationship. In summary, multi-source feature selection is a special case of multi-view feature selection. On the other hand, The multi-view learning is also relevant with cross-domain learning, i.e., to transfer the already learned knowledge from a source domain to a target domain. Then multi-view feature selection can be applied to transfer learning by taking advantage of the typically available multiple views of the data in domains [18].

8.3.6 Multi-Label Feature Selection

Problem: In traditional feature selection, the training sample always has a unique label. However, in many real applications, each instance can be associated with more than one class label. Then feature selection for multi-label data also attracts much attention.

Solution 1: The simplest way to implement feature selection on a multi-label data set is based on transformation, i.e., change the multi-label data set into a single-label one and a traditional feature selection method is used. There are a lot of strategies to transform a multi-label data set into a single-label one, such as:

(1) Simple transformation. Its main idea is to convert a multi-label data set into a single-label one by some label selection operator, such as selecting the most frequent label in the data set (select-max), the least frequent label (select-min), a random label (select-random), or simply discarding every multi-label example (select-ignore).

(2) Copy transformation. This transformation copies each multi-label instance B times, where B is the number of labels associated with that instance. Each copied instance is then assigned one distinct single label from the original B-label set. A slight improvement of the copy transformation is the weighting copy, which assigns a weight $\frac{1}{B}$ to each copied instance.

(3) Label Powerset transformation. Label powerset (LP) considers each subset of labels that exists in the multi-label training data set as one label.

(4) Binary Relevance transformation. Binary relevance (BR) creates a binary training set for each label in the original data set. Besides the classic transformations above, a new transformation based on the entropy measure is

presented in [10], where an instance is assigned to a label according to a certain probability. Then, after the data transformation step, many single-label feature selection techniques can be used. For example, information gain [54], χ^2 statistic [35], and Orthogonal Centroid Feature Selection (OCFS) [73].

Solution 2: The multi-label feature selection methods based on transformation usually suffer from the deficiency that the correlation among the class labels is not taken into account. Furthermore, when there are lots of class labels, the obtained single-label data sets may be too large. Then each imbalanced single-label data set will face the problems of sparse training samples and imbalanced class distribution. So it is desirable to propose feature selection algorithms to deal directly with multi-label data. Most current methods are adaptations of well-known single-label feature selection algorithms. For example, in [38], the well-known algorithm FCBF (Fast Correlation-Based Filter) [79,80] is extended to handle multi-label data through a graphical model to represent the relationships among labels and features. Another example is presented in [51], where a multi-label feature selection approach, gMLC, is designed for graph classification. It is based on an evaluation criterion to estimate the dependence between subgraph features and multiple labels of graphs. Then a branch-and-bound algorithm is proposed to efficiently search for optimal subgraph features by judiciously pruning the subgraph search space using multiple labels. Moreover, a multi-label feature selection method is also described in [23], which is based on the minimization of correlation regularized loss of label ranking [17]. In our recent work [74], we adopted the graph model to capture the label correlation, and proposed a multi-label feature selection algorithm based on graph and large margin theory.

Discussion: Most current multi-label feature selection methods are the extension of traditional single-label feature selection approaches. A future research is to design multi-label feature selection that can directly deal with a multi-label data set without any transformation and sufficiently consider the relationship between labels.

8.3.7   Online Feature Selection

Problem 1: All feature selection methods introduced above assume that all features are known in advance. Now another interesting scenario should be considered where candidate features are sequentially presented to the classifier. In this scenario, the candidate features are generated dynamically and the size of features is unknown. This kind of feature selection for streaming features is also called online feature selection. Online feature selection is significant in many applications. For example, the famous microblogging website Twitter produces more than 250 million tweets per day and many new words (features) are generated such as abbreviations. When we like to select features for tweets, it is impossible to wait until all features have been generated, thus it could be more preferable to use online feature selection.

Solution: Up to now, some online feature selection methods have been proposed in [53, 56, 62, 70, 76, 89]. In general, an online feature selection algorithm will perform the following steps [62]:

Step 1: Generate a new feature.

Step 2: Determine whether the newly generated feature should be added to the currently selected feature subset.

Step 3: Determine whether some features should be removed from the currently selected feature subset when the new feature is added.

Step 4: Repeat Step 1 to Step 3.

Note that different algorithms may have different implementations for Step 2 and Step 3. Step 3 is optional and some online feature selection algorithms only implement Step 2. The correlation model introduced in Section 8.2 is always used in online feature selection to calculate the new feature's relevance and redundancy, which will determine the new feature's inclusion, and the selected feature's deletion.

The general online feature selection algorithms often assume features arrive one by one at a time, however, in some practical applications such as image analysis and email spam filtering, features may arrive in groups. Then the online feature selection should consider the group information. A novel selection approach is proposed in [67] to solve the online group feature selection problem. The proposed approach consists of two stages: online intra-group selection and online inter-group selection. In the intra-group selection, spectral analysis is used to select discriminative features in each group when it arrives. In the inter-group selection, Lasso is adopted to select a globally optimal subset of features. This two-stage procedure continues until no more features arrive or some predefined stopping conditions are met.

Problem 2: On the other hand, we also encounter another scenario in which training instances arrive sequentially, while all features are available before the selection process. Online feature selection in this scenario aims to select a small and fixed number of features in an online learning fashion.

Solution: Taking this problem into account, an approach for this online feature selection is proposed in [66]. When the learner receives a training instance at each time, the classifier will immediately make a prediction of the instance. When the training instance is misclassified, the classifier is first updated by online gradient descent and then projected to an L_2 ball to ensure that the norm of the classifier is bounded. If the resulting classifier has more than K non-zero elements in a weight vector (K is the fixed number of selected features), the algorithm will take a truncate technique, simply keeping the K elements in the classifier with the largest absolute weights.

Problem 3: A new problem for online feature selection is to learn from doubly streaming data where both data volume and feature space increase over time. This problem is always referred to as mining trapezoidal data streams, to which existing online learning, online feature selection and streaming feature selection algorithms are inapplicable.

Solution: A new Sparse Trapezoidal Streaming Data mining algorithm (STSD) that combines online learning and online feature selection to enable learning trapezoidal data streams with infinite training instances and features is introduced in [83]. Specifically, when new training instances carrying new features arrive, the classifier updates the existing features by following the passive-aggressive update rule used in online learning and updates the new features with the structural risk minimization principle. Feature sparsity is also introduced using the projected truncation techniques. The first challenge is to update the classifier with an augmenting feature space. The classifier update strategy is able to learn from new features. The second challenge is to build a feature selection method to achieve a sparse but efficient model, i.e., a sparsity strategy.

The update strategy: On each round, when a training instance is received, the classifier will immediately predict the instance and compute an instantaneous loss of the prediction using some loss function, such as hinge loss. In order to make the classifier learn from new features, the weight vector of the classifier is divided into two parts, one part represents a projection of the original feature space, the other denotes new features that are in the current round but not in the last round. If the prediction is correct, there is not update of the current weight vector. Otherwise, the constrained optimization problem is obtained as the solution to the update strategy. On the one hand, the constrained problem forces the classifier to predict correctly. On the other hand, the constrained problem forces the projection of feature space close to the weight vector obtained in last round with the aim to inherit information and let the weights of new features be small to minimize structural risk and avoid overfitting.

The sparsity strategy: The algorithm uses the truncate technique by introducing a parameter to control the proportion of features. Besides, the algorithm introduces a projection step by projecting the weight vector to an L_1 ball because one single truncation step does not work well.

Discussion: In the big data era, the streaming feature and sample will be encountered in many applications, such as financial analysis, online trading, medical testing, and so on. Static feature selection methods cannot adapt to the characteristics of dynamic data streams, such as continuity, variability, rapidity, and infinity, and can easily lead to the loss of useful information. Therefore, effective theoretical and technical frameworks are needed to support online feature selection. Online feature selection simultaneously considering the streaming feature and streaming sample is an active research topic.

8.3.8   Privacy-Preserving Feature Selection

Problem 1: The goal of privacy-preserving feature selection is to find a feature subset for which a classifier will minimize the classification error in the selected feature space, and the sum of the privacy degree of features in the selected subset will not go beyond the predefined threshold [4]. There exist two key issues in this kind of privacy-preserving feature selection, one is the determination of the privacy degree for each feature and the other is is the optimization of the evaluation criterion with the privacy constraint.

Solution: A privacy-preserving feature selection method was proposed and applied in face detection in [4], which is based on a classification error criterion. This criterion for privacy preservation can be described as follows,

Let us have a training set $D = \{\mathbf{x}_i, y_i\}_{i=1}^n$, and a privacy degree associated with each feature is $\{\omega_a\}_{a=1}^d$. Our goal is to find a feature subset $\mathbf{f} = \{f_1, \cdots, f_\nu\}$ subject to a classifier $\Bbbk(\mathbf{x}(\mathbf{f}))$ that will minimize the classification error $(\Bbbk(\mathbf{x}_i(\mathbf{f})) - y_i)(i = 1, \cdots, n)$, where $\mathbf{x}(\mathbf{f})$ denotes a sample $\mathbf{x}$ that uses only the features in the set $\mathbf{f}$. Formally, we need to minimize:

$$min_\Bbbk \sum_{i=1}^n (\Bbbk(\mathbf{x}_i(\mathbf{f})) - y_i)^2, \qquad (8.6)$$

s. t.

$$\sum_{f_j \in \mathbf{f}} \omega_j \leq \Lambda,$$

where Λ is the threshold for the total feature privacy degree.

Based on the above evaluation criterion, a privacy-preserving feature selection method was proposed and applied to face detection in [4]. The one key problem in this feature selection topic is the determination of the privacy degree for each feature. The authors found it is useful to use the PCA spectrum to measure the amount of privacy information. And specifically, the PCA space of all the face images in the database is computed and maps all the data to that space without reducing dimensionality. Then the privacy degree of all features $\{\omega_a\}_{a=1}^d$ is set to the eigenvalues associated with each dimension in the PCA space. Another issue is the optimization of evaluation criterion with privacy constraints. In the paper, they use a variant of the gentleBoost algorithm [21] to find a greedy solution to the constrained objective function above. Specifically, they use gentleBoost with "stumps" as the weak classifiers where each "stump" works on only one feature. In each iteration they can use features that were already selected or those that, if added, them will not increase the total weight of the selected features beyond the privacy threshold Λ.

Discussion: One key problem in privacy-preserving feature selection above is the determination of the feature privacy degree, which is often determined by domain knowledge or experts. In this aspect, it is similar to cost-sensitive feature selection where the cost of each feature also should be given by domain knowledge or experts [90]. On the other hand, the evaluation criterion of privacy-preserving feature selection described above is the classification error. Of course, other criteria introduced in Section 8.2 can also be used.

Problem 2: The above privacy-preserving feature selection focuses on feature privacy and produces the optimal feature subset with a total privacy degree less than a threshold. There still exists another kind of privacy-preserving feature selection that focuses on the sample privacy.

Solution: The widely used privacy model for this kind of privacy preservation is differential privacy as in Definition 5 [16].

Definition 5. A randomized mechanism A provides ε-*differential privacy*, if, for all data sets D and D' which differ by at most one element, and for all output subsets $S_u \subseteq Range(A)$,

$$Pr[A(D) \in S_u] \leq \exp(\varepsilon) \times Pr[A(D') \in S_u]. \qquad (8.7)$$

Then the algorithm A is said to satisfy differential privacy. The probability Pr is taken over the coin tosses of A, and $Range(A)$ denotes the output range of A. The privacy parameter ε measures the disclosure. Differential privacy means that an adversary, who knows all but one entry of the data set, cannot gain much additional information about this entry by observing the output of the algorithm.

Based on the privacy model above, two privacy-preserving feature selection algorithms are proposed in our recent work [44, 75]. These algorithms are based on output perturbation and objective perturbation, respectively. The output perturbation means adding noise to the feature selection result, and the noise density depends on the sensitivity of the feature selection algorithm. In the paper [75], the sensitivity of local learning–based feature selection with a logistic loss function is analyzed and the proof for meeting ε differential privacy is also given. Objective perturbation aims to enforce the perturbation on the evaluation function of feature selection, and the corresponding privacy-preserving local learning–based feature selection with the associated differential privacy proof is also presented in [44].

Discussion: Certainly, we can enforce privacy-preserving constraints to other traditional feature selection algorithms besides local learning–based feature selection [61]. Some current works focus on such feature selection algorithms whose outputs are feature weighting. On the other hand, it is also of interest to add privacy preservation to other feature selection algorithms whose outputs are feature rankings or feature subsets.

8.3.9 Adversarial Feature Selection

Pattern recognition and machine learning techniques have been increasingly applied to information security areas, such as spam, intrusion, and malware detection. Then we need to analyze the security of machine learning itself [5]. Correspondingly, adversarial machine learning is always mentioned. Adversarial machine learning is the design of machine learning algorithms that can resist some sophisticated attacks, and the study of the capabilities and limitations of attackers [31]. These sophisticated attacks include avoiding detection of attacks, causing benign input to be classified as attack input, launching focused or targeted attacks, or searching a classifier to find blind spots in the algorithm.

Problem: In the previous works focus on adversarial classification and clustering [6], only a few authors have considered the adversarial feature selection.

In fact, for adversarial tasks, feature selection can open the door for the adversary to evade the classification system and misclassify the adversary sample as a normal one [39].

Solution: Current adversarial feature selection works are concerned with two issues: attack and defense. To explore the vulnerability of some classical feature selection algorithms under attacks, [72] sheds light on the issue of whether feature selection may be beneficial or even counterproductive when training data are poisoned by intelligent attackers. It also provides a framework to investigate the robustness of popular feature selection methods, including Lasso, ridge regression and the elastic net, to carefully crafted attacks. Another issue discussed in [82] is to analyze the impact of feature selection results on classifier security against an evasion attack where the attacker's goal is to manipulate malicious data at test time to evade detection. The basic idea of evaluation criterion for this kind of adversarial feature selection is to select a feature subset that not only maximizes the generalization capability of the classifier, but also its security against evasion attacks. Then there are two terms in the criterion: generalization capability and security. The generalization capability of a classifier on a feature subset can be estimated using different performance measures as described in Section 8.2. As for the security term, the robustness against attack is always exploited, i.e., the average minimum number of modifications to a malicious sample to evade detection.

Discussion: Many attacks have been introduced in machine learning systems [5]. Currently, only part of particular attacks are considered in adversarial feature selection. So it is urgent to analyze the vulnerability of many classical feature selections under different attacks, and design robust feature selection algorithms against these attacks.

8.4   Future Work and Conclusion

In this section, we discuss some future work on feature selection.

First, the aim of feature selection is to choose an optimal feature subset. However, the outputs of some feature selection algorithms are feature rankings (weighting). Then it still needs to determine the subset from the ranking result. If the number of important features is known, this determination is very easy; we just need to choose the important features one by one from the ranking set until the number of features meets our requirement. Unfortunately, without any prior knowledge, the number of important features is unknown. The transformation of feature ranking to feature subset is still an open model selection issue in feature selection research.

Second, the research of feature selection closely follows the development of machine learning. When any new machine learning paradigms emerge, the corresponding feature selection topics also will be studied. For example, if

Table 8.3: Summary of properties related to current algorithms in each topic

	Scalability	Stability	Security
Topic 1: Stable feature selection		Y	
Topic 2: Sparsity-based feature selection	Y		
Topic 3: Multi-sources feature selection	Y		
Topic 4: Distributed feature selection	Y		
Topic 5: Multi-view feature selection	Y		
Topic 6: Multi-label feature selection	Y		
Topic 7: Privacy preserving feature selection			Y
Topic 8: Adversarial feature selection			Y
Topic 9: Online feature selection	Y		

adversarial machine learning is the current hot topic, then adversarial feature selection will be studied soon. On the other hand, if different machine learning paradigms are often combined to solve a special problem, then the combination of corresponding feature selection topics is also an interesting topic. For instance, we can study the integration of online feature selection and multi-label feature selection to handle streaming data with multi-labels.

Finally, traditional feature selection algorithms focus on classification or clustering performance, however, some other properties about feature selection deserve more attention, such as scalability, stability, and security, especially in the big data era. We summarize the different properties with respect to current algorithms for each topic in Table 8.3, and Y means current algorithms have this property. From the table, we can observe that most algorithms have one characteristic; the improvement of current feature selection algorithms to acquire other traits is an exciting research direction.

Since deep learning has attracted more attention in feature generation, we also want to discuss the relationship between deep learning and feature selection. Given large amounts of data, instead of designing a handcrafted feature representation, a deep learning algorithm tends to learn a good abstract representation for the current task with a series of nonlinear transformations [30]. So, with the rise of deep learning, it seems that you can do advanced machine learning without any feature selection. However, in some cases where the number of data points is not sufficiently large, deep learning should be combined with feature selection to obtain better learning performance because with a fixed number of instances, removing irrelevant features is equivalent to exponentially increasing the number of instances. So deep learning is expected to face challenges dealing with HDSSS data. Moreover, we give another example to describe the relationship between deep learning and feature selection. In heterogeneous multi-modal information fusion, each independent modality is characterized by a single feature group, and then these different modalities are sent to different branches of the multi-modal deep neural networks, yielding refined feature representations with multiple nonlinear transformations based upon the given original modalities. When all the feature groups are transformed by multi-modal deep neural networks, the outputs of the refined features extracted from the top layer of each branch are concatenated into a new feature vector. Then a feature selection algorithm is adopted to produce an optimal weight vector for this concatenation. According to this weight vector, the most relevant feature groups with respect to the current task are picked out. Finally, these selected features are used in the final recognition task [84]. On the other hand, feature selection is also an important tool for knowledge discovery and has merits on its own. In this case, our goal is to choose the key features rather than serving as a tool for data preprocessing, so we prefer feature selection to deep learning and keep the interpretability of original features. For instance, in microarray analysis, biologists are interested in finding a small number of features (genes or proteins) that explain the mechanisms driving different behaviors of microarray samples. A feature selection algorithm is often used to choose a subset of genes or proteins, while deep learning is not suitable.

Feature selection is an ever-evolving frontier in data mining, machine learning and statistics. Along with the fast development of machine learning, the scope of feature selection research and application are also broadened. In this chapter, we discusses several challenges brought by Big Data, HDSSS problems, multi-label data, privacy preserving, etc., And we selectively discussed some hot topics under these challenges. For each topic, after a brief analysis of the existing problem, the current research findings were summarized and followed by a short discussion. We then introduced some current applications of feature selection, such as bioinformatics, social media and multimedia retrieval. We also discussed some general issues and future work for feature selection. This review was done mostly based on our experience in feature selection of more than fifteen years and performing an automated text mining literature analysis on feature selection similar to [49] is part of our future work.

Bibliography

[1] T. Abeel, T. Helleputte, Y. Van de Peer, P. Dupont, and Y. Saeys. Robust biomarker identification for cancer diagnosis with ensemble feature selection methods. *Bioinformatics*, 26:392–398, 2010.

[2] A.Bhattacharjee, W. G. Richards, J. Staunton, C. Li, and S. Monti. Classification of human lung carcinomas by mRNA expression profiling reveals distinct adenocarcinoma subclasses. *Proceedings of the National Academy of Sciences of the United States of America*, 98:13790–13795, 2001.

[3] U. Alon, N. Barkai, D. A. Notterman, K. Gish, S. Ybarra, D. Mack, and A. J. Levine. Broad patterns of gene expression revealed by clustering analysis of tumor and normal colon cancer tissues probed by oligonucleotide arrays. In *Proceedings of the National Academy of Sciences of the United States of America*, pages 6745–6750, 1999.

[4] S. Avidan and M. Butman. Efficient methods for privacy preserving face detection. In *Advances in Neural Information Processing Systems*, pages 57–64, 2006.

[5] M. Barreno, B. Nelson, A. D. Joseph, and J. D. Tygar. The security of machine learning. *Machine Learning*, 81:121–148, 2010.

[6] B. Biggio, G. Fumera, and F. Roli. Security evaluation of pattern classifiers under attack. *IEEE Transactions on Knowledge and Data Engineering*, 26:984–996, 2014.

[7] A. Blum and P. Langley. Selection of relevant features and examples in machine learning. *Artificial Intelligence*, 1997.

[8] A. L. Blum and R. L. Rivest. Training a 3-node neural networks is NP-complete. *Neural Networks*, 5:117–127, 1992.

[9] B.K. Cao, L. F. He, X. N. Kong, P. S. Yu, Z. F. Hao, and A. B. Ragin. Tensor-based multi-view feature selection with applications to brain diseases. In *Proceedings of the 2014 International Conference on Data Mining*, pages 40–49, 2014.

[10] W. Z. Chen, J. Yan, B. Y. Zhang, Z. Chen, and Q. Yang. Document transformation for multi-label feature selection in text categorization. In *Proceedings of the 7th IEEE Conference on Data Mining*, pages 451–456, 2007.

[11] C. T. Chu, S. K. Kim, Y. A. Lin, Y. Y. Yu, G. Bradski, A. Ng, and K. Olukotun. Map-reduce for machine learning on multicore. In *Proceedings of Advances in Neural Information Processing Systems*, 2007.

[12] K. Crammer, R. G. Bachrach, A. Navot, and N. Tishby. Margin analysis of the LVQ algorithm. In *Proceedings of Advances in Neural Information Processing Systems*, pages 462–469, 2002.

[13] K. Das, K. Bhaduri, and H. Kargupta H. A local asynchronous distributed privacy preserving feature selection algorithm for large peer-to-peer networks. *Knowledge Information System*, 24:341–367, 2010.

[14] M. Dash and H. Liu. Feature selection for classification. *Intelligent Data Analysis*, 1:131–156, 1997.

[15] J. Dean and S. Ghemawat. MapReduce: Simplified data processing on large clusters. *Communications of the ACM*, 51:107–113, 2008.

[16] C. Dwork. Differential privacy. In *Proceedings of International Colloquium on Automata, Languages and Programming*, pages 1–12, 2006.

[17] A. Elisseeff and J. Weston. A kernel method for multi-labelled classification. In *Advances in Neural Information Processing Systems*, pages 681–687, 2001.

[18] Zheng Fang and Zhongfei (Mark) Zhang. Discriminative feature selection for multi-view cross-domain learning. In *Proceedings of ACM International Conference of Information and Knowledge Management*, pages 1321–1330, 2013.

[19] G. Forman. An extensive empirical study of feature selection metrics for text classification. *Journal of Machine Learning Research*, 3:1289–1305, 2003.

[20] A. Frank and A. Asuncion. UCI machine learning repository. In *http://archive.ics.uci.edu/ml*, 2010.

[21] J. Friedman, T. Hastie, and R. Tibshirani. Additive logistic regression: A statistical view of boosting. *Annals of Statistics*, 28, 1998.

[22] T. R. Golub, D. K. Slonim, P. Tamayo, C. Huard, and M. Gaasenbeek. Molecular classification of cancer: Class discovery and class prediction by gene expression monitoring. *Science*, 286:531–537, 1999.

[23] Q. Q. Gu, Z. H. Li, and J. W. Han. Correlated multi-label feature selection. In *Proceedings of the 20th ACM International Conference on Information and Knowledge Management*, pages 1087–1096, 2011.

[24] I. Guyon and A. Elisseeff. An introduction to variable and feature selection. *Journal of Machine Learning Research*, 31:1157–1182, 2003.

[25] I. Guyon, S. Gunn, M. Nikravesh, and L. Zadeh. *Feature Extraction, Foundations and Applications*. Springer, Physica-Verlag, New York, 2006.

[26] I. Guyon, J. Weston, S. Barnhill, and V. Vapnik. Gene selection for cancer classification using support vector machines. *Machine Learning*, 46:389–422, 2002.

[27] M. A. Hall. Correlation-based feature selection for discrete and numeric class machine learning. In *Proceedings of International Conference on Machine Learning*, pages 359–366, 2000.

[28] Y. Han and L. Yu. A variance reduction framework for stable feature selection. In *Proceedings of the International Conference on Data Mining*, pages 206–215, 2010.

[29] Z. Y. He and W. C. Yu. Stable feature selection for biomarker discovery. *Computational Biology and Chemistry*, 34:215–225, 2010.

[30] G. E. Hinton and R. R. Salakhutdinov. Reducing the dimensionality of data with neural networks. *Science*, 313:504–507, 2006.

[31] L. Huang, A. D. Joseph, B. Nelson, B. I. P. Rubinstein, and J. D. Tygar. Adversarial machine learning. In *Proceedings of 4th ACM Workshop on Artificial Intelligence and Security*, pages 43–58, 2011.

[32] G. F. Hughes. On the mean accuracy of statistical pattern recognizers. *IEEE Transactions on Information Theory*, 14:55–63, 1968.

[33] I. Inza, P. Larranaga, R. Blanco, and A. J. Cerrolaza. Filter versus wrapper gene selection approaches in DNA microarray domains. *Artificial Intelligence in Medicine*, 31:91–103, 2004.

[34] R. Jenatton, G. Obozinski, and F. Bach. Structured sparse principal component analysis. In *Proceedings of International Conference on Artificial Intelligence and Statistics*, 2010.

[35] G. V. Kass. An exploratory technique for investigating large quantities of categorical data. *Applied Statistics*, pages 119–127, 1980.

[36] S. Kim and E. P. Xing. Tree-guided group lasso for multi-task regression with structured sparsity. In *Proceedings of the 27th International Conference on Machine Learning*, 2010.

[37] R. Kohavi and G.H. John. Wrappers for feature subset selection. *Artificial Intelligence*, 97:273–324, 1997.

[38] G. Lastra, Oscar Luaces, Jose R. Quevedo, and Antonio Bahamonde. Graphical feature selection for multilabel classification tasks. In *Proceedings of the 10th International Conference on Advances in Intelligent Data Analysis*, pages 281–305, 2011.

[39] B. Li and Y. Vorobeychik. Feature cross-substitution in adversarial classification. In *Proceedings of Advances in Neural Information Processing Systems*, pages 2087–2095, 2014.

[40] J. D. Li, K. W. Cheng, S. H. Wang, F. Morstatter, R. P. Trevino, J. L. Tang, and H. Liu. Feature selection: A data perspective. *arXiv:1601.07996*, 3:1–73, 2016.

[41] Y. Li, S. Y. Gao, and S. C. Chen. Ensemble feature weighting based on local learning and diversity. In *AAAI Conference on Artificial Intelligence*, pages 1019–1025, 2012.

[42] Y. Li, S. S. Huang, S. C. Chen, and J. Si. Stable l2-regularized ensemble feature weighting. In *Proceedings of the 11th International Workshop on Multiple Classifier Systems*, pages 167–178, 2013.

[43] Y. Li, J. Si, G. J. Zhou, S. S. Huang, and S. C. Chen. Frel: A stable feature selection algorithm. *IEEE Transaction on Neural Networks and Learning Systems*, 26:1388–1402, 2015.

[44] Yun Li, Jun Yang, and Wei Ji. Local learning-based feature weighting with privacy preservation. *Neurocomputing*, 174:1107–1115, 2016.

[45] H. Liu and L. Yu. Toward integrating feature selection algorithms for classification and clustering. *IEEE Transactions on Knowledge and Data Engineering*, 17:494–502, 2005.

[46] S. Loscalzo, L. Yu, and C. Ding. Consensus group stable feature selection. In *Proceedings of ACM SIGKDD Conference on Knowledge Discovery and Data Mining*, pages 567–575, 2009.

[47] A. J. Miller. Selection of subsets of regression variables. *Journal of the Royal Statistical Society*, 147:389–425, 1984.

[48] P. Mitra, C. A. Murthy, and S. K. Pal. Unsupervised feature selection using feature similarity. *IEEE Transactions on Pattern Analysis and Machine Intelligence*, 24:301–312, 2002.

[49] Sérgio Moro, Paulo Cortez, and Paulo Rita. Business intelligence in banking: A literature analysis from 2002 to 2013 using text mining and latent Dirichlet allocation. *Expert Systems with Applications*, 42:1314–1324, 2015.

[50] A. Y. Ng. Feature selection, l1 vs. l2 regularization, and rotational invariance. In *Proceedings of International Conference on Machine Learning*, pages 78–85, 2004.

[51] X. N.Kong and P. S. Yu. GMLC: A multi-label feature selection framework for graph classification. *Knowledge Information Systems*, 31:281–305, 2012.

[52] H. C. Peng, F. H. Long, and C. Ding. Feature selection based on mutual information: Criteria of max-dependency, max-relevance, and min-redundancy. *IEEE Transactions on Pattern Analysis and Machine Intelligence*, 27:1226–1238, 2005.

[53] S. Perkins and J. Theiler. Online feature selection using grafting. In *Proceedings of International Conference on Machine Learning*, pages 592–599, 2003.

[54] J. R. Quinlan. Induction of decision trees. *Machine Learning*, 1:81–106, 1986.

[55] Y. Saeys, T. Abeel, and Y. Van de Peer. Robust feature selection using ensemble feature selection techniques. In *Proceedings of the 25th European Conference on Machine Learning and Knowledge Discovery in Databases*, pages 313–325, Banff, Canada, 2008.

[56] Debarka Sengupta, Sanghamitra Bandyopadhyay, and Debajyoti Sinha. A scoring scheme for online feature selection: Simulating model performance without retraining. *IEEE Transaction on Neural Networks and Learning Systems*, 28:405–414, 2017.

[57] D. Singh, P. G. Febbo, and K. Ross. Gene expression correlates of clinical prostate cancer behavior. *Cancer Cell*, 2:203–209, 2002.

[58] A. Smalter, J. Huan, and G. Lushington. Feature selection in the tensor product feature space. In *Proceedings of the 2009 International Conference on Data Mining*, pages 1004–1009, 2009.

[59] M. Snir, S. Otto, S. H. Lederman, D. Walker, and J. Dongarra. *MPI: The Complete Reference*. MIT Press Cambridge, 1 edition, 1995.

[60] A. Strehl and J. Ghosh. Cluster ensembles: A knowledge reuse framework for combining multiple partitions. *Journal of Machine Learning Research*, 3:583–617, 2002.

[61] Y. J. Sun, S. Todorovic, and S. Goodison. Local learning based feature selection for high dimensional data analysis. *IEEE Transactions on Pattern Analysis and Machine Intelligence*, 32:1–18, 2010.

[62] J. L. Tang, S. Alelyani, and H. Liu. Feature selection for classification: A review. *Data Classification: Algorithms and Applications*. Editor: Charu Aggarwal, CRC Press, 2014.

[63] J. L. Tang, X. Hu, H. J. Gao, and Huan Liu. Unsupervised feature selection for multi-view data in social media. In *Proceedings of the 2013 SIAM Conference on Data Mining*, 2013.

[64] R. Tibshirani. Regression shrinkage and selection via the lasso. *Journal of the Royal Statistical Society: Series B (Statistical Methodology)*, 58:267–288, 1996.

[65] J. Wang and J. P. Ye. Safe screening for multi-task feature learning with multiple data matrices. In *Proceedings of the 32nd International Conference on Machine Learning*, 2015.

[66] J. Wang, P. Zhao, S. Hoi, and R. Jin. Online feature selection and its applications. *IEEE Transactions on Knowledge and Data Engineering*, pages 1–14, 2013.

[67] J. Wang, Z. Q. Zhao, X. G. Hu, Y. M. Cheung, M. Wang, and X. D. Wu. Online group feature selection. In *Proceedings of International Joint Conference on Artificial Intelligence*, 2013.

[68] J. Wang, J. Y. Zhou, J. Liu, P. Wonka, and J. P. Ye. A safe screening rule for sparse logistic regression. In *Proceedings of Advances in Neural Information Processing Systems*, pages 1053–1061, 2014.

[69] A. Woznica, P. Nguyen, and A. Kalousis. Model mining for robust feature selection. In *Proceedings of ACM SIGKDD Conference on Knowledge Discovery and Data Mining*, pages 913–921, 2012.

[70] X. Wu, K. Yu, H. Wang, and W. Ding. Online streaming feature selection. In *Proceedings of International Conference on Machine Learning*, pages 1159–1166, 2010.

[71] Xindong Wu, Xingquan Zhu, Gong-Qing Wu, and Wei Ding. Data mining with big data. *IEEE Transactions on Knowledge and Data Engineering*, 26:97–107, 2014.

[72] H. Xiao, B. Biggio, G. Brown, G. Fumera, C. Eckert, and F. Roli. Is feature selection secure against training data poisoning? In *Proceedings of the 32th International Conference on Machine Learning*, 2015.

[73] J. Yan, N. Liu, B. Zhang, S. Yan, Z. Chen, Q. Cheng, W. Fan, and W. Y. Ma. OCFS: Optimal orthogonal centroid feature selection for text categorization. In *Proceedings of the 28th Annual International ACM SIGIR Conference on Research and Development in Information Retrieval*, pages 122–129, 2005.

[74] Peng Yan and Yun Li. Graph-margin based multi-label feature selection. In *European Conference on Machine Learning*, pages 540–555, 2016.

[75] J. Yang and Y. Li. Differential privacy feature selection. In *Proceedings of International Joint Conference on Neural Networks*, pages 4182–4189, 2014.

[76] K. Yu, X. D. Wu, W. Ding, and J. Pei. Towards scalable and accurate online feature selection for big data. In *Proceedings of IEEE Conference on Data Mining*, pages 660–669, 2014.

[77] L. Yu, C. Ding, and S. Loscalzo. Stable feature selection via dense feature groups. In *Proceedings of ACM SIGKDD Conference on Knowledge Discovery and Data Mining*, pages 803–811, 2008.

[78] L. Yu, Y. Han, and M. E. Berens. Stable gene selection from microarray data via sample weighting. *IEEE/ACM Transactions on Computational Biology and Bioinformatics*, 9:262–272, 2012.

[79] L. Yu and H. Liu. Feature selection for high-dimensional data: A fast correlation-based filter solution. In *Proceedings of International Conference on Machine Learning*, pages 856–863, 2003.

[80] L. Yu and H. Liu. Efficient feature selection via analysis of relevance and redundancy. *Journal of Machine Learning Research*, 5:1205–1224, 2004.

[81] M. Yuan and Y. Lin. Model selection and estimation in regression with grouped variables. *Journal of the Royal Statistical Society: Series B (Statistical Methodology)*, 68:49–67, 2006.

[82] F. Zhang, P. P. K. Chan, B. Biggio, D. S. Yeung, and F. Roli. Adversarial feature selection against evasion attacks. *IEEE Transactions on Cybernetics*, 2015.

[83] Qin Zhang, Peng Zhang, Guodong Long, Wei Ding, Chengqi Zhang, and Xindong Wu. Towards mining trapezoidal data streams. In *Proceedings of IEEE International Conference on Data Mining*, pages 1111–1116, 2015.

[84] Lei Zhao, Qinghua Hu, and Wenwu Wang. Heterogeneous feature selection with multi-modal deep neural networks and sparse group lasso. *IEEE Transactions on Multimedia*, 17:1936–1948, 2015.

[85] Z. Zhao. *Spectral Feature Selection for Mining Ultrahigh Dimensional Data*. PhD thesis, Arizona State University, 2010.

[86] Z. Zhao, J. X. Wang, S. Sharma, N. Agarwal, H. Liu, and Y. Chang. An integrative approach to identifying biologically relevant genes. In *Proceedings of SIAM International Conference on Data Mining*, 2010.

[87] Z. Zhao, R. W. Zhang, J. Cox, D. Duling, and W. Sarle. Massively parallel feature selection: An approach based on variance preservation. *Machine Learning*, 92:195–220, 2013.

[88] Z. A. Zhao and H. Liu. *Spectral Feature Selection for Data Mining*. Taylor and Francis Group, 2012.

[89] D. Zhou, J. Huang, and B. Scholkopf. Learning from labeled and unlabeled data on a directed graph. In *Proceedings of International Conference on Machine Learning*, pages 1036–1043, 2005.

[90] Qifeng Zhou, Hao Zhou, and Tao Li. Cost-sensitive feature selection using random forest: Selecting low-cost subsets of informative features. *Knowledge-Based Systems*, 95:1–11, 2016.

[91] H. Zou and T. Hastie. Regularization and variable selection via the elastic net. *Journal of the Royal Statistical Society: Series B (Statistical Methodology)*, 67:301–320, 2005.

Chapter 9

Transformation-based Feature Engineering in Supervised Learning: Strategies toward Automation

Udayan Khurana

IBM Research

The process of predictive modeling requires extensive feature engineering. It often involves the transformation of given feature space, typically using mathematical functions, with the objective of reducing the modeling error for a given target. However, there is no well-defined basis for performing effective feature engineering. It involves domain knowledge, intuition, and most of all, a lengthy process of trial and error. The human attention involved in overseeing this process significantly influences the cost of model generation. Moreover, when the data presented is not well described and labeled, effective manual feature engineering becomes an even more prohibitive task. In this chapter, we discuss ways to algorithmically tackle the problem of feature engineering using transformation functions in the context of supervised learning.

9.1 Introduction

Feature representation plays an important role in the effectiveness of a supervised learning algorithm. For instance, Figure 9.1 depicts two different representations for points belonging to a binary classification dataset. On the left, the instances corresponding to the two classes appear to be present in alternating small clusters along a straight line. For most machine learning algorithms, it is hard to draw a classifier separating the two classes in this representation. However, if the feature x is replaced by its *sine*, as seen in the image on the right, it makes the two classes easily separable. Feature engineering is that *task* or *process* of altering the feature representation of a predictive modeling problem, in order to better fit a training algorithm. The *sine* function is a *transformation* function used to perform feature engineering.

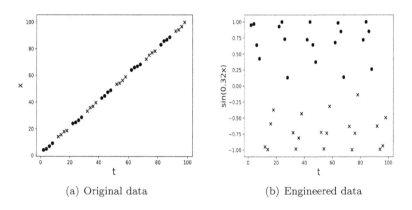

(a) Original data   (b) Engineered data

Figure 9.1: Illustration of two representations of a feature.

Consider the problem of modeling the heart diseases of patients based upon their characteristics such as height, weight, waist, hip, age, gender, amongst others. While the given features serve as important signals to classify the risk of a person, more effective measures, such as BMI (body mass index), and a waist to hip ratio, are actually functions of these base features. To derive BMI, two transformation functions are used – *division* and *square*. Composing new features using multiple functions and from multiple base features is quite common. Consider another example of predicting hourly bike rental count [1] in Figure 9.2. The given features lead to a weak prediction model. However, the addition of several derived features dramatically decreases modeling error. The new features are derived using well-known mathematical functions such as *log*, *reciprocal*, and statistical transformations such as *zscore*. Often, lesser

---

[1] Kaggle bike sharing: https://www.kaggle.com/c/bike-sharing-demand

datetime	season	holiday	workingday	weather	temp	atemp	humidity	windspeed	count
2011-01-01 01:00:00	1	0	0	1	9.84	14.395	81	0	16
2011-01-01 02:00:00	1	0	0	1	9.02	13.635	80	0	40
2011-01-01 03:00:00	1	0	0	1	9.02	13.635	80	1	32

(a) Original features and target (count).

year(datetime)	hour(datetime)	log(humidity)	log(windspeed)	1/humidity	1/log(hour(datetime))	zscore(datetime)
2011	1	4.394449	0	0.0125	0	-1.711228
2011	2	4.382027	0	0.0123	3.3219	-1.711030
2011	3	4.382027	0	0.0123	2.0959	-1.710832

(b) Additionally engineered features using transformation functions.

Figure 9.2: In Kaggle's bike rental count prediction dataset using Random Forest regressor, the addition of new features reduced the Relative Absolute Error from 0.61 to 0.20.

known domain-specific functions prove to be particularly useful in deriving meaningful features as well. For instance, *spatial aggregation*, and *temporal windowing*, are heavily used in spatial and temporal data, respectively. A combination of those—*spatio-temporal aggregation*–can be seen in the problem of predicting rainfall quantities from atmospheric data. The use of the recent weather observations at a station, and surrounding stations, greatly enhance the quality of a model for predicting precipitation. Such features might not be directly available and need aggregation from within the same dataset. [2]

Feature engineering may be viewed as the addition or removal of features to a dataset in order to reduce the modeling error. The removal of a subset of features, called *dimensionality reduction* or *feature selection*, is a relatively well-studied problem in machine learning [7] [16]. The techniques presented in this chapter focus on the feature construction aspects while utilizing feature selection as a black box. In this chapter, we talk about general frameworks to automatically perform feature engineering in supervised learning through a set of transformation functions. The algorithms used in the frameworks are independent of the actual transformations being applied, and are hence domain independent. We begin with somewhat simple approaches for automation, moving on to complex performance-driven, trial-and-error style algorithms. We then talk about optimizing such an algorithm using reinforcement learning, concluding with an approach that learns patterns between feature distributions and effective transformations. First of all, let us talk about what makes either manual or automated feature engineering challenging.

---

[2]NOAA climate datasets: https://www.ncdc.noaa.gov/cdo-web/datasets

9.1.1   Challenges in Performing Feature Engineering

In practice, feature engineering is orchestrated by a data scientist, using hunch, intuition, and domain knowledge. Simultaneously, it involves continuous observation and reaction to the evolution of model performance, in a manner of trial and error. For instance, upon glancing at the bike rental prediction dataset described previously, a data scientist might think of discovering seasonal or daily (day of the week) or hourly patterns. Such insights are obtained by virtue of some past knowledge, obtained either through personal experience or an academic expertise. It is natural for humans to argue that the demand for bike rental has a correlation to the work schedules of people, as well as some relationship to the weather, and so on. This is a collective example of the data scientist applying *hunch, intuition*, and *domain expertise*. Now, all of the proposed patterns do not end up being true or useful in model building. The person conducting the model building exercise would actually try the different options (either independently, or in a certain combinations) by adding new features obtained through transformation functions, followed by training and evaluation. Based on which model trials provide the best performance, the data scientist would deem the corresponding new features useful, and vice versa. This process is an example of *trial and error*. As a result of this process, feature engineering for supervised learning is often time-consuming, and is also prone to bias and error. Due to this inherent dependence on human decision making, it is colloquially referred to as "*an art/science*" [3] [4], making it non-trivial to automate. Figure 9.4 illustrates an abstract feature engineering process centered around a data scientist.

The automation of FE is challenging computationally, as well as in terms of decision making. First, the number of possible features that can be constructed is unbounded; the transformations can be composed and applied recursively to features generated by previous transformations. In order to confirm whether a new feature provides value, it requires training and validation of a new model upon including the feature. It is an expensive step and infeasible to perform with respect to each newly constructed feature. In the examples discussed previously, we witnessed the diversity of functions and possible composition of functions to yield the most useful features. The immense plurality of options available makes it infeasible in practice to try out all options computationally. Consider a scenario with merely $t = 10$ transformation functions and $f = 10$ base features; if the transforms are allowed to be applied up to a depth, $d = 5$, the total number of options are $f \times t^{d+1}$, which is greater than a million choices. If these choices were all evaluated through training and testing, it would take an infeasibly large amount of time for even a relatively small dataset. Secondly, feature engineering involves complex decision making, that is based on

---

[3]http://www.datasciencecentral.com/profiles/blogs/feature-engineering-tips-for-data-scientists

[4]https://codesachin.wordpress.com/2016/06/25/non-mathematical-feature-engineering-techniques-for-data-science/

a variety of factors. Some examples are prioritization of transformations based on the performance with the given dataset or even based on past experience, or whether to *explore* different transformations or *exploit* the combinations of the ones that have shown promise thus far on this dataset, and so on. It is non-trivial to articulate the notions or set of rules that are the basis of such decisions. Hence, it is also non-trivial to write programs to perform the same task.

In this chapter, we take a closer look at the automation of the tasks described above for feature engineering in supervised learning using transformation functions. We specifically look at the strategies that automate the trial-and-error methodology, and those that try to learn patterns of association between features and effective transforms from past experience.

9.2 Terminology and Problem Definition

We are given a predictive modeling task consisting of (1) a set of feature vectors, $F = \{f_1, f_2 \ldots f_m\}$; (2) a target vector, y. The nature of y—categorical or continuous—describes whether it is a classification or regression problem, respectively. Consider a suitable learning algorithm L, that is applicable in the context of given y, and a measure of performance, m. We use $A_L^m(F, y)$ to signify the performance of a the model constructed on given data using the algorithm L through the performance measure m. An example of L is logistic regression for classification and an example of m is average F1-score.

Now consider a set of k transformation functions at our disposal, $\mathcal{T} = \{t_1, t_2 \ldots t_k\}$. The application of a unary transformation, t_i, can be represented as $f_{out} = t_i(f_{in})$, where $f_{in}, f_{out} \in \mathbb{R}^n$, are features of the same dimension. Similar notation extends to binary and k-ary transformations. A variation of the transformations is written with capital letters, such as $T_1, T_2 \ldots T_k$. These are applied on a set of features, F, instead of individual features. They symbolize a separate application of the corresponding function t on each input $f \subseteq F$, such that $t(f)$ is a legal and valid feature. Also, for $F_o = T(F_i)$, F_o includes all the newly generated features besides the original features from F_i. For instance, a *Log* transformation applied to a set of ten numerical features, F, will produce ten new output features, $f_o = log(f_i), \forall f_i \in F$. This extends to k-ary functions, which work on k input features. The entire (open) set of features derived directly or recursively from F using $\mathcal{T}$ is denoted by $\hat{F}_{\mathcal{T}}$.

A $+$ operator on two feature sets (associated with the same target y) is a union of the two feature sets, $F_o = F_1 + F_2 = F_1 \cup F_2$, preserving row order. Note that all operations specified on a feature set $T(F)$, can exchangeably be written for a corresponding dataset, $D = \langle F, y \rangle$, as $T(D)$, where it is implied that the operation is applied on the corresponding feature set. Also, for a binary, such as sum, $D_o = D_1 + D_2$, it is implied that the target is common across the operands and the result. Transformations on feature sets add features or keep the set unchanged; on the other hand, a *feature selection* operator removes features. However, it can be written in the same algebraic notation as set transformations, such as $T_2(FS_1(T_1(D_0)))$ or $T_2.FS_1.T_1(D_0)$.

The goal of feature engineering is stated as follows. Given a set of features, F, and target, y, and a set of transformations, $\mathcal{T}$, find a set of features, $F^* = F_1 \cup F_2$, where $F_1 \subseteq F$ (original) and $F_2 \subset \hat{F}_\mathcal{T}$ (derived), to maximize the modeling accuracy for a given algorithm, L, and measure, m.

$$F^* = \arg\max_{F_1, F_2} A_L^m(F_1 \cup F_2, y) \tag{9.1}$$

9.3   A Few Simple Approaches

One way of constructing new features is to simply apply all transformations to the given data and sum all the resulting datasets. This leads to the generation of a large number of features, a few of which might be useful with respect to the given target. However, training a model over such a large feature set is computationally inefficient and also leads to overfitting. It is possible to reduce the number of features through a feature selector, retaining only a relevant subset of features. This process is illustrated in Figure 9.3(a). This technique is easy to implement and effective in finding features that can be generated from a single layer of transformations on the given features. However, it lacks the capability to generate features from the composition of different transformations, often limiting the scope of the feature space it can discover. Note that not feasible to run this method recursively because of the magnitude of feature expansion. The feature subset selection algorithms can be a performance bottleneck because of their super-linear complexity in the number of features. Note that this technique doesn't explicitly involve training and evaluations; however, they may be performed within the feature selection step. This approach is suggested as a part of the Data Science Machine (DSM) [10] and the OneButton Machine [15]. We refer to this as the *expansion-reduction* approach.

A contrasting approach to the above is to generate one new feature at a time followed by training and evaluation to decide if the new feature is worth keeping or not. While this method is more scalable than the expansion-reduction approach, it is also slower because it involves model trainings and evaluations, over the entire space of features that can be generated. In practice, this method is also only feasible without deep compositions of transforms because of the expensive nature of exploration. ExploreKit [11] describes one such method, where a greedy heuristic logic for feature prioritization is used.

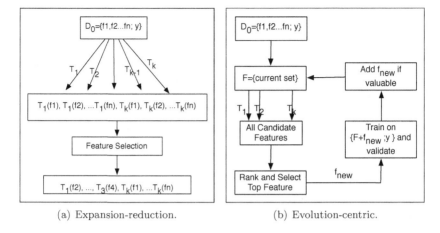

(a) Expansion-reduction.   (b) Evolution-centric.

Figure 9.3: Two basic methods for feature engineering.

We will call this category the *evolution-centric* approach. It is illustrated in Figure 9.3(b).

The two contrasting approaches discussed in the previous section pose their own unique performance challenges. The expansion-reduction method has scalability problems due to its dependence on a feature subset selection module running for a large number of generated features, whereas the evolution-centric approach is fairly time consuming due to the training and evaluation with respect to each new feature. In a way, the two approaches are the opposite of each other and go to different extremes, which also cause each of them to be inefficient in its own way. Recall the example of BMI, which is derived through a composition of two basic transformation functions (square and division) on two measured quantities. Either of the two approaches are unlikely to discover BMI. In the next section, we will explore a middle path, where the newly generated features are batched into groups by applying set transformations on entire datasets.

9.4   Hierarchical Exploration of Feature Transformations

So far we have discussed two algorithmic approaches to feature engineering. In summary, expansion-reduction works by generating a large number of new features, followed by pruning the undesired ones. On the other hand, the evolution-centric method evaluates the addition of one feature at a time. The two approaches stand in contrast to each other in the quantity and timing of generation of new features. Both face performance bottlenecks because of the extremities of their approaches. Additionally, the given approaches do not clearly embrace the composition of transforms. Composition is essential for the discovery of complex relationships. In this section, we discuss an approach that overcomes some of these limitations through *batching* of new feature generation and evaluation. It also performs a *hierarchical composition* of transforms in a performance-driven manner.

The batching is performed per transformation. At each step, one transformation is applied to a dataset (recall the set-level transformations with capital letters), generating a set of new features. At each step, the resulting new dataset is evaluated for accuracy. This is performed recursively, forming a hierarchical structure. The batching of feature generation per transformation is scalable and efficient. It also provides an abstraction for measuring the effectiveness of each transformation on the data. The difference in model accuracy upon applying a transformation is averaged over all instances of its application for the given problem until that moment. Those performance numbers are then used to guide the exploration process, to make the decision of which transformation to apply next, to which version of the dataset. The hierarchical organization is a directed acyclic graph (DAG), known as a Transformation Graph [13]. It is a general framework for performance-based feature engineering. The approaches discussed before this can be expressed as specific formulations of this approach. Further in this section, we formally define the anatomy of the transformation graph, followed by strategies to explore one.

9.4.1   Transformation Graph

A *Transformation Graph*, G, for a given dataset, D_0, and a finite set of transformations, $\mathcal{T}$, is a directed acyclic graph in which each node corresponds to a either D_0 or a dataset derived from D_0 using a transformation path. Hence, every node's dataset contains the same target and row count as D. The nodes are divided into three categories: (a) The start, or the root node, D_0, corresponding to the given dataset; (b) hierarchical nodes, D_i, where $i > 0$, which have one incoming parent node D_j, $j > i$, and the connecting edge from D_j to D_i corresponds to a transformation $T \in \mathcal{T}$ (including feature selection), i.e., $D_j = T(D_i)$. The direction of an edge represents the application of the transformation from the source to a target dataset or node; (c) sum nodes, $D_{i,j}^+ = D_i + D_j$, a result of a dataset sum such that $i \neq j$. Height (h) of the transformation graph is the maximum unweighted distance between the root and any other node. The operator $\theta(G)$ signifies all nodes of graph G. Also, $\lambda(D_i, D_j)$ signifies the transformation T, such that its application on D_i created D_j as its child. A transformation graph is illustrated in Figure 9.4. The best-known solution through a transformation graph is the node with the greatest accuracy: $\arg\max_{D_i} A(D_i)$. A complete transformation graph always contains a global solution to the problem.

Any complete transformation graph is unbounded for a non-empty transformation set. A constrained (with bounded height, h) but complete transformation graph for t transformations contains $t^{h+1} - 2$ hierarchical nodes, and

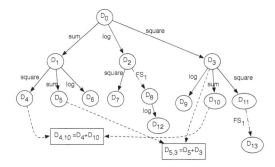

Figure 9.4: Example of a *Transformation Graph*, a directed acyclic graph. The start node D_0 corresponds to the given dataset. The hierarchical nodes are circular and the sum nodes are rectangular. Here we can see three transformations: *log*, *sum*, and *square*, as well as a feature selection operator FS_1.

$\frac{(t^{h+1}-1) \times (t^{h+1}-2)}{2}$ sum nodes. It can be seen that for even a height-bounded tree with a modest number of transformations, the verification of accuracies across the tree is combinatorially large. Therefore, we adopt a *performance-guided exploration* strategy to explore only a tiny subset of the graph which is most likely to contain the required solution, avoiding other nodes. The algorithm works under a budget constraint.

9.4.2 Transformation Graph Exploration

Exhaustive exploration of a transformation graph is not an option, given its massive potential size. For instance, with 20 transformations and a height = 5, the complete graph contains about 3.2 million nodes; an exhaustive search would imply as many model training and testing iterations. On the other hand, there is no known property that allows us to deterministically verify the optimal solution in a subset of the trials. Hence, the focus of this work is to find a performance-driven exploration policy or strategy, which *maximizes expected gain in accuracy* in a *limited time budget*.

Algorithm 2 outlines a general methodology for exploration. At each step, an estimated reward from each possible move, $R(G_i, n, t, \frac{i}{B_{max}})$, is used to rank the options of actions available at each given state of the transformation graph $G_i, \forall i \in [0, B_{max})$, where B_{max} is the total allocated budget in number of steps. The budget can be considered in terms of any quantity that is monotonically increasing in i, such as time elapsed; for simplicity, we work with "number of steps." Note that the algorithm allows for plugging-in of different exploration strategies, through the definition of the function $R(\ldots)$. Any such definition is a function of four basic parameters: (1) current global state of the graph, (2) which transform is being characterized for application, (3) the node on which it is being considered for application, and (4) how much bud-

---

Algorithm 2 General Transformation Graph Exploration

Input: Dataset D_0, Budget B_{max}

  1: Initialize G_0 with root D_0

  2: **while** $i < B_{max}$ **do**

  3:     $\mathcal{N} \leftarrow \theta(G_i)$

  4:     $b_{ratio} \leftarrow \frac{i}{B_{max}}$

  5:     $n^*, t^* \leftarrow \arg\max_{n, t \nexists n' \forall t = \lambda(n, n')} R(G_i, n, t, b_{ratio})$

  6:     $G_{i+i} \leftarrow$ Apply t^* to n^* in G_i

  7:     $i \leftarrow i + 1$

Output: $\underset{D}{\arg\max} \, A(\theta(G_i))$

---

get is remaining. The following is a non-exhaustive list of influential factors (attributes of one or more of the four parameters) in designing an exploration strategy:

1. Node n's Accuracy: Higher accuracy of a node incents further exploration from that node, compared to others.

2. Transformation: t's average or max accuracy improvement until G_i.

3. Number of times transform t has already been used in the path from root node to n. A high or even non-zero number weakens the case for an application of t on n.

4. Accuracy gain for node n (from its parent) and the accuracy gain for n's parent. This tests whether n's cumulative gains are recent or not.

5. Node Depth: A higher value is considered as a sign of relative complexity of the transformation sequence.

6. The fraction of budget exhausted till G_i.

7. Ratio of feature counts in n to the original dataset: This indicates how bloated n is, in comparison to the original dataset.

8. Is the transformation a feature selector (reduces feature count)?

9. Whether the dataset contains (a) numerical features, or (b) date-time features, or (c) string features?

The exploration strategy essentially translates to the design of the reward estimation function, $R(\ldots)$. Some of the handcrafted graph traversal strategies by Cognito [14] are described as follows. In a *depth-first* strategy, the emphasis is on exploring further from the node with the highest accuracy, until saturation or decrease in accuracy is noticed. It is best utilized for finding consolidation on an already-found solution in a somewhat limited budget.

However, it can get stuck in local, deep areas of the graph without exploring other simpler choices. In other words, it lacks the exploration aspect and such a policy may take a long time to stumble upon a simple transformation with high reward. A *breadth-first* strategy is primarily focused on exploring the less explored subtrees of the hierarchical portion of the transformation graph. Other factors are secondary influencers, such as transformation performance, the parent node's accuracy, and the child node's prospective accuracy. This strategy is good for discovering single (or a small sequence) of highly rewarding transforms. However, it performs poorly in consolidating benefits into a single chain of a large number of transforms. A *global* strategy is derived from a mix of the depth- and breadth-oriented policies. It works by first exploring the breadth, followed by a more concentrated exploration of promising depths based upon the initial phase. Figure 9.5 illustrates the breadth-first, depth-first and one of the RL-based strategies (Section 9.5) for the OpenML_618 dataset ($B_{max} = 20$, $h_{max} = 5$), with sum nodes disabled (for visual clarity). In general, it is hard to manually encode all rules that best capture the optimal intent for different situations—at different values of remaining budget, average performance of different transformations and their combinations for a given dataset, and so on. In the next section, we will discuss how to empirically optimize such capture.

9.5   Learning Optimal Traversal Policy

In the previous section, we discussed an algorithmic approach for a performance-based exploration for feature engineering. It was based upon the exploration of a hierarchical set up of the transformation functions in the form of a transformation graph (a directed acyclic graph). We discussed different heuristics to form exploration strategies based on an understanding of the manual trial-and-error process. While it helps achieve good results for feature engineering without human intervention, there is a considerable scope for improving the strategy beyond handcrafted rules.

In this section, we describe a method to improve the exploration strategy from experience. Instead of relying on "human experts" to encode heuristics, we rely on empirical observations and perform *reinforcement learning* to optimize the strategy. Consider a feature engineering *agent* that is continuously monitoring the impact of each transformation applied (call it *action*) on a given transformation graph (*state*) and resulting improvement in performance (*reward*). The goal of reinforcement learning here is for the agent to learn a strategy that optimizes the final or cumulative reward ($A^* - A(D_0)$) for a given dataset in a specified time budget. Similar to the handcrafted strategies discussed previously, the learned strategy can also be thought of as an *action-utility* function to satisfy the expected reward function, R(...) in

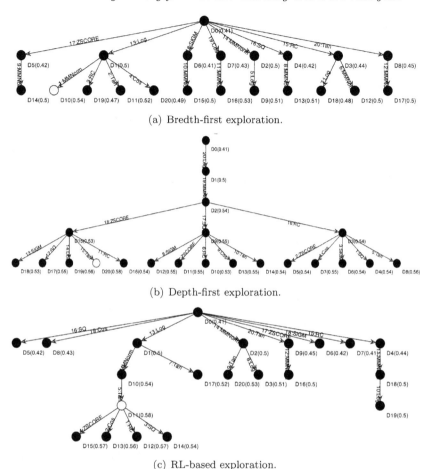

(a) Bredth-first exploration.

(b) Depth-first exploration.

(c) RL-based exploration.

Figure 9.5: Illustration of different exploration policies on a dataset: https://www.openml.org/d/618 dataset. In a $B_{max} = 20$ iteration limit, RL and DF both find the best performance of 0.58 $(1 - Rel.Abs.Error)$, while BF finds only 0.54. RL takes 11 iterations, while DF takes 20 iterations.

Algorithm 2. This simply means the association of any action with a scalar utility or expected reward value. Reinforcement learning is helpful in learning such an action-utility function based upon observing immediate rewards from actions, in the process of optimizing the final or cumulative reward. A tutorial on reinforcement learning is beyond the scope of this chapter, but we encourage the interested reader to refer to Sutton and Barto [26] for a general understanding of the topic. In a nutshell, reinforcement learning is an area of machine learning concerned with training an agent to perform optimal actions in an environment in order to maximize a notion of cumulative reward.

It relies on a reward signal for each action taken in order to guide the agent's behavior, which is different than the supervised learning paradigm, where we are given the ground truth to train the system. Here, we specifically discuss a particular instance of Q-learning with a function approximation method as discussed by Khurana et al. [13]. Q-value learning is a particular kind of reinforcement learning that is useful in the absence of an explicit model of the environment, which in this case translates to the behavior of the learning algorithm. An approximation function is suitable due to the large number of states (recall, millions of nodes in a graph with small depth) for which it is infeasible to learn state-action transitions explicitly. This style of work, where machine learning is aided by the use of other machine learning techniques, is referred to as "learning to learn" or *meta-learning*.

9.5.1 Feature Exploration through Reinforcement Learning

Consider the graph exploration process as a *Markov Decision Process (MDP)* where the *state* at step i is a combination of two components: (a) a transformation graph after i node additions, G_i (G_0 consists of the root node corresponding to the given dataset. G_i contains i nodes); (b) the remaining budge at step i, i.e., $b_{ratio} = \frac{i}{B_{max}}$. Let the entire set of states be S. On the other hand, an *action* at step i is a pair of an existing tree node and a transformation that hasn't already been applied to it, i.e., $< n, t >$ where $n \in \theta(G_t)$, $t \in T$ and $\nexists n \in G_i \forall \lambda(n, n') = t$. Let the entire set of actions be C. A policy, $\Pi : S \to C$, determines which action is taken given a state. Note that the objective here is to learn the optimal policy (exploration strategy) by learning the action-value function, which is explained later.

The described formulation uniquely identifies each state. Considering the "remaining budget" as a factor in the state of the MDP helps address the *runtime exploration versus exploitation* trade-off for a given dataset. Note that this runtime explore/exploit trade-off is not identical to the commonly referred to trade-off in RL training in the context of selecting actions to balance reward and not getting stuck in a local optimum.

At step i, the occurrence of an action results in a new node, n_i, and hence a new dataset on which a model is trained and tested, and its accuracy $A(n_i)$ is obtained. To each step, we attribute an immediate scalar reward:

$$r_i = \max_{n' \in \theta(G_{i+1})} A(n') - \max_{n \in \theta(G_i)} A(n)$$

with $r_0 = 0$, by definition. The cumulative reward over time from state s_i onwards is defined as:

$$R(s_i) = \sum_{j=0}^{B_{max}} \gamma^i . r_{i+j}$$

where $\gamma \in [0, 1)$ is a discount factor, which prioritizes early rewards over the later ones.

We use Q-learning [28] with function approximation to learn the action-value Q-function. For each state, $s \in S$, and action, $c \in C$, the Q-function with respect to policy Π is defined as:

$$Q(s,c) = r(s,c) + \gamma R^{\Pi}(\delta(s,c))$$

where $\delta : S \times C \to S$ is a hypothetical transition function, and $R^{\Pi}(s)$ is the cumulative reward following state s. The optimal policy is achieved as

$$\Pi^*(s) = \arg\max_c [Q(s,c)]. \tag{9.2}$$

However, given the size of S, it is infeasible to learn the Q-function directly. Instead, a linear approximation of the Q-function is used as follows:

$$Q(s,c) = w^c.f(s) \tag{9.3}$$

where w^c is a weight vector for action c and $f(s) = f(g,n,t,b)$ is a vector of the state characteristics described in the previous section and the remaining budget ratio. Therefore, we approximate the Q-functions with linear combinations of the characteristics of a state of the MDP. Note that in the heuristic rule-based strategies described in Section 9.4.2, we used a subset of these state characteristics, in a self-conceived manner. However, in the ML-based approach here, we select the entire set of characteristics and empirically determine the appropriate weights of those characteristics (for different actions). Hence, this approach generalizes the handcrafted approaches.

The update rule for w_c is as follows:

$$w^{c_j} \leftarrow w^{c_j} + \alpha.(r_j + \gamma.\max_{n',t'} Q(g',c') - Q(g,c)).f(g,b) \tag{9.4}$$

where g' is the state of the graph at step $j+1$, and α is the learning rate parameter. The proof follows from [9].

A variation of the linear approximation where the coefficient vector w is independent of the action c, is as follows:

$$Q(s,c) = w.f(s). \tag{9.5}$$

This method reduces the space of coefficients to be learned by a factor of c, and makes it faster to learn the weights. It is important to note that the Q-function in this case is still not independent of the action c, as one of the factors in $f(s)$ or $f(g,n,t,b)$ is actually the average immediate reward for the transform for the present dataset. Hence, the Equation 9.5–based approximation still distinguishes between various actions (t) based on their performance in the transformation graph exploration so far; however, it does not learn a bias for different transformations in general and based on the feature types (factor #9). We refer to this type of strategy as RL_2. In our experiments RL_2 efficiency is somewhat inferior to the strategy learned with Equation 9.3,

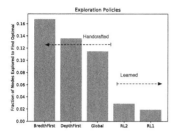
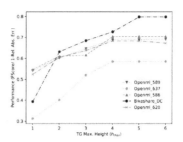

(a) Comparing different exploration policies by an average of nodes explored (in a constrained graph) to find the optimal solution.

(b) Performance of RL_1 exploration on various datasets with varying h_{max}. $h_{max} = 1$ is the base accuracy.

Figure 9.6: Evaluating the performance of hierarchical exploration.

which we refer to as RL_1. However, RL_2 can be learned from fewer examples compared to RL_1, due to the former's smaller space of parameters. In Figure 9.6(a), we see that on an average for 10 datasets, the RL-based strategies are 4 to 8 times more efficient than any handcrafted strategy (*breadth-first, depth-first* and *global* as described in [14]), in finding the optimal dataset in a given graph with 6 transformations and bounded height, $h_{max} = 4$.

For training, Khurana at al. [13] used 48 datasets (not overlapping with test datasets) to select training examples using different values for maximum budget, $B_{max} \in \{25, 50, 75, 100, 150, 200, 300, 500\}$ with each dataset, in a random order. The discount factor $\gamma = 0.99$, and the learning rate parameter $\alpha = 0.05$. The weight vectors, w^c or w, each of size 12, were initialized with 1's. The training example steps were drawn randomly with the probability $\epsilon = 0.15$ and the current policy with probability $1 - \epsilon$.

9.6 Finding Effective Features without Model Training

So far, we have discussed approaches that rely on evaluation of generated features either directly through model construction and testing, or indirectly through feature selection. These tasks are computationally expensive. In this section, we shift the discussion to a paradigm without model construction and evaluation. Consider a binary classification example where one of the features is plotted in Figure 9.7(a). The high degree of overlap between the two classes suggests that this feature is not quite helpful for classification. Upon transformation with a frequency function, the distinction between points from the two classes is more prominent, as can be seen on the right. Hence, without model training and evaluation, we can suggest that the particular

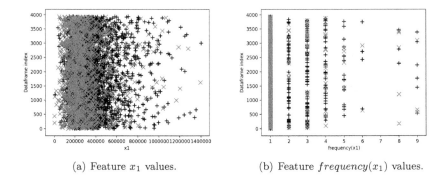

(a) Feature x_1 values.   (b) Feature $frequency(x_1)$ values.

Figure 9.7: Scatterplots juxtaposing values of an original and a transformed feature for several data instances ("dataframe index"). The transformed feature separates the two classes (x / +) better than the original.

transformation has generated additional value for classification with respect to the base feature. Generally, in the presence of a set of other features F, we can only say that a feature f_2 is more suitable than f_1, if

$$\Pr(y|f_2, F) > \Pr(y|f_2, F). \tag{9.6}$$

Determining the validity of Inequation 9.6 is as good as training two models with feature sets $f_1 + F$ and $f_2 + F$, respectively. In practice however, it is still viable to consider only the independent impact of a derived feature with respect to its base feature. This is because amongst a vast pool of features that can be derived, only a small fraction ever end up being beneficial. For a base feature f_1, a transformation, t, and a derived feature, $t(f_1)$, the following condition makes $t(f_1)$ a strong candidate to add value to the problem of predicting y:

$$\Pr(y|t(f_1), f_1) > \Pr(y|f_1). \tag{9.7}$$

A more strict condition than Equation 9.7, but one that is easier to evaluate through proxy functions, is the following:

$$\Pr(y|t(f_1)) > \Pr(y|f_1). \tag{9.8}$$

Consider the case of binary classification. Measuring the overlap of two sets of a feature belonging to different classes provides a reasonable measure of effectiveness of that feature itself in building a classifier. The less the overlap, the better. The degree of lack of overlap can be measured by the magnitude of divergence in the probability distribution functions (PDFs) of the two classes, say $\omega(c_1, c_2)$. If the application of a transformation reduces ω, it is a positive signal to embrace the new feature. One such measure is the symmetric-KL-divergence. It is described below for continuous distributions of the two classes,

$c_1(x)$ and $c_2(x)$, for feature f. There also exists a corresponding expression for discrete distributions.

$$\omega^f_{KL}(c_1, c_2) = \int_{-\infty}^{\infty} (c_1(x) - c_2(x)) \log \frac{c_1(x)}{c_2(x)} dx \qquad (9.9)$$

If $\omega^{f_2} > \omega^{f_1}$, where $f_2 = t(f_1)$ for a base feature f_1, we can infer that $f_2 = t(f_1)$ is a potentially valuable instance of transformation and f_2 should be retained. It is important to note two important points regarding the choice of the measure. First, metrics such as mutual information are not suitable. For our purpose, even identically shaped distributions without a significant overlap are good cases and mutual information does not convey that difference. Secondly, the required measure need not strictly be a metric. This concept extends well to multi-class problems. In case of regression, a measure of correlation between the feature and the target mirrors the objective appropriately.

This approach is efficient because the measures of similarity between PDFs can be approximated more efficiently than training models on the entire data. However, it still needs an enumeration of various feature-transformation choices. While the computed PDF for a feature can be cached (specifically for base features), creating the PDF for each new feature ($|\mathcal{T}| \times |F|$) and computing ω is still quite a bit of work.

9.6.1 Learning to Predict Useful Transformations

We now discuss an approach to predict ω using supervised machine learning instead of computing it. It is based on *learning* the patterns between the distributions of feature vectors, the target vector, and corresponding utility of transformations. Once learned, those patterns are employed for predicting useful transformations for any previously unseen dataset. Its prominent advantage is that it is not dependent on the expensive task of model training and evaluation. It does not even depend on finding the improvement in divergence of PDFs of different classes upon applying a transformation. Instead, it predicts the improvement based on a trained model. Hence, it is much faster at runtime compared to any other method discussed so far. It can also be combined with any of the previously described approaches to prioritize their transformation application in accordance with the predictions. This style of making transformation predictions for a dataset based upon past experience is somewhat analogous to the hunch or intuition used by a data scientist in manual feature engineering.

Nargesian et al. [20] train a set of Multi-Layer Perceptrons (MLP), one for each transformation $t \in \mathcal{T}$. For every given feature-target pair, an MLP learns the impact of its corresponding transformation on the specified prediction task. It generalizes this knowledge across all training examples. A training instance consists of an alternative representation of the feature's PDF as input; the output is a binary value—whether the transformation is useful for accuracy improvement of the model or not. Hundreds of thousands of training examples are used, thanks to the vast array of open dataset repositories for supervised learning problems. Notice that the training data for the supervised meta-learning problem is generated automatically.

Let R_f be the alternate representation for a feature f. Recommending a transformation for f involves applying all $|\mathcal{T}|$ MLPs on R_f. If the highest confidence score obtained from the classifiers that returned a positive output is above a given threshold, the corresponding transformation is recommended for application on feature f. Let $G_k(R_f)$ be the confidence score of the MLP corresponding to transformation t_k, and γ is the threshold for confidence scores which we determined empirically. LFE recommends the transformation t_c, for feature f, as follows:

$$c = \arg\max_k G_k(R_f)$$

$$\text{recommend} : \begin{cases} t_c, & \text{if } G_c(R_f) > \gamma \\ \text{none}, & \text{otherwise.} \end{cases} \quad (9.10)$$

The alternative PDF representation is called a *Quantile Sketch Array (QSA)*. It represents feature f in a dataset with k classes as follows:

$$R_f = \left[Q_f^{(1)}; Q_f^{(2)}; \ldots; Q_f^{(k)} \right] \quad (9.11)$$

where $Q_f^{(i)}$ is a fixed-sized representation of values in f that are associated with class i. QSA uses a *quantile* data sketch [27] to represent feature values associated with a class label. It is a non-parametric representation that enables characterizing the feature PDFs. QSA is similar to a cumulative histogram, where data is summarized into a small number of buckets. Several other approaches for the alternate representation have been tried and QSA has proved to be the most effective for this problem [20].

Let $\mathcal{V}_k$ be the bag of values in a feature, f, that correspond to label c_k and $Q_f^{(i)}$ be the quantile sketch of $\mathcal{V}_k$. First, these values are scaled to a predefined range $[lb, ub]$. To generate $Q_f^{(i)}$, all values in $\mathcal{V}_k$ are bucketing into a set of bins. Given a fixed number of bins, r, the range $[lb, ub]$ is partitioned into r disjoint bins of uniform width $w = \frac{ub-lb}{r}$. The range of the bin b_j ($j \in \{0, 1, \ldots r-1\}$) is $[lb + j * w, lb + (j + 1) * w)$. $P(b_j)$ signifies the number of feature values bucketed in b_j, and $I(b_j) = \frac{P(b_j)}{\sum_{0 \le m < r} P(b_m)}$ is the normalized value of $P(b_j)$ across all bins.

The training samples for transformation MLP classifiers are generated using several classification datasets. For each dataset, each numerical feature, f, is considered and a model is trained using a learning algorithm, L. For each MLP, the corresponding transform t is applied to f and a new model is trained with f and $t(f)$. If the transformation leads to an improvement above a certain threshold, $A_L(\{f, t(f)\}, y) - A_L(\{f\}, y) > \phi$, R_f is considered a *positive* training example; otherwise a *negative* training example.

For a k-class problem, and while using b bins for each quantile data sketch, R_f is a vector of size $k \times b$. For an MLP with one hidden layer having h units, the probability of transformation t being a useful transformation or not for feature f is computed as

$$[p_{t \text{ is useful}}(f), p_{t \text{ is not useful}}(f)] =$$
$$\sigma_2(\mathbf{b}^{(2)} + \mathbf{W}^{(2)}(\sigma_1(\mathbf{b}^{(1)} + \mathbf{W}^{(1)}[Q_f^{(1)}; \ldots; Q_f^{(k)}]))). \tag{9.12}$$

Here, $\mathbf{W}^{(1)}$ and $\mathbf{W}^{(2)}$ are weight matrices and $\mathbf{b}^{(1)}$ and $\mathbf{b}^{(2)}$ are bias vectors. σ_1 and σ_2 are softmax and rectified linear unit (ReLU) functions, respectively. Stochastic Gradient Descent is used to train transformation MLPs. Overfitting should be prevented using regularization and drop-out [24].

At runtime, when a new dataset is presented, computing the QSA and scoring on the MLPs is computationally cheap. Compared to evaluation-based techniques with a large turn-around time, prediction-based techniques can give quick insights to a data scientist. Additionally, their results can be used as an initial bias for any of the exploration-based techniques for faster search. The gains reported by this technique are usually better than the expansion-reduction style of feature engineering [20], but less than a well-tuned transformation graph exploration system.

9.7 Miscellaneous

9.7.1 Other Related Work

The techniques presented in this chapter are representative of the state-of-the-art for automated feature engineering for predictive modeling. There is an additional body of valuable work which should also be of interest for researchers and graduate students working on this topic. We summarize some of the relevant work in this section.

FICUS [18] performs a beam search over the space of possible features, constructing new features by applying "constructor functions" (e.g., inserting an original feature into a composition of transformations). FICUS's search for better features is guided by heuristic measures based on information gain in a decision tree, and other surrogate measures of performance. FICUS is more general than a number of less recent approaches [1, 8, 19, 21, 29].

Fan et al. [4] propose FCTree, which uses a decision tree to partition the data using both original and constructed features as splitting points (nodes in the tree). Similar to FICUS [18], FCTree uses surrogate tree-based information-theoretic criteria to guide the search, as opposed to the true prediction performance. FCTree is capable of generating only simple features, and is not capable of composing transformations, i.e., it is search in a smaller space than our approach. They also propose a weight update mechanism that helps identify good transformations for a dataset, such that they are used more frequently. FEADIS [3] relies on a combination of random feature generation and feature selection. It adds constructed features greedily, and as such requires many expensive performance evaluations.

Certain machine learning methods perform some level of feature engineering implicitly. A recent survey on the topic can be found in Reference [25]. Dimensionality reduction methods such as Principal Component Analysis (PCA) and its non-linear variants (Kernel PCA) [6] aim at mapping the input dataset into a lower-dimensional space with fewer features. Such methods are also known as *embedding* methods [25]. Kernel methods [22] such as Support Vector Machines (SVM) are a class of learning algorithms that use kernel functions to implicitly map the input feature space into a higher-dimensional space.

9.7.2   Research Opportunities

One interesting direction is to view the problem as a hyper-parameter optimization [2]. Each transformation option corresponds to a hyper-parameter and one searches for the hyper-parameter setting that results in the best improvement of predictive performance. For instance, in [23] a genetic algorithm was used to determine a suitable transformation for a given data set. Similarly, in the context of automated ML pipeline configuration (e.g., feature selection and model), the work presented in [5] employs Bayesian optimization to determine a suitable pipeline. While the approach in [23] is limited to determining single transformations and does not search for a sequence of transformations, black-box optimization strategies [17] have, to our knowledge, not been applied to generate novel features based on compositions. A fertile area for improvement is to combine different known methods for feature engineering into one. For instance, using prediction-based techniques to provide quick insights on exploration-based techniques can boost the overall efficiency of the process [12]. Finally, extending the analysis and solutions presented in Section 9.6 from a single base feature to multiple ones and performing a joint-probabilistic analysis is valuable.

9.7.3   Resources

Please refer to an online addendum to this chapter on GitHub `https://github.com/uk2911/FEChapterExtended`. It contains resources for automated feature engineering tools that are described in this chapter. There are demonstrations on various real datasets, including videos and IPython notebooks. It also contains hints on efficiently implementing your own feature engineering program.

Acknowledgments

Thanks to Horst Samulowitz, Fatemeh Nargesian, Elias Khalil, Deepak Turaga, and Tejaswini Pedapati for joint research on different problems which are described in this chapter. Thanks to Biplav Srivastava for helpful discussions on the process of writing the chapter.

Bibliography

[1] Giulia Bagallo and David Haussler. Boolean feature discovery in empirical learning. *Machine Learning*, 5(1):71–99, 1990.

[2] James S. Bergstra, Rémi Bardenet, Yoshua Bengio, and Balázs Kégl. Algorithms for hyper-parameter optimization. In J. Shawe-Taylor, R. S. Zemel, P. L. Bartlett, F. Pereira, and K. Q. Weinberger, editors, *Advances in Neural Information Processing Systems 24*, pages 2546–2554. Curran Associates, Inc., 2011.

[3] Ofer Dor and Yoram Reich. Strengthening learning algorithms by feature discovery. *Information Sciences*, 189(April):176?190, 2012.

[4] Wei Fan, Erheng Zhong, Jing Peng, Olivier Verscheure, Kun Zhang, Jiangtao Ren, Rong Yan, and Qiang Yang. *Generalized and Heuristic-Free Feature Construction for Improved Accuracy*. pages 629–640, 2010.

[5] Matthias Feurer, Aaron Klein, Katharina Eggensperger, Jost Tobias Springenberg, Manuel Blum, and Frank Hutter. Efficient and robust automated machine learning. *NIPS*, 2015.

[6] Imola K Fodor. A survey of dimension reduction techniques, 2002.

[7] Isabelle Guyon and André Elisseeff. An introduction to variable and feature selection. *Journal of Machine Learning Research*, 3(Mar):1157–1182, 2003.

[8] Yuh-Jyh Hu and Dennis Kibler. Generation of attributes for learning algorithms. *AAAI*, 1996.

[9] Marina Irodova and Robert H Sloan. Reinforcement learning and function approximation. In *FLAIRS Conference*, pages 455–460, 2005.

[10] James Max Kanter and Kalyan Veeramachaneni. Deep feature synthesis: Towards automating data science endeavors. *IEEE Data Science and Advanced Analytics*, pages 1–10, 2015.

[11] Gilad Katz, Eui Chul, Richard Shin, and Dawn Song. ExploreKit: Automatic feature generation and selection. In *IEEE ICDM*, pages 979–984, 2016.

[12] Udayan Khurana, Fatemeh Nargesian, Horst Samulowitz, Elias Khalil, and Deepak Turaga. Automating feature engineering. In *Artificial Intelligence for Data Science (NIPS workshop)*, 2016.

[13] Udayan Khurana, Horst Samulowitz, and Deepak Turaga. Feature engineering for predictive modeling using reinforcement learning. *arXiv preprint arXiv:1709.07150*, 2017.

[14] Udayan Khurana, Deepak Turaga, Horst Samulowitz, and Srinivasan Parthasarathy. Cognito: Automated feature engineering for supervised learning. In *IEEE ICDM*, 2016.

[15] Hoang Thanh Lam, Johann-Michael Thiebaut, Mathieu Sinn, Bei Chen, Tiep Mai, and Oznur Alkan. One button machine for automating feature engineering in relational databases. *arXiv preprint arXiv:1706.00327*, 2017.

[16] Jundong Li, Kewei Cheng, Suhang Wang, Fred Morstatter, Trevino Robert, Jiliang Tang, and Huan Liu. Feature selection: A data perspective. *arXiv:1601.07996*, 2016.

[17] Lisha Li, Kevin G. Jamieson, Giulia DeSalvo, Afshin Rostamizadeh, and Ameet Talwalkar. Efficient hyperparameter optimization and infinitely many armed bandits. *CoRR*, abs/1603.06560, 2016.

[18] Shaul Markovitch and Dan Rosenstein. Feature generation using general constructor functions. *Machine Learning*, 2002.

[19] Christopher J Matheus and Larry A Rendell. Constructive induction on decision trees. *IJCAI*, 1989.

[20] Fatemeh Nargesian, Horst Samulowitz, Udayan Khurana, Elias B. Khalil, and Deepak Turaga. Learning feature engineering for classification. In *Proceedings of the Twenty-Sixth International Joint Conference on Artificial Intelligence, IJCAI-17*, pages 2529–2535, 2017.

[21] Harish Ragavan, Larry Rendell, Michael Shaw, and Antoinette Tessmer. Complex concept acquisition through directed search and feature caching. *IJCAI*, 1993.

[22] John Shawe-Taylor and Nello Cristianini. *Kernel Methods for Pattern Analysis*. Cambridge University Press, 2004.

[23] Matthew G. Smith and Larry Bull. *Feature Construction and Selection Using Genetic Programming and a Genetic Algorithm*, pages 229–237. Springer Berlin Heidelberg, Berlin, Heidelberg, 2003.

[24] Nitish Srivastava, Geoffrey Hinton, Alex Krizhevsky, Ilya Sutskever, and Ruslan Salakhutdinov. Dropout: A simple way to prevent neural networks from overfitting. *Journal of Machine Learning*, 15(1):1929–1958, 2014.

[25] Dmitry Storcheus, Afshin Rostamizadeh, and Sanjiv Kumar. A survey of modern questions and challenges in feature extraction. *Proceedings of the 1st International Workshop on Feature Extraction: Modern Questions and Challenges at NIPS*, 2015.

[26] Richard S Sutton and Andrew G Barto. *Reinforcement Learning: An Introduction*, volume 1. MIT Press Cambridge, 1998.

[27] Lu Wang, Ge Luo, Ke Yi, and Graham Cormode. Quantiles over data streams: An experimental study. *SIGMOD*, pages 737–748, 2013.

[28] Christopher JCH Watkins and Peter Dayan. Q-learning. *Machine Learning*, 8(3-4):279–292, 1992.

[29] Der-Shung Yang, Larry Rendell, and G Blix. Fringe-like feature construction: A comparative study and a unifying scheme. *ICML*, 1991.

Chapter 10

Pattern-Based Feature Generation

Yunzhe Jia

School of Computing and Information Systems, The University of Melbourne

James Bailey

School of Computing and Information Systems, The University of Melbourne

Ramamohanarao Kotagiri

School of Computing and Information Systems, The University of Melbourne

Christopher Leckie

School of Computing and Information Systems, The University of Melbourne

10.1   Introduction

Frequent patterns are combinations of feature values that have a high frequency of co-occurrence, which can represent interesting relationships among instances in the dataset. For example, one may find that milk and bread usually appear together in a store's transactions, and thus {milk, bread} is a frequent pattern. Frequent pattern mining is a classic problem in data mining research. In this chapter, we investigate how frequent patterns can be used to generate features.

The intuition behind the idea of generating features using patterns is that feature combinations can be more discriminative than individual features [11] [19] [40]. For example, in the case of document classification, word phrases are more useful than single words. While exhaustive exploration of possible feature combinations is usually computationally infeasible, pattern-based techniques provide a solution to reduce the search space for feature combinations and generate features that have good predictive power.

Besides the discriminative ability of patterns, they can also result in features that are highly interpretable. Compared with similar methods such as Principle Component Analysis (PCA) and other kernel methods, the interpretability of patterns enables users to reason about why a data mining system (e.g., a classifier) yields certain outcomes, especially when the outcomes contradict previous expectations.

Generating features using patterns generally follows three steps:

- Pattern mining. This addresses the question of how to generate patterns from a dataset.

- Pattern selection. This process selects representatives with high quality and removes useless patterns.

- Feature generation. This constructs a new feature space based on patterns. In the new pattern feature space, each instance is usually mapped to an m-dimensional vector, where m is the number of patterns.

This chapter is organized as follows: Definitions and preliminaries are represented in Section 10.2. The framework of pattern-based feature generation is given in Section 10.3. Approaches to generating patterns are discussed in Section 10.4. Techniques to prune large pattern sets are given in Section 10.5.

Table 10.1: Synthetic transaction data

TID	Items
T_1	a, b, c, d
T_2	a, c, e
T_3	b, c, d
T_4	a, e
T_5	a, b, c

Strategies for constructing new features using patterns are discussed in Section 10.6. Applications of pattern-based feature generation for classification and clustering are given in Section 10.7 and Section 10.8 respectively.

10.2   Preliminaries

10.2.1   Data and Patterns

Frequent patterns are usually applied to transaction data, which assumes that there is a universal set of items in a given domain. Let $\mathcal{I} = \{I_1, I_2, \ldots, I_m\}$ be the set of all items. A *transaction* T is a non-empty subset of $\mathcal{I}$ (each transaction may also be associated with a unique transaction identifier tid), and a dataset $\mathcal{T} = \{T_1, T_2, \ldots, T_n\}$ is a set of transactions.

A *pattern* p is also a non-empty subset of $\mathcal{I}$. The length of a pattern is defined by the number of items it contains. A pattern p is sometimes referred to as an *l*-pattern if its length is *l*. A transaction T matches (or satisfies) a pattern p if $p \subseteq T$.

The *matching dataset* of a pattern p in a dataset $\mathcal{T}$ is denoted as $mds(p, \mathcal{T})$, which is a subset of $\mathcal{T}$ where all transactions in the subset match p, and is formally defined as $mds(p, \mathcal{T}) = \{T \in \mathcal{T} | T \text{ matches } p\}$.

The *support* of a pattern in a dataset $\mathcal{T}$ is denoted as $support(p, \mathcal{T})$, which is equal to the proportion of transactions of $mds(p, \mathcal{T})$ in $\mathcal{T}$, and is formally defined as $support(p, \mathcal{T}) = \frac{|mds(p, \mathcal{T})|}{|\mathcal{T}|}$. A pattern p is called frequent if its support is greater than or equal to a user-specified threshold $minSupp$.

Table 10.2.1 depicts a synthetic transaction dataset with five transactions (T_1, T_2, T_3, T_4 and T_5). The first column shows the ID of each transaction, and the second column shows the items in the transaction. Table 10.2.1 depicts the frequent patterns mined from the above dataset with minimum support $minSupp = 0.6$. Each pattern has at least three transactions in its matching dataset. For example, pattern $p_4 = \{a, c\}$ is matched by T_1, T_2 and T_5 and thus its support is 3/5=0.6.

Table 10.2: Frequent pattern set with threshold $minSupp = 0.6$

Pattern	Items	Matching dataset	support
p_1	a	T_1, T_2, T_4, T_5	0.8
p_2	b	T_1, T_3, T_5	0.6
p_3	c	T_1, T_2, T_3, T_5	0.8
p_4	a, c	$T_1.T_2, T_5$	0.6
p_5	b, c	T_1, T_3, T_5	0.6

10.2.2   Patterns for Non-Transactional Data

Patterns for Vector Data

When the data is non-transactional, the definition of a pattern can be extended in a similar way. Vector/tuple data is commonly used in data mining tasks. For vector data, there is a pre-defined set $\{F_1, F_2, \ldots, F_m\}$ of features/attributes, and each feature F_i is associated with a domain $dom(F_i)$, which could be numeric (continuous) or nominal (discrete). Table 10.3 gives an example of vector/tuple data. The dataset consists of three features F_1, F_2 and F_3 (TID helps to identify the instances and is not in the feature set), where F_1, F_2 are nominal and F_3 is numeric. In particular, $dom(F_1) = \{a,b,c\}$, $dom(F_2) = \{yes,no\}$ and $dom(F_3) = [1,10]$.

As most pattern mining algorithms are designed for transactional data, vector data is usually transformed into transactional data with a discretization process for numeric features. For nominal features, the feature-value pair of an instance can be directly transformed to an item in the form of "feature=value." For numeric features, the domain of these features is divided into a finite number of disjunctive intervals, and the feature-value pair of an instance is transformed into an item in the form "feature $\in$ interval," where the value of the numeric feature must belong to the given interval. There are many discretization approaches, including the following commonly used approaches [16]: 1) equal-width, which divides the domain of a numeric feature into intervals of equal width, 2) equal-density, where all intervals have the same number of instances, and 3) entropy-based discretization, which iteratively generates splitting points using information gain [20].

The transformation of the dataset shown in Table 10.3 to the corresponding transactional dataset is given in Table 10.4. Equal-width discretization is used for F_3 where the width is set to 5.

In the case of vector/tuple data types, a pattern is a conjunction of feature-value pairs (e.g., $\{F_1 = a \land F_3 \in [5, 10]\}$).

Table 10.3: Synthetic vector/tuple data

TID	F_1	F_2	F_3
T_1	a	yes	1
T_2	b	no	3
T_3	a	yes	5
T_4	c	yes	9

Table 10.4: Corresponding transactional data

TID	Items
T_1	F_1=a, F_2=yes, $F_3 \in [1,5)$
T_2	F_1=b, F_2=no, $F_3 \in [1,5)$
T_3	F_1=a, F_2=yes, $F_3 \in [5,10]$
T_4	F_1=c, F_2=yes, $F_3 \in [5,10]$

Patterns for Sequence Data

In sequence data, there is also a universal set of items denoted by $\mathcal{I} = \{I_1, I_2, \ldots, I_m\}$. A *sequence* is an ordered list of itemsets, and it is denoted by $\langle s_1, s_2, \ldots, s_l \rangle$, where s_i is an itemset. A pattern in sequence data is represented as a *subsequence*. A sequence $\langle a_1, a_2, \ldots, a_l \rangle$ is a subsequence of $\langle b_1, b_2, \ldots, b_n \rangle$ if there exist integers $1 \leq j_1 \leq j_2 \leq \ldots \leq j_l \leq n$ such that $a_i \subseteq b_{j_i}$ for $i = 1, 2, \ldots l$.

Table 10.2.2 gives an example of a sequence dataset, where the set of items is $\{a, b, c, d, e, f, g\}$. Each sequence is associated with a sequence identifier SID. An itemset within a sequence is represented using brackets, and for brevity, when an itemset contains only one item, the brackets are omitted. The first sequence $\langle a(abc)(be) \rangle$ contains three itemsets: a, (abc) and (be). Sequence $\langle abe \rangle$ is a subsequence of S_1, while $\langle ade \rangle$ is not.

Table 10.5: Synthetic sequence data

SID	Items
S_1	$\langle a(abc)(be) \rangle$
S_2	$\langle a(ce)(bf)g \rangle$
S_3	$\langle (ab)(acd)(be) \rangle$
S_4	$\langle (be)(dg) \rangle$

Patterns for Graph Data

A labeled graph G can be represented using a 4-tuple (V, E, α, β), where V is a vertex set, $E \subseteq V \times V$ is a edge set, α is a function that assigns labels to vertices, and function β assigns a label to edges. A pattern in the scenario of graph data is a *subgraph*. Given two labeled graphs $G = (V, E, \alpha, \beta)$ and $G' = (V', E', \alpha', \beta')$, G is a subgraph of G' iff

- $V \subseteq V'$,

- $\forall v \in V, \alpha(v) = \alpha'(v)$,

- $E \subseteq E'$,

- $\forall(u, v) \in E, \beta(u, v) = \beta'(u, v)$.

Contrast Patterns

Frequent patterns are mined in an unsupervised manner, where no class information is considered. It is natural to extend this concept from a supervised perspective.

Suppose a dataset $\mathcal{T}$ is associated with classes/labels $C_1, C_2, \ldots, C_k$, and $\mathcal{T}$ can be partitioned into k disjoint groups $\mathcal{T}_1, \mathcal{T}_2, \ldots, \mathcal{T}_k$ where all transactions in $\mathcal{T}_i$ have class C_i. A *contrast pattern* or *discriminative pattern* is a pattern that occurs frequently only in one subset with a certain class value while infrequently in the rest. In other words, the support of a contrast pattern differs significantly between the subset of interest and the rest of the dataset.

Assume dataset $\mathcal{T}_p$ labeled as C_p is the subset that is being contrasted or discriminated against the remaining subset $\mathcal{T}_n$, where $\mathcal{T}_n = \bigcup_{i \neq p} \mathcal{T}_i$. There are two common ways to define a contrast pattern: based on growth ratio or based on support delta.

The *growth ratio* of a pattern p is the ratio of the support of p in $\mathcal{T}_p$ to the support of p in $\mathcal{T}_n$: $GrRatio(p, \mathcal{T}_p, \mathcal{T}_n) = support(p, \mathcal{T}_p)/support(p, \mathcal{T}_n)$. The *support delta* of a pattern p is the difference of the support of p in $\mathcal{T}_p$ and the support of p in $\mathcal{T}_n$: $Supp_\delta(p, \mathcal{T}_p, \mathcal{T}_n) = support(p, \mathcal{T}_p) - support(p, \mathcal{T}_n)$. A pattern is called a contrast pattern or discriminative pattern if the chosen measure (growth ratio or support delta) is at least equal to a user-specified threshold. All discussions in this chapter will use the growth ratio to define a contrast pattern, and scenarios based on the support delta extend in a similar way.

Table 10.6: Example dataset $\mathcal{T}$ for contrast patterns

TID	F_1	F_2	F_3	Class
T_1	true	false	1	1
T_2	true	true	2	1
T_3	false	false	5	0
T_4	false	true	3	1

Take the data set $\mathcal{T}$ shown in Table 10.2.2 as an example. Consider two patterns $p = \{F1 = \text{true}, F3 <= 3\}, q = \{F2 = \text{false}\}$. The matching data sets of p, q are $mds(p, \mathcal{T}) = \{T_1, T_2\}$, $mds(q, \mathcal{T}) = \{T_1, T_3\}$, and the corresponding supports are $supp(p, \mathcal{T}) = supp(q, \mathcal{T}) = \frac{2}{4} = 0.5$. Assume the data set is split into $\mathcal{T}_1 = \{T_1, T_2, T_4\}$ and $\mathcal{T}_2 = \{T_3\}$ by the class label, and the task is to find contrast patterns for $\mathcal{T}_1$. Then the growth ratios of p, q are $GrRatio(p, \mathcal{T}_1, \mathcal{T}_2) = \frac{2}{0} = +\infty$, and $GrRatio(q, \mathcal{T}_1, \mathcal{T}_2) = \frac{1}{1} = 1$. Pattern p is called a contrast pattern for $\mathcal{T}_1$ and q is not, if $minRatio$ is set to be greater than 1.

10.3 Framework of Pattern-Based Feature Generation

The framework of pattern-based generation follows three steps: 1) pattern mining, 2) pattern selection, and 3) feature generation. As shown in Figure 10.1, a pattern set Q is first mined from the given dataset. Then Q is pruned to a set P of representative patterns where insignificant and redundant patterns are removed. Finally, the remaining patterns are used to build a new feature space and the original dataset is mapped into the pattern feature space. The new feature space built on patterns is referred to as the *pattern space*.

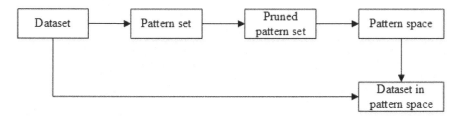

Figure 10.1: Framework of pattern-based generation.

An example of the framework is given in Figure 10.2. The original vector dataset contains n instances represented in feature space $\mathcal{F}^{\lceil} = (F_1, F_2, \ldots, F_d)$. A pattern set Q containing l patterns is first mined from the original dataset. Then the pattern set is pruned to a smaller set $P = \{p_1, p_2, \ldots, p_m\}$, which contains the representative patterns with high quality according to user-specified measures. With the final pattern set P, the new pattern space $\mathcal{F}_p^m = (F_{p_1}, F_{p_2}, \ldots, F_{p_m})$ is built based on these patterns. In the pattern space, each feature is a pattern and its feature value is calculated by a mapping function $\phi_i(x)$, which maps an instance in the original feature space into the feature value for pattern p_i.

For structural data types like sequence data and graph data, one follows the same framework to convert the structural data into vector data, such that existing vector-based algorithms (e.g., SVM) can be directly applied on the transformed data.

10.3.1 Pattern Mining

Pattern mining is the initial step, where the inputs and outputs are described as follows:

- **Input:** $\mathcal{T} = \{t_1, t_2, \ldots, t_n\}$, $minSupp$, (optional) $minRatio$

- **Output:** $Q = \{q_1, q_2, \ldots, q_l\}$

$\mathcal{T} = \{t_1, t_2, \ldots, t_n\}$ is the given dataset, the common types include: 1)

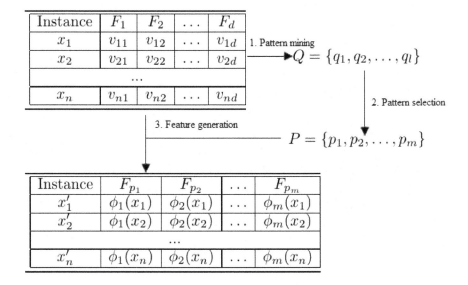

Figure 10.2: Framework of pattern-based generation.

transactional data, 2) vector data, 3) sequence data, and 4) graph data. Transactional data and vector data are usually handled in the same way as they are mutually convertible. For sequence and graph data, extra information such as spatial distance should be taken into consideration.

minSupp is the minimum support threshold. It is used to describe the degree to which a pattern is called frequent in a dataset. Although it is the only required parameter for most pattern mining algorithms, the quality of a pattern can be measured from other perspectives, such as information gain, given different domains. Thus a small *minSupp* is usually desired to avoid information loss.

minRatio is required in the case of contrast pattern mining. It is used to describe the degree to which a pattern is considered significant in a subset while insignificant in the rest of the dataset. Contrast patterns are more widely used for classification as they capture the relationship between features and class labels. The choice of *minRatio* is similar to the choice of *minSupp* and a small value is commonly used.

$Q = \{q_1, q_2, \dots, q_l\}$ is the output of the mining process and is a set containing l patterns.

10.3.2   Pattern Selection

As *minSupp* and *minRatio* are usually set to small values, the pattern set size is usually large and some of the patterns can be noisy and even useless.

This motivates the problem of pruning the pattern set and selecting representative patterns for a given domain and task. The inputs and outputs are:

- **Input**: $Q = \{q_1, q_2, \ldots, q_l\}$, $s(p)$, $r(p_i, p_j)$, $eval(PS)$, k

- **Output**: $P = \{p_1, p_2, \ldots, p_m\}$

$Q = \{q_1, q_2, \ldots, q_l\}$ is a pattern set containing l patterns, which is the output from the previous mining process.

$s(p)$ defines a scoring function for individual patterns, which evaluates the significance of a pattern. Commonly used measures include support, growth ratio and information gain.

$r(p_i, p_j)$ evaluates the redundancy between two patterns p_i and p_j. It could be a distance function or similarity function such as l_1 norm distance or Jaccard similarity.

$eval(PS)$ measures the overall quality of a pattern set PS and it is usually the objective function for the final task such as classification or clustering. It helps to find an optimal or an approximately optimal pattern set in terms of the given tasks.

k is the constraint on the number of patterns, which means that at most k patterns are desired.

$s(p)$, $r(p_i, p_j)$, $eval(Q)$, k are all optional and the definitions of them depend on the specific domains or applications.

$P = \{p_1, p_2, \ldots, p_m\}$ is the output of the reduced pattern set containing m patterns. If k is given, then $m \leq k$.

10.3.3 Feature Generation

When the patterns are available, the next process creates new features based on these patterns, and maps the original data into the new feature space. There are two strategies to build the new feature space: 1) feature extraction, which creates new features using patterns, and 2) feature filtering, which selects a subset of the original features based on pattern information.

Feature generation using patterns creates new features and defines a mapping function from the original feature space to the new pattern space. Assume a dataset has d features and each instance in the dataset is a d-dimensional vector. Let $\mathcal{F}^d = (F_1, F_2, \ldots, F_d)$ denote the original d-dimensional feature space. The pattern set $P = \{p_1, p_2, \ldots, p_m\}$ is used to construct the new pattern space denoted by $\mathcal{F}_p^m = (F_{p_1}, F_{p_2}, \ldots, F_{p_m})$. Then a mapping function $\Phi : x \mapsto x', x \in \mathcal{F}^d, x' \in \mathcal{F}_p^m$ is defined to transform the original d-dimensional instances into m-dimensional vectors in the pattern space, where each feature corresponds to a pattern. After the new pattern space is generated, it could either be used solely or combined with the original feature space for further analysis.

10.4   Pattern Mining Algorithms

Pattern mining is the first step for pattern-based feature generation, and it provides a set of candidate patterns for the next process. This section presents common techniques to generate frequent patterns and contrast patterns. For each discussion, we first consider the cases for transactional data and vector data, then extend to the cases for sequence data and graph data where appropriate.

10.4.1   Frequent Pattern Mining

Common pattern mining algorithms can be categorized into three types and their variants: 1) Apriori, 2) FP-growth, and 3) Eclat. These three basic algorithms are discussed in this section.

Apriori

Apriori [4] uses a level-wise search to find patterns, where l-patterns are used to find $(l + 1)$-patterns. It starts with patterns with length 1, and all patterns in the initial set contain only one item. At each iteration, a pruning procedure is conducted to remove patterns that do not meet the minimum support threshold. The pruning process is based on the Apriori property: all non-empty subsets of a frequent pattern must also be frequent. It stops when no more patterns can be found. The detailed algorithm is given in Algorithm 3.

Algorithm 3 Apriori algorithm

1: **procedure** APRIORI($\mathcal{T}, minSupp$)
2:      $P_1 = \{$length-1 frequent patterns$\}$
3:      $c = 2$
4:      **while** $P_{c-1} \neq \emptyset$ **do**
5:          $Temp_c =$ generate length-c candidates from P_{c-1}
6:          **for** every T in $\mathcal{T}$ **do**
7:              **for** every p in $temp_c$ **do**
8:                  **if** T matches p **then**
9:                      $p.count$++
10:         $P_c = \{p \in temp_c | p.count \geq minSupp * |\mathcal{T}|\}$
11:     Return $\cup_c P_c$.

The inputs include the dataset $\mathcal{T}$ and the minimum support threshold $minSupp$. Line 2 generates all length-1 frequent patterns from the dataset as initial pattern sets. Lines 4–10 repeatedly find length-c candidates from length-$(c-1)$ frequent patterns and remove candidates whose supports are less than $minSupp$.

The main drawback of Apriori is that it needs to scan the entire dataset at every iteration. Many variants [25] have been proposed to improve the efficiency from perspectives like hashing techniques [43], sampling techniques [50] and distributed mining [2].

Sequence patterns also follow the Apriori property: any non-empty subsequence of a frequent sequence pattern must also be frequent. AprioriAll [3] and GSP [48] are two approaches that mine sequence patterns based on the Apriori property.

For graph data, typical Apriori-based techniques [32] [35] [51] discover graph patterns starting with small-size graphs and iteratively increase the size by 1 to generate larger graphs.

FP-growth

Frequent pattern growth (FP-growth) [29] first compresses a dataset into a frequent pattern tree (FP-tree) and then generates patterns directly from the tree. Unlike Apriori that repeatedly scans the whole dataset at each generation of l-patterns and generates a large number of candidates, FP-growth only scans the dataset twice and does not generate candidates that are not frequent.

Given the dataset $\mathcal{T}$ and the minimum support threshold $minSupp$, FP-growth is described in Algorithm 4.

Algorithm 4 FP-growth algorithm

1: **procedure** FP-GROWTH($\mathcal{T}, minSupp$)
2:    Scan the dataset and sort all length-1 patterns in frequency-descending order.
3:    Construct an FP-tree. Start with a root node labeled as "null" and associated with a count 0. Then scan the dataset again. For every transaction, create a path containing all the items in the 1-patterns' order. If the path $\mathcal{P}$ and some branch $\mathcal{B}$ in the tree share a common prefix, increase the counts of all nodes in the prefix by 1, and then create a new branch using the remaining suffix of $\mathcal{P}$ and link it to the last node of $\mathcal{B}$ as a child.
4:    $P = \{\}$.
5:    Generate patterns from the FP-tree. Start with the root node with prefix=$\{\}$, and recursively process the node as follows: concatenate the given prefix with the node being processed to form a new pattern and add it to P, then use the new pattern as the new prefix and pass it to its child nodes whose associated counts satisfy the threshold $minSupp$.
6:    Return P.

Experiments in [29] have shown that FP-growth is efficient and scalable, and is typically an order of magnitude faster than Apriori. Several variants have been proposed to improve FP-growth, and interested readers can refer to [25].

FreeSpan [27] and its extension PrefixSpan [28] are the FP-Growth-like approaches for sequence data. They mine sequence patterns by dividing the dataset into smaller groups and generating longer patterns from shorter patterns recursively.

For graph data, pattern-growth-based algorithms maintain a frequent graph by adding new edges in all possible positions incrementally. gSpan [60] avoids generating duplicates by performing depth-first search and using a right-most-extension technique.

Eclat

Both Apriori and FP-growth mine patterns from datasets in horizontal data format $\{tid : \text{itemset}\}$, where tid is the transaction identifier. Correspondingly, the datasets can be transformed into vertical data format $\{\text{item} : tid\_\text{set}\}$. Elact [63] mines patterns from vertical datasets.

First, the original dataset is transformed into a dataset in vertical form. Similar to Apriori, it repeatedly generates $(l+1)$-patterns from l-patterns using the Apriori principle, and terminates when no patterns can be found. Unlike Apriori, Eclat does not repeatedly scan the original datasets. However, if the tid_set can be quite long, then Eclat faces the same challenges as Apriori. It has also been proven that Eclat works for the situation where a dataset contains many dense and long patterns [26].

SPAD [62] and SPAM [5] transform horizontal sequence datasets into vertical format, and mine frequent sequence patterns based on the Apriori property.

10.4.2   Contrast Pattern Mining

In this stage, the growth ratio is chosen as the threshold parameter to find contrast patterns. The use of other thresholds such as the support delta follows a similar approach.

Indirect Contrast Pattern Mining

An intuitive approach for contrast pattern mining is to mine frequent patterns first, then select patterns that meet the growth ratio threshold. The framework is described in Algorithm 5. The inputs include the frequent pattern set FP, the minimum growth ratio $minRatio$, the positive dataset $\mathcal{T}_p$ and the negative dataset $\mathcal{T}_n$. The procedure first calculates the growth ratios for every pattern and remove the patterns whose ratios are less than $minRatio$.

The methods proposed in [11] [15] [14] [19] [39] [41] all belong to this two-step framework. The major problem of two-step mining is its efficiency.

Algorithm 5 Indirect contrast pattern mining algorithm

1: **procedure** INDIRECTCONTRASTPATTERNMINING($FP, minRatio, \mathcal{T}_p, \mathcal{T}_n$)
2:     $CP = \{\}$
3:     **for** every p in FP **do**
4:         $p.ratio = \frac{support(p_i, \mathcal{T}_p)}{support(p_i, \mathcal{T}_n)}$
5:         **if** $p.ratio \geq minRatio$ **then**
6:             $CP = CP \cup \{p\}$
7:     Return CP

Direct Contrast Pattern Mining

Direct contrast pattern mining directly discovers contrast patterns without generating a large number of candidates, thus it is more efficient than indirect contrast pattern mining.

The work in [17] mines contrast patterns (which are called emerging patterns by the authors) by manipulating the borders (collection of closed patterns and generators).

The method proposed in [7] uses Apriori-like algorithms to generate contrast patterns. When pruning length-k candidates, it also prunes the patterns that do not meet the contrast criteria (support differences are used in this paper). This method suffers the same problem as Apriori, which needs to scan the whole dataset at every iteration.

DDPMine [12] progressively reduces the data size by eliminating instances that are covered by found patterns. It generates one pattern at each iteration and removes the instances that match the pattern, and terminates when the remaining dataset is empty.

HARMONY [55] uses a instance-centric approach to generate patterns. It ensures that every instance is associated with a pattern with the highest confidence.

DPClass [46] generates patterns using a random forest. It first constructs a random forest from the dataset, and then transforms the path from the root to a non-leaf node into a pattern for every tree in the forest. Although it is efficient even with large datasets, the search space is smaller compared with other techniques.

In the scenario where transactions can be inserted and/or deleted over time, repeatedly running the mining algorithms is time-consuming. The works in [38] [6] propose methods to incrementally generate contrast patterns.

For sequence data, a direct mining algorithm is proposed in [33], which generates patterns using depth-first search in a lexicographic sequence tree and checks the supports of patterns using an efficient bitset technique. This algorithm is efficient even with a low support threshold.

For graph data, [49] utilizes the connections of maximal common edge sets and the minimal contrast edge sets to generate contrast graph patterns.

Though direct contrast pattern mining avoids the generation of a complete frequent pattern set, it suffers the problem that some critical contrast patterns may be missing from the search space.

10.5   Pattern Selection Approaches

The choice of the minimum support threshold $minSupp$ has a major impact on the number of frequent patterns mined. The larger $minSupp$ is, the smaller the pattern set size is, and vice versa. In general, a relatively small $minSupp$ is chosen because a large $minSupp$ also results in considerable information loss during the mining process. Thus there are many frequent patterns, and exploiting all of them is redundant and usually computationally infeasible. This calls for pruning these patterns to reduce the number of patterns and choosing the best representatives to preserve the information in the dataset. There are two categories of techniques to prune a pattern set: post-processing pruning and in-processing pruning. Post-processing pruning techniques reduce the number of patterns after pattern candidates are generated. It is independent from the pattern mining algorithm, and thus can be employed for any existing mining algorithms. In-processing pruning techniques prune the pattern size during the mining process. It can avoid generating a large number of candidates, thus improving efficiency.

10.5.1   Post-Processing Pruning

Post-processing pruning follows a pattern mining procedure that typically takes data and a minimum support threshold $minSupp$ as inputs, and outputs a set of pattern candidates denoted as P. The set P is then used as input to the post-processing pruning procedure, optionally together with a threshold k, which means that at most k patterns are desired. The goal of post-processing pruning is to remove weak patterns or redundant patterns and output a pruned pattern set Q, which is a subset of P. The definition of the strength or redundancy of a pattern varies in different domains or scenarios, and is discussed as follows.

Equivalence Class

The concept of an *equivalence class* helps to select representatives and remove redundant patterns [8] [44]. The equivalence class of a pattern p in a dataset $\mathcal{T}$ is the pattern set $EC(p) = \{q|mds(q,\mathcal{T}) = mds(p,\mathcal{T})\}$, where all patterns in $EC(p)$ have the same matching dataset as p. A pattern p is called a *closed pattern* if there exists no superset q of p such that $p \subset q$ and $q \in EC(p)$. Similarly, a pattern p is called a *generator* if there exists no subset q of p such that $q \subset p$ and $q \in EC(p)$. Closed patterns and generators are representatives of an equivalence class. An equivalence class contains one closed pattern and at least one generator.

Table 10.7: Dataset used to illustrate the equivalence class

TID	Items
T_1	a, b, c
T_2	a, b, c, d
T_3	a, b, c, e
T_4	b, g, f
T_5	a, d

Table 10.8: Closed pattern and generator

Equivalence class	{c}, {a, b}, {a, c}, {b, c}, {a, b, c}
Closed pattern	{a, b, c}
Generator	{c},{a, b}

Given the dataset shown in Table 10.7, an equivalence class is illustrated in Table 10.8. Patterns {c}, {a, b}, {a, c}, {b, c}, {a, b, c} are in the same equivalence class and the matching dataset of all of them is $\{T_1, T_2, T_3\}$. Pattern {a} is not in this equivalence class as it is also matched by T_4, which is not in the matching dataset of the others. Pattern {a, b, c} is the closed pattern in this equivalence class and patterns {c},{a, b} are generators.

Though selecting closed patterns and/or generators reduces the pattern set size, the number of patterns mined for further analysis is still large especially when the support threshold is low. Pruning using equivalence class is usually used as the initial step, and closed patterns or generators are commonly selected as pattern candidates for further pruning.

Profile-Based Techniques

A profile-based pruning method is proposed in [59]. It first introduces a statistical model to deal with frequent patterns. Patterns are clustered into k clusters, then all patterns in each cluster are merged into one pattern profile. A probability distribution vector is used to represent a pattern profile. For item set $I = \{a_1, a_2, \ldots, a_k\}$, a pattern profile is represented as $p = \{g(a_1), g(a_2), \ldots, g(a_k)\}$, where $g(a_i)$ is the probability of item a_i occurring in the pattern. Moreover, it uses Kullback-Leibler (KL) divergence to measure the quality of a pattern. By using a probabilistic representation of patterns, it enables the use of a "fuzzy match" which relaxes the strict match that a pattern should be a subset of a transaction. When partitioning patterns into K clusters, it requires the patterns to be strongly correlated in both composition and support.

These pattern profiles are representatives of the pattern clusters, and depend heavily on the applied clustering algorithms (e.g., K means). The whole process requires good design of distance measures for clustering. The interpretability of pattern profiles as new patterns is another issue, as the profiles are just statistical counts of items.

Redundancy-Based Techniques

A redundancy-aware method is proposed in [58]. Quality measurement of pattern redundancy is based on the coverage of the pattern set on the data. This method maximizes the coverage of patterns (or minimizes the number of transactions that are not covered by any pattern). Similarly, another redundancy-based method is KRIMP proposed in [52], which applies the Minimal Description Length Principle (MDL) to find an optimal pattern set to cover the dataset best as well as to reduce the redundancy of patterns. The exact optimizations of these two methods are NP-hard, thus heuristic algorithms are used to approximate the optimal solution. Both methods avoid the problem that similar patterns are ranked closely and pruned results are not diversified. One drawback of these techniques is that they consider significance (e.g., support) and redundancy separately, thus the patterns mined can have low significance.

Probabilistic Model-Based Techniques

In [53], frequent patterns help to construct a graphical model in the form of a Markov Random Field (MRF). During the construction of a MRF, a pattern is pruned if it cannot introduce significant dependency to the current model.

The advantages of using a probabilistic model include: 1) fast inference using existing algorithms (e.g., Chow-Liu tree [13]), and 2) a very good representation. While pattern mining remains a challenge for high-dimensional and time series data, probabilistic models can outperform traditional techniques. However, probabilistic models usually lack interpretability and assume the existence of prior distributions. Current research mainly focuses on using mined patterns to build the probabilistic model, where these patterns are still mined using classical algorithms.

10.5.2   In-processing Pruning

Post-processing pruning can be treated as a two-step procedure, which filters patterns from a large number of candidates that are generated using traditional pattern mining algorithms. To avoid the generation of useless candidates, in-processing pruning techniques are proposed. This is a one-step pattern mining approach, where the pruning strategy is incorporated in the mining process.

Constraint-Based Techniques

A constraint-based method is introduced in [23]. Two levels of constraints are used: local constraints (significance of a pattern, e.g., support, length) are imposed on individual patterns, together with global constraints (redundancy in a pattern set, e.g., distances among patterns, coverage on the data set) on the whole pattern set. It has the advantage that it gives an optimal solution given two levels of constraints. However, it depends heavily on the constraint programming solver and does not scale well to large datasets. On the other hand, it still remains a challenge to design useful but relatively small constraints, as the quality and efficiency is mainly affected by the choice of constraints.

Bayesian Theory-Based Techniques

A classification-oriented technique KRSNB is proposed in [22]. Instead of having an unlimited growing pattern space, this method pre-defines a pattern space, together with a prior distribution on this space. The process of pattern mining becomes extraction of local optima, and each local optima is a pattern. Then these patterns are used as classification rules.

The advantages of this method include: 1) It is a parameter-free method. 2) The resulting classifier has a competitive performance compared with other state-of-the-art pattern-based classifiers. 3) It is novel in the sense that it pre-defines a pattern space, which is different from traditional pattern mining methods. 4) It can apply directly to numeric data without requiring a discretization process.

However, it mainly suffers from problems that include: 1) The optimization process is heuristic and does not guarantee finding patterns that maximize the classification performance. 2) The performance depends heavily on the pre-defined pattern space.

Minimum Description Length (MDL)-Based Techniques

KRIMP [52], introduced earlier, can also be categorized as this type of technique. SLIM [47] is an MDL-based method that directly applies to the data, instead of an existing pattern set. This is also the main difference between KRIMP and SLIM. A code table is proposed to summarize the pattern space, then heuristic optimization using branch-and-bound is applied to mine good patterns following the principle of selecting highly frequent patterns with a short length.

SLIM's main advantages are: 1) It does not need to mine pattern sets using other techniques and can be directly applied to the data, which is efficient compared with post-processing methods. 2) It is parameter free. 3) It guarantees good coverage of the data. Meanwhile, SLIM is computationally expensive, and only performs well on small datasets. When using SLIM on large datasets, given a limited time, early termination is very likely to generate patterns of poor quality.

10.6   Pattern-Based Feature Generation

When the patterns are ready, the next step is then to create new features based on these patterns, and map the original data into the new feature space. Given a dataset $X = \{x_1, x_2, \ldots, x_n\}$, where x_i is a d-dimensional vector and a pattern set $P = \{p_1, p_2, \ldots, p_m\}$, a *mapping function* $\Phi(x)$ is defined to transform the original d-dimensional instances into m-dimensional vectors in the pattern feature space, where each feature corresponds to a pattern. Let $\mathcal{F}^d = (F_1, F_2, \ldots, F_d)$ denote the original d-dimensional feature space, and $\mathcal{F}_p^m = (F_{p_1}, F_{p_2}, \ldots, F_{p_m})$ denote the new pattern space. Then a mapping function $\Phi : x \mapsto x', x \in \mathcal{F}^d, x' \in \mathcal{F}_p^m$ is defined as $\Phi(x) = (\phi_1(x), \phi_2(x), \ldots, \phi_m(x))$, where $\phi_m(x)$ calculates the feature value.

10.6.1   Unsupervised Mapping Functions

Binary Mapping Function

Figure 10.3 gives an example of generating new features using patterns. The original data contains three features, *gender, age* and *pclss*, and the pattern set contains two patterns p_1, p_2. Thus the new feature space consists of two features corresponding to p_1, p_2. For an instance x, the ith value of the corresponding vector in the pattern space is 1 if x matches p_i, and 0 otherwise. The first instance matches p_1 but does not match p_2, thus the new instance is $(p_1 = 1, p_2 = 0)$. Similarly, instance 2 matches p_2 but does not match p_1, thus the new instance is $(p_1 = 0, p_2 = 1)$.

instance	gender	age	pclass
1	male	20	1st
2	female	12	3rd

$+$

$p_1 = (\text{gender} = \text{male, age} \geq 18)$
$p_2 = (\text{pclass} = \text{3rd})$

$=$

instance	p_1	p_2
1	1	0
2	0	1

Figure 10.3: Constructing a pattern space using a binary mapping function.

In the above example, the mapping function is a simple binary function. Formally, given a dataset $X = \{x_1, x_2, \ldots, x_n\}$ and a pattern set $P = \{p_1, p_2, \ldots, p_m\}$, the mapping function is defined as $\Phi(x) = (\phi_1(x), \phi_2(x), \ldots, \phi_m(x))$, where

$$\phi_i(x) = \begin{cases} 1, & \text{if } x \text{ matches } p_i \\ 0, & \text{otherwise.} \end{cases}$$

Binary mapping functions are the most widely used mapping functions for pattern-based feature generation. PatClass [11] and DDPMine [12] use binary mapping functions to calculate the new values in the pattern space for vector data. The work in [61] uses the binary mapping function for sequence classification. The study in [21] transforms a set of graphs to vectors using a binary mapping function.

Frequency-Based Mapping Function

Binary mapping functions treat all patterns as equally important features, which does not hold for many cases. Patterns are either in good quality or poor quality given a user-specified scoring function, and it is natural to use these measures as feature values in the pattern space.

Support or frequency can be used as the indicator of pattern quality. The mapping function based on frequency is defined as $\Phi(x) = (\phi_1(x), \phi_2(x), \ldots, \phi_m(x))$, where

$$\phi_i(x) = \begin{cases} support(p_i), & \text{if } x \text{ matches } p_i \\ 0, & \text{otherwise.} \end{cases}$$

10.6.2 Supervised Mapping Functions

Confidence-Based Mapping Function

When using contrast patterns to build the new feature space, one can evaluate the confidence of a pattern and use it as a new feature value. Given a dataset $\mathcal{T}$ and a contrast pattern p that frequently occurs in a subset with class label c, the confidence of the pattern is

$$confidence(p) = \frac{support(p, \mathcal{T}_c)}{support(p, \mathcal{T})}$$

where $\mathcal{T}_c$ is the subset that contains all instances with class c in $\mathcal{T}$.

A mapping function using confidence is defined as $\Phi(x) = (\phi_1(x), \phi_2(x), \ldots, \phi_m(x))$, where

$$\phi_i(x) = \begin{cases} confidence(p_i), & \text{if } x \text{ matches } p_i \\ 0, & \text{otherwise.} \end{cases}$$

Growth Ratio-Based Mapping Function

Similar to confidence, the growth ratio is another indicator of the predictive power of a pattern. A mapping function using a growth ratio is defined as $\Phi(x) = (\phi_1(x), \phi_2(x), \ldots, \phi_m(x))$, where

$$\phi_i(x) = \begin{cases} GrRatio(p_i), & \text{if } x \text{ matches } p_i \\ 0, & \text{otherwise.} \end{cases}$$

The definition of growth ratio $GrRatio(p_i)$ can be found in Section 10.2.2. Similarly, one can also use the support delta as an alternative to the growth ratio, e.g., the work in [30] uses the support delta to measure the discriminative power of a pattern feature.

Chi-Square-Based Mapping Function

The contingency table of a contrast pattern p associated with class label c is shown in Table 10.9. n_{11} is the number of instances that match p and are labeled as c; n_{12} is the number of instances that match p but are not labeled as c; n_{21} is the number of instances that do not match p but are labeled as c; n_{21} is the number of instances that do not match p and also are not labeled as c.

Table **10.9**: The contingency table for pattern p in dataset $\mathcal{T}$

	c	$\neg c$	Total
p	n_{11}	n_{12}	a_1
$\neg p$	n_{21}	n_{22}	a_2
Total	$|\mathcal{T}_c| = b1$	$|\mathcal{T}_{\neg c}| = b_2$	$|\mathcal{T}| = N$

Given the contingency table of a pattern p, now we can define chi-square χ^2 for the pattern:

$$\chi^2(p) = \sum_{i=1}^{2} \sum_{j=1}^{2} \frac{(n_{ij} - E_{ij})^2}{E_{ij}}$$

where $E_{ij} = \frac{(\sum_{k=1}^{2} n_{ik}) \times (\sum_{k=1}^{2} n_{kj})}{N}$ is the expected frequency count in the corresponding cell of the contingency table.

Then the mapping function using χ^2 is defined as $\Phi(x) = (\phi_1(x), \phi_2(x), \dots, \phi_m(x))$, where

$$\phi_i(x) = \begin{cases} \chi^2(p_i), & \text{if } x \text{ matches } p_i \\ 0, & \text{otherwise.} \end{cases}$$

It is pointed out in CMAR [39] that a higher χ^2 value may favor minority classes, and the authors propose to use a weighted χ^2 measure to address the issue. Interested readers can refer to [39].

Hybrid Mapping Function

The mapping function can also be defined from combinations of different criteria. For example, CAEP [19] and the work in [45] measure the pattern quality from both the frequency and growth ratio. Similarly, the mapping function can be defined as $\Phi(x) = (\phi_1(x), \phi_2(x), \dots, \phi_m(x))$, where

$$\phi_i(x) = \begin{cases} \frac{GrRatio(p_i)}{GrRatio(p_i)+1} * support(p_i), & \text{if } x \text{ matches } p_i \\ 0, & \text{otherwise.} \end{cases}$$

10.6.3 Feature Generation for Sequence Data and Graph Data

The mapping functions discussed above can be directly applied on sequence data and graph data. The process transforms the structured sequences/graphs into vector format, where each sequence/graph is converted to a vector of feature values. Such transformation helps bridge the gap between vector-data-based techniques and sequence/graph data, e.g., an SVM can be directly applied on a transformed graph dataset.

There may be some special considerations for sequence data and graph data, e.g., the spatial distribution of a subsequence/subgraph can carry important information. Here we discuss a solution to build the mapping function using structural information from sequence/graphs.

For example, in sequence data, an important property can be how spread out the subsequences are. This can be defined as a function to measure how many gaps are interspersed within a subsequence. For example, given two strings "fare" and "father," "far" occurs as a subsequence of both, but we may consider that its occurrence in "fare" has more import as it is contiguous.

Given a sequence s and a subsequence pattern p, let $l(s,p)$ denote the length of the minimal contiguous sequence that contains p in s. For example, given the subsequence "far," "far" is the corresponding minimal contiguous sequence in "fare," thus the length is 3, and "father" is the corresponding minimal contiguous sequence in "father" thus the length is 6.

Now, we can define the mapping function as $\Phi(x) = (\phi_1(x), \phi_2(x), \ldots, \phi_m(x))$, where

$$\phi_i(x) = \begin{cases} l(x, p_i), & \text{if } x \text{ matches } p_i \\ 0, & \text{otherwise} \end{cases}$$

10.6.4 Comparison with Similar Techniques

One may consider the difference between frequent patterns and similar methods such as Principle Component Analysis (PCA) and Linear Discriminant Analysis (LDA) that select or construct new features from the original features. PCA produces a new feature space where features are ranked according to the amount of variance they capture in the original feature space, but there is no guarantee that the components also have good discriminative power and new generated features may not be interpretable. LDA aims to reduce the dimensionality of the original features while preserving as much information as possible, but it fails to capture relationships (e.g., correlations) among instances that belong to the same class.

Kernel methods also create new feature spaces and map data into those new spaces. However, designing good kernel functions is not be easy and it usually depends on domain knowledge. The interpretability of newly generated features is another issue, as in most cases they cannot even be understood by domain experts.

Spectrum kernel methods for sequence data and graph data are closely connected to pattern-based feature generation. They differ in the sense that spectrum kernel methods enumerate all possible subsequences/subgraphs up to a maximum length, and do not take the discriminative power of each subsequence/subgraph into consideration. Also, generating all possible subsequences/subtrees is computationally expensive and can require significant tuning afterwards.

10.7 Pattern-Based Feature Generation for Classification

Classification is a major topic in data mining. In a typical classification problem, a classifier is built on a training dataset, where the class information is known, then the classifier is able to give predictions for unseen data where the class information is unknown.

This section presents existing solutions that employ patterns for classification. The approaches fall into two categories: 1) direct classification in the pattern space, which makes predictions directly from the vector value of instances in the pattern space, and 2) indirect classification in the pattern space, which trains a classifier on the transformed dataset and makes a prediction using that classifier.

10.7.1 Problem Statement

Given a dataset $\mathcal{T} = \{t_1, t_2, \ldots, t_n\}$ associated with label set C in feature space $\mathcal{F} = (F_1, F_2, \ldots, F_d)$ shown in Table 10.10, and a pattern set $P = \{p_1, p_2, \ldots, p_m\}$ with new feature space $\mathcal{F}_p^m = (F_{p_1}, F_{p_2}, \ldots, F_{p_m})$ shown in Table 10.11, $\mathcal{T}$ is transformed into $\mathcal{T}' = \{t_1', t_2', \ldots, t_n'\}$ using a mapping function $\Phi(t) = (\phi_1(t), \phi_2(t), \ldots, \phi_m(t))$. **Classification in the pattern space** predicts the class label of an unseen instance t_{new} using its projection in the pattern space.

Table **10.10**: Dataset in original feature space

	F_1	F_2	$\ldots$	F_d	C
t_1	v_{11}	v_{12}	$\ldots$	v_{1n}	c_1
t_2	v_{21}	v_{22}	$\ldots$	v_{2n}	c_2
t_3	v_{31}	v_{32}	$\ldots$	v_{3n}	c_3
$\ldots$					

Table **10.11**: Dataset in pattern space

	F_{p_1}	F_{p_2}	$\ldots$	F_{p_m}	C
t'_1	$\phi_1(t_1)$	$\phi_2(t_1)$	$\ldots$	$\phi_m(t_1)$	c_1
t'_2	$\phi_1(t_2)$	$\phi_2(t_2)$	$\ldots$	$\phi_m(t_2)$	c_2
t'_3	$\phi_1(t_3)$	$\phi_2(t_3)$	$\ldots$	$\phi_m(t_3)$	c_3
$\ldots$					

10.7.2 Direct Classification in the Pattern Space

Every feature in the pattern space can be directly assigned with a class label, e.g., the class that is associated with a contrast pattern. Let c_i denote the class label associated with pattern p_i. Given an unseen instance t_{new} and $t'_{new} = (\phi_1(t_{new}), \phi_2(t_{new}), \ldots, \phi_m(t_{new}))$ in the pattern space, the prediction for t_{new} can be made directly from the feature values of t'_{new}.

The pattern-class $\langle p_i, c_i \rangle$ pair in the pattern space means that if patten p_i is satisfied, then the class label is c_i. Such rules provide **IF...THEN...** reasoning for classification, and can be easily understood by users. Many recent works suggest that such rule-based classifiers have the potential to be highly interpretable [10] [34] [36] [54], which is important for the user to decide whether a model or prediction is trustworthy or not.

Prediction by Most Probable Pattern

One solution is to rank the feature values in t'_{new} and find the feature F_{p_i} with the highest priority, and to assign the class label c_i associated with p_i to t_{new}. Formally:

$$ind = \operatorname*{argmax}_{i}(\phi_i(t_{new}))$$

$$prediction(t_{new}) = c_{ind}.$$

In the case that the values are all 0s in t'_{new}, a default class label is generally desired, and the default class is usually set as the class label that is associated with most instances in the training dataset.

If multiple patterns/features have the same highest value, we can randomly choose one as proposed in CBA [41].

CBA is a method that use only one pattern for direct classification on each given instance.

Prediction by Pattern Set

We can also use the feature values as weights of the corresponding patterns, and compute the weighted votes for each class. This technique leverages the contributions of all patterns. CAEP [19] and iCAEP [64] are earlier methods in this direction.

To predict an unseen instance t_{new}, it first creates a k-dimensional vector *vote*, where k is number of class labels, and then calculates the votes for each class using feature values in the pattern space:

$$vote[i] = \sum_{j:c_j=i} (\phi_j(t_{new}))$$

for $i = 1, 2, \ldots, k$. Then the class label with the highest vote is returned as the prediction for t_{new}.

CMAR [39], CPAR [42], JEP-C [37] and HARMONY [55] all follow this framework for vector data classification. The method in [65] is an implementation for sequence data.

10.7.3   Indirect Classification in the Pattern Space

Though making prediction directly from values in the pattern space is easily interpretable, the accuracy is still a bottleneck for this category of techniques. Another approach achieves better performance at the cost of less interpretability. It is indirect classification that builds a new classifier (it could be any classifier model) on the transformed data and makes predictions using the trained model.

The framework of the training process is shown in Algorithm 6. Given the training dataset $\mathcal{T}$ and a mapping function $\Phi(t)$, all the training instances are transformed into new instances in the pattern space using the mapping function, and a user-specified classifier is trained on the new instances.

Algorithm 6 Training process for indirect classification

1: **procedure** INDIRECTCLASSIFICATION_TRAIN$(cl, \mathcal{T}, \Phi(t))$
2:     $T' = \{\}$
3:     **for** every t in $\mathcal{T}$ **do**
4:         $t' = \Phi(t)$
5:         $T' = T' \cup \{t'\}$
6:     $cl.train(T')$
7:     Return cl

The framework of predicting an unseen instance is described in Algorithm 7. The unseen instance is first projected into the pattern space using the same mapping function used in the training process, and then predicted using the trained classifier cl.

Algorithm 7 Prediction process for indirect classification

1: **procedure** INDIRECTCLASSIFICATION_PREDICT$(cl, t, \Phi(t))$
2:     $t' = \Phi(t)$
3:     Return $cl.predict(t')$

PatClass [11] and DDPMine [12] belong to this framework for vector data. The work in [61] gives an implementation for sequence data, and [31] [21] are proposed for graph data.

For vector data, we can combine the original feature space and pattern space into a larger feature space if the dimensionality is not a concern. The combined feature space preserves the information of the original dataset and adds extra features that are discriminative.

10.7.4   Connection with Stacking Technique

The stacking method [57] trains a combiner classifier on predictions of several other classifiers. Several classifiers (that could be different types, or different parameter settings of the same type) are trained on the given dataset first, then a combiner classifier is trained to make predictions using all predictions of other classifiers as inputs.

Classification in the pattern space belongs to the framework of stacking techniques, as all the pattern features can be treated as special classifiers that always output single labels.

10.8   Pattern-Based Feature Generation for Clustering

The goal of clustering is to divide the data into groups where instances in the same group are similar to each other. Most clustering techniques require the notion of pairwise similarity, e.g., a distance function, which is crucial for their performance. The design of a good distance function usually depends on prior domain knowledge. Recent works [1] [18] have shown that frequent patterns can be used to help define the similarity between two instances, especially for high-dimensional data where distance is not very meaningful [9].

10.8.1   Clustering in the Pattern Space

One of the key steps in clustering is to measure pair-wise similarity between instances in a dataset. While the definition of similarity differs in different data types, transforming the original dataset into the pattern space provides uniform measures in terms of vector values in the pattern space, e.g., [24] measures the similarity of two sequences in the pattern space using cosine distance:

$$sim(s,t) = \frac{s' \cdot t'}{\|s'\|\|t'\|}$$

where s, t are two sequences, and s', t' are vectors that are projections of s, t in the pattern space.

Another commonly used measure is Hamming distance for vectors in the pattern space:

$$sim(s,t) = \sum_{i=1}^{m} |s_i - t_i|$$

where s, t are two sequences, and s', t' are vectors that are projections of s, t in the pattern space.

Clustering in the pattern space is similar to indirect classification in the pattern space, where the given original dataset (which could be transactions, vectors, sequences, graphs) is transformed into vectors in the pattern space, then traditional clustering algorithms (e.g., K-means) are applied on the new dataset [24] [56].

10.8.2 Subspace Clustering

In subspace clustering, no pattern feature space is generated, and patterns are used to filter the original features. The basic idea of subspace clustering is that two instances may not be similar over all attributes, but they are similar over a subset of attributes. A subset of attributes is referred to as a subspace. Defining similarity on the subspace can avoid the influences of "irrelevant attributes." Exhaustive exploration of all possible subspaces is computationally infeasible as there exist $2^d - 1$ subspaces for a d-dimensional dataset. Frequent pattern mining is one approach to help generate subspaces. Reference [1] gives the connection between frequent pattern mining and subspace search as illustrated in Table 10.8.2.

Table 10.12: Connection between frequent pattern mining and subspace search

Frequent pattern mining	Subspace search
Item	Dimension (attribute)
Pattern	Subspace (set of attributes)
Frequent patterns	'Interesting' subspace

Suppose a pattern p is mined as a subspace. Traditional similarity measures such as Euclidean distance and Jaccard distance can be applied on the attributes that occur in pattern p. For example, given two instances $x_1 = \{a, b, c, f\}$, $x_2 = \{b, c, d, e\}$ and a pattern $p = \{b, d\}$, and two instances are mapped to the pattern subspace as $x_1' = \{b\}$, $x_2' = \{b, d\}$, then the Jaccard distance of x_1, x_2 on subspace p is $Jaccard_p(x_1, x_2) = Jaccard(x_1', x_2') = \frac{|x_1 \cap x_2|}{|x_1 \cup x_2|} = \frac{1}{2}$.

10.9 Conclusion

This chapter has discussed the use of frequent patterns as features for data mining tasks. Frequent patterns are interpretable and have the potential to be highly discriminative features. Techniques to generate patterns and to prune a large pattern set were first discussed. Then we described techniques that employ frequent patterns to generate features for classification and clustering. We have also discussed scenarios where the underlying data type is a sequence or graph.

There are still many open questions in this area:

1. Most mapping functions evaluate the feature values in the pattern space solely by the significance of patterns, which can result in the domains of pattern features containing only two values: the significance of patterns and 0. This motivates the research direction to develop instance-level mapping functions that leverage the significance of patterns and that of instances. The gap-based mapping function for sequence data is an example where the same pattern can exhibit different levels of importance for difference instances.

2. Pattern mining techniques have been developed and applied in complex data types such as spatio-temporal data and image data. It is natural to extend the framework of pattern-based feature generation to new data types as well, especially in an efficient way.

3. Interpretability has drawn more and more attention recently. Pattern-based techniques are a promising class of data mining methods which are easy to interpret, while having the capacity to be highly discriminative. It remains a challenge to quantify the interpretability of patterns, and investigate the relationship between interpretability and performance (e.g., accuracy for classification) of patterns.

4. The framework of pattern-based feature generation can be divided into three individual steps: pattern mining, pattern selection and feature generation. In many cases, these three steps are executed separately, which means that the objectives of pattern mining and pruning may not be related to feature generation. It is interesting to see how a pattern mining or pruning approach could directly consider feature generation as the objective.

Bibliography

[1] Charu C Aggarwal and Jiawei Han. *Frequent Pattern Mining*. Springer, 2014.

[2] Rakesh Agrawal and John C Shafer. Parallel mining of association rules. *IEEE Transactions on Knowledge and Data Engineering*, 8(6):962–969, 1996.

[3] Rakesh Agrawal and Ramakrishnan Srikant. Mining sequential patterns. In *Data Engineering, 1995. Proceedings of the Eleventh International Conference on*, pages 3–14. IEEE, 1995.

[4] Rakesh Agrawal, Ramakrishnan Srikant, et al. Fast algorithms for mining association rules. In *Proc. 20th Int. Conf. Very Large Data Bases, VLDB*, volume 1215, pages 487–499, 1994.

[5] Jay Ayres, Jason Flannick, Johannes Gehrke, and Tomi Yiu. Sequential pattern mining using a bitmap representation. In *Proceedings of the Eighth ACM SIGKDD International Conference on Knowledge Discovery and Data Mining*, pages 429–435. ACM, 2002.

[6] James Bailey and Elsa Loekito. Efficient incremental mining of contrast patterns in changing data. *Information Processing Letters*, 110(3):88–92, 2010.

[7] Stephen D Bay and Michael J Pazzani. Detecting group differences: Mining contrast sets. *Data Mining and Knowledge Discovery*, 5(3):213–246, 2001.

[8] Roberto J Bayardo Jr. Efficiently mining long patterns from databases. *ACM Sigmod Record*, 27(2):85–93, 1998.

[9] Kevin Beyer, Jonathan Goldstein, Raghu Ramakrishnan, and Uri Shaft. When is "nearest neighbor" meaningful? In *International Conference on Database Theory*, pages 217–235. Springer, 1999.

[10] Rich Caruana, Yin Lou, Johannes Gehrke, Paul Koch, Marc Sturm, and Noemie Elhadad. Intelligible models for healthcare: Predicting pneumonia risk and hospital 30-day readmission. In *Proceedings of the 21th ACM SIGKDD International Conference on Knowledge Discovery and Data Mining*, pages 1721–1730. ACM, 2015.

[11] Hong Cheng, Xifeng Yan, Jiawei Han, and Chih-Wei Hsu. Discriminative frequent pattern analysis for effective classification. In *Data Engineering, 2007. ICDE 2007. IEEE 23rd International Conference on*, pages 716–725. IEEE, 2007.

[12] Hong Cheng, Xifeng Yan, Jiawei Han, and S Yu Philip. Direct discriminative pattern mining for effective classification. In *Data Engineering, 2008. ICDE 2008. IEEE 24th International Conference on*, pages 169–178. IEEE, 2008.

[13] C Chow and Cong Liu. Approximating discrete probability distributions with dependence trees. *IEEE Transactions on Information Theory*, 14(3):462–467, 1968.

[14] Gao Cong, Kian-Lee Tan, Anthony KH Tung, and Xin Xu. Mining top-k covering rule groups for gene expression data. In *Proceedings of the 2005 ACM SIGMOD International Conference on Management of Data*, pages 670–681. ACM, 2005.

[15] Mukund Deshpande, Michihiro Kuramochi, Nikil Wale, and George Karypis. Frequent substructure-based approaches for classifying chemical compounds. *IEEE Transactions on Knowledge and Data Engineering*, 17(8):1036–1050, 2005.

[16] Guozhu Dong and James Bailey. *Contrast Data Mining: Concepts, Algorithms, and Applications*. CRC Press, 2012.

[17] Guozhu Dong and Jinyan Li. Efficient mining of emerging patterns: Discovering trends and differences. In *Proceedings of the Fifth ACM SIGKDD International Conference on Knowledge Discovery and Data Mining*, pages 43–52. ACM, 1999.

[18] Guozhu Dong and Vahid Taslimitehrani. Pattern-aided regression modeling and prediction model analysis. *IEEE Transactions on Knowledge and Data Engineering*, 27(9):2452–2465, 2015.

[19] Guozhu Dong, Xiuzhen Zhang, Limsoon Wong, and Jinyan Li. Caep: Classification by aggregating emerging patterns. In *International Conference on Discovery Science*, pages 30–42. Springer, 1999.

[20] James Dougherty, Ron Kohavi, Mehran Sahami, et al. Supervised and unsupervised discretization of continuous features. In *Machine Learning: Proceedings of the Twelfth International Conference*, volume 12, pages 194–202, 1995.

[21] Hongliang Fei and Jun Huan. Structure feature selection for graph classification. In *Proceedings of the 17th ACM Conference on Information and Knowledge Management*, pages 991–1000. ACM, 2008.

[22] Dominique Gay and Marc Boullé. A Bayesian approach for classification rule mining in quantitative databases. In *Joint European Conference on Machine Learning and Knowledge Discovery in Databases*, pages 243–259. Springer, 2012.

[23] Tias Guns, Siegfried Nijssen, and Luc De Raedt. k-pattern set mining under constraints. *IEEE Transactions on Knowledge and Data Engineering*, 25(2):402–418, 2013.

[24] Valerie Guralnik and George Karypis. A scalable algorithm for clustering sequential data. In *Data Mining, 2001. ICDM 2001, Proceedings IEEE International Conference on*, pages 179–186. IEEE, 2001.

[25] Jiawei Han, Hong Cheng, Dong Xin, and Xifeng Yan. Frequent pattern mining: current status and future directions. *Data Mining and Knowledge Discovery*, 15(1):55–86, 2007.

[26] Jiawei Han, Jian Pei, and Micheline Kamber. *Data Mining: Concepts and Techniques*. Elsevier, 2011.

[27] Jiawei Han, Jian Pei, Behzad Mortazavi-Asl, Qiming Chen, Umeshwar Dayal, and Mei-Chun Hsu. Freespan: Frequent pattern-projected sequential pattern mining. In *Proceedings of the Sixth ACM SIGKDD International Conference on Knowledge Discovery and Data Mining*, pages 355–359. ACM, 2000.

[28] Jiawei Han, Jian Pei, Behzad Mortazavi-Asl, Helen Pinto, Qiming Chen, Umeshwar Dayal, and MC Hsu. Prefixspan: Mining sequential patterns efficiently by prefix-projected pattern growth. In *Proceedings of the 17th International Conference on Data Engineering*, pages 215–224, 2001.

[29] Jiawei Han, Jian Pei, and Yiwen Yin. Mining frequent patterns without candidate generation. In *ACM Sigmod Record*, volume 29, pages 1–12. ACM, 2000.

[30] Jun Huan, Wei Wang, Deepak Bandyopadhyay, Jack Snoeyink, Jan Prins, and Alexander Tropsha. Mining protein family specific residue packing patterns from protein structure graphs. In *Proceedings of the Eighth Annual International Conference on Resaerch in Computational Molecular Biology*, pages 308–315. ACM, 2004.

[31] Jun Huan, Wei Wang, and Jan Prins. Efficient mining of frequent subgraphs in the presence of isomorphism. In *Data Mining, 2003. ICDM 2003. Third IEEE International Conference on*, pages 549–552. IEEE, 2003.

[32] Akihiro Inokuchi, Takashi Washio, and Hiroshi Motoda. An Apriori-based algorithm for mining frequent substructures from graph data. *Principles of Data Mining and Knowledge Discovery*, pages 13–23, 2000.

[33] Xiaonan Ji, James Bailey, and Guozhu Dong. Mining minimal distinguishing subsequence patterns with gap constraints. *Knowledge and Information Systems*, 11(3):259–286, 2007.

[34] Ron Kohavi. The power of decision tables. *Machine Learning: ECML-95*, pages 174–189, 1995.

[35] Michihiro Kuramochi and George Karypis. Frequent subgraph discovery. In *Data Mining, 2001. ICDM 2001, Proceedings IEEE International Conference on*, pages 313–320. IEEE, 2001.

[36] Benjamin Letham, Cynthia Rudin, Tyler H McCormick, David Madigan, et al. Interpretable classifiers using rules and Bayesian analysis: Building a better stroke prediction model. *The Annals of Applied Statistics*, 9(3):1350–1371, 2015.

[37] Jinyan Li, Guozhu Dong, and Kotagiri Ramamohanarao. Making use of the most expressive jumping emerging patterns for classification. *Knowledge and Information systems*, 3(2):131–145, 2001.

[38] Jinyan Li, Thomas Manoukian, Guozhu Dong, and Kotagiri Ramamohanarao. Incremental maintenance on the border of the space of emerging patterns. *Data Mining and Knowledge Discovery*, 9(1):89–116, 2004.

[39] Wenmin Li, Jiawei Han, and Jian Pei. Cmar: Accurate and efficient classification based on multiple class-association rules. In *Data Mining, 2001. ICDM 2001, Proceedings IEEE International Conference on*, pages 369–376. IEEE, 2001.

[40] Elsa Loekito and James Bailey. Using highly expressive contrast patterns for classification-is it worthwhile? *Advances in Knowledge Discovery and Data Mining*, pages 483–490, 2009.

[41] Bing Liu Wynne Hsu Yiming Ma. Integrating classification and association rule mining. In *Proceedings of the Fourth International Conference on Knowledge Discovery and Data Mining*, 1998.

[42] FP Machado. CPAR: Classification based on predictive association rules. 2003.

[43] Jong Soo Park, Ming-Syan Chen, and Philip S Yu. *An Effective Hash-Based Algorithm for Mining Association Rules*, volume 24. ACM, 1995.

[44] Nicolas Pasquier, Yves Bastide, Rafik Taouil, and Lotfi Lakhal. Discovering frequent closed itemsets for association rules. In *International Conference on Database Theory*, pages 398–416. Springer, 1999.

[45] Kotagiri Ramamohanarao, James Bailey, and Hongjian Fan. Efficient mining of contrast patterns and their applications to classification. In *Intelligent Sensing and Information Processing, 2005. ICISIP 2005. Third International Conference on*, pages 39–47. IEEE, 2005.

[46] Jingbo Shang, Wenzhu Tong, Jian Peng, and Jiawei Han. Dpclass: An effective but concise discriminative patterns-based classification framework. In *Proceedings of the 2016 SIAM International Conference on Data Mining*, pages 567–575. SIAM, 2016.

[47] Koen Smets and Jilles Vreeken. Slim: Directly mining descriptive patterns. In *SDM*, pages 236–247. SIAM, 2012.

[48] Ramakrishnan Srikant and Rakesh Agrawal. Mining sequential patterns: Generalizations and performance improvements. *Advances in Database Technology—EDBT'96*, pages 1–17, 1996.

[49] Roger Ming Hieng Ting and James Bailey. Mining minimal contrast subgraph patterns. In *Proceedings of the 2006 SIAM International Conference on Data Mining*, pages 639–643. SIAM, 2006.

[50] Hannu Toivonen et al. Sampling large databases for association rules. In *VLDB*, volume 96, pages 134–145, 1996.

[51] Natalia Vanetik, Ehud Gudes, and Solomon Eyal Shimony. Computing frequent graph patterns from semistructured data. In *Data Mining, 2002. ICDM 2003. Proceedings. 2002 IEEE International Conference on*, pages 458–465. IEEE, 2002.

[52] Jilles Vreeken, Matthijs Van Leeuwen, and Arno Siebes. KRIMP: Mining itemsets that compress. *Data Mining and Knowledge Discovery*, 23(1):169–214, 2011.

[53] Chao Wang and Srinivasan Parthasarathy. Summarizing itemset patterns using probabilistic models. In *Proceedings of the 12th ACM SIGKDD International Conference on Knowledge Discovery and Data Mining*, pages 730–735. ACM, 2006.

[54] Fulton Wang and Cynthia Rudin. Falling rule lists. In *AISTATS*, 2015.

[55] Jianyong Wang and George Karypis. Harmony: Efficiently mining the best rules for classification. In *Proceedings of the 2005 SIAM International Conference on Data Mining*, pages 205–216. SIAM, 2005.

[56] Jianyong Wang, Yuzhou Zhang, Lizhu Zhou, George Karypis, and Charu C Aggarwal. Discriminating subsequence discovery for sequence clustering. In *Proceedings of the 2007 SIAM International Conference on Data Mining*, pages 605–610. SIAM, 2007.

[57] David H Wolpert. Stacked generalization. *Neural Networks*, 5(2):241–259, 1992.

[58] Dong Xin, Hong Cheng, Xifeng Yan, and Jiawei Han. Extracting redundancy-aware top-k patterns. In *Proceedings of the 12th ACM SIGKDD International Conference on Knowledge Discovery and Data Mining*, pages 444–453. ACM, 2006.

[59] Xifeng Yan, Hong Cheng, Jiawei Han, and Dong Xin. Summarizing itemset patterns: a profile-based approach. In *Proceedings of the Eleventh ACM SIGKDD International Conference on Knowledge Discovery in Data Mining*, pages 314–323. ACM, 2005.

[60] Xifeng Yan and Jiawei Han. gSpan: Graph-based substructure pattern mining. In *Data Mining, 2002. ICDM 2003. Proceedings. 2002 IEEE International Conference on*, pages 721–724. IEEE, 2002.

[61] Osmar R Zaıane, Yang Wang, Randy Goebel, and Gregory Taylor. Frequent subsequence-based protein localization. In *Workshop on Data Mining for Biomedical Applications (BioDM'06), in Conjunction with PAKDD'06*, pages 35–47. Springer, 2006.

[62] Mohammed J Zaki. Spade: An efficient algorithm for mining frequent sequences. *Machine Learning*, 42(1):31–60, 2001.

[63] Mohammed Javeed Zaki. Scalable algorithms for association mining. *IEEE Transactions on Knowledge and Data Engineering*, 12(3):372–390, 2000.

[64] Xiuzhen Zhang, Guozhu Dong, and Kotagiri Ramamohanarao. Building behaviour knowledge space to make classification decision. In *Pacific-Asia Conference on Knowledge Discovery and Data Mining*, pages 488–494. Springer, 2001.

[65] Cheng Zhou, Boris Cule, and Bart Goethals. Pattern based sequence classification. *IEEE Transactions on Knowledge and Data Engineering*, 28(5):1285–1298, 2016.

Chapter 11

Deep Learning for Feature Representation

Suhang Wang

Arizona State University

Huan Liu

Arizona State University

11.1 Introduction

Deep learning methods have become increasingly popular in recent years because of their tremendous success in image classification [19], speech recognition [20] and natural language processing tasks [60]. In fact, deep learning methods have regularly won many recent challenges in these domains [19]. The great success of deep learning mainly comes from specially designed structures of deep nets, which are able to learn discriminative non-linear features that can facilitate the task at hand. For example, the specially designed convolutional layers of CNN allow it to extract translation-invariant features from images while the max pooling layers of CNN help to reduce the parameters to be learned. In essence, the majority of existing deep learning algorithms can be used as powerful feature learning/extraction tools, i.e., the *latent features* extracted by deep learning algorithms are the new learned representations. In this chapter, we will review classical and popular deep learning algorithms and explain how they can be used for feature representation learning. We will also discuss how they are used for hierarchical and disentangled representation learning, and how they can be applied to various domains.

11.2   Restricted Boltzmann Machine

A restricted Boltzmann machine (RBM) is an undirected graphical model that defines a probability distribution over a vector of observed, or visible, variables $\mathbf{v} \in \{0,1\}^m$ and a vector of latent, or hidden, variables $\mathbf{h} \in \{0,1\}^d$, where m is the dimension of input features and d is the dimension of the latent features. It is widely used for unsupervised representation learning. For example, $\mathbf{v}$ can be the bag-of-words representation of documents or the vectorized binary images and $\mathbf{h}$ *is the learned representation for the input data*. A typical choice is that $d < m$, i.e., learning compact representation. Figure 11.1(a) gives a toy example of an RBM. In the figure, each node of the hidden layer is connected to each node in the visible layer, while there are no connections between hidden nodes or visible nodes. Figure 11.1(b) is a simplified representation of RBM, where the connection details between hidden layers and visible layers are simplified. We will begin by assuming both $\mathbf{v}$ and $\mathbf{h}$ as binary vectors, i.e., elements of $\mathbf{v}$ and $\mathbf{h}$ can only take the value of 0 or 1. An extension of real-valued input $\mathbf{x}$ will be introduced 11.2.2. An RBM defines a joint probability over $\mathbf{v}$ and $\mathbf{h}$ as

$$P(\mathbf{v}, \mathbf{h}) = \frac{1}{Z} \exp(-E(\mathbf{v}, \mathbf{h})) \tag{11.1}$$

where Z is the partition function defined as $Z = \sum_{\mathbf{v}} \sum_{\mathbf{h}} \exp(-E(\mathbf{v}, \mathbf{h}))$, and E is an energy function given by

$$E(\mathbf{v}, \mathbf{h}) = -\mathbf{h}^T \mathbf{W} \mathbf{v} - \mathbf{b}^T \mathbf{h} - \mathbf{c}^T \mathbf{v} \tag{11.2}$$

where $\mathbf{W} \in \mathbb{R}^{d \times m}$ is a matrix of pairwise weights between elements of $\mathbf{v}$ and $\mathbf{h}$ (see Figure 11.1(a)), while $\mathbf{b} \in \mathbb{R}^{d \times 1}$ and $\mathbf{c} \in \mathbb{R}^{m \times 1}$ are biases for the hidden and visible variables, respectively.[1]

---

[1] For simplicity, bias terms are not shown in Figure 11.1.

Since there are no explicit connections between hidden units in an RBM, given randomly selected training data $\mathbf{v}$, the hidden units are independent of each other, which gives $P(\mathbf{h}|\mathbf{v}) = \prod_{i=1}^{d} P(h_i|\mathbf{v})$, and the binary state, h_i, $i = 1, \ldots, d$, is set to 1 with conditional probability given as,

$$P(h_i = 1|\mathbf{v}) = \sigma\left(\sum_{j=1}^{m} W_{ij}v_j + b_i\right) \tag{11.3}$$

where $\sigma(\cdot)$ is the sigmoid function defined as $\sigma(x) = (1 + \exp(-x))^{-1}$. Similarly, given $\mathbf{h}$, the visible units are independent of each other. Thus, we have $P(\mathbf{v}|\mathbf{h}) = \prod_{j=1}^{m} P(v_j|\mathbf{h})$, and the binary state, v_j, $j = 1, \ldots, m$, is set to 1 with conditional probability given as

$$P(v_j = 1|\mathbf{h}) = \sigma\left(\sum_{i=1}^{d} W_{ij}h_i + v_j\right). \tag{11.4}$$

With the simple conditional probabilities given by Eq.(11.3) and Eq.(11.4), sampling from $P(\mathbf{h}|\mathbf{v})$ and $P(\mathbf{v}|\mathbf{h})$ becomes very efficient. RBMs have generally been trained using gradient ascent to maximize the log-likelihood $l(\boldsymbol{\theta})$ for some set of training vectors $\mathbf{V} \in \mathbb{R}^{m \times n}$, where $\boldsymbol{\theta} = \{\mathbf{W}, \mathbf{b}, \mathbf{c}\}$ is the set of variables to be optimized. The log-likelihood $l(\boldsymbol{\theta})$ is written as

$$l(\boldsymbol{\theta}) = \frac{1}{n} \log P(\mathbf{V}) = \frac{1}{n} \sum_{i=1}^{n} \log P(\mathbf{v}_i). \tag{11.5}$$

The derivative of $\log P(\mathbf{v})$ w.r.t variable $\mathbf{W}$ is given as

$$\frac{\partial \log P(\mathbf{v})}{\partial \mathbf{W}} = \sum_{\mathbf{h}} P(\mathbf{h}|\mathbf{v})\mathbf{h}\mathbf{v}^T - \sum_{\tilde{\mathbf{v}}} \sum_{\mathbf{h}} P(\tilde{\mathbf{v}}, \mathbf{h})\mathbf{h}\tilde{\mathbf{v}}^T \tag{11.6}$$

where $\tilde{\mathbf{v}} \in \{0, 1\}^m$ is an m-dimensional binary vector. The first term in Eq.(11.6) can be computed exactly. This term is often referred to as the *positive* gradient. It corresponds to the expected gradient of the energy with respect to $P(\mathbf{h}|\mathbf{v})$. The second term in Eq. (11.6) is known as the *negative* gradient, which is expectation over the model distribution $P(\mathbf{v}, \mathbf{h})$. It is intractable to compute the negative gradients exactly. Thus, we need to approximate the negative gradients by sampling $\mathbf{v}$ from $P(\mathbf{v}|\mathbf{h})$ and sampling $\mathbf{h}$ from $P(\mathbf{h}|\mathbf{v})$ by maintaining a Gibbs chain. For more details, we encourage readers to refere to Contrastive Divergence [62].

11.2.1 Deep Belief Networks and Deep Boltzmann Machine

RBMs can be stacked and trained in a greedy manner to form so-called Deep Belief Networks (DBN) [21] . DBNs are graphical models which learn

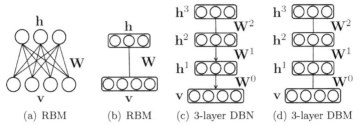

(a) RBM   (b) RBM   (c) 3-layer DBN   (d) 3-layer DBM

Figure 11.1: An illustration of RBM, DBN and DBM.

to extract a deep hierarchical representation of the training data. They model
the joint distribution between observed vector $\mathbf{v}$ and the l hidden layers as:

$$P(\mathbf{x}, \mathbf{h}^1, \mathbf{h}^2, \ldots, \mathbf{h}^l) = \left(\prod_{k=0}^{l-2} P(\mathbf{h}^k | \mathbf{h}^{k+1}) \right) P(\mathbf{h}^{l-1}, \mathbf{h}^l) \qquad (11.7)$$

where $\mathbf{v} = \mathbf{h}^0$. $P(\mathbf{h}^{k-1} | \mathbf{h}^k)$ is a conditional distribution for the visible units
conditioned on the hidden units of the RBM at level k, and $P(\mathbf{h}^{l-1}, \mathbf{h}^l)$ is
the visible-hidden joint distribution in the top-level RBM. This is illustrated
in Figure 11.1(c). DBN is able to learn hierarchical representation [33]. The
low-level hidden representation such as $\mathbf{h}^1$ captures *low-level features* while
the high-level hidden representation such as $\mathbf{h}^3$ captures more complex *high-
level features*. Training of DBN is done by greedy layer-wise unsupervised
training [21]. Specifically, we first train the first layer as an RBM with the
raw input $\mathbf{v}$. From the first layer, we obtain the latent representation as the
mean activations $P(\mathbf{h}^1 | \mathbf{h}^0)$ or samples of $P(\mathbf{h}^1 | \mathbf{h}^0)$, which will then be used
as input to the second layer to update $\mathbf{W}^2$. After all the layers are trained, we
can fine-tune all the parameters of DBN with respect to a proxy for the DBN
log-likelihood, or with respect to a supervised training criterion by adding a
classifier such as the softmax function on top of DBN.

A deep Boltzmann machine (DBM) [51] is another kind of deep generative
model. Figure 11.1(d) gives an illustration of a DBM with 3 hidden layers.
Unlike DBN, it is an entirely undirected model. Unlike RBM, the DBM has
several layers of latent variables (RBMs have just one). Within each layer,
each of the variables are mutually independent, conditioned on the variables
in the neighboring layers. In the case of a deep Boltzmann machine with one
visible layer $\mathbf{v}$, and l hidden layers, $\mathbf{h}^1$, $\mathbf{h}^2$ and $\mathbf{h}^l$, the joint probability is
given by:

$$P(\mathbf{v}, \mathbf{h}^1, \mathbf{h}^2, \ldots, \mathbf{h}^n) = \frac{1}{Z} \exp(-E(\mathbf{v}, \mathbf{h}^1, \mathbf{h}^2, \ldots, \mathbf{h}^n)) \qquad (11.8)$$

where the DBM energy function is defined as

$$E(\mathbf{v}, \mathbf{h}^1, \mathbf{h}^2, \ldots, \mathbf{h}^n) = -\left(\sum_{k=0}^{l-1} \mathbf{h}^k \mathbf{W}^k \mathbf{h}^{k+1} \right) - \sum_k \mathbf{b}^k \mathbf{h}^k \qquad (11.9)$$

and $\mathbf{v} = \mathbf{h}^0$, $\mathbf{W}^k$ is the weight matrix to capture the interaction between $\mathbf{h}^k$ and $\mathbf{h}^{k+1}$, and $\mathbf{b}^k$ is the bias.

The conditional distribution over one DBM layer given the neighboring layers is factorial. In the example of the DBM with two hidden layers, these distributions are $P(\mathbf{v}|\mathbf{h}^1)$, $P(\mathbf{h}^1|\mathbf{v}, \mathbf{h}^2)$ and $P(\mathbf{h}^2|\mathbf{h}^1)$. The distribution over all hidden layers generally does not factorize because of interactions between layers. In the example with two hidden layers, $P(\mathbf{h}^1, \mathbf{h}^2|\mathbf{v})$ does not factorize due to the interaction weights $\mathbf{W}^1$ between $\mathbf{h}^1$ and $\mathbf{h}^2$ which render these variables mutually dependent. Therefore, sampling from $P(\mathbf{h}^1, \mathbf{h}^2|\mathbf{v})$ is difficult while training of DBM using gradient ascent methods require sampling from $P(\mathbf{h}^1, \mathbf{h}^2|\mathbf{v})$. To solve this problem, we use a mean-field approximation to approximate $P(\mathbf{h}^1, \mathbf{h}^2|\mathbf{v})$. Specifically, we define

$$Q(\mathbf{h}^1, \mathbf{h}^2) = \prod_j Q(h_j^1|\mathbf{v}) \prod_k Q(h_k^2|\mathbf{v}) \tag{11.10}$$

The mean field approximation attempts to find a member of this family of distributions that best fits the true posterior $P(\mathbf{h}^1, \mathbf{h}^2|\mathbf{v})$ by minimizing KL-divergence between $Q(\mathbf{h}^1, \mathbf{h}^2)$ and $P(\mathbf{h}^1, \mathbf{h}^2|\mathbf{v})$. With the approximation, we can easily sample $\mathbf{h}^1$ and $\mathbf{h}^2$ from $Q(\mathbf{h}^1, \mathbf{h}^2)$ and then update the parameters using gradient ascents with these samples [51].

11.2.2 RBM for Real-Valued Data

In many real-world applications such as image and audio modeling, the input features $\mathbf{v}$ are often real-valued data. Thus, it is important to extend RBM for modeling real-valued inputs. There are many variants of the RBM which defines the probability over real-valued data such as Gaussian-Bernoulli RBMs [69], mean and variance RBMs [22] and Spike and Slab RBMs [8].

The Gaussian-Bernoulli RBM (GBM) is the most common way to handle real-valued data, which has binary hidden units and real-valued visible units. It assumes the conditional distribution over the visible units being a Gaussian distribution whose mean is a function of the hidden units. Under this assumption, GRBM defines a joint probability over $\mathbf{v}$ and $\mathbf{h}$ as in Eq.(11.1) with the energy function given as

$$E(\mathbf{v}, \mathbf{h}) = -\mathbf{h}^T \mathbf{W}(\mathbf{v} \odot \boldsymbol{\beta}) - \mathbf{b}^T \mathbf{h} - \frac{1}{2}\mathbf{v} - \mathbf{c}^T(\boldsymbol{\beta} \odot (\mathbf{v} - \mathbf{c})) \tag{11.11}$$

where $\boldsymbol{\beta} \in \mathbb{R}^{m \times 1}$ is the precision vector with the i-th element β_i being the precision of v_i. $\odot$ is the Hadamard operation. Then the conditional probability of $P(\mathbf{v}|\mathbf{h})$ and $P(\mathbf{h}|\mathbf{v})$ are

$$P(\mathbf{h}|\mathbf{v}) = \prod_{i=1}^d P(h_i|\mathbf{v}) = \prod_{i=1}^d \sigma(b_i + \sum_{j=1}^m W_{ij} v_i \beta_i) \tag{11.12}$$

$$P(\mathbf{v}|\mathbf{h}) = \prod_{j=1}^{m} P(v_j|\mathbf{h}) = \prod_{j=1}^{m} \mathcal{N}\left(v_j\Big|b_j + \sum_{i=1}^{d} W_{ij}h_i, \beta_i^{-1}\right) \qquad (11.13)$$

where $\mathcal{N}(v_j|b_j + \sum_{i=1}^{d} W_{ij}h_i, \beta_i^{-1})$ is the Gaussian distribution with mean $b_j + \sum_{i=1}^{d} W_{ij}h_i$ and variance β_i^{-1}.

While the GRBM has been the canonical energy model for real-valued data, it is not well suited to the statistical variations present in some types of real-valued data, especially natural images [31]. The problem is that much of the information content present in natural images is embedded in the covariance between pixels rather than in the raw pixel values. To solve these problems, alternative models have been proposed that attempt to better account for the covariance of real-valued data. Mean and Covariance RBM (mcRBM) is one of the alternatives. The mcRBM uses its hidden units to independently encode the conditional mean and covariance of all observed units. Specifically, the hidden layer of mcRBM is divided into two groups of units: binary mean units $\mathbf{h}^{(m)}$ and binary covariance units $\mathbf{h}^{(c)}$. The energy function of mcRBM is defined as the combination of two energy functions:

$$E_{mc}(\mathbf{v}, \mathbf{h}^{(m)}, \mathbf{h}^{(c)}) = E_m(\mathbf{v}, \mathbf{h}^{(m)}) + E_c(\mathbf{v}, \mathbf{h}^{(c)}) \qquad (11.14)$$

where $E_m(\mathbf{v}, \mathbf{h}^{(m)})$ is the standard Gaussian-Bernoulli energy function defined in Eq.(11.11), which models the interaction between real-valued $\mathbf{v}$ input and hidden units $\mathbf{h}^{(m)}$; and $E_c(\mathbf{v}, \mathbf{h}^{(c)})$ models the conditional covariance information, which is given as

$$E_c(\mathbf{v}, \mathbf{h}^{(c)}) = \frac{1}{2}\sum_{j} h_j^{(c)}(\mathbf{v}^T\mathbf{r}^{(j)})^2 - \sum_{j} b_j^{(c)} h_j^{(c)}. \qquad (11.15)$$

The parameter $\mathbf{r}^{(j)}$ corresponds to the covariance weight vector associated with $h_j^{(c)}$ and $\mathbf{b}^{(c)}$ is a vector of covariance offsets.

11.3   AutoEncoder

An autoencoder (AE) is a neural network trained to learn latent representation that is good at reconstructing its input [4]. Generally, an autoencoder is composed of two parts, i.e., an encoder $f(\cdot)$ and a decoder $g(\cdot)$. An illustration of autoencoder is shown in Figure 11.2(a). The encoder maps the input $\mathbf{x} \in \mathbb{R}^m$ to latent representation $\mathbf{h} \in \mathbb{R}^d$ as $\mathbf{h} = f(\mathbf{x})$ and $f(\cdot)$ is usually a one-layer neural network, i.e., $f(\mathbf{x}) = s(\mathbf{Wx} + \mathbf{b})$, where $\mathbf{W} \in \mathbb{R}^{d \times m}$ and $\mathbf{b} \in \mathbb{R}^d$ are the weights and bias of the encoder. $s(\cdot)$ is a non-linear function such as sigmoid and tanh. A decoder maps back the latent representation $\mathbf{h}$ into a reconstruction $\tilde{\mathbf{x}} \in \mathbb{R}^m$ as $\tilde{\mathbf{x}} = g(\mathbf{h})$ and $g(\cdot)$ is given as $g(\mathbf{h}) = s(\mathbf{W}'\mathbf{h} + \mathbf{b}')$, where $\mathbf{W}' \in \mathbb{R}^{m \times d}$ and $\mathbf{b} \in \mathbb{R}^m$ are the weights and bias of the decoder. Note that the prime symbol does not indicate matrix transposition. The parameters of the autoencoder, i.e., $\theta = \{\mathbf{W}, \mathbf{b}, \mathbf{W}', \mathbf{b}'\}$ are optimized to minimize the reconstruction error. Depending on the appropriate distribution assumptions of the input, the reconstruction error can be measured in many ways. The most widely used reconstruction error is the squared error $\mathcal{L}(\mathbf{x}, \tilde{\mathbf{x}}) = \|\mathbf{x} - \tilde{\mathbf{x}}\|_2^2$. Alternatively, if the input is interpreted as either bit vectors or vectors of bit probabilities, cross-entropy of the reconstruction can be used

$$\mathcal{L}_H(\mathbf{x}, \tilde{\mathbf{x}}) = -\sum_{k=1}^{d}[\mathbf{x}_k \log \tilde{\mathbf{x}}_k + (1 - \mathbf{x}_k \log(1 - \tilde{\mathbf{x}}_k))]. \qquad (11.16)$$

By training an autoencoder that is good at reconstructing input data, we hope that the latent representation $\mathbf{h}$ can capture some useful features. The identity function seems a particularly trivial function to try to learn, when it doesn't result in useful features. Therefore, we need to add constraints to the autoencoder to avoid trivial solution and learn useful features.

The autoencoder can be used to extract useful features by forcing $\mathbf{h}$ to have smaller dimension than $\mathbf{x}$, i.e., $d < m$. An autoencoder whose latent dimension is less than the input dimension is called an undercomplete autoencoder. Learning an undercomplete representation forces the autoencoder to capture the most salient features of the training data [15]. In other words, the latent representation $\mathbf{h}$ is a distributed representation which captures the coordinates along the main factors of variation in the data [15]. This is similar to the way that the projection on principal components would capture the main factors of variation in the data. Indeed, if there is one linear hidden layer, i.e., no activation function applied, and the mean squared error criterion is used to train the network, then the d hidden units learn to project the input in the span of the first d principal components of the data. If the hidden layer is non-linear, the autoencoder behaves differently from PCA, with the ability to capture multi-modal aspects of the input distribution.

Another choice is to constrain $\mathbf{h}$ to have a larger dimension than $\mathbf{x}$, i.e., $d > m$. An autoencoder whose latent dimension is larger than the input dimension is called an overcomplete autoencoder. However, due to the large dimension, the encoder and decoder are given too much capacity. In such cases, even a linear encoder and linear decoder can learn to copy the input to the output without learning anything useful about the data distribution. Fortunately, we can still discover interesting structure, by imposing other constraints on the network. One of the most widely used constraints is the sparsity constraint on $\mathbf{h}$. An overcomplete autoencoder with sparsity constraint is called a sparse autoencoder, which will be discussed next.

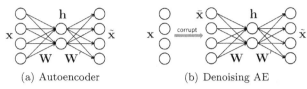

(a) Autoencoder   (b) Denoising AE

Figure 11.2: An illustration of an autoencoder and a denoising autoencoder.

11.3.1 Sparse Autoencoder

A sparse autoencoder is an overcomplete authoencorder which tries to learn sparse overcomplete codes that are good at reconstruction [43]. A sparse overcomplete representation can be viewed as an alternative "compressed" representation: it has implicit straightforward compressibility due to the large number of zeros rather than an explicit lower dimensionality. Given the training data $\mathbf{X} \in \mathbb{R}^{m \times N}$, the objective function is given as

$$\min_{\mathbf{W}, \mathbf{b}, \mathbf{W}', \mathbf{b}'} \frac{1}{N} \sum_{i=1}^{N} \mathcal{L}(\mathbf{x}_i, \tilde{\mathbf{x}}_i) + \alpha \Omega(\mathbf{h}_i) \tag{11.17}$$

where N is the number of training instances, $\mathbf{x}_i$ is the i-th training instance, and $\mathbf{h}_i$ and $\tilde{\mathbf{x}}_i$ are the corresponding latent representation and reconstructed features. $\Omega(\mathbf{h}_i)$ is the sparsity regularizer to make $\mathbf{h}_i$ sparse and α is a scalar to control the sparsity. Many sparsity regularizers can be adopted. One popularly used is the ℓ_1-norm, i.e., $\Omega(\mathbf{h}_i) = \|\mathbf{h}_i\|_1 = \sum_{j=1}^{d} |h_i(j)|$. However, the ℓ_1-norm is non-smooth and not appropriate for gradient descent. An alternative is to use the smooth sparse constraint based on KL-divergence. Let $\rho_j, j = 1, \ldots, d$ be the average activation of hidden unit j (averaged over the training set) as

$$\rho_j = \frac{1}{N} \sum_{i=1}^{N} \mathbf{h}_i(j). \tag{11.18}$$

The essential idea is to force ρ_j to be close to ρ, where ρ is a small value close to zero (say $\rho = 0.05$). By forcing ρ_j be close to ρ, we would like the average activation of each hidden neuron j to be close to 0.05 (say). This constraint is satisfied when the hidden unit activations are mostly near 0. To achieve that ρ_j is close to ρ, we can use the KL-divergence as

$$\sum_{j=1}^{d} KL(\rho \| \rho_j) = \sum_{j=1}^{d} \rho \log \frac{\rho}{\rho_j} + (1 - \rho) \log \frac{1 - \rho}{1 - \rho_j}. \tag{11.19}$$

$KL(\rho \| \rho_j)$ is a convex function with its minimum of when $\rho_j = \rho$. Thus, minimizing this penalty term has the effect of causing ρ_j to be close to ρ, which achieves the sparse effect.

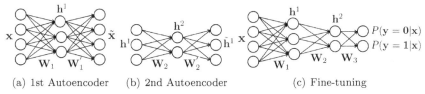

(a) 1st Autoencoder (b) 2nd Autoencoder (c) Fine-tuning

Figure 11.3: An illustration of 2-layer stacked autoencoder.

11.3.2 Denoising Autoencoder

The aforementioned autoencoders add constraints on latent representations to learn useful features. Alternatively, denoising the autoencoder uses the denoising criteria to learn useful features. In order to force the hidden layer to discover more robust features and prevent it from simply learning the identity, the denoising autoencoder trains the autoencoder to reconstruct the input from a corrupted version of it [63]. An illustration of denoising autoencoder is shown in Figure 11.2(b). In the figure, the clean data $\mathbf{x}$ is first corrupted as a noisy data $\bar{\mathbf{x}}$ by means of a stochastic mapping $q_D(\bar{\mathbf{x}}|\mathbf{x})$. The corrupted data $\bar{\mathbf{x}}$ is then used as input to an autoencoder, which outputs the reconstructed data $\tilde{\mathbf{x}}$. The training objective of a denoising autoencoder is then to make reconstructed data $\tilde{\mathbf{x}}$ close to the clean data $\mathbf{x}$ as $\mathcal{L}(\mathbf{x}, \tilde{\mathbf{x}})$.

There are many choices of the stochastic mapping such as (1) additive isotropic Gaussian noise (GS): $\bar{\mathbf{x}}|\mathbf{x} \sim N(\mathbf{x}, \sigma\mathbf{I})$; this is a very common noise model suitable for real-valued inputs. (2) Masking noise (MN): a fraction ν of the elements of x (chosen at random for each example) is forced to 0. (3) Salt-and-pepper noise (SP): a fraction ν of the elements of $\mathbf{x}$ (chosen at random for each example) is set to their minimum or maximum possible value (typically 0 or 1) according to a fair coin flip. The masking noise and salt-and-pepper noise are natural choices for input domains which are interpretable as binary or near binary such as black-and-white images or the representations produced at the hidden layer after a sigmoid squashing function [63].

11.3.3 Stacked Autoencoder

Denoising autoencoders can be stacked to form a deep network by feeding the latent representation of the DAE found on the layer below as input to the current layer as shown in Figure 11.3, which are generally called stacked denoising autoencoders (SDAEs). The unsupervised pre-training of such an architecture is done one layer at a time. Each layer is trained as a DAE by minimizing the error in reconstructing its input. For example, in Figure 11.3(a), we train the first layer autoencoder. Once the first layer is trained, we can train the 2nd layer with the latent representation of the first autoencoder, i.e., $\mathbf{h}^1$, as input. This is shown in Figure 11.3(b). Once all layers are pre-trained, the network goes through a second stage of training called fine-tuning, which is typically to minimize prediction error on a supervised task. For fine-tuning, we first add a logistic regression layer on top of the network as shown in Figure 11.3(c) (more precisely on the output code of the output layer). We then train the entire network as we would train a multilayer perceptron. At this point, we only consider the encoding parts of each autoencoder. This stage is supervised, since now we use the target class during training.

11.4   Convolutional Neural Networks

The Convolutional Neural Network (CNN or ConvNet) has achieved great success in many computer vision tasks such as image classification [32], segmentation [36] and video action recognition [55]. The specially designed architecture of the CNN is very powerful in extracting visual features from images, which can be used for various tasks. An example of a simplified CNN is shown in Figure 11.4. It is comprised of three basic types of layers, which are convolutional layers for extracting translation-invariant features from images, pooling layers for reducing the parameters and fully connected layers for classification tasks. CNNs are mainly formed by stacking these layers together. Recently, dropout layers [56] and residual layers [19] are also introduced to prevent CNN from overfitting and to ease the training of deep CNNs, respectively. Next, we will introduce the basic building blocks of CNNs and how CNNs can be used for feature learning.

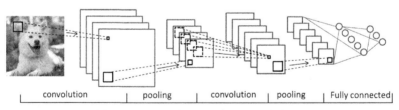

Figure 11.4: An illustration of CNN.

The Convolutional Layer: As the name implies, the Conv layer is the core building block of a CNN. The essential idea of a Conv layer is the observation that natural images have the property of being "stationary," which means that the statistics of one part of the image are the same as any other part. For example, a dog can appear in any location of an image. This suggests that the dog feature detector that we learn at one part of the image can also be applied to other parts of the image to detect dogs, and we can use the same features at all locations. More precisely, having learned features over small (say 3x3) patches sampled randomly from the larger image, we can then apply this learned 3x3 feature detector anywhere in the image. Specifically, we can take the learned 3x3 features and "convolve" them with the larger image, thus obtaining a different feature activation value at each location in the image. The feature detector is called a filter or kernel in ConvNet and the feature obtained is called a feature map. Figure 11.5 gives an example of a convolution operation with the input as the 5x5 matrix and the kernel as the 3x3 matrix. The 3x3 kernel slides over the 5x5 matrix from left to right and from the top to down, which generates the feature map shown on the right. The convolution is done by multiplying the kernel by the sub-patch of the input feature map and then sum together. For example, the calculation of the gray sub-patch in the 5x5 matrix with the kernel is given in the figure. There

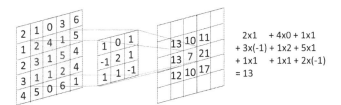

Figure 11.5: An illustration of convolution operation.

are three parameters in a Conv layer, i.e., the *depth, stride* and *zero-padding.* *Depth* corresponds to the number of filters we would like to use. A Conv layer can have many filters, each learning to look for something different in the input. For example, if the first Conv layer takes as input the raw image, then different neurons along the depth dimension may activate in the presence of various oriented edges, or blobs of color. In the simple ConvNet shown in Figure 11.4, the depth of the first convolution and second convolution layers are 4 and 6, respectively. *Stride* specifies how many pixels we skip when we slide the filter over the input feature map. When the stride is 1, we move the filters one pixel at a time as shown in Figure 11.5. When the stride is 2, the filters jump 2 pixels at a time as we slide them around. This will produce smaller output volumes spatially. It will be convenient to pad the input volume with zeros around the border, which is called *zero-padding.* The size of this zero-padding is a hyperparameter. The nice feature of zero-padding is that it will allow us to control the spatial size of the output volumes. Let the input volume be $W \times H \times K$, where W and H are width and height of the feature map and K is the number of feature maps. For example, for a color image with RGB channels, we have $K = 3$. Let the receptive field size (filter size) of the Conv Layer be F, number of filters be $\tilde{K}$, the stride with which they are applied be S, and the amount of zero padding used on the border be P; then the output volume after convolution is $\tilde{W} \times \tilde{H} \times \tilde{K}$, where $\tilde{W} = (W - F + 2P)/S + 1$ and $\tilde{H} = (H - F + 2P)/S + 1$. For example, for a $7 \times 7 \times 3$ input and a $4 \times 3 \times 3$ filter with stride 1 and pad 0, we would get a $5 \times 5 \times 4$ output.

Convolution using filters is a linear operation. After the feature maps are obtained in a Conv layer, a nonlinear activation function will be applied on these feature maps to learn non-linear features. Rectified linear unit (ReLU) is the most widely used activation function for ConvNet, which is demonstrated

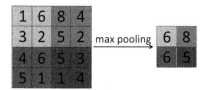

Figure 11.6: An illustration of a max pooling operation.

to be effective in alleviating the gradient vanishing problem. A rectifier is defined as $f(x) = \max(0, x)$.

The Pooling Layer: Pooling layers are usually periodically inserted between successive Conv layers in a CNN. They aim to progressively reduce the spatial size of the representation, which can help reduce the number of parameters and computation in the network, and hence also control overfitting. The pooling layer operates independently over each activation map in the input, and scales its dimensionality using the *max* function. The most common form is a pooling layer with filters of size 2x2 applied with a stride of 2, which downsamples every depth slice in the input by 2 along both width and height, discarding 75% of the activations. Every max operation would, in this case, be taking a max over 4 numbers and the maximum value of the 4 numbers will go to the next layer. An example of a max pooling operation is shown in Figure 11.6. During the forward pass of a pooling layer it is common to keep track of the index of the max activation (sometimes also called the switches) so that gradient routing is efficient during backpropagation.

Though max pooling is the most popular pooling layer, a CNN can also contain general pooling. General pooling layers are comprised of pooling neurons that are able to perform a multitude of common operations including L1/L2-normalization, and average pooling. An example of max pooling

The Fully Connected Layer: Neurons in a fully connected layer have full connections to all activations in the previous layer, as shown in Figure 11.4. The fully connected layers are put at the end of a CNN architecture, i.e., after several layers of Conv layer and max pooling layers. With the high-level features extracted by the previous layers, fully connected layers will then attempt to produce class scores from the activations, to be used for classification. The output of the fully connected layer will then be put in a softmax for classification. It is also suggested that ReLu may be used as the activation function in a fully connected layer to improve performance.

11.4.1   Transfer Feature Learning of CNN

In practice, training an entire Convolutional Network from scratch (with random initialization) is rare as (1) it is very time consuming and requires many computation resources and (2) it is relatively rare to have a dataset of sufficient size to train a ConvNet. Therefore, instead, it is common to pre-train a ConvNet on a very large dataset (e.g., ImageNet, which contains 1.2 million images with 1000 categories), and then use the ConvNet either as an initialization or a fixed feature extractor for the task of interest [53]. There are mainly two major Transfer Learning scenarios, which are listed as follows:

- ConvNet as a fixed feature extractor: In this scenario, we take a ConvNet pretrained on ImageNet, remove the last fully connected layer, then treat the rest of the ConvNet as a fixed feature extractor for the new dataset. With the extracted features, we can train a linear classifier such as Linear SVM or logistic regression for the new dataset. This is usually used when the new dataset is small and similar to the original dataset. For such datasets, training or fine-tuning a ConvNet is not practical as ConvNets are prone to overfitting to small datasets. Since the new dataset is similar to the original dataset, we can expect higher-level features in the ConvNet to be relevant to this dataset as well.

- Fine-tuning the ConvNet: The second way is to not only replace and retrain the classifier on top of the ConvNet on the new dataset, but to also fine-tune the weights of the pretrained network using backpropagation. The essential idea of fine-tuning is that the earlier features of a ConvNet contain more generic features (e.g., edge detectors or color blob detectors) that should be useful in many tasks, but later layers of the ConvNet become progressively more specific to the details of the classes contained in the original dataset. If the new dataset is large enough, we can fine-tune all the layers of the ConvNet. If the new dataset is small but different from the original dataset, then we can keep some of the earlier layers fixed (due to overfitting concerns) and only fine-tune some higher-level portion of the network.

11.5 Word Embedding and Recurrent Neural Networks

Word embedding and recurrent neural networks are the state-of-the-art deep learning models for natural language processing tasks. Word embedding learns word representation and recurrent neural networks utilize word embedding for sentence or document feature learning. Next, we introduce the details of word embedding and recurrent neural networks.

11.5.1 Word Embedding

Word embedding, or distributed representation of words, is to represents each word as a low-dimensional dense vector such that the vector representation of words can capture synthetic and semantic meanings of words. The low-dimensional representation can also alleviate the curse of dimensionality and data sparsity problems suffered by traditional representations such as bag-of-words and N-gram [66]. The essential idea of word embedding is the distributional hypothesis that "you shall know a word by the company it keeps" [13]. This suggests that a word has close relationships with its neighboring words. For example, the phrases *win the game* and *win the lottery* appear very frequently; thus the pair of words *win* and *game* and the pair of words *win* and *lottery* could have a very close relationship. When we are only given the word *win*, we would highly expect the neighboring words to be words like *game* or *lottery* instead of words as *light* or *air*. This suggests that a good word representation should be useful for predicting its neighboring words, which is the essential idea of Skip-gram [41]. In other words, the training objective of the Skip-gram model is to find word representations that are useful for predicting the surrounding words in a sentence or a document. More formally, given a sequence of training words $w_1, w_2, \ldots, w_T$, the objective of the Skip-gram model is to maximize the average log probability

$$\frac{1}{T} \sum_{t=1}^{T} \sum_{-c \leq j \leq c, j \neq 0} \log P(w_{t+j}|w_t) \qquad (11.20)$$

where c is the size of the training context (which can be a function of the center word w_t). Larger c results in more training examples and thus can lead to higher accuracy, at the expense of training time. The basic Skip-gram formulation defines $P(w_{t+j}|w_t)$ using the softmax function:

$$P(w_O|w_I) = \frac{\exp(\mathbf{u}_{w_O}^T \mathbf{v}_{w_I})}{\sum_{w=1}^{W} \exp(\mathbf{u}_w^T \mathbf{v}_{w_I})} \qquad (11.21)$$

where $\mathbf{v}_w$ and $\mathbf{u}_w$ are the "input" and "output" representations of w, and W is the number of words in the vocabulary. Learning the representation is usually done by gradient descent. However, Eq.(11.21) is impractical because the cost of computing $\nabla \log P(w_O|w_I)$ is proportional to W, which is often large. One way of making the computation more tractable is to replace the softmax in Eq. (11.21) with a hierarchical softmax. In a hierarchical softmax, the vocabulary is represented as a Huffman binary tree with words as leaves. With the Huffman tree, the probability of $P(w_O|w_I)$ is the probability of walking the path from root node to leaf node w_O given the word w_I, which is calculated as decision making in each node along the path with a simple function. Huffman trees assign short binary codes to frequent words, and this further reduces the number of output units that need to be evaluated. Another alternative to make the computation tractable is negative sampling [41]. The essential idea of negative sampling is that w_t should be more similar to its neighboring words, say w_{t+j}, than randomly sampled words. Thus, the objective function of negative sampling is to maximize the similarity between w_t and w_{t+j} and minimize the similarity between w_t and randomly sampled words. With negative sampling, Eq. (11.21) is approximated as

$$\log \sigma(\mathbf{u}_{W_O}^T \mathbf{v}_{w_I}) + \frac{1}{K} \sum_{i=1}^{K} \log \sigma(-\mathbf{u}_{W_i}^T \mathbf{v}_{w_I}) \tag{11.22}$$

where K is the number of negative words sampled for each input word w_I. It is found that skip-gram with negative sampling is equivalent to implicitly factorizing a word-context matrix, whose cells are the pointwise mutual information (PMI) of the respective word and context pairs, shifted by a global constant [34].

Instead of using the center words to predict the context (surrounding words in a sentence), Continuous Bag-of-Words Model (CBOW) predicts the current word based on the context. More precisely, CBOW uses each current word as an input to a log-linear classifier with a continuous projection layer, and predicts words within a certain range before and after the current word [39]. The objective function of CBOW is to maximize the following log-likelihood function

$$\frac{1}{T} \sum_{t=1}^{T} \log P(w_t | w_{t-c}, \dots, w_{t-1}, w_{t+1}, \dots, w_{t+c}) \tag{11.23}$$

and $P(w_t | w_{t-c}, \dots, w_{t-1}, w_{t+1}, \dots, w_{t+c})$ is defined as

$$P(w_t | w_{t-c}, \dots, w_{t-1}, w_{t+1}, \dots, w_{t+c}) = \frac{\exp(\mathbf{u}_{w_t}^T \tilde{\mathbf{v}}_t)}{\sum_{w=1}^{W} \exp(\mathbf{u}_w^T \tilde{\mathbf{v}}_t)} \tag{11.24}$$

where $\tilde{\mathbf{v}}_t$ is the average representation of the contexts of w_t, i.e., $\tilde{\mathbf{v}}_t = \frac{1}{2c} \sum_{-c \le j \le c, j \ne 0} \mathbf{v}_{t+j}$.

Methods like skip-gram may do better on the analogy task, but they poorly utilize the statistics of the corpus since they train on separate local context windows instead of on global co-occurrence counts. Based on this observation, GloVe, proposed in [46], uses a specific weighted least squares model that trains on global word-word co-occurrence counts and thus makes efficient use of statistics. The objective function of GloVe is given as

$$\min \sum_{i,j} f(X_{ij})(\mathbf{w}_i^T \tilde{\mathbf{w}}_j - \log X_{ij})^2 \tag{11.25}$$

where X_{ij} tabulates the number of times word j occurs in the context of word i. $\mathbf{w}_i \in \mathbb{R}^d$ is the word representation of w_i and $\tilde{\mathbf{w}}_j$ is a separate context word vector. $f()$ is the weighting function.

Word embedding can capture syntactic and semantic meanings of words. For example, it is found that vec(queen) is the closest vector representation to vec(king) - vec(man) + vec(woman), which implies that word representation learned by Skip-gram encodes semantic meanings of words. Word embedding can also be used for document representation by averaging the word vectors of words appearing in a document as the vector representation of the documents.

Following the distributional representation idea of word embedding, many network embedding algorithms are proposed. The essential idea of network embedding is to learn vector representations of network nodes that are good at predicting the neighboring nodes.

Since word representation learned by word embedding algorithms are low-dimensional dense vectors that capture semantic meanings, they are widely used as a preprocessing step in deep learning methods such as recurrent neural networks and recursive neural networks. Each word will be mapped to a vector representation before it is used as input to deep learning models.

11.5.2   Recurrent Neural Networks

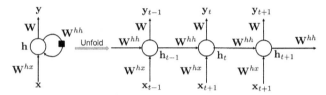

Figure 11.7: An illustration of an RNN.

Recurrent neural networks (RNN) are powerful concepts that allow the use of loops within the neural network architecture to model sequential data such as sentences and videos. Recurrent networks take as input a sequence of inputs, and produce a sequence of outputs. Thus, such models are particularly useful for sequence-to-sequence learning.

Figure 11.7 gives an illustration of the RNN architecture. The left part of the figure shows a folded RNN, which has a self-loop, i.e., the hidden state $\mathbf{h}$ is used to update itself given an input $\mathbf{x}$. To better show how RNN works, we unfold the RNN as a sequential structure, which is given in the right part of Figure 11.7. The RNN takes a sequence, $\mathbf{x}_1, \mathbf{x}_2, \ldots, \mathbf{x}_t, \ldots, \mathbf{x}_T$ as input, where at each step t, $\mathbf{x}_t$ is a d-dimensional feature vector. For example, if the input is a sentence, then each word w_i of the sentence is represented as a vector $\mathbf{x}_i$ using word embedding methods such as Skip-gram. At each time-step t, the output of the previous step, $\mathbf{h}_{t-1}$, along with the next word vector in the document, $\mathbf{x}_t$, are used to update the hidden state $\mathbf{h}_t$ as

$$\mathbf{h}_t = \sigma(\mathbf{W}^{hh}\mathbf{h}_{t-1} + \mathbf{W}^{hx}\mathbf{x}_t) \qquad (11.26)$$

where $\mathbf{W}^{hh} \in \mathbb{R}^{d \times d}$ and $\mathbf{W}^{hx} \in \mathbb{R}^{d \times d}$ are the weights for inputs $\mathbf{h}_{t-1}$ and $\mathbf{x}_t$, respectively. *The hidden states $\mathbf{h}_t$ is the feature representation of the sequence up to time t for the input sequence.* The initial states $\mathbf{h}_0$ are usually initialized as all 0. Thus, we can utilize $\mathbf{h}_t$ to perform various tasks such as sentence completion and document classification. For example, for a sentence completion task, we are given the partial sentence, "The weather is..." and

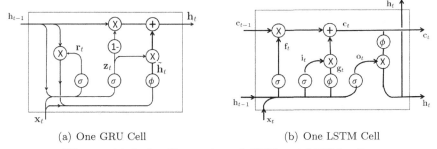

(a) One GRU Cell   (b) One LSTM Cell

Figure 11.8: An illustration of GRU and LSTM cells.

we want to predict the next word. We can predict the next word as

$$\mathbf{y}_t = softmax(\mathbf{W}\mathbf{h}_t + \mathbf{b}), \quad y_t = \arg\max \mathbf{y}_t \tag{11.27}$$

where $\mathbf{W} \in \mathbb{R}^{V \times d}$ are the weights of the softmax function with V being the size of the vocabulary and b the bias term. $\mathbf{y}_t$ is the predicted probability vector and y_t is the predicted label. We can think of an RNN as modeling the likelihood probability as $P(\mathbf{y}_t | \mathbf{x}_1, \ldots, \mathbf{x}_t)$.

Training of RNNs is usually done using Backpropagation Through Time (BPTT), which back propagates the error from time t to time 1 [70].

11.5.3 Gated Recurrent Unit

Though in theory, RNN is able to capture long-term dependency, in practice, the old memory will fade away as the sequence becomes longer. To make it easier for RNNs to capture long-term dependencies, gated recurrent units (GRUs) [7] are designed to have more persistent memory. Unlike an RNN, which uses a simple affine transformation of $\mathbf{h}_{t-1}$ and $\mathbf{h}_t$ followed by $tanh$ to update $\mathbf{h}_t$, GRU introduces the Reset Gate to determine if it wants to forget past memory and the Update Gate to control if new inputs are introduced to $\mathbf{h}_t$. The mathematical equations of how this is achieved are given as follows and an illustration of a GRU cell is shown in Figure 11.8(a):

$$
\begin{aligned}
\mathbf{z}_t &= \sigma(\mathbf{W}_{zx}\mathbf{x}_t + \mathbf{W}_{zh}\mathbf{h}_{t-1} + \mathbf{b}_z) && \text{(Update gate)} \\
\mathbf{r}_t &= \sigma(\mathbf{W}_{rx}\mathbf{x}_t + \mathbf{W}_{rh}\mathbf{h}_{t-1} + \mathbf{b}_r) && \text{(Reset gate)} \\
\tilde{\mathbf{h}}_t &= \tanh(\mathbf{r}_t \odot \mathbf{U}\mathbf{h}_{t-1} + \mathbf{W}\mathbf{x}_t) && \text{(New memory)} \\
\mathbf{h}_t &= (1 - \mathbf{z}_t) \odot \tilde{\mathbf{h}}_t + \mathbf{z}_t \odot \mathbf{h}_{t-1} && \text{(Hidden state)} \tag{11.28}
\end{aligned}
$$

From the above equation and Figure 11.8(a), we can treat the GRU as four fundamental operational stages, i.e., new memory, update gate, reset gate and hidden state. A new memory $\tilde{h}_t$ is the consolidation of a new input word $\mathbf{x}_t$ with the past hidden state $\mathbf{h}_{t-1}$, which summarizes this new word in light of the contextual past. The reset signal $\mathbf{r}_t$ is used to determining how important

$\mathbf{h}_{t-1}$ is to the summarization $\tilde{\mathbf{h}}_t$. The reset gate has the ability to completely diminish a past hidden state if it finds that $\mathbf{h}_{t-1}$ is irrelevant to the computation of the new memory. The update signal $\mathbf{z}_t$ is responsible for determining how much of past state $\mathbf{h}_{t-1}$ should be carried forward to the next state. For instance, if $\mathbf{z}_t \approx 1$, then $\mathbf{h}_{t-1}$ is almost entirely copied out to $\mathbf{h}_t$. The hidden state $\mathbf{h}_t$ is finally generated using the past hidden input $\mathbf{h}_t$ and the new memory generated $\tilde{\mathbf{h}}_t$ with the control of the update gate.

11.5.4   Long Short-Term Memory

Long Short-Term Memories, LSTMs [23], are another variant of the RNN, which can also capture long-term dependency. Similar to GRUs, an LSTM introduces more complex gates to control if it should accept new information or forget previous memory, i.e., the input gate, forget gate, output gate and new memory cell. The update rules of LSTMs are given as follows:

$$
\begin{aligned}
\mathbf{i}_t &= \sigma(\mathbf{W}_{ix}\mathbf{x}_t + \mathbf{W}_{ih}\mathbf{h}_{t-1} + \mathbf{b}_i) && \text{(Input gate)} \\
\mathbf{f}_t &= \sigma(\mathbf{W}_{fx}\mathbf{x}_t + \mathbf{W}_{fh}\mathbf{h}_{t-1} + \mathbf{b}_f) && \text{(Forget gate)} \\
\mathbf{o}_t &= \sigma(\mathbf{W}_{ox}\mathbf{x}_t + \mathbf{W}_{oh}\mathbf{h}_{t-1} + \mathbf{b}_o) && \text{(Output gate)} \\
\mathbf{g}_t &= \tanh(\mathbf{W}_{gx}\mathbf{x}_t + \mathbf{W}_{gh}\mathbf{h}_{t-1} + \mathbf{b}_g) && \text{(New memory cell)} \\
\mathbf{c}_t &= \mathbf{f}_t \odot \mathbf{c}_{t-1} + \mathbf{i}_t \odot \mathbf{g}_t && \text{(Final memory cell)} \\
\mathbf{h}_t &= \mathbf{o}_t \odot \tanh(\mathbf{c}_t) && (11.29)
\end{aligned}
$$

where $\mathbf{i}_t$ is the input gate, $\mathbf{f}_t$ is the forget gate, $\mathbf{o}_t$ is the forget fate, $\mathbf{c}_t$ is the memory cell state at t and $\mathbf{x}_t$ is the input features at t. $\sigma(\cdot)$ means the sigmoid function and $\odot$ denotes the Hadamard product. The main idea of the LSTM model is the memory cell $\mathbf{c}_t$, which records the history of the inputs observed up to t. $\mathbf{c}_t$ is a summation of (1) the previous memory cell $\mathbf{c}_{t-1}$ modulated by a sigmoid gate $\mathbf{f}_t$, and (2) $\mathbf{g}_t$, a function of previous hidden states and the current input modulated by another sigmoid gate $\mathbf{i}_t$. The sigmoid gate $\mathbf{f}_t$ is to selectively forget its previous memory while $\mathbf{i}_t$ is to selectively accept the current input. $\mathbf{i}_t$ is the gate controlling the output. The illustration of a cell of LSTM at the time step t is shown in Figure 11.8(b).

11.6   Generative Adversarial Networks and Variational Autoencoder

In this section, we introduce two very popular deep generative models proposed recently, i.e., generative adversarial networks and the variational autoencoder.

11.6.1 Generative Adversarial Networks

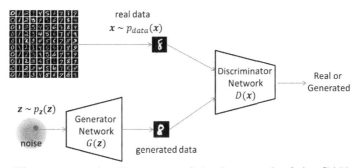

Figure 11.9: An illustration of the framework of the GAN.

The generative adversarial network (GAN) [16] is one of the most popular generative deep models. The core of a GAN is to play a min-max game between a discriminator D and a generator G, i.e., adversarial training. The discriminator D tries to differentiate if a sample is from the real world or generated by the generator, while the generator G tries to generate samples that can fool the discriminator, i.e., make the discriminator believe that the generated samples are from the real world. Figure 11.9 gives an illustration of the framework of the GAN. The generator takes a noise $\mathbf{z}$ sampled from a prior distribution $p_\mathbf{z}(\mathbf{z})$ as input, and maps the noise to the data space as $G(\mathbf{z}; \theta_g)$. Typical choices of the prior $p(\mathbf{z})$ can be a uniform distribution or Gaussian distribution. We also define a second multilayer perceptron $D(\mathbf{x}; \theta_d)$ that outputs a single scalar. $D(\mathbf{x})$ represents the probability that $\mathbf{x}$ came from the real-world data rather than generated data. D is trained to maximize the probability of assigning the correct label to both training examples and samples from G. We simultaneously train G to minimize $\log(1 - D(G(\mathbf{z})))$. In other words, D and G play the following two-player minimax game with value function $V(D, G)$:

$$\min_G \max_D V(D, G) = \mathbb{E}_{\mathbf{x} \sim p_{data}(\mathbf{x})}[\log D(\mathbf{x})] + \mathbb{E}_{\mathbf{z} \sim p_\mathbf{z}(\mathbf{z})}[\log(1 - D(G(\mathbf{z})))].$$

$$(11.30)$$

The training of a GAN can be done using minibatch stochastic gradient descent training by updating the parameters of G and D alternatively. *After the model is trained without supervision, we can treat the discriminator as a feature extractor*: The first few layers of D extract features from $\mathbf{x}$ while the last few layers are to map the features to the probability that $\mathbf{x}$ is from real data. Thus, we can remove the last few layers, then the output of D is the features extracted. In this sense, we treat GANs as unsupervised feature learning algorithms, though the main purpose of the GAN is to learn $p(\mathbf{x})$.

The GAN is a general adversarial training framework, which can be used for various domains by designing a different generator, discriminator and loss function [6, 65, 74]. For example, InfoGAN [6] learns disentangled representation by dividing the noise into two parts, i.e., disentangled codes **c** and incompressible noise **z** so that the disentangled codes **c** can control the properties such as the identity and illumination of the images generated. SeqGAN [74] models the data generator as a stochastic policy in reinforcement learning and extends the GAN for text generation.

11.6.2   Variational Autoencoder

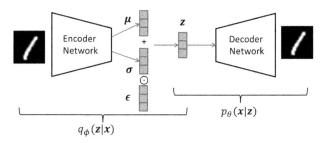

Figure 11.10: An illustration of the framework of the VAE.

The variational autoencoder (VAE) [30] is a popular generative model for unsupervised representation learning. It can be trained purely with gradient-based methods. Typically, a VAE has a standard autoencoder component which encodes the input data into a latent code space by minimizing reconstruction error, and a Bayesian regularization over the latent space, which forces the posterior of the hidden code vector to match a prior distribution. Figure 11.10 gives an illustration of a VAE. To generate a sample from the model, the VAE first draws a sample **z** from the prior distribution $p_\theta(\mathbf{z})$. The sample **z** is used as input to a differentiable generator network $g(\mathbf{z})$. Finally, **x** is sampled from a distribution $p_\theta(\mathbf{x}|g(\mathbf{z})) = p_\theta(\mathbf{x}|\mathbf{z})$. During the training, the approximate inference network, i.e., encoder network $q_\phi(\mathbf{z}|\mathbf{x})$, is then used to obtain **z** and $p_\theta(\mathbf{x}|\mathbf{z})$ is then viewed as a decoder network. The core idea of variational autoenoder is that they are trained by maximizing the variational lower bound $\mathcal{L}(\theta, \phi; \mathbf{x})$:

$$\mathcal{L}(\theta, \phi; \mathbf{x}) = -D_{KL}(q_\phi(\mathbf{z}|\mathbf{x})||p_\theta(\mathbf{z})) + \mathbb{E}_{q_\phi(\mathbf{z}|\mathbf{x})}[\log p_\theta(\mathbf{x}|\mathbf{z})] \le \log p_\theta(\mathbf{x})$$
$$(11.31)$$

where $D_{KL}(q_\phi(\mathbf{z}|\mathbf{x})||p_\theta(\mathbf{z}))$ is the KL divergence which measures the similarity of two distributions $q_\phi(\mathbf{z}|\mathbf{x})$ and $p_\theta(\mathbf{z})$. ϕ and θ are the variational parameters and generative parameters, respectively. We want to differentiate and optimize the lower bound w.r.t both the ϕ and θ. However, directly using a gradient estimator for the above objective function will exhibit high variance. Therefore, VAE adopts the reparametric trick. That is, under certain mild conditions for a chosen approximate posterior $q_\phi(\mathbf{z}|\mathbf{x})$, the random variable $\tilde{z} \sim q_\phi(\mathbf{z}|\mathbf{x})$ can be parameterized as

$$\tilde{z} = g_\phi(\epsilon, \mathbf{x}) \quad \text{with} \quad \epsilon \sim p(\epsilon)$$
$$(11.32)$$

where $g_\phi(\epsilon, \mathbf{x})$ is a differentiable transformation function of a noise variable ϵ. The nonparametric trick is also shown in Figure 11.10. With this technique, the variational lower bound in Eq.(11.31) can be approximated as

$$L^A(\theta, \phi; \mathbf{x}) = \frac{1}{L} \sum_{l=1}^{L} \log p_\theta(\mathbf{x}, \mathbf{z}^{(l)}) - \log q_\phi(\mathbf{z}^{(l)}|\mathbf{x})$$

$$\tilde{z}^{(l)} = g_\phi(\epsilon^{(l)}, \mathbf{x}) \quad \text{with} \quad \epsilon^{(l)} \sim p(\epsilon).$$

(11.33)

Then the parameters can be learned via stochastic gradient descent efficiently. It is easy to see that the encoder is a feature extractor which learns latent representations for $\mathbf{x}$.

11.7 Discussion and Further Readings

We have introduced representative deep learning models for feature engineering. In this section, we'll discuss how they can be used for hierarchical representation learning and disentangled representation, and how they can be used for popular domains such as text, image and graph.

Table 11.1: Hierarchical and disentangled representation learning

Method	Hierarchical Fea. Rep.	Disentangled Fea. Rep.
RBM/DBM	[59]	[48]
DBN	[33]	N/A
AE/DAE/SDAE	[37]	[28]
RNN/GRU/LSTM	[68, 73]	[11, 54]
CNN	[12, 14]	[25, 49]
GAN	[47]	[6, 38]
VAE	[75]	[54, 72]

Hierarchical Representation Generally, hierarchical representation lets us learn features of hierarchy and combine top-down and bottom-up processing of an image (or text). For instance, lower layers could support object detection by spotting low-level features indicative of object parts. Conversely, information about objects in the higher layers could resolve lower-level ambiguities in the image or infer the locations of hidden object parts. Features at different hierarchy levels may be good for different tasks. The high-level features captures the main objects, resolve ambiguities, and thus are good for classification, while mid-level features include many details and may be good for segmentation. Hierarchical feature representation is very common in deep learning models. We list some representative literature on how the introduced model can be used for hierarchical feature learning in Table 11.1.

Disentangled Representation Disentangled representation is a popular way to learn explainable representations. The majority of existing representation learning frameworks learn representation $\mathbf{h} \in \mathbb{R}^{d \times 1}$, which is difficult to explain, i.e., the d-latent dimensions are entangled together and we don't know the semantic meaning of the d-dimensions. Instead, disentangled representation learning tries to disentangle the latent factors so we know the semantic meaning of the latent dimensions. For example, for handwritten digits such as the MNIST dataset, we may want to disentangle the digit shape from writing style so that some part of $\mathbf{h}$ controls digit shapes while the other part represents writing style. The disentangled representation not only explains latent representation but also helps generate controlled realistic images. For example, by changing the part of codes that controls digit shape, we can generate new images of target digit shapes using a generator with this new latent representation. Therefore, disentangled representation learning is attracting increasing attention. Table 11.1 also lists some representative deep learning methods for disentangled representation learning. This is still a relatively new direction that needs further investigation.

Table 11.2: Deep learning methods for different domains

Method	Text	Image	Audio	Linked Data) (Graph)
RBM/DBM	[57, 58]	[57]	[9]	[67]
DBN	[52]	[33]	[42]	N/A
AE/DAE/SDAE	[3]	[63]	[44]	[64]
CNN	[29]	[19, 45, 71]	[1]	[10]
Word2Vec	[35, 41]	N/A	N/A	[61, 66]
RNN/GRU/LSTM	[27, 40, 60]	[2]	[17, 50]	N/A
GAN	[74]	[6, 47]	[74]	N/A
VAE	[5, 26]	[18, 30]	[24]	N/A

Deep Feature Representation for Various Domains Many deep learning algorithms were initially developed for specific domains. For example, the CNN was initially developed for image processing and Word2Vec was initially proposed for learning word representation. Due to the great success of these methods, they were further developed to be applicable to other domains. For example, in addition to images, the CNN has also been successfully applied on texts, audio and linked data. Each domain has its own unique property. For example, text data are inherently sequential and graph data are non-i.i.d. Thus, directly applying CNN is impractical. New architectures are proposed to adapt the CNN for these domains. The same holds for the other deep learning algorithms. Therefore, we summarize the application of the discussed deep learning models in four domains in Table 11.2. We encourage interested users to read these papers for further understanding.

Combining Deep Learning Models We have introduced various deep learning models, which can be applied to different domains. For example, LSTM is mainly used for dealing with sequential data such as texts while the CNN is powerful for images. It is very common that we need to work on tasks which are related to different domains. In such cases, we can combine different deep learning models to propose a new framework that can be applied for the task at hand. For example, for an information retrieval task given a text query, we want to retrieve images that match the query. We will need to use LSTM or Word2Vec to learn a representation that captures the semantic meanings of the query. At the same time, we need to use CNN to learn features that describe the image. We can then train LSTM and CNN so that the similarity of the representations for the matched query-image pairs are maximized while the similarity of the representations for the non-matched query-image pairs are minimized. Another example is video action recognition, where we want to classify the action of the video. Since the video is composed of frames and nearby frames have dependency, a video is inherently sequential data and LSTM is a good fit for modeling such data. However, LSTM is not good at extracting images. Therefore, we will first need to use CNN to extract features from each frame of the video, which are then used as input to LSTM for learning representation of the video [68]. Similarly, for image captioning, we can use CNN to extract features and use LSTM to generate image captions based on the image features [71]. We just list a few examples and there are many other examples. In general, we can treat deep learning algorithms as feature extracting tools that can extract features from certain domains. We can then design a loss function on top of these deep learning algorithms for the problem we want to study. One thing to note is that when we combine different models together, they are trained end-to-end. In other words, we don't train these models separately. Instead, we treat the new model as a unified model. This usually gives better performance than training each model separately and then combining them.

Bibliography

[1] Ossama Abdel-Hamid, Abdel-Rahman Mohamed, Hui Jiang, Li Deng, Gerald Penn, and Dong Yu. Convolutional neural networks for speech recognition. *IEEE/ACM Transactions on Audio, Speech, and Language Processing*, 22(10):1533–1545, 2014.

[2] Stanislaw Antol, Aishwarya Agrawal, Jiasen Lu, Margaret Mitchell, Dhruv Batra, C. Lawrence Zitnick, and Devi Parikh. VQA: Visual question answering. In *CVPR*, pages 2425–2433, 2015.

[3] Sarath Chandar AP, Stanislas Lauly, Hugo Larochelle, Mitesh Khapra, Balaraman Ravindran, Vikas C Raykar, and Amrita Saha. An autoencoder approach to learning bilingual word representations. In *NIPS*, pages 1853–1861, 2014.

[4] Yoshua Bengio et al. Learning deep architectures for AI. *Foundations and Trends in Machine Learning*, 2(1):1–127, 2009.

[5] Samuel R Bowman, Luke Vilnis, Oriol Vinyals, Andrew M Dai, Rafal Jozefowicz, and Samy Bengio. Generating sentences from a continuous space. *CoNLL*, 2016.

[6] Xi Chen, Yan Duan, Rein Houthooft, John Schulman, Ilya Sutskever, and Pieter Abbeel. Infogan: Interpretable representation learning by information maximizing generative adversarial nets. In *NIPS*, pages 2172–2180, 2016.

[7] Kyunghyun Cho, Bart Van Merriënboer, Caglar Gulcehre, Dzmitry Bahdanau, Fethi Bougares, Holger Schwenk, and Yoshua Bengio. Learning phrase representations using RNN encoder-decoder for statistical machine translation. *arXiv preprint arXiv:1406.1078*, 2014.

[8] Aaron Courville, James Bergstra, and Yoshua Bengio. A spike and slab restricted boltzmann machine. In *AISTAS*, pages 233–241, 2011.

[9] George Dahl, Abdel-Rahman Mohamed, Geoffrey E Hinton, et al. Phone recognition with the mean-covariance restricted Boltzmann machine. In *NIPS*, pages 469–477, 2010.

[10] Michaël Defferrard, Xavier Bresson, and Pierre Vandergheynst. Convolutional neural networks on graphs with fast localized spectral filtering. In *NIPS*, pages 3844–3852, 2016.

[11] Emily Denton and Vighnesh Birodkar. Unsupervised learning of disentangled representations from video. pages 4417–4426, NIPS 2017.

[12] Clement Farabet, Camille Couprie, Laurent Najman, and Yann LeCun. Learning hierarchical features for scene labeling. *IEEE TPAMI*, 35(8):1915–1929, 2013.

[13] John R Firth. *A Synopsis of Linguistic Theory*, 1930-1955. 1957.

[14] Ross Girshick, Jeff Donahue, Trevor Darrell, and Jitendra Malik. Rich feature hierarchies for accurate object detection and semantic segmentation. In *CVPR*, pages 580–587, 2014.

[15] Ian Goodfellow, Yoshua Bengio, and Aaron Courville. *Deep Learning*. MIT Press, 2016.

[16] Ian Goodfellow, Jean Pouget-Abadie, Mehdi Mirza, Bing Xu, David Warde-Farley, Sherjil Ozair, Aaron Courville, and Yoshua Bengio. Generative adversarial nets. In *NIPS*, pages 2672–2680, 2014.

[17] Alex Graves, Abdel-Rahman Mohamed, and Geoffrey Hinton. Speech recognition with deep recurrent neural networks. In *ICASSP*, pages 6645–6649. IEEE, 2013.

[18] Karol Gregor, Ivo Danihelka, Alex Graves, Danilo Jimenez Rezende, and Daan Wierstra. Draw: A recurrent neural network for image generation. *arXiv preprint arXiv:1502.04623*, 2015.

[19] Kaiming He, Xiangyu Zhang, Shaoqing Ren, and Jian Sun. Deep residual learning for image recognition. In *CVPR*, pages 770–778, 2016.

[20] Geoffrey Hinton, Li Deng, Dong Yu, George E Dahl, Abdel-Rahman Mohamed, Navdeep Jaitly, Andrew Senior, Vincent Vanhoucke, Patrick Nguyen, Tara N Sainath, et al. Deep neural networks for acoustic modeling in speech recognition: The shared views of four research groups. *IEEE Signal Processing Magazine*, 29(6):82–97, 2012.

[21] Geoffrey E Hinton. Deep belief networks. *Scholarpedia*, 4(5):5947, 2009.

[22] Geoffrey E Hinton et al. Modeling pixel means and covariances using factorized third-order Boltzmann machines. In *CVPR*, pages 2551–2558. IEEE, 2010.

[23] Sepp Hochreiter and Jürgen Schmidhuber. Long short-term memory. *Neural Computation*, 9(8):1735–1780, 1997.

[24] Wei-Ning Hsu, Yu Zhang, and James R. Glass. Learning latent representations for speech generation and transformation. Annual Conference of the International Speech Communication Association, (INTER-SPEECH). pages 1273–1277, 2017.

[25] Wei-Ning Hsu, Yu Zhang, and James R. Glass. Unsupervised learning of disentangled and interpretable representations from sequential data. In *NIPS*, 2017.

[26] Zhiting Hu, Zichao Yang, Xiaodan Liang, Ruslan Salakhutdinov, and Eric P Xing. Toward controllable text generation. In *ICML*, 2017.

[27] Ozan Irsoy and Claire Cardie. Opinion mining with deep recurrent neural networks. In *EMNLP*, pages 720–728, 2014.

[28] Michael Janner, Jiajun Wu, Tejas Kulkarn, Ilker Yildirim, and Josh Tenenbaum. Learning to generalize intrinsic images with a structured disentangling autoencoder. In *NIPS*, 2017.

[29] Nal Kalchbrenner, Edward Grefenstette, and Phil Blunsom. A convolutional neural network for modelling sentences. In *ACL*, 2014.

[30] Diederik P Kingma and Max Welling. Auto-encoding variational Bayes. *arXiv preprint arXiv:1312.6114*, 2013.

[31] Alex Krizhevsky, Geoffrey E Hinton, et al. Factored 3-way restricted Boltzmann machines for modeling natural images. In *AISTATS*, pages 621–628, 2010.

[32] Alex Krizhevsky, Ilya Sutskever, and Geoffrey E Hinton. Imagenet classification with deep convolutional neural networks. In *NIPS*, pages 1097–1105, 2012.

[33] Honglak Lee, Roger Grosse, Rajesh Ranganath, and Andrew Y Ng. Unsupervised learning of hierarchical representations with convolutional deep belief networks. *Communications of the ACM*, 54(10):95–103, 2011.

[34] Omer Levy and Yoav Goldberg. Neural word embedding as implicit matrix factorization. In *NIPS*, pages 2177–2185, 2014.

[35] Yang Li, Quan Pan, Tao Yang, Suhang Wang, Jiliang Tang, and Erik Cambria. Learning word representations for sentiment analysis. *Cognitive Computation*, 2017.

[36] Jonathan Long, Evan Shelhamer, and Trevor Darrell. Fully convolutional networks for semantic segmentation. In *CVPR*, pages 3431–3440, 2015.

[37] Jonathan Masci, Ueli Meier, Dan Cireşan, and Jürgen Schmidhuber. Stacked convolutional auto-encoders for hierarchical feature extraction. *Artificial Neural Networks and Machine Learning–ICANN 2011*, pages 52–59, 2011.

[38] Michaël Mathieu, Junbo Jake Zhao, Pablo Sprechmann, Aditya Ramesh, and Yann LeCun. Disentangling factors of variation in deep representation using adversarial training. In *NIPS*, pages 5041–5049, 2016.

[39] Tomas Mikolov, Kai Chen, Greg Corrado, and Jeffrey Dean. Efficient estimation of word representations in vector space. *arXiv preprint arXiv:1301.3781*, 2013.

[40] Tomas Mikolov, Martin Karafiát, Lukás Burget, Jan Cernocký, and Sanjeev Khudanpur. Recurrent neural network based language model. In *INTERSPEECH*, pages 1045–1048, 2010.

[41] Tomas Mikolov, Ilya Sutskever, Kai Chen, Greg S Corrado, and Jeff Dean. Distributed representations of words and phrases and their compositionality. In *NIPS*, pages 3111–3119, 2013.

[42] Abdel-Rahman Mohamed, George Dahl, and Geoffrey Hinton. Deep belief networks for phone recognition. In *NIPS Workshop on Deep Learning for Speech Recognition and Related Applications*, 2009.

[43] Andrew Ng. Sparse autoencoder. *CS294A Lecture Notes*, 72(2011):1–19, 2011.

[44] Jiquan Ngiam, Aditya Khosla, Mingyu Kim, Juhan Nam, Honglak Lee, and Andrew Y Ng. Multimodal deep learning. In *ICML*, pages 689–696, 2011.

[45] Maxime Oquab, Leon Bottou, Ivan Laptev, and Josef Sivic. Learning and transferring mid-level image representations using convolutional neural networks. In *CVPR*, pages 1717–1724, 2014.

[46] Jeffrey Pennington, Richard Socher, and Christopher D Manning. Glove: Global vectors for word representation. In *EMNLP*, volume 14, pages 1532–1543, 2014.

[47] Alec Radford, Luke Metz, and Soumith Chintala. Unsupervised representation learning with deep convolutional generative adversarial networks. *arXiv preprint arXiv:1511.06434*, 2015.

[48] Scott Reed, Kihyuk Sohn, Yuting Zhang, and Honglak Lee. Learning to disentangle factors of variation with manifold interaction. In *ICML*, pages 1431–1439, 2014.

[49] Salah Rifai, Yoshua Bengio, Aaron Courville, Pascal Vincent, and Mehdi Mirza. Disentangling factors of variation for facial expression recognition. *ECCV*, pages 808–822, 2012.

[50] Haşim Sak, Andrew Senior, and Françoise Beaufays. Long short-term memory recurrent neural network architectures for large scale acoustic modeling. In *Fifteenth Annual Conference of the International Speech Communication Association*, 2014.

[51] Ruslan Salakhutdinov and Geoffrey Hinton. Deep Boltzmann machines. In *Artificial Intelligence and Statistics*, pages 448–455, 2009.

[52] Ruhi Sarikaya, Geoffrey E. Hinton, and Anoop Deoras. Application of deep belief networks for natural language understanding. *IEEE/ACM Trans. Audio, Speech & Language Processing*, 22(4):778–784, 2014.

[53] Ali Sharif Razavian, Hossein Azizpour, Josephine Sullivan, and Stefan Carlsson. CNN features off-the-shelf: an astounding baseline for recognition. In *CVPR Workshops*, pages 806–813, 2014.

[54] N. Siddharth, Brooks Paige, Jan-Willem van de Meent, Alban Desmaison, Frank Wood, Noah D. Goodman, Pushmeet Kohli, and Philip H. S. Torr. Learning disentangled representations with semi-supervised deep generative models. In *NIPS*, 2017.

[55] Karen Simonyan and Andrew Zisserman. Two-stream convolutional networks for action recognition in videos. In *NIPS*, pages 568–576, 2014.

[56] Nitish Srivastava, Geoffrey E Hinton, Alex Krizhevsky, Ilya Sutskever, and Ruslan Salakhutdinov. Dropout: A simple way to prevent neural networks from overfitting. *Journal of Machine Learning Research*, 15(1):1929–1958, 2014.

[57] Nitish Srivastava and Ruslan R Salakhutdinov. Multimodal learning with deep Boltzmann machines. In *NIPS*, pages 2222–2230, 2012.

[58] Nitish Srivastava, Ruslan R Salakhutdinov, and Geoffrey E Hinton. Modeling documents with deep Boltzmann machines. In *UAI*, 2013.

[59] Heung-Il Suk, Seong-Whan Lee, Dinggang Shen, Alzheimer's Disease Neuroimaging Initiative, et al. Hierarchical feature representation and multimodal fusion with deep learning for AD/MCI diagnosis. *NeuroImage*, 101:569–582, 2014.

[60] Ilya Sutskever, Oriol Vinyals, and Quoc V Le. Sequence to sequence learning with neural networks. In *NIPS*, pages 3104–3112, 2014.

[61] Jian Tang, Meng Qu, Mingzhe Wang, Ming Zhang, Jun Yan, and Qiaozhu Mei. Line: Large-scale information network embedding. In *WWW*, pages 1067–1077, 2015.

[62] Tijmen Tieleman. Training restricted Boltzmann machines using approximations to the likelihood gradient. In *ICML*, pages 1064–1071. ACM, 2008.

[63] Pascal Vincent, Hugo Larochelle, Isabelle Lajoie, Yoshua Bengio, and Pierre-Antoine Manzagol. Stacked denoising autoencoders: Learning useful representations in a deep network with a local denoising criterion. *Journal of Machine Learning Research*, 11(Dec):3371–3408, 2010.

[64] Daixin Wang, Peng Cui, and Wenwu Zhu. Structural deep network embedding. In *SIGKDD*, pages 1225–1234. ACM, 2016.

[65] Jun Wang, Lantao Yu, Weinan Zhang, Yu Gong, Yinghui Xu, Benyou Wang, Peng Zhang, and Dell Zhang. Irgan: A minimax game for unifying generative and discriminative information retrieval models. In *SIGIR*, 2017.

[66] Suhang Wang, Jiliang Tang, Charu Aggarwal, and Huan Liu. Linked document embedding for classification. In *CIKM*, pages 115–124. ACM, 2016.

[67] Suhang Wang, Jiliang Tang, Fred Morstatter, and Huan Liu. Paired restricted Boltzmann machine for linked data. In *CIKM*, pages 1753–1762. ACM, 2016.

[68] Yilin Wang, Suhang Wang, Jiliang Tang, Neil O'Hare, Yi Chang, and Baoxin Li. Hierarchical attention network for action recognition in videos. *CoRR*, abs/1607.06416, 2016.

[69] Max Welling, Michal Rosen-Zvi, and Geoffrey E Hinton. Exponential family harmoniums with an application to information retrieval. In *NIPS*, volume 4, pages 1481–1488, 2004.

[70] Paul J Werbos. Backpropagation through time: What it does and how to do it. *Proceedings of the IEEE*, 78(10):1550–1560, 1990.

[71] Kelvin Xu, Jimmy Ba, Ryan Kiros, Kyunghyun Cho, Aaron Courville, Ruslan Salakhudinov, Rich Zemel, and Yoshua Bengio. Show, attend and tell: Neural image caption generation with visual attention. In *ICML*, pages 2048–2057, 2015.

[72] Xinchen Yan, Jimei Yang, Kihyuk Sohn, and Honglak Lee. Attribute2image: Conditional image generation from visual attributes. In *ECCV*, pages 776–791. Springer, 2016.

[73] Zichao Yang, Diyi Yang, Chris Dyer, Xiaodong He, Alexander J Smola, and Eduard H Hovy. Hierarchical attention networks for document classification. In *HLT-NAACL*, pages 1480–1489, 2016.

[74] Lantao Yu, Weinan Zhang, Jun Wang, and Yong Yu. Seqgan: Sequence generative adversarial nets with policy gradient. In *AAAI*, pages 2852–2858, 2017.

[75] Shengjia Zhao, Jiaming Song, and Stefano Ermon. Learning hierarchical features from deep generative models. In *ICML*, pages 4091–4099, 2017.

Part III

Feature Engineering in Special Applications

Chapter 12

Feature Engineering for Social Bot Detection

Onur Varol

Indiana University, Bloomington, IN, USA

Clayton A. Davis

Indiana University, Bloomington, IN, USA

Filippo Menczer

Indiana University, Bloomington, IN, USA

Alessandro Flammini

Indiana University, Bloomington, IN, USA

12.1 Introduction

Social media platforms connect millions of individuals and allow dissemination of information. Properties of social media make it the ideal tool for communication, however, entities with malicious intentions have strong motives to abuse online social networks to profit or gain power by boosting their popularity, manipulating online discussions, and targeting certain groups for attack [27, 29, 74].

Increasing evidence suggests that social platforms like Twitter accommodate an increasing number of autonomous entities known as social bots [4, 29]. A recent study estimates that between 9% and 15% of the accounts on Twitter display bot-like behaviors [78]. These autonomous entities are controlled by software that generates content and establishes interactions with other accounts. It is fair to point out that not all bots have malicious intentions; many are used for benign tasks, such as dissemination of news and publications [41, 56] and coordination of volunteer activities [73]. But there is a growing record of vicious application of social bots.

Examples of malicious social-bot use include emulating human behavior to manufacture fake grassroots political support [34, 72], promoting terrorist propaganda and recruitment [5, 7, 31, 43], manipulating stock and advertisement markets [19, 27], and disseminating rumors and conspiracy theories [6].

The magnitude of the problem is underscored by a social bot–detection challenge recently organized by DARPA to study information dissemination mediated by automated accounts and to detect deceptive activities carried out by these bots [76]. Researchers also point to the possibility of social bot involvement in online discourse about the US presidential election in 2016 [7, 43].

12.2 Social Bot Detection

Social bot activity, the broader implications for social network platforms, and the detection of these accounts are becoming central research avenues [8, 12, 20, 29, 50, 83]. Previous research categorized various types and *modus operandi* of social bots [46, 63, 66].

Mainstream research efforts have focused on three approaches to detect social bots: holistic, pairwise, and egocentric analysis. Each approach presents its own advantages and disadvantages to analyze the activities of users.

12.2.1   Holistic Approach

In terms of performance and accuracy, the holistic approach performs better than other methodologies, since it captures more information about accounts and their interactions. However, capturing a complete picture of social networking systems is not practical outside of the companies that own the platforms themselves.

Having complete information about social network structure, user interactions, and online activities allows social media companies to build operational systems. Examples of studies discussing holistic solutions focus on clustering behavioral patterns of users [80] and classifying accounts using supervised learning techniques [50,83]. For instance, Beutel *et al.* extract behavioral similarities by decomposing event data in time, user, and activity dimensions [8].

Advantages of this approach over other methodologies come from the availability of complete data. Other methodologies lack full knowledge of social ties that are hard to collect due to their dynamic nature. Companies can also track user behaviors such as impressions on each post, time spent on user profiles, and usage statistics of the website to extract useful features. Such behavioral features have been studied to measure the credibility of online information [33] and purchasing behaviors [40].

A limitation of this approach is the computational complexity of analyzing such massive data in real or near-real time with limited resources. Recent advances in deep learning and reinforcement learning may help mitigate these limitations.

12.2.2   Pairwise Account Comparison

Evidence of so-called *botnets*—coordinated collectives of software-controlled fake accounts—has been observed in support of the Syrian War [1] as well as in seemingly aimless activities [26]. The comparisons of temporal or content patterns among pairs of accounts can reveal significant similarities that are unlikely to emerge organically.

The idea is to enumerate all elements of certain account features, such as friends, followers, URLs, hashtags, and so on. Pairwise comparison between sets defined for each user can then be used to compute account similarities. Such methodology has also been applied to cluster memes on social media [28, 44].

The pairwise comparison methodology has been used to detect abnormally correlated user activities [16]. An advantage of this approach is that the computed similarity matrix can be employed in both supervised and unsupervised learning frameworks [62,77]. However, the computation of pairwise similarities in huge networks is very costly without some heuristics to narrow down the possible pairs.

12.2.3   Egocentric Analysis

Egocentric analysis captures and evaluates information about a single user at a given point in time. When performed by users, as opposed to the platform owners themselves, one is usually restricted to collecting the public subset of information about other accounts. However the trade-off between computational complexity and accuracy favors this simpler approach in many cases.

In the literature, we have observed several examples of systems designed to operate with limited information resources by considering single accounts [17, 18, 20, 50]. Most of the research in this direction relies on annotations by experts and crowd-sourcing workers to train supervised learning algorithms and evaluate the consistency and effectiveness of different detection systems.

12.3   Online Bot Detection Framework

In this section, we present an online bot detection system, Botometer (`botometer.iuni.iu.edu`), that is freely available for academic and public use as part of the Observatory on Social Media (OSoMe) project [23]. Our system extracts 1150 features from a collection of tweets related to a given Twitter account and uses them in a machine-learning framework to classify the account as being operated by a bot or a human [24, 78]. Accessible via a website and an API, our system served over 30 million requests in the first several months after its public release in 2016, as shown in Fig. 12.1.

Our desire to build a bot detection system for public use informed the choices of criteria for building feature sets and training classifiers. As a publicly available service, we require the system to be simultaneously fast and reliable. Single-request speed is important in order for the website to feel responsive, while reliability is critical for API users submitting requests in bulk.

With single-request speed in mind, we took computational efficiency into account as well as accuracy when selecting a feature set. Details of the features implemented are discussed in Sec. 12.3.1.

Additionally we limit analysis to only the most recent activity from a given account. This is a result of strict rate limits on the Twitter API; each evaluation by Botometer only requires a single call to each Twitter API endpoint used, thus maximizing the number of account analyses possible per unit time and minimizing the total time required to classify a single account.

Besides speed and reliability, public availability necessitates that our system be useful without any special data or permission from the platform owners. As such, we only use public data from the Twitter API according to its terms of service.

Considering factors of computational efficiency, performance, and information access, the egocentric approach to classification best fits our design goals.

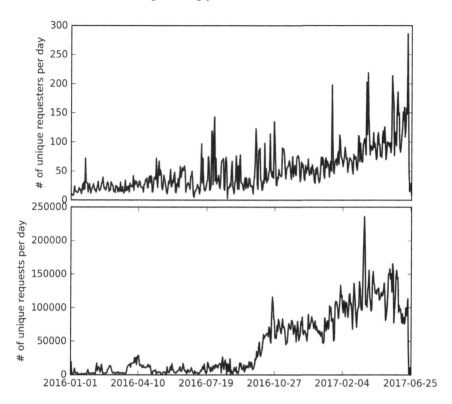

Figure 12.1: Number of daily requests (bottom) and unique requesters (top) served by the Botometer system.

12.3.1 Feature Extraction

Our approach to egocentric classification of a given Twitter user leverages three main types of data obtained from the Twitter REST API[1]: the user profile, tweets produced and broadcasted (retweeted) by the user, and tweets authored by other accounts mentioning the target user.

Quotas on the number of requests per unit time to each Twitter API endpoint present a trade-off between accuracy and classification volume: more API calls per user yield more data, which may improve accuracy, but proportionally decrease the number of accounts one can analyze before reaching the quota. Our system harnesses the most recent 200 tweets by the user and 100 tweets mentioning the user. These quantities correspond to the maximum number of tweets that can be collected with a single API request to each endpoint (each endpoint is individually rate-limited). Therefore this choice is a natural trade-off between data volume (performance) and accuracy.

---

[1]`dev.twitter.com/rest/public`

The public data and meta-data about the target user, collected using the Twitter API, is distilled into 1,150 features. These features are roughly categorized as friends, tweet content and sentiment, network patterns, and activity time series. Next we present details about the individual features in each class.

12.3.1.1   User-Based Features

As with other systems analyzing Twitter users and behavior, we leverage user meta-data features extracted from meta-data [29, 60]. First we count the length and number of digits in the user's `screen_name` and `user_name` (these can differ on Twitter). Users can also provide a textual `description` of themselves; we consider the length of this field as well as the number of unique descriptions observed in tweets from users connected via retweet, mention, *etc.*

User activity and connectivity in its simplest form can also provide signals for classification. We extract numerical features about number of `friends` and `followers`, as well as of different activity types such as `tweet`, `retweet`, `mention`, and `reply`. We consider both the total number of tweets in each type as well as their temporal rate. Further discussion of these social relations and tweet types can be found in the next section.

When a new account is created on Twitter, default values are used for some profile fields, such as profile image, until changed by the user. We use binary features indicating whether or not a given account has each of these `default` `properties`. We also extract features about `account age` and `time-zone`. For a complete list of features in this category see Table 12.1.

12.3.1.2   Friend Features

Twitter actively encourages social connectivity by `following` other accounts. Users can follow any public profile, and the follow relation need not be reciprocal. The reverse of the `follower` relation is the `friend` relation: if A follows B, then B is a friend of A.

In this setting, content can disseminated by users rebroadcasting other users' tweets via `retweets`. A tweet can be addressed to one or more specific users by `mention`ing the target users' screen names. We consider four types of links: retweet, mention, being retweeted, and being mentioned. Grouping tweets by their link type, we extract *friend-features* for each group separately.

Groupwise distributions of user meta-data are then extracted for accounts in the group. We compute distributions for number of friends, followers, and tweets, length of profile description, account age, and time-zone offset. For each distribution we compute mean, maximum, minimum, and median values, along with skewness, kurtosis, and entropy.

We also consider the number of unique languages represented in the group as well as entropy of language use as features. The fraction of those users with default profile information is also included. All of the features in this category are listed in Table 12.2.

Table 12.1: List of features extracted from user profile.

List of `user-features`
Screen name length
Number of digits in screen name
User name length
Time offset (sec.)
Default profile (binary)
Default picture (binary)
Account age (days)
Number of unique profile descriptions among connected users
(*) Profile description lengths for connected users
(*) Number of friends distribution
(*) Number of followers distribution
(*) Number of favorites distribution
Number of friends (signal-noise ratio and rel. change)
Number of followers (signal-noise ratio and rel. change)
Number of favorites (signal-noise ratio and rel. change)
Number of tweets (per hour and total)
Number of retweets (per hour and total)
Number of mentions (per hour and total)
Number of replies (per hour and total)
Number of retweeted (per hour and total)

(*) Distribution types. The following statistics are computed and used as individual features: min, max, median, mean, std. deviation, skewness, kurtosis, and entropy.

Table 12.2: List of features extracted from neighbors of user. We consider four types of users: retweeting, mentioning, retweeted, and mentioned.

List of `friend-features`
Number of distinct languages
Entropy of language use
(*) Account age distribution
(*) Time offset distribution
(*) Number of friends distribution
(*) Number of followers distribution
(*) Number of tweets distribution
(*) Description length distribution
Fraction of users with default profile
Fraction of users with default picture

(*) Distribution types. The following statistics are computed and used as individual features: min, max, median, mean, std. deviation, skewness, kurtosis, and entropy.

Table 12.3: List of features extracted from interaction and hashtag co-occurrence networks. We consider three types of network: retweet, mention, and hashtag co-occurrence networks.

List of `network-features`
Number of nodes
Number of edges (also for reciprocal)
(*) Strength distribution
(*) In-strength distribution
(*) Out-strength distribution
Network density (also for reciprocal)
(*) Clustering coeff. (also for reciprocal)

(*) Distribution types. The following statistics are computed and used as individual features: min, max, median, mean, std. deviation, skewness, kurtosis, and entropy.

12.3.1.3   Network Features

Network structure can contain information useful for characterizing different types of communication. Network features have notably been leveraged in the context of astroturf detection [72]. Our system constructs three types of networks: `retweet`, `mention`, and `hashtag co-occurrence`.

Retweet and mention networks are represented as weighted, directed networks with users as nodes and retweets/mention tweets as links. The link direction corresponds to the information flow: toward the user retweeting or being mentioned. The edge weight represents the frequency of interaction.

A hashtag is a word prefixed with the hash (#) symbol, and is used in Twitter as a topic identifier. Hashtag co-occurrence networks are weighted, undirected networks with hashtags as the nodes. Two hashtags are linked when they occur together in a given tweet, and the edge is weighted according to the frequency of the co-occurrence in tweets.

Given the local nature of egocentric data collection, we utilize simple network features that quantify local interactions. These measures also happen to be the least expensive to compute. The most straight forward features we consider are number of nodes and edges, as well as the density of the network. We also include features extracted from distributions of local clustering coefficients and (in-/out-)strength, or weighted degree. Subgraphs of the retweet and mention networks that contain only reciprocal links are additionally considered and used for feature extraction. The complete list of features in this category can be found in Table 12.3.

12.3.1.4   Content and Language Features

Content and linguistic analysis of tweets have been used for a wide variety of applications [13,21,22,51,58,64]. The simplest content features we use come from word counts and text entropy.

Table 12.4: List of features extracted from content of tweets.

List of `content-features`
(*,**) Frequency of POS tags in a tweet
(*,**) Proportion of POS tags in a tweet
(*) Number of words in a tweet
(*) Entropy of words in a tweet

(*) Distribution types. The following statistics are computed and used as individual features: min, max, median, mean, std. deviation, skewness, kurtosis, and entropy. (**) Part-of-Speech (POS) tag. There are nine POS tags: verbs, nouns, adjectives, modal auxiliaries, pre-determiners, interjections, adverbs, wh-, and pronouns.

Other content features are extracted by applying the *Part-of-Speech* (POS) tagging technique, which identifies different types of natural language components. We consider 9 types of POS tags: verbs, nouns, adjectives, modal auxiliaries, pre-determiners, interjections, adverbs, wh-, and pronouns. Distributions of POS tag occurrences are used to extract features to reflect use of different language styles [15]. For a complete list of features in this category, see Table 12.4.

12.3.1.5 Sentiment Features

Sentiment analysis is used to describe the emotions conveyed by a piece of text, or more broadly, the attitude or mood of an entire conversation. Sentiment extracted from social media conversations has been used to forecast offline events including financial market fluctuations [11] and is known to affect information spreading and social structure [10, 32, 61].

Our framework leverages several sentiment extraction techniques to generate various sentiment features:

- **ANEW**: Arousal, valence, and dominance scores are selected for analysis of mood and sentiment based on theoretical foundations of these dimensions [81]. Crowd-sourcing is used to annotate over 14k words along each of the three dimensions.

- **Happiness**: To quantify happiness in a text, we use a dataset of over 10k words identified and annotated by researchers [48]. This word list contains the most frequent words collected from Google books, *New York Times* articles, music lyrics, and Twitter messages.

- **Polarization and strength**: This measure identifies a phrase as neutral or polar and then disambiguates the polarity of the polar expressions [82].

- **Emoticon**: Pictorial representations of different facial expressions are popular on social media. We used a lexicon of such symbols and character sequences to identify positively and negatively associated text [2]. This does not include emoji, although recent work exploring the popularity of emojis in social media [3, 59] suggests that their inclusion would be possible.

All these techniques rely on a lexicon to compute scores for each type of content and there exist several alternatives one could consider [36]. One could extend this analysis by adopting machine learning models trained solely to extract features about sentiment. The complete list of sentiment features is found in Table 12.5.

We note that both content and sentiment features are language-specific and were trained on corpora of English-language tweets. Language-agnostic evaluation is possible by using models trained without these two categories.

12.3.1.6   Temporal Features

Temporal signatures are shown to be useful in the context of analyzing content production and consumption, identification of online campaigns, and evolution of online discussion [16, 30, 35, 79].

Basic temporal features indicate how frequently an account is active; a human is unlikely to tweet hundreds of times per day. These features are listed in the user class. More sophisticated temporal features are extracted using distributions of time intervals between consecutive tweets, retweets, and mentions. Table 12.6 lists the features in this category.

12.3.2   Possible Directions for Feature Engineering

As Twitter introduces new functionalities and usage patterns evolve over time, one may consider creating new features to leverage these additional behaviors. For example, Twitter has recently introduced *quoted tweets*, which are essentially a retweet with additional user-supplied commentary.

Modern machine learning techniques can also be applied to extract more sophisticated features from the existing data. Deep learning and vector embeddings are promising technologies that one can employ to extract features for network structure [39, 69] and language and sentiment [25, 37, 57]. Research in this area may lead to features that capture not only basic statistics but also semantics expressed by textual content [42, 49]. Of course, these more sophisticated analyses come with computational costs that must be weighed against one's desire for fast classification results. We discuss implications of recent technologies using deep learning more in detail in Sec. 12.4.

12.3.3   Feature Analysis

With such a wide range of signals from various domains of available data and meta-data, we want to quantify the interactions among features. Upon examination of the pairwise correlations between features, we do notice that

Table 12.5: List of features extracted from sentiment analysis of content.

List of `sentiment-features`
Mean of happiness scores of aggregated tweets
Standard deviation of happiness scores of aggregated tweets
(***) Happiness scores of aggregated tweets
Mean of valence scores of aggregated tweets
Standard deviation of valence scores of aggregated tweets
(***) Valence scores of aggregated tweets
Mean of arousal scores of aggregated tweets
Standard deviation of arousal scores of aggregated tweets
(***) Arousal scores of aggregated tweets
Mean of dominance scores of aggregated tweets
Standard deviation of dominance scores of aggregated tweets
(***) Dominance scores of single tweets
(*) Happiness score of single tweets
(*) Valence score of single tweets
(*) Arousal score of single tweets
(*) Dominance score of single tweets
(*) Polarization score of single tweets
(*) Entropy of polarization scores of single tweets
(*) Positive emoticons entropy of single tweets
(*) Negative emoticons entropy of single tweets
(*) Emoticons entropy of single tweets
(*) Positive and negative score ratio of single tweets
(*) Number of positive emoticons in single tweets
(*) Number of negative emoticons in single tweets
(*) Total number of emoticons in single tweets
Ratio of tweets that contain emoticons

(*) Distribution types. The following statistics are computed and used as individual features: min, max, median, mean, std. deviation, skewness, kurtosis, and entropy.

(***) For each feature, we compute mean and std. deviation of the weighted average across words in the lexicon.

Table 12.6: List of features extracted from temporal information.

List of `temporal-features`
(*) Time between two consecutive tweets
(*) Time between two consecutive retweets
(*) Time between two consecutive mentions

(*) Distribution types. The following statistics are computed and used as individual features: min, max, median, mean, std. deviation, skewness, kurtosis, and entropy.

some of these features are correlated and thus possibly redundant in the context of social bot detection.

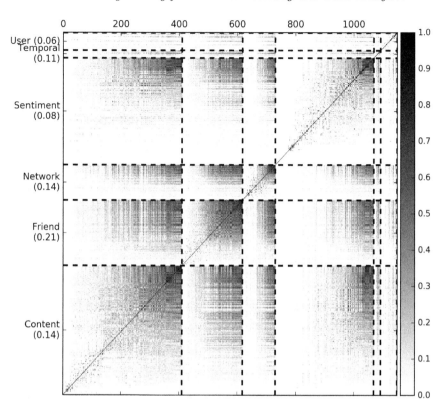

Figure 12.2: Intensities of pairwise correlation between feature values across the dataset. Average pairwise correlations are also reported for the features within each class.

The magnitude of pairwise correlations is shown in Fig. 12.2. Features in this representation are grouped by classes and sorted by average correlation within each group.

The degree of correlation varies depending on the feature category. On average we observe 0.21 correlation among friends features, which is largely due to dependencies between profile meta-data. Content and network features also exhibit some redundancy.

These correlated features demonstrate the importance of feature selection: they suggest that we may be able to retain accuracy while extracting only a subset of our features. The next section introduces different feature selection methods and examines how they perform in identifying a subset of representative features.

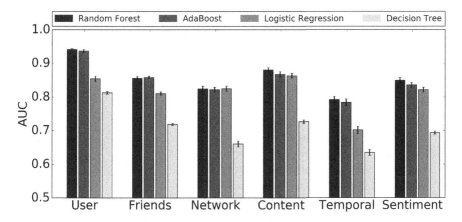

Figure 12.3: Performance comparison for different feature classes and classification methods.

12.3.4 Feature Selection

We built a pipeline to evaluate classification models using subsets of our features. This pipeline uses several off-the-shelf benchmark algorithms provided in the *scikit-learn* library [67]. Our models are trained and evaluated using two different datasets: a honeypot dataset collected by Lee *et al.* [50] and a manually annotated collection [78]. We combine these two datasets to capture both simpler and more sophisticated bot behaviors, along with examples of human accounts, from different time intervals. A model's accuracy is evaluated by measuring the Area Under the receiver operating characteristic Curve (AUC) with 5-fold cross validation, and computing the average AUC score across the folds using Random Forests, AdaBoost, Logistic Regression, and Decision Tree classifiers.

12.3.4.1 Feature Classes

To compare the discriminatory power of the different feature types, we trained models using each class of features alone. We repeated the performance evaluation experiments considering independently only the user, friends, network, content, temporal, and sentiment feature classes. Fig. 12.3 presents the performance of the classifiers using the different feature subsets in isolation.

We achieved the best performance with user meta-data features. Content features are also effective. Both yielded an AUC above 0.9. Other feature classes yielded an AUC above 0.8. In addition to giving the best overall accuracy when all features are considered, Random Forest models produce scores at least as good as every other method when restricting to single feature classes.

Table 12.7: Top features according to Random Forests algorithm.

User number of friends
User number of favorites
Mentioned friends' mean tweet count
User number of follower
User account age
Mentioned friends' mean account age
Mention network mean edge strength
Mentioned friends' mean profile description length
Tweet content mean adjective count
Mentioned friends' mean number of followers

12.3.4.2   Top Individual Features

Given the performance of Random Forest models as compared to the other models, as well as its interpretability and robustness to overfitting, we use Random Forests in the rest of this analysis. This is also the algorithm used in the production Botometer service.

The Random Forest method builds a number of decision trees. In each tree, nodes represent a single condition about a feature value, designed to split the dataset into two so that similar response values end up in the same set. The split criterion can be either Gini impurity or information gain/entropy.

To enrich our understanding about important features, we extend our analysis beyond studying classes of features. To compute the importance of a single feature in Random Forests, one can average across trees the contribution of that feature in reducing impurity. We list the top features identified using this method in Table. 12.7.

Below we briefly describe a few additional feature selection methods inspired by information theory. Further details can be found in a recent review by Li *et al.* [54].

- **CIFE**: Conditional Informative Feature Extraction introduces class-relevant redundancy to maximize the joint class-relevant information by explicitly reducing the class-relevant redundancies among features [55].

- **FCBF**: The Fast Correlation-Based Feature solution tries to identify pairs of features correlating with each other [84]. Once a group of correlated features is identified, this method selects the subset of these features that have smaller inter-dependencies.

- **MRMR**: This method aims to achieve feature selection by controlling the quality of features that satisfy Maximum dependency and Relevance, and Minimum Redundancy [68].

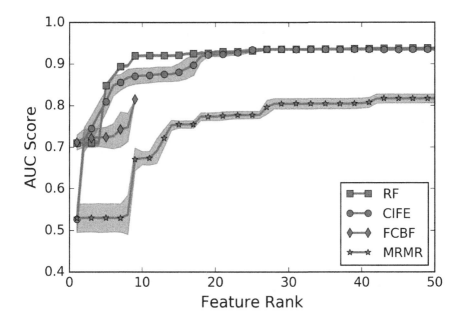

Figure 12.4: Classifier accuracy given by the AUC of models trained using top N features, as ranked by different feature selection methods.

Fig. 12.4 shows that the best accuracy can be obtained using as few as 20 features selected by CIFE or Random Forests (RF). In terms of accuracy, RF and CIFE perform equally well. The MRMR and FCBF methods do not perform as well. Comparing the top features chosen by each algorithm, CIFE algorithms tend to pick network, content, and friend features; MRMR and FCBF prefer content and sentiment features. Since FCBF is a subset selection method, only a small set of features is identified by the algorithm. The Random Forest model ranks friend and user features more highly, as listed in Table 12.7.

12.4 Conclusions

While bots can be harmless or even useful parts of the social media ecosystem, bot accounts that are not clearly identified as such can be used for nefarious purposes. Since social bots can broadcast at a high rate and in coordination with other bots, they can skew the online conversation by amplifying the "volume" of the bot controller's message and creating the appearance that the message is coming from many independent sources. This can in turn influence public opinion by overwhelming our capacity to discriminate quality information [70] and by leveraging cognitive biases that lead people to pay attention to what is popular [65] and to trust content that seems to be shared by social connections [45] or in a social group [47]. Given the amount of public discourse taking place on social media platforms, it becomes crucial for users and platforms to be able to distinguish such activities as early and as accurately as possible.

Research on social bot detection aims to provide tools for identifying autonomous entities. While the arms race between humans and deceptive bots is likely to continue for years, advances in feature engineering and in the identification of weaknesses of different classes of social bots will be key to preserving our stance against malicious bot activities.

In this chapter, we presented the most common approaches used in systems for identifying social bots. We focused on egocentric analysis methodology due to its advantages with respect to data collection and algorithmic complexity. Our system, Botometer, analyzes public information about a Twitter account, extracting over a thousand features describing the account and its neighbors [78]. Using these features, we created a classifier that scores an account's likelihood of being a bot. We examined the extracted features in terms of their contribution to overall performance and redundancy within the feature set.

Feature selection is as essential as feature engineering for improving the performance of bot detection systems, especially when taking into consideration trade-offs between accuracy and computational speed. Some machine learning methods such as Random Forests can measure the importance of features intrinsically by using ensembles of weak learners [14]. We analyzed the top features identified by the Random Forest algorithm and also evaluated other feature selection mechanisms in the recent literature [54]. Our analysis points out that Random Forests can achieve over 90% accuracy, as measured by the AUC, using fewer than 20 features.

Let us discuss some future directions that one can pursue to design better and semi-autonomous systems for social bot detection. Deep learning presents natural extensions to some of our feature extraction methods [49]. Architectures of deep neural networks (DNNs) can capture important patterns and use those as features for learning algorithms. As such, DNNs may be useful in identifying increasingly sophisticated bots.

Research into the use of these modern techniques for bot detection becomes even more critical when considering how they may be used by bot *creators*. Recent advances in DNN technologies accelerate fake persona generation [9,52] and conversation models for social bots [53,75]. Generative adversarial nets can be used to simultaneously learn generative models for social bots and how to trick detection systems [38,71].

The task of social bot detection exhibits the characteristics of an arms race. Both bot creators and the bot detection community work towards improving their existing systems and try to exploit weaknesses of the adversary group. It is our hope that the work presented here will provide a key advantage in the arms race against deceptive bot creators. By working together and sharing public tools and data[2] we won't have to fight this battle alone.

Bibliography

[1] Norah Abokhodair, Daisy Yoo, and David W McDonald. Dissecting a social botnet: Growth, content and influence in twitter. In *Proc. of the ACM Intl. Conf. on Computer Supported Cooperative Work & Social Computing*, pages 839–851. ACM, 2015.

[2] Apoorv Agarwal, Boyi Xie, Ilia Vovsha, Owen Rambow, and Rebecca Passonneau. Sentiment analysis of Twitter data. In *Proc. of the Workshop on Languages in Social Media*, pages 30–38. ACL, 2011.

[3] Wei Ai, Xuan Lu, Xuanzhe Liu, Ning Wang, Gang Huang, and Qiaozhu Mei. Untangling emoji popularity through semantic embeddings. In *Proc. of the Intl. Conf. on Web and Social Media*, pages 2–11, 2017.

[4] Luca Aiello, Martina Deplano, Rossano Schifanella, and Giancarlo Ruffo. People are strange when you're a stranger: Impact and influence of bots on social networks. In *Proc. of the Intl. Conf. on Web and Social Media*, 2012.

[5] J Berger and Jonathan Morgan. The ISIS Twitter census: Defining and describing the population of ISIS supporters on Twitter. *The Brookings Project on US Relations with the Islamic World*, 3:20, 2015.

[6] Alessandro Bessi, Mauro Coletto, George Alexandru Davidescu, Antonio Scala, Guido Caldarelli, and Walter Quattrociocchi. Science vs conspiracy: Collective narratives in the age of misinformation. *PLoS ONE*, 10(2):e0118093, 02 2015.

[7] Alessandro Bessi and Emilio Ferrara. Social bots distort the 2016 us presidential election online discussion. *First Monday*, 21(11), 2016.

[8] Alex Beutel, Wanhong Xu, Venkatesan Guruswami, Christopher Palow, and Christos Faloutsos. Copycatch: Stopping group attacks by spotting lockstep behavior in social networks. In *Proc. ACM Intl. Conf. on World Wide Web*, pages 119–130, 2013.

[9] Parminder Bhatia, Marsal Gavalda, and Arash Einolghozati. soc2seq: Social embedding meets conversation model. Preprint 1702.05512, arXiv, 2017.

---

[2]A public repository of social bot datasets and tools is available on the Botometer website and we invite the community to contribute.

[10] Johan Bollen, Bruno Gonçalves, Ingrid van de Leemput, and Guangchen Ruan. The happiness paradox: Your friends are happier than you. *EPJ Data Science*, 6(1):4, 2017.

[11] Johan Bollen, Huina Mao, and Xiaojun Zeng. Twitter mood predicts the stock market. *Journal of Computational Science*, 2(1):1–8, 2011.

[12] Yazan Boshmaf, Ildar Muslukhov, Konstantin Beznosov, and Matei Ripeanu. The socialbot network: When bots socialize for fame and money. In *Proc. of the Annual Conf. on Computer Security Applications*, 2011.

[13] Federico Botta, Helen Susannah Moat, and Tobias Preis. Quantifying crowd size with mobile phone and twitter data. *Royal Society Open Science*, 2(5):150162, 2015.

[14] Leo Breiman. Random forests. *Machine Learning*, 45(1):5–32, 2001.

[15] R Sherlock Campbell and James W Pennebaker. The secret life of pronouns flexibility in writing style and physical health. *Psychological Science*, 14(1):60–65, 2003.

[16] Nikan Chavoshi, Hossein Hamooni, and Abdullah Mueen. Identifying correlated bots in Twitter. In *Proc. Intl. Conf. on Social Informatics*, pages 14–21, 2016.

[17] Zi Chu, Steven Gianvecchio, Haining Wang, and Sushil Jajodia. Who is tweeting on Twitter: Human, bot, or cyborg? In *Proc. of the Annual Conf. on Computer Security Applications*, pages 21–30, 2010.

[18] Zi Chu, Steven Gianvecchio, Haining Wang, and Sushil Jajodia. Detecting automation of twitter accounts: Are you a human, bot, or cyborg? *IEEE Tran Dependable & Secure Comput*, 9(6):811–824, 2012.

[19] Eric Clark, Chris Jones, Jake Williams, Allison Kurti, Michell Nortotsky, Christopher Danforth, and Peter Dodds. Vaporous marketing: Uncovering pervasive electronic cigarette advertisements on Twitter. Preprint 1508.01843, arXiv, 2015.

[20] Eric Clark, Jake Williams, Chris Jones, Richard Galbraith, Christopher Danforth, and Peter Dodds. Sifting robotic from organic text: A natural language approach for detecting automation on Twitter. *Journal of Computational Science*, 16:1–7, 2016.

[21] Cristian Danescu-Niculescu-Mizil, Robert West, Dan Jurafsky, Jure Leskovec, and Christopher Potts. No country for old members: User lifecycle and linguistic change in online communities. In *Proc. of the Intl. Conf. on World Wide Web*, pages 307–318, 2013.

[22] Abimanyu Das, Sreenivas Gollapudi, Emre Kiciman, and Onur Varol. Information dissemination in heterogeneous-intent networks. In *Proc. ACM Intl. Conf. on Web Science*, 2016.

[23] Clayton A Davis, Giovanni Luca Ciampaglia, Luca Maria Aiello, Keychul Chung, Michael D Conover, Emilio Ferrara, Alessandro Flammini, Geoffrey C Fox, Xiaoming Gao, Bruno Gonçalves, et al. OSoMe: The IUNI observatory on social media. *PeerJ Computer Science*, 2:e87, 2016.

[24] Clayton Allen Davis, Onur Varol, Emilio Ferrara, Alessandro Flammini, and Filippo Menczer. BotOrNot: A system to evaluate social bots. In *Proc. of the Intl. Conf. Companion on World Wide Web*, pages 273–274, 2016.

[25] Cícero Nogueira Dos Santos and Maira Gatti. Deep convolutional neural networks for sentiment analysis of short texts. In *Proc. Intl. Conf. on Computational Linguistics (COLING)*, pages 69–78, 2014.

[26] Juan Echeverría and Shi Zhou. The "Star Wars" botnet with >350k Twitter bots. Preprint 1701.02405, arXiv, 2017.

[27] Emilio Ferrara. Manipulation and abuse on social media. *SIGWEB Newsletter*, Spring(4):1–9, 2015.

[28] Emilio Ferrara, Mohsen JafariAsbagh, Onur Varol, Vahed Qazvinian, Filippo Menczer, and Alessandro Flammini. Clustering memes in social media. In *Proc. IEEE/ACM Intl. Conf. on Advances in Social Networks Analysis and Mining*, pages 548–555. IEEE, 2013.

[29] Emilio Ferrara, Onur Varol, Clayton Davis, Filippo Menczer, and Alessandro Flammini. The rise of social bots. *Communications of the ACM*, 59(7):96–104, 2016.

[30] Emilio Ferrara, Onur Varol, Filippo Menczer, and Alessandro Flammini. Detection of promoted social media campaigns. In *Proc. of the Intl. Conf. on Web and Social Media*, 2016.

[31] Emilio Ferrara, Wen-Qiang Wang, Onur Varol, Alessandro Flammini, and Aram Galstyan. Predicting online extremism, content adopters, and interaction reciprocity. In *Proc. of the Intl. Conf. on Social Informatics*, pages 22–39, 2016.

[32] Emilio Ferrara and Zeyao Yang. Quantifying the effect of sentiment on information diffusion in social media. *PeerJ Computer Science*, 2015.

[33] Andrew J Flanagin and Miriam J Metzger. The role of site features, user attributes, and information verification behaviors on the perceived credibility of web-based information. *New Media & Society*, 9(2):319–342, 2007.

[34] Michelle C Forelle, Philip N Howard, Andrés Monroy-Hernández, and Saiph Savage. Political bots and the manipulation of public opinion in Venezuela. Technical Report 2635800, SSRN, 2015.

[35] Rumi Ghosh, Tawan Surachawala, and Kristina Lerman. Entropy-based classification of retweeting activity on Twitter. In *Proc. of KDD Workshop on Social Network Analysis*, August 2011.

[36] CJ Hutto Eric Gilbert. Vader: A parsimonious rule-based model for sentiment analysis of social media text. In *Proc. of the Intl. Conf. on Weblogs and Social Media*, 2014.

[37] Xavier Glorot, Antoine Bordes, and Yoshua Bengio. Domain adaptation for large-scale sentiment classification: A deep learning approach. In *Proc. of the Intl. Conf. on Machine Learning*, pages 513–520, 2011.

[38] Ian Goodfellow, Jean Pouget-Abadie, Mehdi Mirza, Bing Xu, David Warde-Farley, Sherjil Ozair, Aaron Courville, and Yoshua Bengio. Generative adversarial nets. In *Advances in Neural Information Processing Systems*, pages 2672–2680, 2014.

[39] Aditya Grover and Jure Leskovec. node2vec: Scalable feature learning for networks. In *Proc. of the ACM SIGKDD Intl. Conf. on Knowledge Discovery and Data Mining*, pages 855–864. ACM, 2016.

[40] Angela V Hausman and Jeffrey Sam Siekpe. The effect of web interface features on consumer online purchase intentions. *Journal of Business Research*, 62(1):5–13, 2009.

[41] Stefanie Haustein, Timothy D Bowman, Kim Holmberg, Andrew Tsou, Cassidy R Sugimoto, and Vincent Larivière. Tweets as impact indicators: Examining the implications of automated "bot" accounts on Twitter. *Journal of the Association for Information Science and Technology*, 67(1):232–238, 2016.

[42] Karl Moritz Hermann, Tomas Kocisky, Edward Grefenstette, Lasse Espeholt, Will Kay, Mustafa Suleyman, and Phil Blunsom. Teaching machines to read and comprehend. In *Advances in Neural Information Processing Systems*, pages 1693–1701, 2015.

[43] Philip N Howard and Bence Kollanyi. Bots, #StrongerIn, and #Brexit: computational propaganda during the UK-EU Referendum. Technical Report 2798311, SSRN, 2016.

[44] Mohsen JafariAsbagh, Emilio Ferrara, Onur Varol, Filippo Menczer, and Alessandro Flammini. Clustering memes in social media streams. *Social Network Analysis and Mining*, 4(1):1–13, 2014.

[45] T. Jagatic, N. Johnson, M. Jakobsson, and F. Menczer. Social phishing. *Communications of the ACM*, 50(10):94–100, October 2007.

[46] Yuede Ji, Yukun He, Xinyang Jiang, Jian Cao, and Qiang Li. Combating the evasion mechanisms of social bots. *Computers & Security*, 58:230–249, 2016.

[47] Youjung Jun, Rachel Meng, and Gita Venkataramani Johar. Perceived social presence reduces fact-checking. *Proceedings of the National Academy of Sciences*, 114(23):5976–5981, 2017.

[48] Isabel M Kloumann, Christopher M Danforth, Kameron Decker Harris, Catherine A Bliss, and Peter Sheridan Dodds. Positivity of the english language. *PLoS ONE*, 7(1):e29484, 2012.

[49] Yann LeCun, Yoshua Bengio, and Geoffrey Hinton. Deep learning. *Nature*, 521(7553):436–444, 2015.

[50] Kyumin Lee, Brian David Eoff, and James Caverlee. Seven months with the devils: A long-term study of content polluters on Twitter. In *Proc. of the AAAI Intl. Conf. on Web and Social Media*, 2011.

[51] Adrian Letchford, Helen Susannah Moat, and Tobias Preis. The advantage of short paper titles. *Royal Society Open Science*, 2(8):150266, 2015.

[52] Jiwei Li, Michel Galley, Chris Brockett, Georgios P Spithourakis, Jianfeng Gao, and Bill Dolan. A persona-based neural conversation model. Preprint 1603.06155, arXiv, 2016.

[53] Jiwei Li, Will Monroe, Alan Ritter, Michel Galley, Jianfeng Gao, and Dan Jurafsky. Deep reinforcement learning for dialogue generation. Preprint 1606.01541, arXiv, 2016.

[54] Jundong Li, Kewei Cheng, Suhang Wang, Fred Morstatter, Trevino Robert, Jiliang Tang, and Huan Liu. Feature selection: A data perspective. Preprint 1601.07996, arXiv, 2016.

[55] Dahua Lin and Xiaoou Tang. Conditional infomax learning: An integrated framework for feature extraction and fusion. In Aleš Leonardis, Horst Bischof, and Axel Pinz, editors, *Proc. 9th European Conference on Computer Vision (ECCV), Part I*, pages 68–82. Springer, 2006.

[56] Tetyana Lokot and Nicholas Diakopoulos. News bots: Automating news and information dissemination on Twitter. *Digital Journalism*, 4(6):682–699, 2016.

[57] Andrew L Maas, Raymond E Daly, Peter T Pham, Dan Huang, Andrew Y Ng, and Christopher Potts. Learning word vectors for sentiment analysis. In *Proc. of the 49th Annual Meeting of the Association for Computational Linguistics: Human Language Technologies*, pages 142–150, 2011.

[58] Julian McAuley and Jure Leskovec. From amateurs to connoisseurs: Modeling the evolution of user expertise through online reviews. In *Proc. 22nd Intl. ACM Conf. World Wide Web*, pages 897–908, 2013.

[59] Hannah Miller, Jacob Thebault-Spieker, Shuo Chang, Isaac Johnson, Loren Terveen, and Brent Hecht. "Blissfully happy" or "ready to fight": Varying interpretations of emoji. *Proc. of the Intl. Conf. on Web and Social Media*, 2016, 2016.

[60] Alan Mislove, Sune Lehmann, Yong-Yeol Ahn, Jukka-Pekka Onnela, and J Niels Rosenquist. Understanding the demographics of Twitter users. In *Proc. of the Intl. AAAI Conf. on Weblogs and Social Media*, 2011.

[61] Lewis Mitchell, Kameron Decker Harris, Morgan R Frank, Peter Sheridan Dodds, and Christopher M Danforth. The geography of happiness: Connecting Twitter sentiment and expression, demographics, and objective characteristics of place. *PLoS ONE*, 8(5):e64417, 2013.

[62] Pabitra Mitra, CA Murthy, and Sankar K. Pal. Unsupervised feature selection using feature similarity. *IEEE Transactions on Pattern Analysis and Machine Intelligence*, 24(3):301–312, 2002.

[63] Silvia Mitter, Claudia Wagner, and Markus Strohmaier. A categorization scheme for socialbot attacks in online social networks. In *Proc. of the ACM Intl. Conf. on Web Science*, 2013.

[64] Delia Mocanu, Andrea Baronchelli, Nicola Perra, Bruno Gonçalves, Qian Zhang, and Alessandro Vespignani. The Twitter of Babel: Mapping world languages through microblogging platforms. *PLoS ONE*, 8(4):e61981, January 2013.

[65] Azadeh Nematzadeh, Giovanni L. Ciampaglia, Filippo Menczer, and Alessandro Flammini. How algorithmic popularity bias hinders or promotes quality. Preprint 1707.00574, arXiv, 2017.

[66] Richard J Oentaryo, Arinto Murdopo, Philips K Prasetyo, and Ee-Peng Lim. On profiling bots in social media. In *Proc. Intl. Conf. on Social Informatics*, pages 92–109. Springer, 2016.

[67] F. Pedregosa, G. Varoquaux, A. Gramfort, V. Michel, B. Thirion, O. Grisel, M. Blondel, P. Prettenhofer, R. Weiss, V. Dubourg, J. Vanderplas, A. Passos, D. Cournapeau, M. Brucher, M. Perrot, and E. Duchesnay. Scikit-learn: Machine learning in Python. *Journal of Machine Learning Research*, 12:2825–2830, 2011.

[68] Hanchuan Peng, Fuhui Long, and Chris Ding. Feature selection based on mutual information criteria of max-dependency, max-relevance, and min-redundancy. *IEEE Transactions on Pattern Analysis and Machine Intelligence*, 27(8):1226–1238, 2005.

[69] Bryan Perozzi, Rami Al-Rfou, and Steven Skiena. Deepwalk: Online learning of social representations. In *Proc. of the Intl. Conf. on Knowledge Discovery and Data Mining*, pages 701–710. ACM, 2014.

[70] Xiaoyan Qiu, Diego F. M. Oliveira, Alireza Sahami Shirazi, Alessandro Flammini, and Filippo Menczer. Limited individual attention and online virality of low-quality information. *Nature Human Behavior*, 1:0132, 2017.

[71] Alec Radford, Luke Metz, and Soumith Chintala. Unsupervised representation learning with deep convolutional generative adversarial networks. Preprint 1511.06434, arXiv, 2015.

[72] J. Ratkiewicz, M. Conover, M. Meiss, B. Goncalves, A. Flammini, and F. Menczer. Detecting and tracking political abuse in social media. In *Proc. Intl. Conf. on Weblogs and Social Media ICWSM)*, pages 297–304, 2011.

[73] Saiph Savage, Andres Monroy-Hernandez, and Tobias Höllerer. Botivist: Calling volunteers to action using online bots. In *Proc. of the Intl. Conf. on Computer-Supported Cooperative Work & Social Computing*, pages 813–822. ACM, 2016.

[74] Chengcheng Shao, Giovanni Luca Ciampaglia, Onur Varol, Alessandro Flammini, and Filippo Menczer. The spread of fake news by social bots. Preprint 1707.07592, arXiv, 2017.

[75] Alessandro Sordoni, Michel Galley, Michael Auli, Chris Brockett, Yangfeng Ji, Margaret Mitchell, Jian-Yun Nie, Jianfeng Gao, and Bill Dolan. A neural network approach to context-sensitive generation of conversational responses. Preprint 1506.06714, arXiv, 2015.

[76] VS Subrahmanian, Amos Azaria, Skylar Durst, Vadim Kagan, Aram Galstyan, Kristina Lerman, Linhong Zhu, Emilio Ferrara, Alessandro Flammini, Filippo Menczer, et al. The DARPA Twitter Bot Challenge. *IEEE Computer*, 6(49):38–46, 2016.

[77] Wei Tang, Zhengdong Lu, and Inderjit S Dhillon. Clustering with multiple graphs. In *Proc. IEEE Intl. Conf. on Data Mining*, pages 1016–1021. IEEE, 2009.

[78] Onur Varol, Emilio Ferrara, Clayton A Davis, Filippo Menczer, and Alessandro Flammini. Online human-bot interactions: Detection, estimation, and characterization. In *Proc. of the Intl. Conf. on Web and Social Media*, 2017.

[79] Onur Varol, Emilio Ferrara, Filippo Menczer, and Alessandro Flammini. Early detection of promoted campaigns on social media. *EPJ Data Science*, 6(1):13, 12 2017.

[80] Gang Wang, Tristan Konolige, Christo Wilson, Xiao Wang, Haitao Zheng, and Ben Y Zhao. You are how you click: Clickstream analysis for sybil detection. In *Proc. USENIX Security*, pages 1–15. Citeseer, 2013.

[81] Amy Beth Warriner, Victor Kuperman, and Marc Brysbaert. Norms of valence, arousal, and dominance for 13,915 English lemmas. *Behavior research methods*, pages 1–17, 2013.

[82] Theresa Wilson, Janyce Wiebe, and Paul Hoffmann. Recognizing contextual polarity in phrase-level sentiment analysis. In *Proc. of the Intl. Conf. on Human Language Techn & Empirical Methods in NLP*, pages 347–354. ACL, 2005.

[83] Zhi Yang, Christo Wilson, Xiao Wang, Tingting Gao, Ben Y Zhao, and Yafei Dai. Uncovering social network sybils in the wild. *ACM Trans. Knowledge Discovery from Data*, 8(1):2, 2014.

[84] Lei Yu and Huan Liu. Feature selection for high-dimensional data: A fast correlation-based filter solution. In *ICML*, volume 3, pages 856–863, 2003.

12.5   Glossary

Social bot: A social bot, also known as a sybil account, is a computer algorithm that automatically produces content and interacts with humans on social media.

Botnet: Coordinated collectives of software-controlled fake accounts operating on social media.

ROC: Receiver Operating Characteristic curve serves as a tool to visually evaluate the performance of a binary classifier as the value of the threshold is varied.

AUC: A measure of quality for a classification system by computing the area under the ROC curve.

Chapter 13

Feature Generation and Engineering for Software Analytics

Xin Xia

Faculty of Information Technology, Monash University, Australia

David Lo

School of Information Systems, Singapore Management University, Singapore

13.1   Introduction

As developers work on a project, they leave behind many digital artifacts. These digital trails can provide insights into how software is developed and provide a rich source of information to help improve development practices. For instance, GitHub hosts more than 57M repositories, and is currently used by more than 20M developers [1]. As another example, Stack Overflow has more than 3.9M registered users, 8.8M questions, and 41M comments [58]. The productivity of software developers and testers can be improved using information from these repositories.

There have been a number of studies in software engineering which focus on building predictive models by mining a wide variety of software data collected from systems, their repositories and relevant online resources [3, 6, 35, 59, 60]. For example, in defect prediction [35, 60], developers aim to predict whether a module/class/method/change contains bugs, and they build a predictive model by extracting features from historical modules/classes/methods/changes with known labels (i.e., buggy or clean). In bug priority prediction [53], developers aim to predict the priority level of a bug when it is submitted, and they build a predictive model by leveraging features from historical bug reports with known priority levels. In practice, the performance of a predictive model will be largely affected by the features used to build the model. For example, Rahman and Devanbu investigated different types of features on the performance of defect prediction, and they found that process features performed better than the code features in defect prediction [45]. However, feature identification and generation from software artifacts and repositories is challenging since (1) software engineering data are complex, and (2) it requires domain knowledge to identify effective features.

Features can be extracted from various types of software artifacts, e.g., source code, bug reports, code reviews, commit logs, and email lists. Even in the same software artifacts, there are various ways to extract features. For example, to extract features from source code, trace features (e.g., statement coverage) can be extracted by running the source code and analyzing its execution trace, code features (e.g., code complexity) by leveraging static analysis tools (e.g., SciTool[1]), textual features (e.g., readability and term frequency) by using text mining techniques, and process features (e.g., number of developers who changed the code) by mining the change history of the code.

In this chapter, we aim to provide an introduction on feature generation and engineering for software analytics, and show how domain-specific features are extracted and used for three software engineering use cases, i.e., defect prediction, crash release prediction, and developer turnover prediction. These three case studies extract different kinds of features from software artifacts,

---

[1]https://scitools.com/

and build predictive models based on these features. Some features used in these three case studies are related, while others are problem specific.

The remainder of the chapter is structured as follows. Section 13.2 describes features used in defect prediction. Section 13.3 presents features used in crash release prediction for apps. Section 13.4 discusses features generated from a monthly report for developer turnover prediction. Section 13.5 concludes the chapter and discusses future directions.

13.2 Features for Defect Prediction

Defect prediction techniques are proposed to help prioritize software testing and debugging; they can recommend likely defective code to developers. Most defect prediction studies propose prediction models built on various types of features (e.g., process or code features), and predict defects at a coarse granularity level (e.g., file), which is referred to as file-level defect prediction [17,19,28,39,45,54,60]. Besides file-level defect prediction, Mockus and Weiss proposed a prediction model which focuses on identifying defect-prone software changes instead of files or packages [37], which was also referred to as just-in-time (JIT) defect prediction by Kamei et al. [24].

The difference between file-level and just-in-time defect prediction lies in the development phase when they are employed. File-level defect prediction is usually conducted before a product release. It aims to be a quality control step before a release [63]. Just-in-time defect prediction is conducted when each change is submitted. It aims to be a continuous activity of quality control, which leads to smaller amounts of code to be reviewed, and developers can review and test these risky changes while they are still fresh in their minds (i.e., at commit time) [21]. They can complement each other to improve the quality of the upcoming release. Considering the difference in the usage scenarios of these two types of defect prediction techniques, their corresponding features are different. In the remaining sections, the details of features for these two types of defect prediction techniques are introduced.

13.2.1 File-level Defect Prediction

In general, there are two types of features for file-level defect prediction: code features, which measure properties of the code (e.g., code complexity, and lines of code), and process features (e.g., developer experience, and number of changes), which are extracted from the software development process. A number of papers in the software engineering literature have investigated the effectiveness of each feature type. Menzies et al. concluded that code metrics are effective for defect prediction [36]. Moser et al. compared the performance of code and process features on Eclipse JDT project, and they found that process features outperform code features [38]. Arisholm et al. performed an empirical study on various types of features and techniques on several releases of a Java middleware system named COS, and they found that process and code features perform similarly in terms of AUC, but process features are cost-effective [4]. Finally, Rahman and Devanbu performed a large-scale empirical study to investigate why and how process features performed better than code features [45].

13.2.1.1   Code Features

Jureczko and Madeyski proposed 20 code features to predict defective files [23]. These features have been empirically demonstrated to be effective in defect prediction [8, 23, 41]. They can be categorized according to the researchers who first proposed them as follows:

1. **Features proposed by Chidamber and Kemerer [9]:**

    1. **Weighted methods per class (WMC):** the number of methods used in a given class.

    2. **Depth of Inheritance Tree (DIT):** the maximum distance from a given class to the root of an inheritance tree.

    3. **Number of Children (NOC):** the number of children of a given class in an inheritance tree.

    4. **Coupling between object classes (CBO):** the number of classes that are coupled to a given class.

    5. **Response for a Class (RFC):** the number of distinct methods invoked by code in a given class.

    6. **Lack of cohesion in methods (LCOM):** the number of method pairs in a class that do not share access to any class attributes.

2. **A Feature proposed by Henderson-Sellers [20]:**

    1. **Lack of cohesion in methods (LCOM3):** another type of LCOM metric proposed by Henderson-Sellers [20], i.e.,

$$LOCM3 = \frac{\frac{1}{a}\sum_{j=1}^{a} m(A_j) - m}{1 - m}.$$
(13.1)

    In the above equation, m is the number of methods in a class, a is the number of attributes in a class, and $m(A)$ is the number of methods that access the attribute A.

3. Features proposed by Bansiy and Davis [5]:

1. **Number of Public Methods (NPM):** the number of public methods in a given class.

2. **Data Access Metric (DAM):** the ratio of the number of private/protected attributes to the total number of attributes in a given class.

3. **Measure of Aggregation (MOA):** the number of attributes in a given class which are of user-defined types.

4. **Measure of Functional Abstraction (MFA):** the number of methods inherited by a given class divided by the total number of methods that can be accessed by the member methods of the given class.

5. **Cohesion Among Methods of Class (CAM):** the ratio of the sum of the number of different parameter types of every method in a given class to the product of the number of methods in the given class and the number of different method parameter types in the whole class.

4. Features proposed by Tang et al. [52]:

1. **Inheritance Coupling (IC):** the number of parent classes to which a given class is coupled.

2. **Coupling between Methods (CBM):** the total number of new or overwritten methods to which all inherited methods in a given class are coupled.

3. **Average Method Complexity (AMC):** the average size of methods in a given class.

5. Features proposed by Martin [29]:

1. **Afferent couplings (Ca):** number of classes that depend upon a given class.

2. **Efferent couplings (Ce):** number of classes on which a given class depends.

6. Features proposed by McCabe [32]:

1. **McCabe's cyclomatic complexity (CC):** CC is equal to the number of different paths in a method (function) plus one. The cyclomatic complexity of a method is defined as: $CC_M = E \times \times N + P$; where E is the number of edges of the graph, N is the number of nodes of the graph, and P is the number of connected components. Based on CC_M, two variants of CC can be computed for a class as follows:

(a) **Maximum McCabe's cyclomatic complexity (MAX_CC)**: maximum McCabe's cyclomatic complexity (CC) score of methods in a given class.

(b) **Average McCabe's cyclomatic complexity (AVG_CC)**: arithmetic mean of the McCabe's cyclomatic complexity (CC) scores of methods in a given class.

7. Others:

1. **Lines of Code (LOC)**: a popular feature in defect prediction, which calculates the number of lines of code of a class under investigation.

These 20 code features can also be categorized on other categories. Table 13.1 categorizes these features based on how they are derived, including complexity, coupling, cohesion, abstraction, and encapsulation.

Table 13.1: List of code features

Category	Code Features
Complexity	Lines of Code (LOC)
	Weighted Methods per Class (WMC)
	Number of Public Methods (NPM)
	Average Method Complexity (AMC)
	Max McCabe's Cyclomatic Complexity (Max_cc)
	Avg McCabe's Cyclomatic Complexity (Avg_cc)
	Measure of Aggregation (MOA)
Coupling	Coupling between object classes (CBO)
	Response of a Class (RFC)
	Afferent Couplings (CA)
	Efferent Couplings (CE)
	Inheritance Coupling (IC)
	Coupling Between Methods (CBM)
Cohesion	Lack of cohesion in methods (LCOM)
	Lack of cohesion in methods (LCOM3)
	Cohesion Among Methods of Class (CAM)
Abstraction	Depth of Inheritance Tree (DIT)
	Number Of Children (NOC)
	Measure of Functional Abstraction (MFA)
Encapsulation	Data Access Metric (DAM)

13.2.1.2   Process Features

Various process features can be extracted for a source code file, and generally they can be grouped into 3 categories: developer's behavior, change entropy, and commit history [45].

1. Developer's Behavior: Since source code files are created/revised by different developers, features extracted from developers' commit behavior can potentially be used to predict likely buggy files. Many developer behavior features have been proposed in prior studies [4, 7, 37, 43, 45]; they include the following:

1. Number of commits made to a file (COM)

2. Number of developers who changed a file (NumDev)

3. Number of distinct developers who contributed to a file (DisDev)

4. Number of lines of code added or deleted or modified in a file in the previous release (AddLoc, DelLoc, and ModiLoc)

5. Geometric mean of experiences of all developers working on a file (Exp)

2. Change Entropy: Scattered changes could be more complex to manage, and a prior study showed that scattered changes are good indicators of defects [19]. Rahman and Devenbu proposed a simple line-based change entropy feature named SCTR, which measures the scattering of changes to a file [45]. SCTR is the standard position deviation of changes from the geographical center theme.

3. Commit History: Features extracted from the commit history of a source code file can also potentially help to predict defective files [25]. Features in this category include:

1. Number of defects in previous version (NDPV), which measures the number of defects reported in a given file in the previous release of a project

2. Number of commits which modified a file in the previous release (NCOM)

3. Number of commits which aimed to fix bugs in a file in the previous release (NCOMBUG)

13.2.2 Just-in-time Defect Prediction

In general, the features used by file-level defect prediction can also be adapted for just-in-time defect prediction. Also, there are some specific features for just-in-time defect prediction. Kamei et al. proposed 14 features for just-in-time defect prediction, which are divided into five dimensions: diffusion, size, purpose, history, and experience [24]. Table 13.2 presents the details of these 14 features. Features in the diffusion, size, history, and experience dimensions are similar to those originally defined for file-level defect prediction, while the feature FIX in the purpose dimension is unique to just-in-time defect prediction.

The features in the diffusion dimension characterize the distribution of a change. Previous studies showed that a highly distributed change is more likely to be defective [19,37,40]. The features in size dimension characterize the size of a change, and a larger change is more likely to be defective since more code has to be changed or implemented [38]. The purpose dimension only consists of FIX, and it is believed that a defect-fixing change is more likely to introduce a new defect [14,16,44]. The features in the history dimension demonstrate how developers interacted with different files in the past. As stated by Yang et al. [66], a change was more likely to be defective if the touched files have been modified by more developers [30], by more recent changes [14], or by more unique last changes [19]. The experience dimension measures a developer's experience based on the number of changes made by the developer in the past. In general, a change made by a more experienced developer is less likely to introduce defects [37].

Table 13.2: Summary of features for JIT defect prediction

Category	Feature	Definition
Diffusion	NS	Number of subsystems touched by the current change
	ND	Number of directories touched by the current change
	NF	Number of files touched by the current change
	Entropy	Distribution across the touched files
Size	LA	Lines of code added by the current change
	LD	Lines of code deleted by the current change
	LT	Lines of code in a file before the current change
Purpose	FIX	Whether or not the current change is a defect fix
History	NDEV	Number of developers that changed the files
	AGE	Average time interval between the last and current change
	NUC	Number of unique last changes to the files
Experience	EXP	Developers experience (number of files modified)
	REXP	Developers experience in recent years
	SEXP	Developer experience on a subsystem

13.2.3   Prediction Models and Results

Various prediction models can be built on these features to perform file-level or just-in-time defect prediction. Table 13.3 summaries the 31 supervised models, which are grouped into six categories, namely Function, Lazy, Rule, Bayes, Tree and Ensemble. These supervised models are commonly used in defect prediction studies [13,18,27,34,36]. All of them were investigated in Yang et al.'s work [66], and most of them (except Random Forest) were revisited in Ghotra et al.'s work [13].

The function category contains regression models, neural networks and a support vector machine, including EALR [24] (i.e., Effort-Aware Linear Regression), Simple Logistic (SL), Radial Basis Functions Network (RBFNet), and Sequential Minimal Optimization (SMO). The Lazy family represents lazy learning methods, and the K-Nearest Neighbor (IBk) method is used in this category. The Rule family represents models based on rules, including propositional rules (JRip) and ripple-down rules (Ridor). The Bayes family represents probability-based models, and the most popular one, namely Naive Bayes (NB), is included in this category. The Tree family represents decision tree–based methods, including J48, the Logistic Model Tree (LMT) and Random Forest (RF). In the last family, four ensemble learning methods are investigated: Bagging, Adaboost, Rotation Forest and Rotation Subspace. Different from other models, ensemble learning models are built with multiple base classifiers.

Yang et al. compared the performance of different prediction models on just-in-time defect prediction, and they found that EALR showed better performance than the other prediction models—it can detect 33% defective changes when inspecting 20% LOC [66]. Similar results were found by Yan et al.'s study [63], and they found EALR achieved the best performance in file-level defect prediction—it can detect 34% defective files when inspecting 20% LOC.

13.3   Features for Crash Release Prediction for Apps

The quality of mobile applications has a vital impact on their user's experience, ratings and ultimately, overall success. Compared with traditional applications, mobile apps tend to have more releases. In many cases, mobile developers may release versions of the app that are of poor quality, e.g., crash releases which cause the app to crash [61]. A crashing release is likely to cause users to uninstall an app, potentially giving it a negative rating, which in turn impacts the app's revenue. Thus, identifying crashing releases early on (e.g., before the release date), can help warn mobile app developers about a

Table 13.3: Summary of prediction models

Category	Model	Abbreviation
Function	Linear Regression	EALR
	Simple Logistic	SL
	Radial basis functions network	RBFNet
	Sequential Minimal Optimization	SMO
Lazy	K-Nearest Neighbor	IBk
Rule	Propositional rule	JRip
	Ripple down rules	Ridor
Bayes	Naive Bayes	NB
Tree	J48	J48
Ensemble	Logistic Model Tree	LMT
	Random Forest	RF
	Bagging	BG+LMT, BG+NB, BG+SL, BG+SMO, and BG+J48
	Adaboost	AB+LMT, AB+NB, AB+SL, AB+SMO, and AB+J48
	Rotation Forest	RF+LMT, RF+NB, RF+SL, RF+SMO, and RF+J48
	Random subspace	RS+LMT, RS+NB, RS+SL, RS+SMO, and RS+J48

potential crashing version before it is released and reduce the number of crashing releases.

Various features can be extracted to predict crashing releases. Our previous study proposed 20 features which were grouped into six unique dimensions: complexity, time, code, diffusion, commit, and text [61]. All of these features are derived from the source control repository data of a mobile application. Table 13.4 presents a summary of the features.

13.3.1   Complexity Dimension

If source code in a release is too complex (e.g., high number of data or control flows in an applications), the code will be harder to write and maintain, which may increase the chance of a crashing release. Also, prior studies showed complexity (e.g., cyclomatic complexity) was a good predictor of defect-prone modules [32,40,51]. As shown in Table 13.4, McCabe's cyclomatic complexity is used in the complexity dimension, which is measured directly from the source code in the current release using a standard static analysis tool.

Table **13.4**: Features used to identify crashing releases

Dimension	Name	Definition
Complexity	Cyclomatic	The number of branching paths within code in all the source code files in a release
Time	PreDays	The number of days since the previous release
Code	LA	Number of lines added in a release
	LD	Number of lines deleted in a release
	SIZE	Total number of lines of code in the current release
	SAME	Number of source code files that are modified by both the current and the previous release
	CUR_file	Number of source code files in the current release
	PREV_file	Number of modified source code files in the previous release
Diffusion	Top_NS	Number of unique subsystems changed between two releases
	Bottom_NS	Number of unique subsystems changed between two releases
	NF	Number of unique files that have changed between two releases
	File_entropy	Distribution of modified files across the release
	Churn_entropy	Distribution of modified code across the application
Commit	NC	Number of commits
	NFC	Number of commits which fix bugs
Text	Fuzzy_score	Fuzzy set scores of commit logs
	NB_score	Naive Bayes scores of commit logs
	NBM_score	Naive Bayes Multinomial scores of commit logs
	DMN_score	Discriminative naive Bayes Multinomial scores of commit logs
	COMP_score	Complement naive Bayes scores of commit logs

13.3.2   Time Dimension

If the time period between the two releases is short, the current release may have a high chance to be a non-crash release since it may fix the crash bugs which appear in the previous release. Based on this, the number of days since the previous release (PreDays) is used as a feature to predict a crashing release. It is computed by counting the number of days between the previous and current release.

13.3.3   Code Dimension

If many lines of code have been added/deleted/modified between the current and previous release, the current release is more likely to be a crash release. This is the case since many new features may have been added, which increases the likelihood of a feature malfunction that causes a crash [38]. Also, if the current release modifies many of the same source code files as the previous release, it may indicate that many repairs have been done, and in turn indicate that the current release is a good release. As shown in Table 13.4, six features make up this dimension; they can be extracted from the source control repository by comparing the difference between two releases.

13.3.4   Diffusion Dimension

Intuitively, if too many different source code files are changed during a release, this release might be more difficult to understand, and require more work to inspect all the locations that are changed. In defect prediction literature, prior studies found that the number of subsystems touched is an indicator of defects [37], and scattered changes was a good indicator of defects [19]. Also, the more functionalities there are in a release, the more prone it is to fail. Thus, subsystems are used as proxies to features. Releases that contain many modifications at the subsystem level are more likely to be crash releases. Table 13.4 shows five features that make up the diffusion dimension.

Top directory name and bottom directory name as the subsystem name are used to measure Top_NS and Bottom_NS, respectively. For example, if changes are committed to a file in the path src/app/token/main.java, then its top directory name is "src/," and the bottom directory name is "src/app/token/." For the ith release, the set of top and bottom directory names are denoted as Top_i and $Bottom_i$, respectively. Then, for two consecutive releases (i^{th} and $(i+1)^{th}$ releases), Top_NS= $|Top_i \cap Top_{i+1}|$, and Bottom_NS $=|Bottom_i \cap Bottom_{i+1}|$.

Entropy aims to measure the distribution of a release across different files or the lines of code in the files. Releases with high entropy are more likely to be crash releases, since a developer needs to inspect a large number of scattered changes across files. Two kinds of entropies were proposed, i.e., file and churn entropy [19]. Entropy is computed as: $H(P) = - \sum_{k=1}^{n} (p_k \times log_2\ p_k)$, where n is the number of files changed in the release, $p_k \geq 0$ is the probability for a file k, and p_k satisfies $(\sum_{k=1}^{n} p_k) = 1$. To compute file entropy, p_k is computed as the proportion of commits between the current release and the previous release that include changes to file k. To compute churn entropy, p_k is computed as the proportion of the number of lines of code between the current release and the previous release that include changes to file k.

13.3.5   Commit Dimension

If there are many commits between the current and previous release, the current release may have a high probability of being a crashing release. This is the case since more commits means more changes (e.g., bug fixes, new functionalities) to an app, which may introduce more problems (e.g., bugs) in the release. In Table 13.4, two features are proposed in this dimension: number of commits (NC), and number of bug fixing commits (NFC). NC is computed by counting the number of commits in the current release, and NFC is computed by counting the number of commits whose logs contain one of the following keywords: strings "fix," "error," "fault," "crash," "issue," or "bug" [25, 46, 49].

13.3.6   Text Dimension

During the release of an app, many commits may be submitted to fix defects or implement new features. The textual features are first extracted from the commit messages by tokenization, stop-word removal, and stemming. The resulting textual tokens and the number of times each token appears in the commit logs of a release are used to represent the textual features. Since there are many unique words in commit logs, and to avoid the text features crowding out the other features, the words that appear in commit logs are converted into a small number of features. In total, five different features are proposed in the text dimension, which correspond to the textual scores outputted by five different classifiers.

To come up with the scores for the different textual features, all the collected data are divided into a training set and a testing set. Then, the training data set is split into two training subsets by leveraging stratified random sampling, so that the distribution and number of non-crashing and crashing releases in both training subsets is the same [55]. A classifier is trained with the first training subset, and it is used to obtain the textual scores on the second training subset. Besides, a second classifier is trained with the second training subset, and it is used to obtain the textual scores on the first training subset. In the prediction phase, for a new release, text mining classifiers are built on all of the training releases to compute the values of the textual features. Different text mining classifiers can be used to build the textual features; our prior study used 5 types of textual classifiers to calculate the scores of the textual features, including a fuzzy set classifier [67], a naive Bayes classifier [33], a naive Bayes multinomial classifier [33], a discriminative naive Bayes multinomial classifier [50], and a complement naive Bayes classifier [47].

Table **13.5**: Examples of monthly reports

	Example 1	**Example 2**
Month	2013-03	2015-08
Employee ID	1	11
Employee Name	D1	D2
Project Name	P1	P2
Tasks	1. fix bugs on UI 2. implement 5 new functionalities (ID XXX)	Write unit tests on the model XXX
Working Hours	168	128

13.3.7   Prediction Models and Results

Similar to defect prediction studies, various prediction models can be used to predict crash releases. In Xia et al.'s study [61], they built prediction models by using four different classification algorithms, namely Naive Bayes, decision tree, kNN, and Random Forest. They found Naive Bayes achieved the best performance, which corresponds to an F1 and an AUC of 0.30 and 0.64, respectively. Considering that only a small number of releases are crash releases, predicting them accurately is a difficult problem.

13.4   Features from Mining Monthly Reports to Predict Developer Turnover

Developers are a key asset of an Information Technology (IT) company. Unfortunately, in an IT company, the influx and retreat of software developers, which is referred to as *turnover*, are often very frequent. Prior studies found the turnover rate in IT companies varies from 20% to 48% [22, 42, 57]. To help companies better manage developer turnover, it would be interesting to predict who is likely to leave.

Many companies require their employees to write a monthly report, reporting their estimated number of working hours[2] and what they have done in the month. Table 13.5 presents two example monthly reports. Although the structure of a monthly report is often simple, various features can be extracted from such reports.

Our prior work extracted 67 features from monthly reports that developers write in the first six months of them joining a company [6], which were divided

---

[2]This is especially true for outsourcing companies that charge clients based on the number of hours their developers spent on a project.

into three categories: working hours, task report, and project. The details of the features in these categories are presented in the following sections.

13.4.1 Working Hours

In this category, eleven features corresponding to the working hours of developers in each of the first six months are collected. Working hours are related to a developer's workload. Software developers might be asked to take a heavy workload or have tight deadlines. A heavy workload might cause a developer to leave a company. On the other hand, if a developer's working hours are less than normal, he/she might not be interesting in the job, which is an indicator of his/her eventual departure. Thus, the working hours of a developer in the first six months are used as the first six features in this category.

Summary statistics based on a developer's first six months' working hours are also collected. Another five features are proposed in this category, i.e., *sum, mean, median, standard deviation* and *maximum* of a developer's working hours for the six months.

13.4.2 Task Report

In this category, features which are based on the text information in the task report written by the developers are collected. The written style of task report could be different for different developers, which is related to a developer's character and working attitude. For example, a developer, who writes the monthly report in much detail, is usually very conscientious. Otherwise, a simple task report might imply that the developer does not focus on his/her work or is dissatisfied with the work. One such feature is based on the length of the text in the monthly task report and based on five kind of statistics including the sum, mean, median, standard deviation, and maximum text length for each developer. Sometimes, "lazy" developers copy the text of previous task reports or write similar task reports. Thus, after tokenizing and stemming the text of the task report, the *sum, mean, median, standard deviation* and *maximum* number of tokens in the monthly report for each developer are calculated. In total, 11 features are proposed in this category:

1. *task_len_sum*: the sum of the lengths of the text of the task reports.

2. *task_len_mean*: the mean length of the text of the task reports.

3. *task_len_median*: the median length of the text of the task reports.

4. *task_len_std*: the standard deviation of the length of the text of the task reports.

5. *task_len_max*: the maximum length of the text of the task reports.

6. *task_zero*: the number of monthly reports whose task length is 0.

7. *token_sum*: the sum of the token number of task reports.

8. *token_mean*: the mean of the token number of task reports.

9. *token_median*: the median of the token number of task reports.

10. *token_std*: the standard deviation of the token number of task reports.

11. *token_max*: the maximum of the token number of task reports.

Readability features, which refers to the ease with which a reader can understand the task report, are collected. The readability of text is measured by the number of syllables per word and the length of sentences. Readability measures can be used to tell how many years of education a reader should have before reading the text without difficulties [11, 12]. Amazon.com uses readability measures to inform customers about the difficulty of books. Readability features of the task report are used to complement of statistics features of the task report since readability could also be an indicator of a developer's working attitude. Following the prior study on state-of-the-art readabilty, nine readability features are used, i.e., Flesh [12], SMOG (simple measure of gobbledygook) [31], Kincaid [26], Coleman-Liau [10], Automated Readability Index [48], Dale-Chall [11], difficult words [11], Linsear Write [2], and Fog [15]. These readability features can be extracted by using a Python package named *textstat*.[3]

13.4.3   Project

In this category, these features represent information about a project which a developer is working on for each month. The working environment and other members in the project might have a very important effect on a developer's working experience. For example, good collaboration with other members in the project can improve a developer's work efficiency and experience. For each month, the following measures of the project on which the developer is working on are calculated: the number of project members, the sum, the mean and standard deviation of working hours of project members, and the number of changed developers. The number of project members is an indicator of project size. Small project size usually means more workload on each individual in the project. The working hours of project members could reflect the overall workload in the project. And the number of changed developers might indicate the stability of the project. The developers often prefer stay at a stable project. In total, 30 features are proposed in this dimension:

1. *p{N}_person*: the number of persons in the project that the developer is working for in the Nth month, where N is from 1 to 6.

---

[3]https://pypi.python.org/pypi/textstat

2. $p\{N\}\_hour\_mean$: the mean number of working hours of project members in the Nth month.

3. $p\{N\}\_hour\_sum$: the sum of working hours of project members in the Nth month.

4. $p\{N\}\_hour\_std$: the standard deviation of working hours of project members in the Nth month.

5. $p\{N\}\_person\_change$: the number of changed persons compared with the previous month in the Nth month.

Summary statistics based on projects that a developer joins in their first six months are also collected. In total, six features are proposed, i.e., project_num, multi_project, avg_person_change, less_zero, equal_zero, and larger_zero. Project_num refers to the number of projects in the first six months for each developer, and multi_project refers to whether a developer takes part in more than one project in a month. These two features are proposed since the experience of working for multiple projects is different from that of working for only one project and multiple projects might mean higher workload. The number of developer changes in the project which a developer works for (avg_person_change, less_zero, equal_zero, larger_zero) are also counted, since the stability of the project might have an impact on the working experience of a developer.

13.4.4   Prediction Models and Results

Based on the features described in the previous subsections, Bao et al. used five different classification algorithms to build prediction models [6], namely Naive Bayes, Support Vector Machine (SVM), decision tree, kNN, and Random Forest. They performed experiments on monthly reports collected from two companies in China, and Random Forest achieved the best performance, which corresponded to F1-scores for retained and not-retained developers of 0.86 and 0.65, respectively.

13.5   Summary

In this chapter, we presented three case studies to demonstrate how features can be generated from different software artifacts for different software engineering problems. The generated features can be used as input to a machine learning engine (e.g., a classification algorithm) to automate some software tasks or better manage projects. We hope our chapter can inspire more researchers and developers to dig into software artifacts to generate more powerful features, to further improve the performance of existing software analytics solutions or build new automated solutions that address pain points of software developers.

Nowadays, the performance of many predictive models developed to improve software engineering tasks is highly dependent manually on the constructed features. However, significant expert knowledge is required to identify domain-specific features. It would be interesting to investigate methods to automatically generate features from raw data. Deep learning is a promising direction that can be used to automatically learn advanced features from the multitude of raw data available in software repositories, APIs, blog posts, etc. Some of recent studies have shown the potential of deep learning to solve many software analytics problems (e.g., defect prediction [56,65], similar bug detection [64], and linkable knowledge detection [62]) with promising results. Thus, it would be interesting to use deep learning techniques to relieve the heavy workload involved in manually crafting domain-specific features for various software engineering tasks and applications.

Bibliography

[1] Celebrating nine years of GitHub with an anniversary sale. *https://goo.gl/4tXxUu*, Retrieved on May 30, 2017.

[2] Linsear write. http://www.csun.edu/~vcecn006/read1.html#Linsear.

[3] John Anvik, Lyndon Hiew, and Gail C. Murphy. Who should fix this bug? In *Proceedings of the 28th international conference on Software Engineering*, pages 361–370. ACM, 2006.

[4] Erik Arisholm, Lionel C. Briand, and Eivind B. Johannessen. A systematic and comprehensive investigation of methods to build and evaluate fault prediction models. *Journal of Systems and Software*, 83(1):2–17, 2010.

[5] Jagdish Bansiya and Carl G. Davis. A hierarchical model for object-oriented design quality assessment. *IEEE Trans. Software Eng.*, 28(1):4–17, 2002.

[6] Lingfeng Bao, Zhenchang Xing, Xin Xia, David Lo, and Shanping Li. Who will leave the company? A large-scale industry study of developer turnover by mining monthly work report. In *Proceedings of the 14th International Conference on Mining Software Repositories*, pages 170–181. IEEE Press, 2017.

[7] Christian Bird, Nachiappan Nagappan, Brendan Murphy, Harald Gall, and Premkumar Devanbu. Don't touch my code! Examining the effects of ownership on software quality. In *Proceedings of the 19th ACM SIGSOFT symposium and the 13th European Conference on Foundations of Software Engineering*, pages 4–14. ACM, 2011.

[8] Cagatay Catal, Banu Diri, and Bulent Ozumut. An artificial immune system approach for fault prediction in object-oriented software. In *Dependability of Computer Systems, 2007. DepCoS-RELCOMEX'07. 2nd International Conference on*, pages 238–245. IEEE, 2007.

[9] Shyam R. Chidamber and Chris F. Kemerer. A metrics suite for object oriented design. *IEEE Trans. Software Eng.*, 20(6):476–493, 1994.

[10] Meri Coleman and Ta Lin Liau. A computer readability formula designed for machine scoring. *Journal of Applied Psychology*, 60(2):283, 1975.

[11] Edgar Dale and Jeanne S Chall. A formula for predicting readability: Instructions. *Educational Research Bulletin*, pages 37–54, 1948.

[12] Rudolf Franz Flesch. *How to Write Plain English: A Book for Lawyers and Consumers*. HarperCollins, 1979.

[13] Baljinder Ghotra, Shane McIntosh, and Ahmed E Hassan. Revisiting the impact of classification techniques on the performance of defect prediction models. In *ICSE*, pages 789–800. IEEE Press, 2015.

[14] Todd L. Graves, Alan F. Karr, James S. Marron, and Harvey Siy. Predicting fault incidence using software change history. *IEEE Transactions on Software Engineering*, 26(7):653–661, 2000.

[15] Robert Gunning. {The Technique of Clear Writing}. 1952.

[16] Philip J. Guo, Thomas Zimmermann, Nachiappan Nagappan, and Brendan Murphy. Characterizing and predicting which bugs get fixed: An empirical study of Microsoft windows. In *Software Engineering, 2010 ACM/IEEE 32nd International Conference on*, volume 1, pages 495–504. IEEE, 2010.

[17] Tibor Gyimothy, Rudolf Ferenc, and Istvan Siket. Empirical validation of object-oriented metrics on open source software for fault prediction. *IEEE Transactions on Software Engineering*, 31(10):897–910, 2005.

[18] Tracy Hall, Sarah Beecham, David Bowes, David Gray, and Steve Counsell. A systematic literature review on fault prediction performance in software engineering. *TSE*, 38(6):1276–1304, 2012.

[19] Ahmed E. Hassan. Predicting faults using the complexity of code changes. In *Proceedings of the 31st International Conference on Software Engineering*, pages 78–88. IEEE Computer Society, 2009.

[20] B. Henderson-Sellers. *Object-Oriented Metrics, Measures of Complexity.* Prentice Hall, 1996.

[21] Qiao Huang, Xin Xia, and David Lo. Supervised vs unsupervised models: A holistic look at effort-aware just-in-time defect prediction. In *Proceedings of the 33nd International Conference on Software Maintenance and Evolution.* IEEE, 2017, to appear.

[22] James J. Jiang and Gary Klein. Supervisor support and career anchor impact on the career satisfaction of the entry-level information systems professional. *Journal of Management Information Systems*, 16(3):219–240, 1999.

[23] Marian Jureczko and Lech Madeyski. Towards identifying software project clusters with regard to defect prediction. In *Proceedings of the 6th International Conference on Predictive Models in Software Engineering*, page 9. ACM, 2010.

[24] Yasutaka Kamei, Emad Shihab, Bram Adams, Ahmed E. Hassan, Audris Mockus, Anand Sinha, and Naoyasu Ubayashi. A large-scale empirical study of just-in-time quality assurance. *IEEE Transactions on Software Engineering*, 39(6):757–773, 2013.

[25] Sunghun Kim, Thomas Zimmermann, E. James Whitehead Jr, and Andreas Zeller. Predicting faults from cached history. In *Proceedings of the 29th International Conference on Software Engineering*, pages 489–498. IEEE Computer Society, 2007.

[26] J. Peter Kincaid, Robert P. Fishburne Jr, Richard L. Rogers, and Brad S. Chissom. Derivation of new readability formulas (automated readability index, fog count and Flesch reading ease formula) for Navy enlisted personnel. Technical report, DTIC Document, 1975.

[27] Stefan Lessmann, Bart Baesens, Christophe Mues, and Swantje Pietsch. Benchmarking classification models for software defect prediction: A proposed framework and novel findings. *IEEE Transactions on Software Engineering*, 34(4):485–496, 2008.

[28] Paul Luo Li, James Herbsleb, Mary Shaw, and Brian Robinson. Experiences and results from initiating field defect prediction and product test prioritization efforts at ABB Inc. In *Proceedings of the 28th International Conference on Software Engineering*, pages 413–422. ACM, 2006.

[29] R. Martin. OO design quality metrics: An analysis of dependencies. *IEEE Trans. Software Eng.*, 20(6):476–493, 1994.

[30] Shinsuke Matsumoto, Yasutaka Kamei, Akito Monden, Ken-ichi Matsumoto, and Masahide Nakamura. An analysis of developer metrics for fault prediction. In *Proceedings of the 6th International Conference on Predictive Models in Software Engineering*, page 18. ACM, 2010.

[31] G. Harry Mc Laughlin. Smog grading: A new readability formula. *Journal of Reading*, 12(8):639–646, 1969.

[32] T.J. McCabe. A complexity measure. *IEEE Trans. Software Eng.*, 2(4):308–320, 1976.

[33] Andrew McCallum, Kamal Nigam, et al. A comparison of event models for naive Bayes text classification. In *AAAI-98 Workshop*.

[34] Thilo Mende and Rainer Koschke. Revisiting the evaluation of defect prediction models. In *Proceedings of the 5th International Conference on Predictor Models in Software Engineering*, page 7. ACM, 2009.

[35] Tim Menzies, Andrew Butcher, David Cok, Andrian Marcus, Lucas Layman, Forrest Shull, Burak Turhan, and Thomas Zimmermann. Local versus global lessons for defect prediction and effort estimation. *IEEE Transactions on Software Engineering*, 39(6):822–834, 2013.

[36] Tim Menzies, Jeremy Greenwald, and Art Frank. Data mining static code attributes to learn defect predictors. *IEEE Transactions on Software Engineering*, 33(1):2–13, 2007.

[37] Audris Mockus and David M. Weiss. Predicting risk of software changes. *Bell Labs Technical Journal*, 5(2):169–180, 2000.

[38] Raimund Moser, Witold Pedrycz, and Giancarlo Succi. A comparative analysis of the efficiency of change metrics and static code attributes for defect prediction. In *Proceedings of the 30th International Conference on Software Engineering*, pages 181–190. ACM, 2008.

[39] John C. Munson and Taghi M. Khoshgoftaar. The detection of fault-prone programs. *IEEE Transactions on Software Engineering*, 18(5):423–433, 1992.

[40] Nachiappan Nagappan, Thomas Ball, and Andreas Zeller. Mining metrics to predict component failures. In *Proceedings of the 28th International Conference on Software Engineering*, pages 452–461. ACM, 2006.

[41] Hector M. Olague, Letha H. Etzkorn, Sampson Gholston, and Stephen Quattlebaum. Empirical validation of three software metrics suites to predict fault-proneness of object-oriented classes developed using highly iterative or agile software development processes. *IEEE Transactions on Software Engineering*, 33(6), 2007.

[42] Nancy Pekala. Holding on to top talent. *Journal of Property Management*, 66(5):22–22, 2001.

[43] Daryl Posnett, Vladimir Filkov, and Premkumar Devanbu. Ecological inference in empirical software engineering. In *Proceedings of the 2011 26th IEEE/ACM International Conference on Automated Software Engineering*, pages 362–371. IEEE Computer Society, 2011.

[44] Ranjith Purushothaman and Dewayne E. Perry. Toward understanding the rhetoric of small source code changes. *IEEE Transactions on Software Engineering*, 31(6):511–526, 2005.

[45] Foyzur Rahman and Premkumar Devanbu. How, and why, process metrics are better. In *Proceedings of the 2013 International Conference on Software Engineering*, pages 432–441. IEEE Press, 2013.

[46] Foyzur Rahman, Daryl Posnett, Abram Hindle, Earl Barr, and Premkumar Devanbu. BugCache for inspections: Hit or miss? In *Proceedings of the 19th ACM SIGSOFT Symposium and the 13th European Conference on Foundations of Software Engineering*, pages 322–331. ACM, 2011.

[47] Jason D. Rennie, Lawrence Shih, Jaime Teevan, David R. Karger, et al. Tackling the poor assumptions of naive Bayes text classifiers. In *ICML*, 2003.

[48] R.J. Senter and Edgar A. Smith. Automated readability index. Technical report, DTIC Document, 1967.

[49] Jacek Śliwerski, Thomas Zimmermann, and Andreas Zeller. When do changes induce fixes? In *ACM SIGSOFT Software Engineering Notes*, volume 30, pages 1–5. ACM, 2005.

[50] Jiang Su, Harry Zhang, Charles X. Ling, and Stan Matwin. Discriminative parameter learning for Bayesian networks. In *ICML*, 2008.

[51] Ramanath Subramanyam and Mayuram S. Krishnan. Empirical analysis of CK metrics for object-oriented design complexity: Implications for software defects. *IEEE Transactions on Software Engineering*, 29(4):297–310, 2003.

[52] Mei-Huei Tang, Ming-Hung Kao, and Mei-Hwa Chen. An empirical study on object-oriented metrics. In *METRICS*, pages 242–249, 1999.

[53] Yuan Tian, David Lo, Chengnian Sun, and Xin XIA. Automated prediction of bug report priority using multi-factor analysis. *Empirical Software Engineering*, 20(5):1354, 2015.

[54] Burak Turhan, Tim Menzies, Ayşe B. Bener, and Justin Di Stefano. On the relative value of cross-company and within-company data for defect prediction. *Empirical Software Engineering*, 14(5):540–578, 2009.

[55] Harold Valdivia Garcia and Emad Shihab. Characterizing and predicting blocking bugs in open source projects. In *Proceedings of the 11th Working Conference on Mining Software Repositories*, pages 72–81. ACM, 2014.

[56] Song Wang, Taiyue Liu, and Lin Tan. Automatically learning semantic features for defect prediction. In *Proceedings of the 38th International Conference on Software Engineering*, pages 297–308. ACM, 2016.

[57] Aja Whitaker. What causes it workers to leave. *Management Review*, 88(9):8, 1999.

[58] Xin Xia, David Lo, Denzil Correa, Ashish Sureka, and Emad Shihab. It takes two to tango: Deleted stack overflow question prediction with text and meta features. In *Computer Software and Applications Conference (COMPSAC), 2016 IEEE 40th Annual*, volume 1, pages 73–82. IEEE, 2016.

[59] Xin Xia, David Lo, Ying Ding, Jafar M Al-Kofahi, Tien N Nguyen, and Xinyu Wang. Improving automated bug triaging with specialized topic model. *IEEE Transactions on Software Engineering*, 43(3):272–297, 2017.

[60] Xin Xia, David Lo, Sinno Jialin Pan, Nachiappan Nagappan, and Xinyu Wang. Hydra: Massively compositional model for cross-project defect prediction. *IEEE Transactions on Software Engineering*, 42(10):977–998, 2016.

[61] Xin Xia, Emad Shihab, Yasutaka Kamei, David Lo, and Xinyu Wang. Predicting crashing releases of mobile applications. In *Proceedings of the 10th ACM/IEEE International Symposium on Empirical Software Engineering and Measurement*, page 29. ACM, 2016.

[62] Bowen Xu, Deheng Ye, Zhenchang Xing, Xin Xia, Guibin Chen, and Shanping Li. Predicting semantically linkable knowledge in developer online forums via convolutional neural network. In *Proceedings of the 31st IEEE/ACM International Conference on Automated Software Engineering*, pages 51–62. ACM, 2016.

[63] Meng Yan, Yicheng Fang, David Lo, Xin Xia, and Xiaohong Zhang. File-level defect prediction: Unsupervised vs. supervised models. In *Proceedings of the 11th ACM/IEEE International Symposium on Empirical Software Engineering and Measurement*. IEEE, 2017, to appear.

[64] Xinli Yang, David Lo, Xin Xia, Lingfeng Bao, and Jianling Sun. Combining word embedding with information retrieval to recommend similar bug reports. In *Software Reliability Engineering (ISSRE), 2016 IEEE 27th International Symposium on*, pages 127–137. IEEE, 2016.

[65] Xinli Yang, David Lo, Xin Xia, Yun Zhang, and Jianling Sun. Deep learning for just-in-time defect prediction. In *Software Quality, Reliability and Security (QRS), 2015 IEEE International Conference on*, pages 17–26. IEEE, 2015.

[66] Yibiao Yang, Yuming Zhou, Jinping Liu, Yangyang Zhao, Hongmin Lu, Lei Xu, Baowen Xu, and Hareton Leung. Effort-aware just-in-time defect prediction: Simple unsupervised models could be better than supervised models. In *Proceedings of the 2016 24th ACM SIGSOFT In-*

ternational Symposium on Foundations of Software Engineering, pages 157–168. ACM, 2016.

[67] H.J. Zimmermann. *Fuzzy Set Theory and Its Applications Second, Revised Edition.* 1992.

Chapter 14

Feature Engineering for Twitter-Based Applications

Sanjaya Wijeratne, Amit Sheth, Shreyansh Bhatt, Lakshika Balasuriya, Hussein S. Al-Olimat, Manas Gaur, Amir Hossein Yazdavar, Krishnaprasad Thirunarayan

Kno.e.sis Center, Wright State University, Dayton, OH, USA

14.1 Introduction

Social media websites have become extremely popular among online users in recent years. Surveys performed by Pew Research Center in 2016 claimed that social networking sites are visited by 69% of the total U.S. population where 76% of them daily check those websites.[1] These online activities generate large amounts of user-generated content that can be mined to understand user interests and recommend products to online users, develop targeted marketing campaigns for products, understand the user's perspectives on a product, etc. Among many online social networking websites, Twitter has gained popularity due to the fact that users can follow any other user's activities, by accessing their short text messages, called 'tweets,' posted to the Twitter network. For example, Twitter users can follow their favorite celebrities to learn what they share publically, in real-time. Currently, Twitter has grown to a social network of 328 million active users who post around 500 million messages collectively everyday.[2]

With this rapid growth, Twitter has become a useful source for researchers and application developers to conduct studies and develop applications that analyze the pulse and nature of the populace. Researchers have studied the content shared on Twitter to understand the demographics of Twitter users [42,57], their preference for a selected product or service [57], their sentiments [14], and emotions [79]. By letting Twitter users share text, images, and video, Twitter provides an environment that supports sharing of multimodal data. In order to glean insights from tweets, it is critical to design and learn suitable features from the raw data and rank order them based on their effectiveness for analysis or the predictive task at hand. In the past, researchers have studied feature selection for specific problems such as sentiment analysis [45,61] and rumor detection [75], where they have used Twitter as a data source. These studies focus only on a specific task at hand, but these features can be reused or generalized for addressing diverse problems. Thus, identifying features that can work well on a range of Twitter-related applications could help researchers in feature selection and engineering tasks.

This chapter presents an analysis of feature engineering for Twitter-based applications. We begin with a discussion of how Twitter data can be downloaded from the Twitter Application Programming Interface (API). Then we describe different types of data available in tweets downloaded from the Twitter API. Specifically, we discuss the data related to tweet text, Twitter users and other metadata which exist in Twitter JSON objects. Then, we define and discuss various textual features, image and video features, Twitter metadata-related features and network features that can be extracted from them. We also discuss applications that use different feature types along with a justification for why certain features perform well in the context of informal short text messages such as tweets. Then we discuss five Twitter-based applications that utilize the different feature types and highlight the features that perform well in the corresponding application setting. Finally, we conclude the chapter by discussing Twitris, a real-time semantic social web analytics platform that has already been commercialized, and its use of Twitter features.

---

[1]http://www.pewinternet.org/fact-sheet/social-media/
[2]https://www.omnicoreagency.com/twitter-statistics/

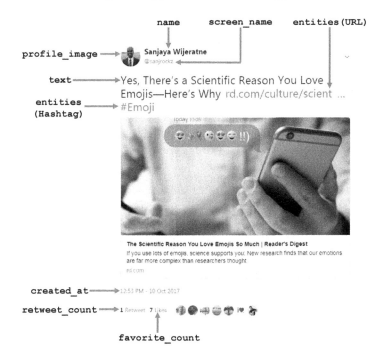

Figure 14.1: An example tweet.

14.2 Data Present in a Tweet

Twitter provides two main APIs, namely, the Streaming API[3] and the REST API[4] to access tweets published by Twitter users in real time. Application developers can use the Twitter Streaming API to collect a random sample of tweets, or a sample of tweets that match a particular keyword, or a set of tweets that originate from a particular geographical location. The Twitter REST API can be used to collect a user's past tweets, friends and followers, and user profile information among many other attributes. Both APIs provide the facility to download Twitter data in the JSON format. We analyze the different data types present in a tweet JSON object (shown in Figure 14.1), with a special focus on the data related to the tweeted text, the user who authored the tweet, location names and URLs in the tweet text, etc.

---

[3]https://dev.twitter.com/streaming/overview
[4]https://dev.twitter.com/rest/public

14.2.1   Tweet Text-Related Data

This section discusses the textual data available in a Twitter JSON object. Data fields corresponding to tweet text that are commonly used in Twitter-based applications are discussed below with pointers to applications that use them.

1. `text`: `text` field in the Twitter JSON object holds the textual content present in a tweet. Tweet text and features derived from it (e.g., part-of-speech tags of the words) are extensively used in Twitter-based applications [4, 14, 28, 79, 90].

2. `entities`: This field contains *hashtags, URLs* and *user_ mentions* present in a tweet. *Hashtags* were introduced as a way of organizing Twitter conversations by topics, thus, they are extensively used for collecting topic-specific tweets. In addition to that, they have been used in various Twitter content analysis studies, including information propagation [76]. *URLs* can also contain valuable information to enrich the content, and thus, are used in studies related to Twitter content analysis [28]. *User_ mentions* contain all Twitter usernames mentioned in a tweet. User mentions can be helpful in building user interaction networks to find influential users [62].

3. `retweeted`: This field indicates whether the current tweet is a retweet of a previous tweet.

4. `retweeted_status`: If the current tweet is a retweet, then this field contains all the information about the original tweet including the text of the tweet and information about the user who originally tweeted it. Retweets of retweets are not captured in this field, but only the original tweet. Data present in the `retweeted_status` field are commonly used in studies that analyze tweet text [8], retweet networks [50,56], influence, and information propagation on Twitter [10]. Past research has also shown that having hashtags and URLs in a tweet make it more likely to be retweeted by others [73].

5. `retweet_count`: This field indicates the number of times that the current tweet has been retweeted. Retweet count can be helpful to predict the popularity of a tweet [9].

6. `quoted_status`: This field carries information about quoted tweets. Quoted tweets are a special form of retweets where a Twitter user gets to write his/her own tweet/message while retweeting a tweet. Information present in a quoted tweet can also be used in applications that analyze Twitter content (e.g., understanding political discourse [30]).

7. `favorite_count`: This field records how many people have liked the current tweet. This information has been used as a feature for predicting the popularity of a tweet [9].

8. `in_reply_to_screen_name`: If the current tweet is a reply to another tweet, this field holds the screen name of the user to whom the current tweet responded. This field can be helpful in building user interaction networks to find influential users [62].

9. `place`: This field will carry information about the places associated with a tweet. Users choose a place to be attached to a tweet from a list of pre-defined places. Thus, this does not necessarily represent the place from which the tweet originated.

14.2.2   Twitter User-Related Data

This section discusses the data available in a Twitter JSON object that corresponds to the user who authored the tweet.

1. `description`: This field records the user-provided description of a Twitter profile. In general, Twitter users use the description of their Twitter profiles to provide a short biography about themselves. Thus, applications that classify Twitter profiles use the content extracted from this field to build classifiers [4, 62, 82, 90].

2. `screen_name`: This field holds the user's screen name. A screen name or a Twitter handle is a unique name that a Twitter user selects to identify him/herself on Twitter. This name starts with an @ symbol and can go up to 15 characters. `screen_name` is used to uniquely identify Twitter users.

3. `name`: This field holds the Twitter user's name. This field can act as a label to refer to users, but the same `name` can be shared by many Twitter users; thus, this field should not be used as a unique way to refer to Twitter users.

4. `location`: This field holds a Twitter user-provided location. Twitter users can enter any value as their location; thus, this field will not always carry a valid physical location of a Twitter user. For example, some invalid physical locations can include "worldwide," "someone's heart," "in the middle of nowhere," and "here." However, whenever possible, Twitter applications that try to predict the location of a Twitter user utilize the text specified in this field when trying to arrive at a meaningful physical location of a user [71].

5. `geo_enabled`: This field records whether the user has decided to share the geo-coordinates of the tweet's originating location with the tweet or not.

6. `profile_image_url`: This field records the profile image URL used in a given Twitter profile.

7. `profile_banner_url`: This field records the cover image URL used in a given Twitter profile.

8. `followers_count`: This field indicates the number of followers that a given Twitter user has.

9. `friends_count`: This field indicates the number of friends that a given Twitter user has.

14.2.3   Other Metadata

This section discusses the metadata available in a Twitter JSON object that corresponds to either tweet text or the user who tweeted it.

1. `id`: The `id` field in the Twitter JSON object represents the unique ID associated with a tweet. Twitter applications can use this ID to uniquely identify and retrieve tweets.

2. `coordinates`: The `coordinates` field contains the longitude and the latitude of a tweet's location, which identifies the exact location of the user at the time of authoring the tweet.

3. `lang`: This field holds the machine-detected language of a tweet text. Note that this does not necessarily represent the language used in the Twitter profile.

4. `created_at`: This field records the Coordinated Universal Time (UTC) of the tweet creation. This field can be helpful for temporal trend analysis and for applications that try to predict a Twitter user's location.

5. `time_zone`: This field records the time zone associated with a Twitter user profile. A Twitter user can specify the time zone information at the time of their Twitter profile creation.

14.3   Common Types of Features Used in Twitter-Based Applications

This section presents a list of features that are commonly used in Twitter-based applications. It also discusses how the features are defined and why they are important for those applications. The features are categorized into several groups based on what type of content is present in them such as text, image, and video (examples are given in Table 14.1 for selected feature types). This section also emphasizes why those features tend to perform well with certain types of Twitter applications.

Table 14.1: Different feature types extracted from the example tweet shown in Figure 14.1.

Feature Type	Example
Unigrams	Yes, There, 's, a, Scientific, Reason, You, Love, Emojis, Here, 's, Why
Bigrams	Yes There, There 's, 's a, a Scientific, Scientific Reason, Reason You, You Love, Love Emojis, Emojis Here, Here 's, 's Why
Part-of-Speech	Yes/UH, There/EX, 's/VBZ, a/DT, Scientific/NNP, Reason/NNP, You/PRP, Love/VBD, Emojis/NNP, Here/RB, 's/VBZ, Why/WRB
Named Entities	Emojis
Hashtags	#Emoji
URLs	https://www.rd.com/culture/scientific-reason-love-emojis
Image Tags	Male, Person
Creation Time	12:53 PM - 10 Oct 2017
Language	English

14.3.1 Textual Features

This section discusses textual features that can be extracted from Twitter data. As discussed in Section 14.2, a Twitter JSON object contains many fields that hold information in the form of text such as tweet text and profile description of a Twitter user. Next, we define and discuss different types of features that can be extracted from the textual content present in a tweet.

1. **Word n-grams**: Word n-grams are defined as contiguous sequences of n words that appear in a text fragment. Popular n-grams are unigrams containing one word and bigrams containing two words. For example, if we consider the tweet text "I am feeling happy today", the set of all unigrams extracted from the tweet text include the words {I, am, feeling, happy, today"}, while the set of all bigrams extracted from the same tweet include {I am, am feeling, feeling happy, happy today}. Word n-grams are very popular in many Twitter-based applications that analyze textual features, including applications that are designed for sentiment analysis [14, 28], emotion analysis [79], and user profile classification [4, 65, 82]. Past research on sentiment analysis has shown that unigram features perform best when Twitter data is used as training data [11], whereas bigram features outperform unigrams when longer text fragments such as product reviews are used for training [77].

2. **Part-of-Speech (PoS) Tags**: In linguistics, a Part-of-Speech (PoS) is defined as a category of words that exhibit similar properties or functions based on how words are used in the language. PoS tags are commonly used in many natural language processing applications including

language parsing and word sense disambiguation [36]. For example, if we consider the tweet text "I'm feeling happy today", a PoS tagger would categorize the word I as a personal pronoun (I/PRP), 'm as a verb which is non-3rd person singular present ('m/VBP), feeling as a verb, which as a gerund or present participle (feeling/VBG), happy as an adjective (happy/JJ), and today as a singular or mass noun (today/NN). PoS tags are widely used in Twitter-based sentiment and emotion analysis applications and have been shown to improve the performance of the baseline sentiment analysis models that are based on word n-gram features [14,28,79]. Prior research has shown that natural language processing (NLP) tools that are trained on well-formed text corpora might not work well with social media text due to language variations [67,84]. Therefore, social media-specific Part-of-Speech (PoS) tagging software has been used in Twitter-based applications [32].

3. **Named Entities**: Named entities are real word objects such as persons, places or organizations that are identified by proper names. Named entities can act as important features for traditional applications such as information retrieval and search, as well as Twitter-based applications such as target-specific sentiment analysis [14]. Named entities are usually extracted from the tweet text [14], profile descriptions [62], and user location [71]. Similar to PoS tag extraction from tweets, named entity extraction from tweets also require specially designed tools due to the informal nature of the language used in Twitter [24,67]. For example, Twitter users prefer abbreviations and unconventional shortened versions of person names in tweets (e.g., "0bama" and "OBMA" to refer to "Barack Obama") due to the 140 character limitation imposed by Twitter.[5] Thus, many features that are used in named entity extraction tasks in well-formed text such as capitalization of the first letters of words, and punctuation would not work in Twitter settings. This has resulted in building Twitter-specific named entity recognition tools [67]. Cultural entities, which are a special form of named entities that refer to artifacts of culture such as music albums, movie names, and book names are also common among Twitter conversations [49]. Those could also play an important role in Twitter applications that are targeted for fans of the music artists, movies or books.

4. **Implicit Entities**: Implicit entities are the "entities that are mentioned in text without an explicit mention of their names nor synonyms/aliases/abbreviations or co-references in the same text" [58]. Implicit entities are a common occurrence. For example, past research has found that nearly 21% of movie mentions and 40% of book mentions are implicit in tweets [59]. For example, consider the tweet "Aren't we gonna talk about how ridiculous the new

---

[5]Twitter is planning to support up to 280 characters for selected languages in near future.

`space movie of Sandra Bullock is?`''. It contains an implicit reference to the movie *Gravity*. Past research has shown that external knowledge bases such as DBpedia and Wikipedia can be successfully utilized to identify implicit entity mentions in clinical narratives [58] and tweets [59].

5. **Emoticons**: Emoticons are the pictorial representations of facial expressions (e.g., :-), :-D, :-(etc.) composed mainly using punctuation marks and letters. They are commonly used to express the emotion of the message sender or to convey other non-verbal cues [54]. Emoticons are commonly treated as sentiment-bearing terms in sentiment analysis applications and emotion-bearing terms in emotion analysis applications. They have been shown to improve the performance of sentiment and emotion analysis on short text such as tweets [79].

6. **Emoji**: With the rise of social media, pictographs, commonly referred to as "emoji" have become one of the world's fastest-growing forms of communication.[6] Users of social media platforms use emoji to express their emotions and other non-verbal cues, making them important features for applications that analyze sentiment and emotion [53]. Similar to emoticons, emoji are rarely seen in well-formed, lengthy texts. Thus, they can act as effective features in short text processing applications that utilize them for brevity. Past research on sentiment and emotion analysis on tweets has reported that the accuracy of the two tasks can be improved by using emoji as features [53, 87]. These studies further state that the sentiment polarity of emoji increases with the distance of their appearance from the start of the text in a sentence. Recent research has shown that emoji can also act as an indicator of sarcasm [29]. Many Twitter-based studies convert emoji into their text equivalents (i.e., using "face_with_tears_of_joy" as a feature instead of processing the image of the emoji) using third-party software [4, 82].

7. **Hashtags**: A hashtag is a special kind of word that starts with the symbol #. They were introduced as a way of organizing conversations by topics on Twitter (e.g., #HurricaneSandy hashtag groups all tweets posted on Hurricane Sandy) and are much more commonly seen on social media platforms than in grammatical text such as news articles. Hashtags can be essential elements for information retrieval and search from social media sites. They have been extensively used in many real-world applications including disaster management and relief coordination [63], and information propagation [76].

8. **User Mentions**: A user mention is a mention of a username in a tweet, which starts with the special character @ followed by the username of the Twitter user (i.e., @username). User mentions are used on Twitter

---

[6]https://goo.gl/jbeRYW

to refer to another Twitter user, whereas real names are used in grammatical text. User mentions are often used as binary features in social media text analysis applications (i.e., existence or non-existence of a @username in a tweet is regarded as a feature). Social network analysis applications use user mentions to build user networks [62].

9. **URLs**: A Uniform Resource Locator, or a URL, is a unique address that locates a resource (e.g., a Web page) on a computer network (e.g., the World Wide Web). Since many users use social media websites to read and share news and other interesting web resources they find online, sharing URL links is a common practice in social media websites including Twitter. Twitter users mainly share links to other web resources in their profile descriptions and tweets. Twitter-based content processing applications such as sentiment analysis applications often treat the existence of a URL in a tweet as a binary feature [14], whereas other content processing applications may process the information present in the resource linked to the URL as well [28].

10. **Repeated Letters and Punctuation**: Twitter users often use multiple repeating letters in a word as a way of conveying and emphasizing the emotion or sentiment associated with a tweet. For example, the tweet ''I looooved the movie'' expresses a positive sentiment about a movie viewing experience of a Twitter user. Thus, repetition of letters and punctuation marks have been used as features for Twitter content analysis. These informal language styles are rarely seen in well-formed text, thus, these features do not play a special role in grammatical text analysis.

14.3.2   Image and Video Features

This section discusses image and video features that can be extracted from Twitter posts and user profile data. Twitter users can upload images to their Twitter profiles using three main ways, namely, (i) uploading an image as the profile image, (ii) uploading an image as the cover image, and (iii) uploading an image as part of a tweet. The only option to post a video to Twitter is through a tweet. Twitter API disseminates image and video URLs with Twitter JSON objects if images or videos are present in a Twitter profile or in a Twitter message. Below, we define two main types of features that can be extracted from image and video content present in a tweet or a Twitter profile.

1. **Image Tags**: Image tags are the labels or names associated with images. These names or labels are usually assigned by human annotators so the annotations and images can be later used to build image classification models. For example, an image of a car could be associated with a label

"car," which will then be used to train a machine learning classifier that can automatically tag images of cars. Images extracted from Twitter profiles are used as features in studies that attempt to predict the gender of a Twitter user [68] or Twitter user groups [4, 82].

2. **Video Titles and Text in Video Comments**: Twitter users also post videos along with their tweets and those can provide additional information for tasks at hand. For example, past work on gang member Twitter profile identification suggest that textual features extracted from YouTube video titles and comments can act as useful features to identify gang member profiles [4, 82].

14.3.3   Twitter Metadata-Related Features

This section discusses features that can be extracted from various metadata related to a tweet. Twitter metadata provide useful information that explain different events related to a tweet such as the tweet originating time, tweet originating location, and tweet language. Below, we discuss several metadata-related features that are commonly used in Twitter-based applications.

1. **Geo-coordinates of a Tweet**: The geo-coordinates of a tweet are the longitude and the latitude of the tweet's originating location. This feature will be available in the Twitter JSON object only if the Twitter user who posted the tweet had already agreed to share the location of the tweet's originating location in the tweet. Geo-coordinates of a tweet are very valuable for any Twitter-based application that requires the location of a Twitter user or a tweet as they can provide the exact tweet originating location. Thus, geo-coordinates are commonly used in location-based Twitter applications [27, 71].

2. **Tweet Creation Time**: Tweet creation time records the Coordinated Universal Time (UTC) of the tweet creation. This can be a helpful feature to organize a collection of tweets chronologically for further processing. For example, dialog processing systems that process tweets can benefit from this feature whose organizing the messages exchanged among a group of users before further processing them to glean contextual information related to the discussion among Twitter users.

3. **Language of a Tweet**: Twitter also provides the machine-detected language of a tweet. This can be a helpful feature for information filtering when collecting tweets using a given language. This could also be helpful for Twitter-based user demography studies.

14.3.4   Network Features

This section discusses features that can be extracted from various Twitter networks. We define network-based features as the features extracted from the Twitter user network and the metadata associated with them. A network (graph) is a set of nodes (vertices) connected by a set of edges (arcs) where the connections among nodes symbolize a relationship among them. For example, a simple Twitter-based network could be a graph of a user's friends on Twitter where Twitter users are represented by the nodes in the graph and the friendships among users are represented using the edges. There are two main types of networks available in Twitter, namely, user interaction-based networks and friend-follower networks [39]. Different types of relationships among Twitter users generate Twitter networks, thus, they can yield different types of features based on the relationships that generate the networks.

1. **Retweet**: Retweet is the task of sharing an existing tweet so that the tweet reaches the followers of the user who shares the tweet. This has become a very common practice among many Twitter users [50]. Retweets can be used to identify influential users [3,10,62]. For example, a retweet pattern among a set of Twitter users can be used to derive features that can help identify influential users and how influence propagates.

2. **Reply**: A reply is a tweet that is targeted to a Twitter user in response to a previous tweet posted by the user. Replies typically start with @username followed by the message posted as the reply. Replies are commonly used to construct the interaction networks among Twitter users. Twitter reply-based networks can be used to derive additional features [88,91], that can be helpful in deciding the influential users and clustering Twitter users based on their interests.

3. **Followers and Friends**: A Twitter follower is a Twitter user that a particular Twitter user follows. If two Twitter users follow each other, they are called friends. Friends and followers networks have been used in many applications for the identification of a Twitter user's social ties, a user's influence on others and information propagation.

14.4   Twitter Feature Engineering in Selected Twitter-Based Studies

This section discusses how different features extracted from Twitter can be used in real-world applications. Specifically, this section discusses studies ranging from Twitter user profile classification and prediction to gleaning the sentiment and emotion of Twitter users.

14.4.1 Twitter User Profile Classification

Twitter user profile classification is a well-studied problem where a class label is assigned to a Twitter profile from a set of pre-defined labels. Concrete examples of Twitter profile classification include user political affiliation classification [57], ethnicity classification [57], gender identification [42], brand loyalty prediction [57], and user occupation classification [65]. Most of these applications rely only on textual features extracted from content posted on Twitter or user profiles. Balasuriya *et al.* recently studied how to identify the Twitter profiles of street gang members where they used different types of content-based features and user-based features [4, 82]. This problem was motivated by the recent increase in the number of gang violence–involved homicides which were traced back to the fights that first started on online social media [86].

Balasuriya *et al.* first curated a large dataset of gang member profiles on Twitter that consists of 400 authentic gang member profiles and 2,865 non-gang member profiles [4]. For each Twitter profile in their dataset, they collected up to 3,200 of the most recent tweets that were associated with those profiles along with profile descriptions and images (profile and cover photos) of every gang and non-gang member profile. They analyzed the text in the tweets and profile descriptions (unigrams) of those Twitter profiles, emoji use, profile images, and music interests. In their analysis, they found that 5.72% of all words posted by gang members were curse words, which is nearly five times more than the average curse word usage on Twitter among the general population [80]. They also noticed that the gang members often talk about drugs and money with terms such as *smoke, high, hit*, and *money*, while ordinary users hardly speak about finances and drugs. Ordinary users often vocalize their feelings with terms such as *new, like, love, know, want, look, make, us*. These differences give a clear indication that the words used by gang and non-gang members could act as important features for gang member profile classification. They found that the terms *rip* and *free* appear in approximately 12% of all gang member Twitter profile descriptions, which suggests that gang members use their profile descriptions as a space to grieve for their fallen or incarcerated gang members. They also found that 51.25% of the gang members in their dataset had a tweet that linked to a YouTube video and 76.58% of those tweets were related to gangster rap music. Emoji analysis revealed that the fuel pump emoji was the most frequently used emoji by the gang members, where it was often used in the context of selling or consuming marijuana. The pistol emoji was the second most frequent emoji, which was often used with the police cop emoji in an "emoji chain" to reflect anger at police officers. They reported that 32.25% of gang members had chained together the police and the pistol emoji, compared to just 1.14% of non-gang members. Gang members were often seen holding or pointing weapons in groups displaying gangster culture, or showing off graffiti, hand signs, tattoos, and bulk cash in their profile or cover pictures.

Balasuriya *et al.* used four different classification models for their task: a Naive Bayes net (NB), a Logistic Regression (LR), a Random Forest (RF), and a Support Vector Machine (SVM). These four models were chosen because they are known to perform well over text features, which is the dominant type of feature considered. They used 10-fold cross validation for training and evaluating the classifier models. First, they trained a series of classifier models by using features extracted from a single feature type (i.e., tweet text, emoji, profile, image, or YouTube) as training data. The classifiers that use a single feature type were intended to help them study the quality of the predictive power of those features alone. Then they also trained another series of classifier models that consider all types of features combined. Their results reported that the RF classifier model trained on the unigram features extracted from tweets perform reasonably well, with an $F1$-score of 0.72 for the "gang" class. NB classifiers trained on the unigram features extracted from YouTube videos and emoji shared in tweets were the next best classifier models with $F1$-scores of 0.65 and 0.61, respectively, for the "gang" class. They reported that the performance of the classifier models improved when different types of features were combined ($F1$–score of 0.77 for RF classifier). In a later study, Wijeratne *et al.* improved the above classification models ($F1$–score of 0.78) using word embeddings [82].

14.4.2   Assisting Coordination during Crisis Events

Social media, specifically Twitter, has proven to be an effective medium for sharing information during crisis events such as Hurricane Sandy and Typhoon Yolanda. The shared information often includes important messages such as requests for help (seekers) as well as responses (suppliers) to such requests. However, extracting seeker and supplier information can be challenging as crisis events tend to produce large amounts of data within a short period of time [64]. Thus, locating tweets with seeker and supplier information becomes a high-priority task for the disaster coordination teams who monitor Twitter during disaster events. To assist online disaster coordination teams with extracting supplier and seeker information, Purohit *et al.* studied the problem of matching resource requests (seekers) with responses to help (suppliers) as an intent classification problem [64] where an intent is defined as a purposeful action. Intent mining on social media can be challenging, a specially in the context of disaster relief coordination due to numerous reasons, including but not limited to:

1. Informal language use causes ambiguity in interpreting user expressions in short-text messages, weakening predictor-class relationships (e.g., "wanna help" appears as a strong intent signal but exists in messages of two complementary intent classes, "seeking" and "offering").

2. The sparsity of instances of specific intent classes in the corpus creates data imbalance (e.g., [63] showed that expressions of "offering" intent

were only a fraction of those with "requesting" intent (1:7 ratio) during Hurricane Sandy event in 2012).

3. Both intent of "seeking" and "offering" may co-occur within a single message. The limited motives pertain to the transactional intent of buying and selling, which are different from the critical actions involved in our problem context of cooperation.

Table 14.2: Examples of short-text documents and potential intents.

Short-text Document	Intent
What is the location of the nearest #Redcross? I wanna give blood to help victims of the Hurricane	Offering Help
@Zurora wants to help @Network4Good with Hurricane relief. TEXT Sandy 8088 & donate $10 to @redcross	Seeking Help
Would like to urge all the citizens to make proper preparations for the Hurricane	Advising
Thx to all in Dayton who brought supplies for those who affected by Hurricane Sandy.	Acknowledging

Table 14.2 exemplifies a few tweets which show seeker/supplier behavior. Past research has investigated simple pattern-based approaches to identify seekers and suppliers and reported that pattern-based methods alone cannot address issues such as ambiguity in the informal language used in seeker/supplier tweets [63]. Thus, Purohit *et al.* have used machine learning models with three different types of features extracted from seeker-/supplier-related tweets and expert knowledge (e.g., features extracted from common messages patterns in a disaster-related event), which are discussed below.

1. Bottom-up: They are unigram features extracted from the tweet text.

2. Top-down: Features based on knowledge-guided patterns, social knowledge–guided patterns, and contrast mining–guided patterns. Knowledge-guided patterns rely on semantic-syntactic knowledge of intent expression. For example, a subject with the main verb "have" and any noun suggests an offering intent. However, the same text preceded by the auxiliary verb "do" and the pronoun "you" suggests a seeking intent. Similarly, word order such as verb-subject position also plays a crucial role in intent expression. Such patterns for expressing intent can help address the ambiguity challenge by endorsing the likelihood of an intent association for a short-text document. The pattern design leverages a lexicon of verbs, given that verbs imply a plan for action. Using Schankâ's P-Trans primitive [69], which reflects the transfer of property, Purohit *et al.* acquire seeking-offering intent related verb classes. Their verb lexicon includes the Levin verb [41] categories of {give, future, having, send, slide, carry, sending/carrying, put, removing, exerting

force, change of possession, hold/keep, contact, combining/attaching, creation/transformation, perception, communication}. Their patterns also include classes of auxiliary verbs (e.g., be, do, have), the models (e.g., can, could, may, might), question words ('wh'-words and how), and the conditional (if). They extend the seed patterns by an exhaustive representation of synonymous verbs preserving the tense, using the WordNet knowledge base [47]. Each pattern is treated as a binary feature. Social conversation can help further differentiate the intent, especially during a crisis event. During crisis events, citizens usually get involved in conversations regarding resource seeking and supply. As a part of this, stop words, which are often discarded, are considered as a conversation indicator for the social knowledge–guided patterns. The full list of the social knowledge–guided patterns used in this study is available in [64]. To learn contrast mining–guided patterns, Purohit *et al.* used a state-of-the-art emerging pattern detection algorithm [25,43], which is capable of identifying patterns in tweet text that are dominant in one class (e.g., seeker) but not often seen in the other class (e.g., supplier).

3. Hybrid: In the hybrid feature selection, both the top-down and bottom-up features were combined and used in the classification process.

Purohit *et al.* used two datasets for their experiments. The first dataset (Dataset 1) consisted of 4.9 million tweets for the event of Hurricane Sandy in the U.S. in 2012 and the second dataset (Dataset 2) consisted of 1.9 million tweets for the event of Typhoon Yolanda in the Philippines in 2013. Their training dataset consisted of 3,135 tweets extracted from Dataset 1 and 2,000 tweets extracted from Dataset 2. Three human judges were asked to annotate each tweet in the training dataset using six labels {Request to get, Offer to give, Both request and offer, Report of past donations, None of the above, Cannot judge} for ground truth data creation. They merged the labels to design the intent classes {seeking, offering, none (i.e., neither seeking nor offering)}. They used Random Forest algorithm (RF) to train classifier models and used 10-fold cross validation to evaluate them. They reported that the classifier models trained using the hybrid features outperformed the classifier models trained on the top-down and bottom-up features alone. The absolute gain in the $F1$-score and accuracy for the hybrid approach are up to 7% and 6%, respectively, compared to the next best performing classifier models trained using top-down and bottom-up features [64]. They also reported that more than half of the most discriminating, best ranked 1% features belong to the top-down (knowledge-based) processing representation, which shows the importance of encoding world knowledge into improving the machine learning classifiers [70].

14.4.3 Location Extraction from Tweets

The location extraction or location identification problem in Twitter is an important problem where the focus can be either to identify the Twitter user's location or the tweet's originating location or both. Knowing the location of a Twitter user or tweet origination can be beneficial in many applications. For example, Carmen *et al.* [27], extract location names from tweets for a surveillance application of influenza by tapping on the spatial extents of tweets and their content. A wide range of applications also use the location information extracted from tweets such as to study U.S. elections [14], users' religiosity [15], analysis of drug use across geographies in the USA [19, 20], the effect of governmental decisions on the legalization of drugs and the perception of Twitter users on such decisions [40], and even cross-cultural differences and their effect on the mental illness of Twitter users [23]. All of the above studies and use cases only need coarse-level location information (such as country, state, or neighborhood levels) as opposed to other studies which require finer levels of location information (such as neighborhood, street, or building). Crisis-related applications have a critical need for fine-grained location information. For example, to study the inter-dependencies between resources and needs during a disaster, Bhatt *et al.* [6] exploited location mentions in text and other information about the resource needs to better facilitate disaster relief efforts. Anantharam *et al.* [2] used a knowledge base of location names (gazetteer) to help in extracting spatiotemporal proximity of city events such as traffic and road closures due to accidents. State-of-the-art social media data processing systems, such as Twitris [71], support spatio-temporal-thematic analysis of events on social media with real-time monitoring. The first item of the analysis triple is the spatial context of each event, allowing users to filter those events based on their locations. There are four types of location information available on Twitter:

1. A Twitter user can specify his/her location in the user's profile and this can be retrieved from the `location` field in a Twitter JSON object.

2. A Twitter user can share the tweet's originating location (longitude and latitude) along with the Tweet. This information can be retrieved from the `coordinates` field in a Twitter JSON object.

3. A Twitter user can choose a location/place from a list of pre-defined places to be attached to tweets. This information, which consists of the place name and the place bounding box, can be retrieved from the `place` field in a Twitter JSON object.

4. A Twitter user can include location names in the tweet. There's no guarantee that the place names extracted from tweet text is the Twitter user's or tweet's originating location, however prior research has shown that the location names [38] and linguistic clues [16] extracted from tweet text can be used to improve Twitter user location prediction.

The exploitation of the geo-coordinates (longitude and latitude) of a tweet becomes a straightforward task if the Twitter user authorizes Twitter to share the tweet's originating location. However, since only around 2% of the tweets contain such information, studies tend to exploit other means to infer the location of a tweet or a Twitter user. This is a non-trivial problem. Finding the user profile location or extracting the tweet originating location from tweet content might not result in the actual tweet's originating location for many reasons. For example, Twitter users might be traveling, thus their tweets could be authored from different locations than what is specified in their Twitter profiles. Similarly, the tweet content might be about a remote location that the user is interested in but does not reflect the user's actual location or the tweet's originating location. Studies have adopted different features extracted from tweets, and user profiles to estimate the location of a Twitter user or a tweet. Carmen *et al.* [27] infer the location of Twitter users and tweets from the user's profile location specified in a Twitter profile. After identifying the irregularities in the Twitter naming scheme in specifying the location names, they used a list of location name synonyms to map lexical variants of a location name to a common location name. They also developed methods to normalize location name acronyms such as "NYC" to "New York City" and filtered out location names such as "Neverland." Finally, they used Yahoo's PlaceFinder API[7] to find the geo-coordinates of the remaining location names. Exploiting the information from the users and their follower/followee network data, the state-of-the-art geo-localization tool Pigeo [66] finds the location of users given their textual messages and their interactions with other users. The tool uses pre-trained geo-location models to predict the user geolocation and achieves on average around 65% accuracy. Notably, Mourad *et al.* [48] found that the language (and its coverage) of a Twitter user highly influences the accuracy of geolocating the user.

Twitris [71], a real-time social media event monitoring tool computes the location of a tweet using the tweet location and the user profile location discussed earlier. For example, if a tweet is not associated with exact geo-coordinates of the tweet originating location, Twitris tries to utilize the user's profile information. This two-step process results in assigning tweet originating locations for up to 25% of tweets. Extracting location names from the tweet text is the most difficult task among the four types of location extraction methods discussed earlier. Similar to other NER tasks, extracting location names starts with delimiting the location names in text (i.e., identifying the mention of the word "London" as a possible location name), linking them with a gazetteer or a knowledge base of location names and disambiguating the identified location names (i.e., deciding whether the mention of London refers to "London, Ohio" or "London, England"). Prior research has shown that natural language processing (NLP) tools trained on well-formed text corpora might not work well with social media text due to language variations [67,84].

---

[7]https://developer.yahoo.com/geo/placefinder/

Therefore, social media-specific NLP methods have been developed for NER and Part-of-Speech (PoS) tagging, which is commonly used in NER to improve the performance [7, 31, 67]. Other techniques for NER include phrase mining or noun-phrase extraction, and n-gram matching [31, 44, 46]. Methods such as those in [46] pre-load a list of location names of an area of interest to improve the accuracy of the location name extraction process. Additionally, methods such as those in [35] have devised semi-supervised methods which use beam-search and the structured perceptron to extract and link location names to their respective Foursquare records. The state-of-the-art methods such as those in [1] extract location names from tweets and link them to open street map gazetteers using statistical language models. The method discussed in [1] achieved a combined F1-Score of 81% by avoiding the use of unreliable syntactic and orthographic features of tweets.

14.4.4 Studying the Mental Health Conditions of Depressed Twitter Users

With the rise of social media, millions of people are routinely expressing their moods, feelings, and daily struggles with mental health issues on social media platforms like Twitter. Unlike traditional observational cohort studies conducted through questionnaires and self-reported surveys, mining social media for depressive symptoms expressed in tweets provides a new way to capture behavioral attributes such as mood and day-to-day activities that are related to one's thinking patterns. Thus, much progress has been made in studying mood and mental health conditions through the lens of social media, recently [5, 22, 37, 52, 89, 90]. The vast collection of mental health studies on social media can be grouped into two major categories, namely, lexicon-based [37, 51] and supervised modeling [21, 22, 52]. These studies suggest that the people's language style, emotion, ego-network, and user engagement can be used as discriminating features to recognize depression-indicative posts. In particular, these distinguishing characteristics can be used to build a model to predict the likelihood of depression expressed in a post [22] or in an individual [21]. In another study, Nguyen *et al.* [52] employ affective aspect, linguistic style and topics as features for characterizing depressed communities. The LIWC[8] program has been employed to capture linguistic style signals, including auxiliary verbs, conjunctions, adverbs, functional words, and prepositions as well as the number of positive and negative words. Wang *et al.* [81] utilize various features including sentence polarity for the detection of depressed individuals in Twitter. By training a text classifier that identifies three different mood states (anxiety, anger, and depression), Reis *et al.* [26] study the effect of exercise on mental health. They use n-grams extracted from tweet text, psychological categories, and emoticons as features. Similarly, Shuai *et*

---

[8]http://liwc.wpengine.com/

al. [72] build a model for identifying potential cases of social network mental disorders.

Moreover, Coppersmith *et al.* [17] created a dataset of 1,800 Twitter profiles that can be used to develop methods to automatically identify depressed users on Twitter. A system that uses topic modeling and bag-of-words extracted from tweet text, LIWC features, metadata, and clustering features achieved state-of-the-art performance [60] when applied to the above dataset of 1,800 depressed Twitter users. Another related line of research which is similar to identifying depressed users on Twitter is studying suicide and self-harm signals from Twitter posts [33, 34, 74]. By studying the tweets posted by individuals attempting to commit suicide, Coppersmith *et al.* [18] reports quantifiable signals of suicide ideations. On the other hand, in the context of lexicon-based approaches, Karmen *et al.* [37] leverage a dictionary-based approach for assigning an overall depression score to each subject. They simply count all the existing phrases that are matched with depression indicators. In another related study, Park *et al.* [55] report the usage of the keyword "depression" in tweets. They show that individuals tweet about their depression and even disclose updates about their mental health treatment on Twitter. They found an association between excessive use of negative emotions-related words and having a major depressive disorder (MDD). In contrast, no relation has been found in the use of positive emotions-related words and depression.

Similarly, Neuman *et al.* [51] report a natural language processing approach for identification of depression by utilizing a depression lexicon incorporating both metaphorical and non-metaphorical words and phrases. They perform a web search to seek documents containing text patterns such as "depression is like *," where "*" can be any word. Employing a dependency parser, they extract phrases which could possibly describe the sources of depression and expand them by their first- and the second-degree synonyms obtained from a depression lexicon used in the study. However, in natural language, words can be ambiguous. For instance, depression may be used to express different concepts such as "economic depression," "depression era," "great depression," and "tropical depression." Moreover, neurotypical people use this term to express their transient sadness. An example of a neurotypical user tweeting about depression could be ``I am depressed, I have a final exam tomorrow''. Furthermore, the experience of depression may be expressed implicitly making a lexicon-based approach insufficient for accurate fine-grained analysis of depression symptoms over time. Another inherent drawback of all lexicon-based methods is their high precision at the expense of low recall and lack of context sensitivity. For example, "sleep forever" indicates suicidal thoughts rather than sleeping activity.

In contrast with lexicon-based approaches, supervised approaches require labor-intensive annotation of a large dataset for reliable training. More recently, Yazdavar *et al.* [90] developed a statistical model for linguistic analysis of social media content authored by a subject by seeking depression indicators and their variation over time. Particularly, they developed a probabilistic topic modeling over user tweets with partial supervision (by leveraging seeded clusters), named semi-supervised topic modeling over time (ssToT), to monitor depression symptoms. Their experimental results revealed that there are significant differences in the discussion topic preferences and word usage patterns in the self-declared depressed user on Twitter versus non-depressed users. Their model showed promising results with an accuracy of 68% and a precision of 72% for capturing depression symptoms per user over a period of time [90].

14.4.5 Sentiment and Emotion Analysis on Twitter

Identifying people's attitude with respect to a specific topic, context, or interaction, and analyzing subjective experiences have fueled research interest in sentiment analysis/opinion mining [14, 28, 78, 79]. Many opinion mining models and tools have been developed to glean the attitudes of people towards products, people, topics, product attributes (e.g., display screen of a phone: big screen size can be a positive feature for a phone) and aspects (e.g., a feature and a range of values that an attribute can take such as {screen, big, small, medium}) in various contexts. Below, we discuss recent studies on opinion mining and emotion analysis on Twitter.

In opinion mining tasks, a subjective experience (e.g., sentiment, emotion, intent etc.) is defined as a quadruple *(h, s, e, c)*, where h is an individual who holds the experience, s is a stimulus (or target) that elicits the experiences (an entity or an event), e is a set of expressions that are used to describe the experiences (the sentiment words/phrases or the opinion claims), and c is a classification or assessment that characterizes or measures the experiences [11]. In this problem setting, our interest is the user's sentiment or emotion expressed in a tweet, and the opinion holder h is the author of the tweet. More recent methods extract the opinion target s of a subjective experience based on clustering, where product attributes and aspects present in the opinionated text are simultaneously clustered to find the opinion target s [12]. To understand the problem setting of extracting opinion targets, consider the following example product reviews where **explicit** and *implicit* product attributes are shown (in boldface and italics, respectively) along with groups of aspects extracted from the opinionated text below.

1. The phone runs *fast* and *smooth*, and has great **price**.

2. Good **features** for an *inexpensive* android. The **screen** is *big* and *vibrant*. Great **speed** makes *smooth* viewing of TV programs or sports.

In review 1, price is an explicit product attribute, and opinion words "smooth" and "fast" imply the implicit product attribute "speed." The task is to identify both explicit and implicit features, and group them into aspects such as speed, fast, smooth, size, big, price, and inexpensive. Given a set of product reviews, Chen *et al.* [12] first use part-of-speech tagging to identify nouns/noun phrases, verbs and adjectives as candidate product attributes that need to be clustered. Then they calculate seed terms for each cluster by taking the most frequently appearing candidate words in text. The remaining candidate words are placed in the closest cluster. To group product attributes into aspect groups that are related to a particular domain of interest, they have proposed a novel domain-specific similarity measure incorporating both statistical association and semantic similarity between a pair of candidate attributes. Their algorithm identifies the aspect groups along with the product attributes of each aspect group. In another study, Chen *et al.* have also developed techniques to extract sentiment-related expressions *e* from opinionated text [13,14]. They have trained several machine learning classifiers that utilize the information extracted from opinionated text and have successfully used them to predict the outcome of the 2012 presidential election of the USA [14]. Chen *et al.* reported that the textual features extracted from the tweets such as n-grams and part-of-speech tags played a prominent role when building the sentiment analysis classifiers for the U.S. election outcome prediction task.

Emotion analysis is a similar problem to sentiment analysis where the opinion holder has expressed his/her opinion as an emotion in the opinionated text. We have also developed automatic methods to extract large collections of labeled data using emotion-related hashtags used in Twitter and trained classifiers to identify seven emotion categories, namely, joy, sadness, anger, love, fear, thankfulness, and surprise [78,79]. Using 131 emotion-related hashtags, Wang *et al.* collected and filtered out nearly 2.5 million tweets that belong to the seven emotion categories listed above. Then they analyzed the content-based features extracted from tweet text and used them to train a Multinomial Naive Bayes (MNB) and a LIBLINEAR classifier. Specifically, they looked at unigrams, bigrams, trigrams extracted from tweets, the location of the n-grams (Wang *et al.* hypothesized that the words that are located towards the end of a tweet contribute more towards the emotion expressed in it), emotion words that appeared in tweets as identified by multiple sentiment and emotional bearing word dictionaries such as LIWC, MPQA Lexicon,[9] and WordNet-Affect, and part-of-speech tags of words in tweets. They reported that combining unigrams and bigrams yields better performance than using unigrams alone and that the positional information of the n-grams did not contribute to improving the classification accuracy. They further reported that adding emotion lexicon-based features and part-of-speech features did improve the performance of the classifiers by a small margin. They achieved the best accuracy of the MNB classifier of 61.15% and 61.63% of the LIBLINEAR classifier when they combined unigrams, bigrams, emotion lexicon-based features and part-of-speech features. In the above studies, Wang *et al.* did not explore emoji features. However, emoji are very commonly used in social media and emoji features have shown promising results in improving sentiment [53] and emotion [87] analysis tasks. Specifically, with the recent introduction of emoji sense knowledgebases [83,84] and the utilization of emoji embeddings for

---

[9]http://mpqa.cs.pitt.edu/

sentiment analysis tasks [85], we have shown that the results of the sentiment analysis could be further improved using emoji features.

14.5 Twitris: A Real-Time Social Media Analysis Platform

This section discusses how the Twitter features discussed earlier were used in building a real-time social media analysis platform called Twitris [71]. Twitris is a semantic social web platform that facilitates understanding of social perceptions about real-world events by analyzing user-generated content on social media. It supports analysis of social media data on multiple dimensions including the Spatio-Temporal-Thematic (STT), People-Content-Network (PCN) and Sentiment-Emotion-Intent (SEI) dimensions. It has been used in analyzing events on Twitter that are related to brand loyalty identification [62], disaster relief and coordination [6, 63, 64], elections and other political phenomena [14, 28], identifying instances of cyberbullying,[10] understanding the severity of depression [89, 90], and monitoring marijuana-related chatter [19, 20, 40]. Twitris's major success stories include predicting the outcomes of the 2012[11] and 2016[12] U.S. presidential elections and Brexit,[13] among many others. Next, we briefly discuss the different types of features that are being used in STT, PCN and SEI dimensions to demonstrate how feature selection can be incorporated into building comprehensive tweet processing systems.

Spatio-Temporal-Thematic data analysis supports (i) collecting user-generated tweets pertaining to an event from Twitter, along with associated news, multimedia, and Wikipedia content, (ii) processing the collected tweets to extract strong event descriptors such as key phrases, and entities associated with the event to learn the event context, and (iii) presenting summarized data and visualizations including interactive maps. STT processing uses textual features extracted from tweets such as unigrams and bigrams, named entities, hashtags, user mentions, and URLs, to identify key phrases and entities associated with an event (thematic processing). The textual features are further processed using event-specific machine learning classifiers to remove irrelevant data about an event and semantically enhance by linking them with the DBpedia knowledgebase. STT dimension also uses Twitter metadata-related features such as geo-coordinates extracted from tweets and profile descriptions to identify a tweet's location (spatial processing). It also uses tweet creation

---

[10]https://goo.gl/A1XYDJ
[11]https://goo.gl/8UR4Ku
[12]https://goo.gl/SctCb7
[13]https://goo.gl/itofGP

time to analyze tweets generated during a user-selected time period to support temporal queries.

The people-Content-Network dimension supports the analysis of social media users (People), the data shared on social media websites (Content), and the network of social media users (Network) related to an event. It facilitates studying the information propagation and identification of influential Twitter users in an event-specific user interaction network [62,65]. For each event that is being monitored, retweets, replies and user mentions in the collected tweets are used as features to create reply, user mention, and retweet networks. Then, different centrality measures such as degree centrality, betweenness centrality, and PageRank centrality are derived as features to identify the influential users. These networks also facilitate analysis of strongly or weakly connected users, which help in assessing coordination and engagement in the network. PCN processing has been extensively used in disaster relief coordination efforts.

Sentiment-Emotion-Intent extraction supports analyzing social media content to extract insights about a user's sentiment related to products and events [12–14], mood or emotion related to seven emotions categories [79], and intent behind an action [6,64]. Twitris supports target-specific sentiment analysis where the sentiment of a tweet is evaluated with respect to a target entity [13,14]. It identifies seven emotion categories, namely, joy, sadness, anger, love, fear, thankfulness, and surprise in users' tweets [79]. Sentiment and emotion analysis in Twitris use textual features extracted from tweets such as unigrams and bigrams, part-of-speech tags, named entities, and emoticons. Intent mining on Twitris is mainly supported in the context of disaster relief and coordination. It supports identifying the intents of information seekers and resource donors (suppliers) and helps to connect them. Intent mining uses textual features such as unigrams, linguistic features and patterns extracted from disaster-related tweets. Section 14.4.2 provides an in-depth discussion of the features used in intent mining in Twitris.

Figure 14.2 depicts selected capabilities of Twitris where the tool is set up to analyze tweets that are related to depression. Item (1) shows the Twitris control panel to navigate between different widgets dedicated to visualizing different data analysis methods used in Twitris. Item (2) shows how to select date and range (day, week, month, year), keywords and population density to narrow down data analysis. Item (3) shows country-level view of depression data, color coded by sentiments expressed in the tweets (Twitris can analyze data for different locations granularities such as country, state, and county level). Item (4) shows depression data for counties in California, color-coded by sentiments expressed in the tweets. Item (5) shows the total number of depression-related tweets and the most popular topics discussed on October 6th, 2014 in Los Angeles, CA (also show per capita GDP, unemployment rate). Item (6) shows a sample of depression related tweets on October 6th, 2014 from Los Angeles, CA. Item (7) shows emotion analysis on six emotions (anger, fear, sadness, joy, disgust, surprise) for depression-related tweets collected from

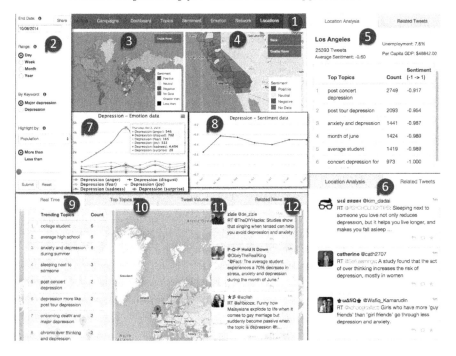

Figure 14.2: Data processing and visualization using Twitris

September 29th, 2014 to October 5th, 2014. Item (8) shows sentiment analysis for depression-related tweets collected from September 29th, 2014 to October 5th, 2014. Item (9) shows trending topics based on the analysis of real-time tweets as of October 6th, 2014. Item (10) shows the most popular topics related to depression in general, not specific to a location. Item (11) shows the tweet volume over a period of time (day, week, month), and (12) shows the depression-related news extracted from tweets.

14.6 Conclusion

This chapter discussed feature engineering for Twitter-based applications. In doing so, it first examined the different types of data fields available in a Twitter JSON object. Then it defined different types of features that can be extracted from tweets and Twitter user profiles. It also discussed the Twitter-specific features and why they would perform well with short text. It then discussed five Twitter-based applications where those features are used along with other computational techniques to solve real-world problems, while highlighting the features that lead to achieving the best results in each problem setting. Finally, the chapter concluded by discussing Twitris, a real-time semantic social web analytics platform that has already been commercialized, and its use of Twitter features. More information about Twitris and the Twitter-based applications covered in the text, along with their corresponding publications, can be found at http://knoesis.org/projects.

14.7   Acknowledgment

We acknowledge partial support from the National Institutes of Health (NIH) award: MH105384-01A1: "Modeling Social Behavior for Healthcare Utilization in Depression," the National Science Foundation (NSF) awards: CNS-1513721: "Context-Aware Harassment Detection on Social Media", and EAR 1520870: "Hazards SEES: Social and Physical Sensing Enabled Decision Support for Disaster Management and Response". Points of view or opinions in this document are those of the authors and do not necessarily represent the official position or policies of the NIH or NSF.

Bibliography

[1] Hussein S Al-Olimat, Krishnaprasad Thirunarayan, Valerie Shalin, and Amit Sheth. Location name extraction from targeted text streams using gazetteer-based statistical language models. *arXiv preprint arXiv:1708.03105*, 2017.

[2] Pramod Anantharam, Payam Barnaghi, Krishnaprasad Thirunarayan, and Amit Sheth. Extracting city traffic events from social streams. *ACM Transactions on Intelligent Systems and Technology (TIST)*, 6(4):43, 2015.

[3] Eytan Bakshy, Jake M Hofman, Winter A Mason, and Duncan J Watts. Everyone's an influencer: Quantifying influence on Twitter. In *Proceedings of the Fourth ACM International Conference on Web Search and Data Mining*, pages 65–74. ACM, 2011.

[4] Lakshika Balasuriya, Sanjaya Wijeratne, Derek Doran, and Amit Sheth. Finding street gang members on twitter. In *2016 IEEE/ACM International Conference on Advances in Social Networks Analysis and Mining (ASONAM)*, volume 8, pages 685–692, San Francisco, CA, USA, August 2016.

[5] Adrian Benton, Margaret Mitchell, and Dirk Hovy. Multitask learning for mental health conditions with limited social media data. In *Proceedings of the 15th Conference of the EACL*, volume 1, pages 152–162, 2017.

[6] Shreyansh P Bhatt, Hemant Purohit, Andrew Hampton, Valerie Shalin, Amit Sheth, and John Flach. Assisting coordination during crisis: A domain ontology based approach to infer resource needs from tweets. In *Proceedings of the 2014 ACM Conference on Web Science*, pages 297–298. ACM, 2014.

[7] Kalina Bontcheva, Leon Derczynski, Adam Funk, Mark A Greenwood, Diana Maynard, and Niraj Aswani. TwitIE: An open-source information extraction pipeline for microblog text. In *RANLP*, pages 83–90, 2013.

[8] Danah Boyd, Scott Golder, and Gilad Lotan. Tweet, tweet, retweet: Conversational aspects of retweeting on twitter. In *2010 43rd Hawaii International Conference on System Sciences (HICSS)*, pages 1–10. IEEE, 2010.

[9] Carlos Castillo, Mohammed El-Haddad, Jürgen Pfeffer, and Matt Stempeck. Characterizing the life cycle of online news stories using social media reactions. In *Computer Supported Collaborative Work and Social Computing (CSCW)*, pages 211–223. ACM, 2014.

[10] Meeyoung Cha, Hamed Haddadi, Fabricio Benevenuto, and P Krishna Gummadi. Measuring user influence in twitter: The million follower fallacy. *4th International AAAI Conference on Web and Social Media (ICWSM)*, 10(10-17):30, 2010.

[11] Lu Chen. Mining and analyzing subjective experiences in user generated content. 2016.

[12] Lu Chen, Justin Martineau, Doreen Cheng, and Amit Sheth. Clustering for simultaneous extraction of aspects and features from reviews. In *Proceedings of the 2016 Conference of the North American Chapter of the Association for Computational Linguistics: Human Language Technologies*, pages 789–799. ACL, 2016.

[13] Lu Chen, Wenbo Wang, Meenakshi Nagarajan, Shaojun Wang, and Amit P Sheth. Extracting diverse sentiment expressions with target-dependent polarity from twitter. In *6th International AAAI Conference on Web and Social Media (ICWSM)*, volume 2, pages 50–57, 2012.

[14] Lu Chen, Wenbo Wang, and Amit P Sheth. Are twitter users equal in predicting elections? A study of user groups in predicting 2012 US Republican presidential primaries. In *4th International Conference on Social Informatics (SocInfo)*, pages 379–392. Springer, 2012.

[15] Lu Chen, Ingmar Weber, and Adam Okulicz-Kozaryn. U.s. religious land-scape on twitter. In *6th International Conference on Social Informatics (SocInfo)*. Springer, 2014.

[16] Zhiyuan Cheng, James Caverlee, and Kyumin Lee. You are where you tweet: A content-based approach to geo-locating twitter users. In *Proceedings of the 19th ACM International Conference on Information and Knowledge Management*, pages 759–768. ACM, 2010.

[17] Glen Coppersmith, Mark Dredze, Craig Harman, Kristy Hollingshead, and Margaret Mitchell. Clpsych 2015 shared task: Depression and PTSD on twitter. In *Proceedings of the 2015 Conference of the North American Chapter of the Association for Computational Linguistics: Human Language Technologies*, pages 31–39, 2015.

[18] Glen Coppersmith, Kim Ngo, Ryan Leary, and Anthony Wood. Exploratory analysis of social media prior to a suicide attempt. In *Proceedings of the 2016 Conference of the North American Chapter of the Association for Computational Linguistics: Human Language Technologies*, pages 106–117, 2016.

[19] Raminta Daniulaityte, Robert Carlson, Farahnaz Golroo, Sanjaya Wijeratne, Edward W Boyer, Silvia S Martins, Ramzi W Nahhas, and Amit P Sheth. "time for dabs." analyzing twitter data on butane hash oil use. *Drug & Alcohol Dependence*, 156:e53–e54, 2015.

[20] Raminta Daniulaityte, Ramzi W Nahhas, Sanjaya Wijeratne, Robert G Carlson, Francois R Lamy, Silvia S Martins, Edward W Boyer, G Alan Smith, and Amit Sheth. "time for dabs." analyzing twitter data on marijuana concentrates across the US. *Drug and Alcohol Dependence*, 155:307–311, 2015.

[21] Munmun De Choudhury, Scott Counts, and Eric Horvitz. Social media as a measurement tool of depression in populations. In *Proceedings of the 5th Annual ACM Web Science Conference*, pages 47–56. ACM, 2013.

[22] Munmun De Choudhury, Michael Gamon, Scott Counts, and Eric Horvitz. Predicting depression via social media. *7th International AAAI Conference on Web and Social Media (ICWSM)*, 13:1–10, 2013.

[23] Munmun De Choudhury, Sanket S Sharma, Tomaz Logar, Wouter Eekhout, and René Clausen Nielsen. Gender and cross-cultural differences in social media disclosures of mental illness. *ACM Conference on Computer Supported Cooperative Work and Social Computing (CSCW)*, pages 353–369, 2017.

[24] Leon Derczynski, Diana Maynard, Giuseppe Rizzo, Marieke van Erp, Genevieve Gorrell, Raphaël Troncy, Johann Petrak, and Kalina

Bontcheva. Analysis of named entity recognition and linking for tweets. *Information Processing & Management*, 51(2):32–49, 2015.

[25] Guozhu Dong and Jinyan Li. Efficient mining of emerging patterns: Discovering trends and differences. In *Proceedings of the 5th ACM SIGKDD International Conference on Knowledge Discovery and Data Mining*, pages 43–52. ACM, 1999.

[26] Virgile Landeiro Dos Reis and Aron Culotta. Using matched samples to estimate the effects of exercise on mental health from twitter. In *Proceedings of the Twenty-Ninth AAAI Conference on Artificial Intelligence*, pages 182–188, 2015.

[27] Mark Dredze, Michael J Paul, Shane Bergsma, and Hieu Tran. Carmen: A twitter geolocation system with applications to public health. In *AAAI Workshop on Expanding the Boundaries of Health Informatics Using AI (HIAI)*, pages 20–24. Citeseer, 2013.

[28] Monireh Ebrahimi, Amir Hossein Yazdavar, and Amit Sheth. On the challenges of sentiment analysis for dynamic events. *IEEE Intelligent Systems*, 2017.

[29] Bjarke Felbo, Alan Mislove, Anders Søgaard, Iyad Rahwan, and Sune Lehmann. Using millions of emoji occurrences to learn any-domain representations for detecting sentiment, emotion and sarcasm. *arXiv preprint arXiv:1708.00524*, 2017.

[30] Kiran Garimella, Ingmar Weber, and Munmun De Choudhury. Quote rts on twitter: Usage of the new feature for political discourse. In *Proceedings of the 8th ACM Conference on Web Science*, pages 200–204. ACM, 2016.

[31] Judith Gelernter and Wei Zhang. Cross-lingual geo-parsing for non-structured data. In *Proceedings of the 7th Workshop on Geographic Information Retrieval*, pages 64–71. ACM, 2013.

[32] Kevin Gimpel, Nathan Schneider, Brendan O'Connor, Dipanjan Das, Daniel Mills, Jacob Eisenstein, Michael Heilman, Dani Yogatama, Jeffrey Flanigan, and Noah A Smith. Part-of-speech tagging for twitter: Annotation, features, and experiments. In *Proceedings of the 49th Annual Meeting of the Association for Computational Linguistics: Human Language Technologies*, pages 42–47. ACL, 2011.

[33] John F Gunn and David Lester. Twitter postings and suicide: An analysis of the postings of a fatal suicide in the 24 hours prior to death. *Suicidologi*, 17(3), 2015.

[34] Jared Jashinsky, Scott H Burton, Carl L Hanson, Josh West, Christophe Giraud-Carrier, Michael D Barnes, and Trenton Argyle. Tracking suicide risk factors through twitter in the US. *Crisis*, 2014.

[35] Zongcheng Ji, Aixin Sun, Gao Cong, and Jialong Han. Joint recognition and linking of fine-grained locations from tweets. In *Proceedings of the 25th International Conference on World Wide Web*, pages 1271–1281. WWW, 2016.

[36] Daniel Jurafsky and James H Martin. *Speech and Language Processing: An Introduction to Natural Language Processing, Computational Linguistics, and Speech Recognition*, Prentice Hall, 2000.

[37] Christian Karmen, Robert C Hsiung, and Thomas Wetter. Screening internet forum participants for depression symptoms by assembling and enhancing multiple nlp methods. *Computer Methods and Programs in Biomedicine*, 120(1):27–36, 2015.

[38] Revathy Krishnamurthy, Pavan Kapanipathi, Amit P Sheth, and Krishnaprasad Thirunarayan. Knowledge enabled approach to predict the location of twitter users. In *European Semantic Web Conference*, pages 187–201. Springer, Cham, 2015.

[39] Shamanth Kumar, Fred Morstatter, and Huan Liu. *Twitter Data Analytics*. Springer, 2014.

[40] Francois R Lamy, Raminta Daniulaityte, Amit Sheth, Ramzi W Nahhas, Silvia S Martins, Edward W Boyer, and Robert G Carlson. "those edibles hit hard." exploration of twitter data on cannabis edibles in the us. *Drug and Alcohol Dependence*, 164:64–70, 2016.

[41] Beth Levin. *English Verb Classes and Alternations: A Preliminary Investigation*. University of Chicago Press, 1993.

[42] Wendy Liu and Derek Ruths. What's in a Name? Using First Names as Features for Gender Inference in Twitter. *AAAI Spring Symposium: Analyzing Microtext*, 2013.

[43] Elsa Loekito and James Bailey. Using highly expressive contrast patterns for classification: Is it worthwhile? *Advances in Knowledge Discovery and Data Mining*, pages 483–490, 2009.

[44] Shervin Malmasi and Mark Dras. Location mention detection in tweets and microblogs. In *International Conference of the Pacific Association for Computational Linguistics (PACL)*, pages 123–134. Springer, 2015.

[45] Riham Mansour, Mohamed Farouk Abdel Hady, Eman Hosam, Hani Amr, and Ahmed Ashour. Feature selection for twitter sentiment analysis: An experimental study. In *International Conference on Intelligent Text Processing and Computational Linguistics*, pages 92–103. Springer, 2015.

[46] Stuart E Middleton, Lee Middleton, and Stefano Modafferi. Real-time crisis mapping of natural disasters using social media. *The Institute of Electrical and Electronics Engineers (IEEE) Intelligent Systems*, 29(2):9–17, 2014.

[47] George A Miller. Wordnet: A lexical database for English. *Communications of the ACM*, 38(11):39–41, 1995.

[48] Ahmed Mourad, Falk Scholer, and Mark Sanderson. *Language Influences on Tweeter Geolocation*, pages 331–342. Springer, Cham, 2017.

[49] Meena Nagarajan, Amit Sheth, and Selvam Velmurugan. Citizen sensor data mining, social media analytics and development centric web applications. In *Proceedings of the 20th International Conference Companion on World Wide Web*, WWW '11, pages 289–290, New York, NY, USA, 2011. ACM.

[50] Meenakshi Nagarajan, Hemant Purohit, and Amit P Sheth. A qualitative examination of topical tweet and retweet practices. *4th International AAAI Conference on Web and Social Media (ICWSM)*, 2(010):295–298, 2010.

[51] Yair Neuman, Yohai Cohen, Dan Assaf, and Gabbi Kedma. Proactive screening for depression through metaphorical and automatic text analysis. *Artificial Intelligence in Medicine*, 56(1):19–25, 2012.

[52] Thin Nguyen, Dinh Phung, Bo Dao, Svetha Venkatesh, and Michael Berk. Affective and content analysis of online depression communities. *IEEE Transactions on Affective Computing*, 5(3):217–226, 2014.

[53] Petra Kralj Novak, Jasmina Smailović, Borut Sluban, and Igor Mozetič. Sentiment of emojis. *PloS one*, 10(12):e0144296, 2015.

[54] Jaram Park, Vladimir Barash, Clay Fink, and Meeyoung Cha. Emoticon style: Interpreting differences in emoticons across cultures. In *7th International AAAI Conference on Web and Social Media (ICWSM)*, 2013.

[55] Minsu Park, David W McDonald, and Meeyoung Cha. Perception differences between the depressed and non-depressed users in twitter. In *7th International AAAI Conference on Web and Social Media (ICWSM)*, volume 9, pages 217–226, 2013.

[56] Huan-Kai Peng, Jiang Zhu, Dongzhen Piao, Rong Yan, and Ying Zhang. Retweet modeling using conditional random fields. In *2011 IEEE 11th International Conference on Data Mining Workshops (ICDMW)*, pages 336–343. IEEE, 2011.

[57] Marco Pennacchiotti and Ana-Maria Popescu. A Machine Learning Approach to Twitter User Classification. *5th International AAAI Conference on Web and Social Media (ICWSM)*, pages 281–288, 2011.

[58] Sujan Perera, Pablo Mendes, Amit Sheth, Krishnaprasad Thirunarayan, Adarsh Alex, Christopher Heid, and Greg Mott. Implicit entity recognition in clinical documents. In *Proceedings of the 4th Joint Conference on Lexical and Computational Semantics (*SEM)*, pages 228–238, 2015.

[59] Sujan Perera, Pablo N Mendes, Adarsh Alex, Amit Sheth, and Krishnaprasad Thirunarayan. Implicit entity linking in tweets. In *Extended Semantic Web Conference (ESWC)*, pages 118–132, Greece, 2016.

[60] Daniel Preotiuc-Pietro, Johannes Eichstaedt, Gregory Park, Maarten Sap, Laura Smith, Victoria Tobolsky, H Andrew Schwartz, and Lyle Ungar. The role of personality, age and gender in tweeting about mental illnesses. In *Proceedings of the 2015 Conference of the North American Chapter of the Association for Computational Linguistics: Human Language Technologies*, volume 2015, page 21, 2015.

[61] Joseph D Prusa, Taghi M Khoshgoftaar, and David J Dittman. Impact of feature selection techniques for tweet sentiment classification. In *FLAIRS Conference*, pages 299–304, 2015.

[62] Hemant Purohit, Jitendra Ajmera, Sachindra Joshi, Ashish Verma, and Amit Sheth. Finding influential authors in brand-page communities. In *6th International AAAI Conference on Web and Social Media (ICWSM)*. AAAI, 2012.

[63] Hemant Purohit, Carlos Castillo, Fernando Diaz, Amit Sheth, and Patrick Meier. Emergency-relief coordination on social media: Automatically matching resource requests and offers. *First Monday*, 19(1), 2013.

[64] Hemant Purohit, Guozhu Dong, Valerie Shalin, Krishnaprasad Thirunarayan, and Amit Sheth. Intent classification of short-text on social media. In *2015 IEEE International Conference on Smart City/SocialCom/SustainCom (SmartCity)*, pages 222–228. IEEE, 2015.

[65] Hemant Purohit, Alex Dow, Omar Alonso, Lei Duan, and Kevin Haas. User taglines: Alternative presentations of expertise and interest in social media. In *2012 International Conference on Social Informatics (SocInfo), Washington, D.C., USA, December 14-16*, pages 236–243, 2012.

[66] Afshin Rahimi, Trevor Cohn, and Timothy Baldwin. pigeo: A python geotagging tool. *Proceedings of ACL-2016 System Demonstrations*, pages 127–132, 2016.

[67] Alan Ritter, Sam Clark, Oren Etzioni, et al. Named entity recognition in tweets: An experimental study. In *Proceedings of the Conference on Empirical Methods in Natural Language Processing*, pages 1524–1534. ACL, 2011.

[68] Shigeyuki Sakaki, Yasuhide Miura, Xiaojun Ma, Keigo Hattori, and Tomoko Ohkuma. Twitter user gender inference using combined analysis of text and image processing. *V&L Net*, 2014:54, 2014.

[69] Roger C Schank. Conceptual dependency: A theory of natural language understanding. *Cognitive Psychology*, 3(4):552–631, 1972.

[70] Amit Sheth, Sujan Perera, Sanjaya Wijeratne, and Krishnaprasad Thirunarayan. Knowledge will propel machine understanding of content: Extrapolating from current examples. In *Proceedings of the International Conference on Web Intelligence, Leipzig, Germany, August 23-26, 2017*, pages 1–9. ACM, 2017.

[71] Amit Sheth, Hemant Purohit, Gary Alan Smith, Jeremy Brunn, Ashutosh Jadhav, Pavan Kapanipathi, Chen Lu, and Wenbo Wang. Twitris: A system for collective social intelligence. In Reda Alhajj and Jon Rokne, editors, *Encyclopedia of Social Network Analysis and Mining*, pages 1–23, New York, 05/2018 2018. Springer-Verlag New York.

[72] Hong-Han Shuai, Chih-Ya Shen, De-Nian Yang, Yi-Feng Lan, Wang-Chien Lee, Philip S Yu, and Ming-Syan Chen. Mining online social data for detecting social network mental disorders. In *Proceedings of the 25th International Conference on World Wide Web*, pages 275–285, 2016.

[73] Bongwon Suh, Lichan Hong, Peter Pirolli, and Ed H Chi. Want to be retweeted? Large scale analytics on factors impacting retweet in twitter network. In *2010 IEEE Second International Conference on Social computing (SocialCom)*, pages 177–184. IEEE, 2010.

[74] Paul Thompson, Chris Poulin, and Craig J Bryan. Predicting military and veteran suicide risk: Cultural aspects. In *Proceedings of the Workshop on Computational Linguistics and Clinical Psychology: From Linguistic Signal to Clinical Reality*, pages 1–6, 2014.

[75] Laura Tolosi, Andrey Tagarev, and Georgi Georgiev. An analysis of event-agnostic features for rumour classification in twitter. In *10th International AAAI Conference on Web and Social Media*, 2016.

[76] Oren Tsur and Ari Rappoport. What's in a hashtag? Content based prediction of the spread of ideas in microblogging communities. In *Proceedings of the Fifth ACM International Conference on Web Search and Data Mining*, pages 643–652. ACM, 2012.

[77] Sida Wang and Christopher D Manning. Baselines and bigrams: Simple, good sentiment and topic classification. In *Proceedings of the 50th Annual Meeting of the ACL*, pages 90–94. ACL, 2012.

[78] Wenbo Wang, Lu Chen, Ming Tan, Shaojun Wang, and Amit P Sheth. Discovering fine-grained sentiment in suicide notes. *Biomedical Informatics Insights*, 5(Suppl 1):137, 2012.

[79] Wenbo Wang, Lu Chen, Krishnaprasad Thirunarayan, and Amit P Sheth. Harnessing twitter "big data" for automatic emotion identification. In *Privacy, Security, Risk and Trust (PASSAT), 2012 International Conference on and 2012 International Conference on Social Computing (SocialCom)*, pages 587–592. IEEE, 2012.

[80] Wenbo Wang, Lu Chen, Krishnaprasad Thirunarayan, and Amit P. Sheth. Cursing in English on twitter. In *Proceedings of the 17th ACM Conference on Computer Supported Cooperative Work & Social Computing*, CSCW '14, pages 415–425, New York, NY, USA, 2014. ACM.

[81] Xinyu Wang, Chunhong Zhang, Yang Ji, Li Sun, Leijia Wu, and Zhana Bao. A depression detection model based on sentiment analysis in microblog social network. In *Pacific-Asia Conference on Knowledge Discovery and Data Mining*, pages 201–213. Springer, 2013.

[82] Sanjaya Wijeratne, Lakshika Balasuriya, Derek Doran, and Amit Sheth. Word embeddings to enhance twitter gang member profile identification. In *IJCAI Workshop on Semantic Machine Learning (SML)*, pages 18–24, New York City, 07 2016.

[83] Sanjaya Wijeratne, Lakshika Balasuriya, Amit Sheth, and Derek Doran. Emojinet: Building a machine readable sense inventory for emoji. In *8th International Conference on Social Informatics (SocInfo)*, pages 527–541, Bellevue, WA, USA, November 2016.

[84] Sanjaya Wijeratne, Lakshika Balasuriya, Amit Sheth, and Derek Doran. Emojinet: An open service and API for emoji sense discovery. In *11th International AAAI Conference on Web and Social Media (ICWSM)*, pages 437–446, Montreal, Canada, May 2017.

[85] Sanjaya Wijeratne, Lakshika Balasuriya, Amit Sheth, and Derek Doran. A semantics-based measure of emoji similarity. In *Proceedings of the International Conference on Web Intelligence, Leipzig, Germany, August 23-26, 2017*, pages 646–653, 2017.

[86] Sanjaya Wijeratne, Derek Doran, Amit Sheth, and Jack L. Dustin. Analyzing the social media footprint of street gangs. In *IEEE International Conference on Intelligence and Security Informatics (ISI), 2015*, pages 91–96, May 2015.

[87] Ian. D. Wood and Sebastian Ruder. Emoji as emotion tags for tweeter. In *Proceedings of the LREC 2016 Workshop on Emotion and Sentiment Analysis*, 2016.

[88] Shaomei Wu, Jake M Hofman, Winter A Mason, and Duncan J Watts. Who says what to whom on twitter. In *Proceedings of the 20th International Conference on World Wide Web*, pages 705–714. ACM, 2011.

[89] Amir Hossein Yazdavar, Hussein S Al-Olimat, Tanvi Banerjee, Krishnaprasad Thirunarayan, and Amit P Sheth. Analyzing clinical depressive symptoms in twitter. *23rd NIMH Conference on Mental Health Services Research (MHSR): Harnessing Science to Strengthen the Public Health Impact.* 2016

[90] Amir Hossein Yazdavar, Hussein S. Al-Olimat, Monireh Ebrahimi, Goonmeet Bajaj, Tanvi Banerjee, Krishnaprasad Thirunarayan, Jyotishman Pathak, and Amit Sheth. Semi-supervised approach to monitoring clinical depressive symptoms in social media. In *2017 IEEE/ACM International Conference on Advances in Social Networks Analysis and Mining (ASONAM)*, Sydney, Australia, 2017.

[91] Shaozhi Ye and Shyhtsun Felix Wu. Measuring message propagation and social influence on twitter.com. *2nd International Conference on Social Informatics (SocInfo)*, 10:216–231, 2010.

Index

Printed in the United States
by Baker & Taylor Publisher Services